UITGAVEN VAN HET

NEDERLANDS HISTORISCH-ARCHAEOLOGISCH INSTITUUT TE İSTANBUL

Publications de l'Institut historique et archéologique néerlandais de Stamboul

sous la direction de

A. A. KAMPMAN et MACHTELD J. MELLINK

XXXIV, 1

GNOSTIC STUDIES

I

GNOSTIC STUDIES

I

BY

GILLES QUISPEL
Professor of Early Church History, Utrecht
Visiting Professor, Catholic University of Louvain

İSTANBUL
Nederlands Historisch-Archaeologisch Instituut
in het Nabije Oosten
1974

188092 *273·1*

Q HP

1

Printed in the Netherlands

TABLE OF CONTENTS

VOLUME I

PREFACE

My good friend Prof. Dr. A. A. Kampman asked me recently to publish a contribution on Gnosticism in the series of the Dutch Institute at Istanbul. I readily accepted his offer and collected some of my articles written since 1945.

This period has seen enormous changes in the field of Gnosticism, mainly due to the discovery of gnostic manuscripts in the neighbourhood of Nag Hammadi in Upper Egypt.

Before this we knew very little about such an important thinker as Valentinus. But now owing to the Jung Codex and other books from Nag Hammadi we have original writings, perhaps of Valentinus himself, certainly of some of his most brilliant pupils. This had led some scholars to say that Valentinus now turns out to be as important as Origen and Plotinus; moreover, it seems most probable that this gifted Gnostic influenced both this philosopher and this theologian.

Even before this discovery an attempt was made to reconstruct the primitive doctrine of Valentinus: it was then pointed out that this system must have been strictly christocentric, in fact a christianization of an already existing non-christian gnostic myth.

Many of these tentative hypotheses were confirmed by François Sagnard [1] and by the publication of the *Apocryphon of John* [2]. Of course it must be kept in mind that only the main outlines of the primitive myth can be reconstructed with some degree of probability. But I still do think that the pupils of Valentinus, Ptolemy and Heracleon, profoundly changed the views of their master, because they had a greater appreciation of Catholic Christianity, or, as they put it, the "psychic" element. This will be shown in the forthcoming edition of the fourth treatise of the Jung Codex, the so-called *Tractatus Tripartitus*. The latter writing in its turn throws a new and unexpected light upon the great theologian Origen, who was not only a biblical scholar but also owed not a little to Valentinian Gnosis. There is a road which leads from Valentinus to Heracleon and from Heracleon to Origen.

My view that Gnosticism is of Jewish origin has met with stubborn opposition

---

[1] F. M. M. Sagnard, *La Gnose valentinienne et le Témoignage de S. Irénée*, Paris, 1947.

[2] W. C. Till, *Die gnostischen Schriften des koptischen Papyrus Berolinensis 8502*, TU 60, Berlin, 1955. M. Krause and P. Labib, *Die drei Versionen des Apokryphon des Johannes im Koptischen Museum zu Alt-Kairo*, Abhandlungen des Deutschen Archäologischen Instituts Kairo, Koptische Reihe, I, Wiesbaden, 1962.

from different quarters. At the time that the theory was launched, Judaism
was often identified, and is even now, with Pharisaeism and rabbinical Judaism.
It was, however, a great privilege for me to become familiar with the works of
Gershom Scholem at an early date. He opened my eyes for the mystical, and
even gnostic aspects of the Jewish religion. Perhaps I have made some mistakes
in dealing with this problem, which more qualified scholars should have studied.
But new material from Nag Hammadi, now becoming gradually available, seems
to prove without any doubt that even the characteristic distinction between the
highest God and the lower Demiurge has its roots in Jewish soil [3]. And the
Mani Codex acquired by the University of Cologne shows that Mani, the
founder of a gnostic world religion, from his fourth to his twentyfifth year lived
in a Jewish Christian community and was once a circumcised, law-abiding
Jewish boy himself [4]. It has become very clear in the course of time that
Gnosticism grew by reaction out of a Jewish milieu.

A new development took place when in 1956 we managed to bring photocopies
of the *Gospel of Thomas* with us from Egypt. It is understandable that this
writing needed a discussion. For the first time in history a complete collection
of Sayings of Jesus had come to light and there was a possibility that some of
them were both unknown and authentic. And yet after so many years I think
that some New Testament scholars have reason to blush about the level of
their polemics. They ought to have been familiar with the methods of form-
criticism and therefore to have seen immediately that at least some of these
Sayings represent a tradition independent of the New Testament. Perhaps I
went too far when I ascribed all the logia of the synoptic type to the Jewish
Christian *Gospel of the Hebrews,* or rather to the *Gospel of the Nazorees.* But
that is not the real issue. Helmuth Koester, the master of form-criticism, has
shown decisively that these sayings were taken from a free tradition, in some
cases even more primitive than the wording of Q, the common source of
Matthew and Luke.

Now it is an established fact that this same tradition has much in common
with the Gospel quotations of the Pseudo-Clementine writings, the Western
Text of the New Testament and the Diatessaron of Tatian. Our conclusion
can only be that these texts must also contain traces of the same free tradition.
Moreover, these Sayings contained certain indications that they were trans-

---

[3] B. A. Pearson, 'Jewish haggadic Traditions in *The Testimony of Truth* from Nag
Hammadi (CG IX, 3)', in *Ex Orbe Religionum* (Festschrift G. Widengren), I, Leiden, 1972,
457-470.
[4] A. Henrichs and L. Koenen, 'Ein griechischer Mani-Codex', *Zeitschrift für Papyrologie und
Epigraphik,* 5, 1970, 97-216.

mitted in a Jewish Christian milieu (the primacy of James, the keeping of the Sabbath, etc.).

Even before this discovery H.-J. Schoeps and Jean Daniélou had underlined the importance of Jewish, as distinguished from Gentile Christianity. It had already been pointed out that Edessa, the center of Syriac Christianity owed its special brand of religion to Jewish Christianity of Palestine. Now that the Gospel of Thomas can be localized in Edessa, the importance of Jewish Christianity becomes much clearer:

1. Aramaic Christianity, as distinguished from Greek and Latin Christianity, had its own features from the very beginning. In fact it almost never was Catholic, but Jewish Christian and Encratitic in its beginnings, Monophysitic or Nestorian in a later period.

2. The mysticism of the influential Syrian monk Macarius turned out to be the revival of a very archaic and indigenous spirituality. Macarius was read by Gregory of Nyssa, who played a rather prominent part at the Oecumenical Council of Constantinople in 381, where it was stated that the Holy Spirit is God. It is possible that the Fathers did so also to consecrate the outburst of spiritual life in Mesopotamia at that time [5].

3. It became increasingly clear that Tatian, when writing his Diatessaron, not only used the four canonical Gospels but also some Jewish Christian, extra-canonical tradition such as is contained in the *Gospel of Thomas*. Evidence of the use of the Diatessaron was discovered in such writers as Philoxenus of Mabbug and Augustine (who as a Manichee read the Diatessaron), and also in the *Heliand* and, recently, in the anonymous *Vita Marie et Salvatoris Rhythmica* (± 1225) and in the *Vita Jesu Christi* of Ludolph of Saxony (± 1350)[6]. And as often as not, echoes of the Jewish Christian tradition, transmitted through the intermediary of Tatian, could be identified in these writings.

Let me quote just two examples:

a. Ludolph of Saxony's description of the baptism of Jesus reflects some peculiar Jewish Christian traditions:

Vita Jesu Christi I, 21, 11-12	*Testament of Levi*, 18, 6-7
(ed. Rigollot I, 186)	(ed. Charles 62-63)
apertum est coelum, id est *inaes-*	Οἱ οὐρανοὶ ἀνοιγήσονται, καὶ
timabilis splendor factus est	ἐκ τοῦ ναοῦ τῆς δόξης ἥξει

---

[5] See my article 'Gregorius van Nyssa en de mystiek', *Nederlands Theologisch Tijdschrift*, 24, 1970-1971, 250-255.

[6] See the forthcoming article by R. van den Broek, 'A Latin Diatessaron in the Vita Beate Virginis Marie et Salvatoris Rhythmica' (to be published in *New Testament Studies*).

circa Christum et tantus fulgor
circumfulsit eum . . . .
Et descendit Spiritus Sanctus visi-
biliter corporali specie, sicut
columba in ipsum, ac *requievit*
super eum, sedens super caput ipsius.

ἐπ' αὐτὸν ἁγιάσμα μετὰ φωνῆς
πατρικῆς ὡς ἀπὸ Ἀβραὰμ πρὸς
Ἰσαάκ. Καὶ δόξα ὑψίστου ἐπ'
αὐτὸν ῥηθήσεται, καὶ πνεῦμα
συνέσεως καὶ ἁγιασμοῦ κατα-
παύσει ἐπ' αὐτὸν ἐν τῷ ὕδατι.

The appearance of a glorious light at Jesus' baptism and the reading *requievit* are both found in the Jewish Christian Gospel tradition [7].

b. The Saying of Matth. 8, 20 and Luke 9, 58:

Vita Jesu Christi I, 45, 2
(ed. Rigollot II, 6-7)
Vulpes foveas habent, ad quiescendum
et latitandum, et volucres coeli nidos
habent ad quos ascendunt et confugiunt,
Filius autem hominis, id est virginis . . . .
non habet
domicilium proprium, ubi caput *suum*
reclinet, *ad pausandum* [8].

Gospel of Thomas, log. 86

The foxes have their holes
and the birds have their nest,
but the Son of Man has no *place*
to lay *his* head *and to rest.*

I must confess that only now I can visualize this Saying. Foxes have dens, where they can lay down their head on their legs for a little while, and birds have nests, where they can rest, but the Son of Man can not lay down his head, like a fox can do in his den, nor can he rest, like a bird can do in his nest. It is clear that the version of the Gospel of Thomas is shorter and more pictoresque than that of the canonical Gospels. But the question remains whether Jesus is designating himself or the situation of restless man in general. Must we translate the Aramaic expression Son of Man with "Man" or "man"? [9].

In any case there can be no doubt that medieval Diatessarons, even of late date, sometimes preserve a more primitive version of a Saying of Jesus than the canonical Gospels.

---

[7] Cf. the *Gospel of the Ebionites* (Epiphanius, *Pan.,* 30, 13, 7 ff.): περιέλαμψε τὸν τόπον φῶς μέγα and the *Gospel of the Nazorees* (Jerome, In *Esaiam* IV, ad 11, 2): "descendit fons omnis Spiritus Sancti, et *requievit* super eum". For a more detailed discussion of these traditions, see van den Broek's article.

[8] A. Strobel, 'Textgeschichtliches zum Thomas-Logion 86', *Vigiliae Christianae,* 17, 1963, 211-224, has shown that e.g. the readings "no *place*" and "to lay his head *and to rest*" only have parallels in the early Syriac Gospel tradition.

[9] Cf. Strobel, 222, n. 27, who refers to the Palestinian Syriac Lectionary: brh dgbr', "the son of the man", and to the Tuscan Diatessaron: "il figliuolo della *vergine*" cf. Ludolph: "Filius autem hominis, id est *virginis*".

4. So the *Gospel of Thomas* has given rise to a new science, practised with consummate skill by F. M. Boismard, which pays for the first time due attention to the extra-canonical tradition. It has long been known that the Gospel quotations of Justin Martyr, the Pseudo-Clementines, and the Diatessaron contain a consistent tradition. Moreover, certain traditions of quite a few Church Fathers have preserved valuable versions of a Saying. The *Gospel of Thomas* has enabled Boismard to write a new and complete History of the Synoptic Tradition, based upon the fundamental insight that the extra-canonical tradition can help us to get behind the sources of the canonical Gospels [10]. In fact we know quite a lot about Jesus quite apart from the Gospels of the Church.

The manuscripts from Nag Hammadi are now published at great speed, mainly owing to the exertions of James M. Robinson of Claremont, California. It is now clear that not all the writings found there are gnostic. One book turned out to be a very bad translation of a passage in the *Republic of Plato*. Moreover, there are fragments of the *Sentences of Sextus,* certainly not a gnostic writing. The *Teachings of Silvanus* reflect the philosophical atmosphere of early Alexandrian Christianity, without a trace of Gnosticism [11]. The writing *Bronté or the Perfect Nous* contains a pre-Christian and pre-gnostic self-proclamation of Sophia, very much in the style of the Isis inscription at Heliopolis [12]. Even the *Exegesis of the Soul,* on the androgynous nature of the soul, is not necessarily gnostic. There can be more surprises, agreeable and not so agreeable.

This means that much in this book may be refuted by new discoveries. We all know that whoever devotes himself to scholarship, sacrifices himself to anonymity. It is however a great satisfaction to have been personally in the midst of these important events and to have perhaps contributed to the development of research in this field. Here and there I had to change a word, to cancel a passage which would seem to have been not quite correct. A reader may get the impression that the author tends to be repetitive. Then he must remember that one has to repeat oneself, when the opponent does not want to listen.

---

[10] P. Benoit and M.-E. Boismard, *Synopse des quatre Évangiles en français,* II, Paris, 1972.
[11] J. Zandee, 'Die Lehren des Silvanus. Stoischer Rationalismus und Christentum im Zeitalter der frühkatholischen Kirche', in *Essays on the Nag Hammadi Texts in Honour of Alexander Böhlig* (Nag Hammadi Studies III), Leiden, 1972, 144-155.
[12] Edited by M. Krause and P. Labib, *Gnostische und hermetische Schriften aus Codex II und Codex VI,* Abhandlungen des Deutschen Archäologischen Instituts Kairo, Koptische Reihe, II, Glückstadt, 1971, 122-132.

Owing to the new discoveries the image of the history of the Early Church has changed completely. And nobody dares to speak anymore about the "Dutch Radical School" or „die religionsgeschichtliche Schule", which dominated this field of research at the time that the present author started his career.

It is not, however, only that the old theories have been refuted; it also has become more and more clear that both primitive and early Christianity have known a pluriformity unheard of by former generations.

I

VALENTINIAN GNOSIS
AND THE JUNG CODEX

THE JUNG CODEX AND ITS SIGNIFICANCE

It is more than possible that our notions about the beginnings of Christianity will need to be considerably revised in consequence of three recent finds. Of these the discovery of the Dead Sea Scrolls is that most widely known. And rightly so, since it seems clear that these MSS. will have much to contribute towards a better understanding of the origins of the Christian religion. For professed scholars the recovery of the writings of Origen at Toura is also a find of much importance, since these texts enrich our knowledge of the teaching and life of the great theologian of the Greek Church whose thought has left its unmistakable mark on Eastern Orthodoxy right down to the present time; though in this case Origen's teaching is so well known from his surviving works that the new documents could not completely overthrow the existing view of him.

In the case of the forty-eight Gnostic books found at Nag Hammadi the situation is different again. Christian Gnosticism is so fragmentarily known, and chiefly from the works of its opponents, that there has hitherto been the greatest uncertainty about the character of this astonishing heresy. And although the information which has so far reached us about the writings at Nag Hammadi indicates that their contents belong for the most part to the vulgar Gnosis of the Sethians, and not to the learned Gnosis of a Valentinus and Basilides which for the history of Christianity is of infinitely more importance, and although the dating of the writings still presents the greatest uncertainties, it may yet be said that through these discoveries at Nag Hammadi a forgotten religion, viz. the heretical Gnosticism which was once a great influence and has not lost its importance for the understanding of European cultural history (e.g. of German Idealism), has come to light.

An interested outsider will necessarily ask whether some connexion does not exist between the finds near the Dead Sea, the discovery of writings of Origen at Toura and the Gnostic writings found at Nag Hammadi. This question, though wholly reasonable, must be put on a broader basis. We must inquire: Does there exist any connexion between Jewish heterodoxy as it finds expression, e.g. in the 'Essene' documents from the Dead Sea, heretical Gnosis which flows in the ancient world as a broad river at the side of Greek philosophy and orthodox Christianity, and the 'true', that is the orthodox, Gnosis of the Alexandrians? The answer to this question, which is of great importance, prejudges a number of problems which confront the student of the New Testament, and will, perhaps, give the death-sentence to Bultmann's hypothesis of a pre-Christian Gnostic Redeemer and to Harnack's basic thesis that early Catholicism was the Hellenization of primitive

Christianity. Was there, then, any connexion between Jewish heterodoxy, heretical Gnosis in the second century and the orthodox Gnosis of the Alexandrians? To this question the available material has hitherto provided no clue.

The Dead Sea Scrolls are still being recovered and are as yet only very partially published. Of the manuscripts of Origen *cum suis* from Toura there has so far been printed only a single ecclesiastical discourse taken down in shorthand. A great part of the find has not yet been bought and at the moment is being offered for sale, now here, now there, by all kinds of mysterious ways at fantastic figures. The Gnostic codices of Nag Hammadi have reposed for some years sealed up in the Coptic Museum at Cairo where they are inaccessible to scientific investigation, so that there can be no question of the MSS. being published in the near future. Everywhere the unrest in the Near East raises insuperable barriers to science.

And nevertheless — or so it seems to me — the question raised above as to the connexion of the three discoveries will from now on be the fundamental issue and govern the interpretation of the new *data*. The reason for this is that a Codex from Nag Hammadi, which *mirabile dictu* contains not the vulgar Gnosticism but the authentic Gnosis of the Valentinian school, is now at the disposal of students. It is quite possible that the contents of this Codex will enable us to draw conclusions both as to the relations between the great Origen and this heretical Gnosis and also as to the dependence of this heretical Gnosis on a pre-Christian Jewish form of heresy.

To introduce these important problems conveniently to my readers, it may be well to divide our subject as follows. I will first describe briefly the contents of the Codex and then discuss the questions how far this Codex can be a missing-link and how far we can draw conclusions from it about the connexion between Jewish heresy, heretical Gnosis and Origenistic theology.

A. HISTORY OF THE DISCOVERY

It was on 10 May, 1952, that I acquired at Brussels a Coptic codex of a hundred pages which contained four unknown writings from the second century A.D., one of them a heretical Gospel. This is how it came to pass.

In the spring of 1948 I received at Leyden vague reports from Jean Doresse about an important discovery of Coptic MSS. in Egypt. Since I had myself been engaged for several years on a study of Valentinus, the most important Gnostic from the middle of the second century A.D., and as I considered it possible that Valentinian texts were included among these writings, I gave M. Doresse the address of an institution with which I was acquainted, the Bollingen Foundation at New York, with the request that it be handed over to a person in Egypt. At the same time, viz. in August 1948, I urged on Jack D. Barrett, the Secretary of the Foundation, the purchase of the Gnostic writings. Such was the beginning of laborious negotiations and investigations which lasted for several years and can be reported only briefly here.

What happened was that in the winter of 1948-9 the possessor of a Gnostic Codex appeared at the offices of the Bollingen Foundation and sought to interest Mr. Barrett in its purchase. He asked 12,000 dollars for it, saying that the University of Michigan had already offered him 6,000 dollars. If American scholars really had the Codex previously in their hands, it is not easily conceivable that they would not have paid the price demanded. At a later date the same person inquired, after he had failed to sell the Codex, whether he might store it in the safe of the Bollingen Foundation. This request was naturally refused in view of the responsibility involved for its safety and the owner returned to Europe.

The situation was extremely delicate. The rumour went round — which later turned out to be correct — that its owner had died. It was not known where the Codex was to be found, what it contained and who was its new owner. It was no imaginary risk that the MS. might remain inaccessible to investigation for a great many years, and perhaps for good. Such writings sometimes happen to disappear mysteriously from the market. Moreover, at a time when foreign currencies were scarce, who could make such a large sum available for a papyrus codex?

The only possibility seemed to be that the generous Bollingen Foundation should interest itself in the matter. With this end in view I approached Professor C. G. Jung of Zürich who with great willingness wrote several letters to the members of the Board of the Bollingen Foundation, in which he emphasized the importance of the Codex and urged the Foundation to buy it.
In the meantime it had become known that the MS. contained a collection of four writings, one of them with the title: *The Gospel of Truth*. More than the title, however, was hardly known. And yet all our passionate exertions rested on the supposition that this *Gospel of Truth* was identical with the 'Evangelium Veritatis' about which the Church Father Irenaeus, writing *c.* 180 A.D., tells us that it was in use among the disciples of the Gnostic Valentinus.

The result of all these negotiations was that in August 1950 I instituted some investigations at Paris on behalf of the Bollingen Foundation and could establish that the Codex reposed in a safe at Brussels. On 19 July, 1951, Dr. C. A. Meier of Zürich succeeded in discovering the address of the new owner and the price which he asked for the Codex. It was accordingly decided at Ascona in August 1951 that the Bollingen Foundation should provide the money for the purchase and I was commissioned to investigate whether or not the writings had been forged and if they were of value. For even if the writings were genuine it remained a possibility that their contents were Gnostic speculations of little worth, whereas what we primarily hoped for was the writings of Valentinus. The expert examination took place at the beginning of March 1952 at St. Idesbald (Coxyde). Although it was not possible to unpack the papyri, and such indeed was not justified because of the dilettante way in which they had been packed up, the reading of a single page convinced me that it was Valentinian. Hence, despite a certain risk, I ventured to recommend their purchase. This, however, did not happen forthwith. The owner suddenly asked for delay, and there were also alarming signs which seemed to indicate that other interested parties, if not offering a higher sum, were at any rate negotiating. At the same time the Bollingen Foundation made certain very understandable stipulations about furnishing the purchase money, which it was not possible at that moment of pressing urgency to comply with. It appeared as if our exertions spread over four years had all come to nothing and our endeavours had failed.

It was at this juncture that Dr. C. A. Meier, acting with great decision, rendered a real service to learning. He put the situation before George H. Page of Wallisellen, who proved a new Maecenas and made available the money for the purchase. The result was than on 10 May, 1952, I bought the Codex at Brussels on behalf of the C. G. Jung Institute at Zürich. At the request of its previous owner, this acquisition was not to be made known until 10 November, 1953. The study of the papyrus, however, could be immediately taken in hand. It appeared that the *Gospel of Truth* beyond doubt came from the school of Valentinus and was identical with the writing which was referred to by Irenaeus of Lyons *c.* 180 A.D. A new heretical Gospel, the only one of its kind which is as yet available to students, had been discovered. Our surmise has proved to have been correct.

There still remained one great source of anxiety for us. In the examination of the MS. at St. Idesbald in March 1952 it was stated that it showed a lacuna of about forty pages. Moreover, during this examination it became clear, as we had suspected, that a photograph of the Codex had already been made in Egypt in 1947 or thereabouts and had somehow come into the hands of a French student, and it was our hope that this photograph would also give us the missing sheets. The owner requested the student in question to restore the photograph to its rightful possessor. The latter stated in a letter his unwillingness to do this, but he sent it none the less. It seems, however, that this photograph contained nothing that was not in our Codex. So there remains the by no means easy task of finding our whether or not these missing pages still repose in Egypt and whether there is any way in which they are, or can be made, accessible.

On closer examination it appeared that the four writings in the MS. were all translations from the Greek. Three of them are without doubt Gnostic and come from the school of Valentinus. Professor Henry-Charles Puech of the Collège de France and myself have been commissioned to edit them while Professor W. C. van Unnik will concern himself with the significance of the discovery for the study of the New Testament. Professor M. Malinine of Paris is primarily entrusted with the constitution of the Coptic text. In particular, the *Gospel of Truth*, which was written round about A.D. 150, appears to be of special importance.

B. CONTENTS OF THE CODEX

The Codex extends, roughly, to about a hundred pages, for the most part numbered. At least thirty-eight pages are wanting. It contains:

1. A *Letter of James* (p. 1, 1-p. 16, 29);

2. The *Gospel of Truth* (p. 16, 30-p. 43, 24);

3. The *Letter to Rheginos* (pp. 43, 25-p. 48 end; continuation and conclusion wanting);

4. A *Treatise on the Three Natures* (a very elaborate exposition, of which the pp. 59-90 are wanting: pp. 51, 1-134 end);

5. Two very damaged pages of the *Prayer of the Apostle*.

1. *The Letter of James*

The opening words of the first writing, which reproduce a commonplace phrasing of Greek epistolography, at once make it clear that the letter was translated from the Greek. It professes, however, by an artifice sufficiently familiar from other instances, to be the translation of a Hebrew letter, written by James, the Lord's Brother, and to contain esoteric revelations which Christ is said to have communicated to James and Peter before His Ascension. This was a form and kind of fiction practised by other Gnostics. But Clement of Alexandria also mentions that James, Peter and John were said to have transmitted a secret Gnosis. Now we may inquire: Did the writer really draw on this more or less ecclesiastical Gnosis, or did he under the cover of an Apostolic tradition communicate his own conceptions or those of the particular sect to which he belonged? The history of the Egyptian Church in the second century is too little known to enable us to answer this question. Moreover, the work contains too few data which would enable us to say with certainty whether its contents are Gnostic or more or less orthodox. It appears as if the

author were anxious to give an answer to the burning questions of his own
age, the second century. He refers to the persecutions, which in his view were
willed by God and must be willingly embraced by men, thus taking part in a
debate which was being carried on at Alexandria in the second century. He
also speaks of prophecy, which was brought to its end by John the Baptist, in
a way which recalls the interpretation of Origen and the Manichees. Also on
the matter of faith, love and works, the author freely expresses his thought.
He says [1]:

For the Word is first of all the origin of faith, secondly of love, thirdly of
works. For herein life consists. For the Word is like a grain of wheat. If any
one has sown it, he has faith in it, and if it has germinated he loves it, since
he sees many grains in the place of one and while he works he is being saved,
since he can prepare it for a meal and further has enough over in order to sow.
This is the way whereby it is possible for you to receive the Kingdom of
Heaven. If you do not receive it by Gnosis, you will not find it.

This appears to be an elaboration of the word of St. Paul on faith which works
through love (*Gal.* v. 6). The writer touches on a number of other subjects in
much the same way.

When the revelations have come to an end Christ rises to Heaven in a chariot
of Pneuma. Peter and James kneel down and give thanks. They raise their
hearts to Heaven and hear a sound of war, the sound of a trumpet and
confusion.

When they rise higher still and lift up their Noûs, they hear hymns and songs
by angels and heavenly spirits. But when they intend to raise their Pneuma
higher still and to penetrate to God Himself, they are not permitted to hear
or see anything. Thereupon James sends out the Twelve and returns alone to
Jerusalem.

We must leave for closer examination the question whether this letter of James
is a product of the school of Valentinus, like the other three writings in the
MS. Provisionally we have no indication that it is not; the writing may well
be Valentinian.

2.   *The Gospel of Truth*

The Gospel of Truth is the joy of those who have received from the Father of
Truth the grace to know Him through the Power of the Logos who has come
from the Pleroma, which is in the Thought and the Thinking of the Father,
[and] who is named Redeemer because He is the Messenger who was destined
to come for the redemption of those who knew not the Father.

---

[1]   The translations in the present paper are provisional.

So begins the second writing in the Codex, a work of the highest importance for the study both of Gnosticism and the history of the New Testament Canon and one which is sure to attract attention from a wide circle.

The existence of a Valentinian writing named the 'Gospel of Truth' had long been known. Writing c. A.D. 180 in his *Adversus Haereses* III, xi. 9, Irenaeus states:

But those who are from Valentinus, being, on the other hand, altogether reckless, while they put forth their own compositions, boast that they possess more Gospels than there really are. Indeed, they have arrived at such a pitch of audacity, as to entitle their comparatively recent writing 'the Gospel of Truth', although it agrees in nothing with the Gospels of the Apostles, so that they have really no Gospel which is not full of blasphemy. For if what they have published is the Gospel of truth, and yet is totally unlike those which have been handed down to us by the Apostles, any who please may learn, as is shown by the Scriptures themselves, that that which has been handed down from the Apostles can no longer be reckoned the Gospel of truth.

Is is possible that the *Gospel of Truth* is also referred to when, in Tertullian, *De Praescriptione Haereticorum*, ch. 25, Valentinians speak of 'a secret Gospel': indeed, the Gospel which has been recovered in our Codex is an esoteric writing. Its name, contents and the way in which Irenaeus speaks about it all indicate that the writing sought a position next to the four canonical Gospels. The 'True Gospel' thus aimed at being a *Fifth Gospel*.

From time to time various theories have been put forward about the 'Gospel of Truth'.

Johannes Kreyenbühl, one of the authorities of Robert Eisler, published two bulky volumes, each of them of some 800 pages, under the title *Das Evangelium der Wahrheit* [2]. Here he endeavoured to show that the Valentinian 'Gospel of Truth', of which only the title was then known, was identical with the canonical Gospel of St. John, which he held had been written by a Gnostic. 'On ne pouvait se tromper si lourdement, ni si longuement' (H.-Ch. Puech). For though the 'Gospel of Truth' has borrowed more than a little from the Gospel of St. John, as from a writing which was already old and held in high repute, it is in fact totally different in content and spirit.

The thesis of G. A. van den Bergh van Eysinga [3], that the four canonical Gospels are the outcome of a historicization of an unhistorical Gnostic Alexandrian Gospel, is also challenged. This theory was put forward at a time

---

[2] J. Kreyenbühl, *Das Evangelium der Wahrheit*. Neue Lösung der johanneischen Frage (2 vols., 1900-5).

[3] *Voorchristelyk Christendom* (Zeist, 1918); *Begin en Beginselen van het Christendom* (1924).

when no Gnostic Gospel was known. It is now possible to check the assertions
of van den Bergh van Eysinga. For we now have in our possession an actual
Alexandrian Gnostic Gospel. And what do we find? That its writer, round
about A.D. 150, was acquainted not only with the Synoptic Gospels and the
Gospel of St. John, but also with the Epistles of St. Paul and even with the
Epistle to the Hebrews and the Apocalypse of St. John, already existing as a
collection. This is exactly the opposite of what van den Bergh van Eysinga
had maintained: we find not that the Canonical Gospels rest on a Gnostic
Gospel but that the Gnostic Gospels rest on the Canonical Gospels.

That the *Gospel of Truth* comes from the school of Valentinus, the most
important Gnostic of *c.* A.D. 90-160, there is not the least doubt. But certain
data in the work enable us to go a step further. It appears that the opinions
which it embodies reflect a stage in the development of doctrine prior to the
division of Valentinianism into different schools. That means that our *Gospel
of Truth* is very old and must have been written about A.D. 150, presumably
by Valentinus himself. We should well consider what it means to have in our
possession a heretical Gospel from A.D. 150, the only one as yet known to us
and one which appears to come from the hand of the most gifted and influential
of the Gnostics, Valentinus.

That the work was translated later from Greek into Coptic is not remarkable.
Epiphanius, an anti-heretical writer of the fourth century, tells us that there
were still Valentinians in Egypt in his time, especially in the Thebaid (Upper
Egypt). It was towards the end of the same fourth century that the Codex
which contains the *Gospel of Truth* was written. By its format, language and
Valentinian content, our collection stands in contrast with the bulk of MSS.
which were found at Nag Hammadi. These last seem to have formed the
library of a Sethian vulgar-Gnostic community which dwelt in the neighbourhood of the ancient Chenoboskion and used mainly the Sahidic dialect. It
would thus appear that our Codex was written elsewhere and later received
into the library which this community assembled in the course of the third and
fourth centuries. Nothing prevents us from supposing that the Codex originated
in a community of Valentinians which dwelt at the same time in the Thebaid,
or, if the use of the Subakhmîmic dialect justifies this conjecture, somewhat
to the north of it.

The writing is a summons to Introspection and Life, to that turning to oneself
and to God, which is Gnosis, to the discovery and winning of ourselves at the
same time as the knowledge of God and the return to Him in Whom our
proper being has its beginning and end. The whole character of the work can
best be indicated by two citations.

The state of ignorance, which is emptiness and nothingness, incoherent illusion and nightmare, which delivers man over to phantasmagoria, to foolishness, to the fears and the terrors of his unconscious, is described in a passage as fine as it is moving. The being 'who has no root', still immersed in his nothingness, thinks thus of himself: 'I am as the shadows and spectral appearances of the night'.

But when the light appears, he comes to recognize that the fear which took hold of him was nothing. Thus men were in ignorance concerning the Father, Him Whom they saw not. When [this ignorance] inspired them fear and confusion left them uncertain and hesitant, divided and torn into shreds, there were many vain illusions and empty and absurd fictions which tormented them, like sleepers who are a prey to nightmares. One flees one knows not where or one remains at the same spot when endeavouring to go forward, in the pursuit of one knows not whom. One is in a battle, one gives blows, one receives blows. Or one falls from a great height or one flies through the air without having wings. At other times it is as if one met death at the hands of an invisible murderer, without being pursued by anyone. Or it seems as if one were murdering one's neighbours: one's hands are full of blood. Down to the moment when those who have passed through all this wake up. Then they see nothing, those who have passed through all this, for all those dreams were ... nought. Thus they have cast their ignorance far away from them, like the dream which they account as nought.

It is a curious fact that this moving passage in our heretical Gospel is inspired by the *Iliad* of Homer, **XXII**, 199-201:

ὡς δ' ἐν ὀνείρῳ οὐ δύναται φεύγοντα διώκειν·
οὔτ' ἄρ' ὁ τὸν δύναται ὑποφεύγειν οὔθ' ὁ διώκειν.
ὡς ὁ τὸν οὐ δύνατο μάρψαι ποσὶν οὐδ' ὃς ἀλύξαι.

Thus the elect, i.e. 'the Living who stand written in the Book of Life' (lit. 'of the Living'), receive through the Gospel which Christ brings the voice of revelation which wakes them from this Oblivion of Being and of Self. They are called by their names. This very impressive figurative language, which ultimately goes back to Isaiah xliii. 1 ('I have called thee by thy name, thou art mine') but by this time had been greatly developed, is worked out as follows:

The Pneumatici turn to God, Who is fulfilment of the All, because they are those 'whose names the Father has known from the beginning' and 'who are called to that end, as someone who knows that he it is whose name the Father has uttered'.

Therefore he who knows is a being from above. When he is called, he hears; he answers; he directs himself to Him Who calls him and returns to Him; he apprehends how he is called. By possessing Gnosis, he carries out the will of Him Who called him and seeks to do what pleases Him. He receives the repose .... He who thus possesses knowledge knows whence he comes and whither he goes. He understands as some one who makes himself free and awakes from the drunkenness wherein he lived and returns to himself.

Thus Christianity for this Gnostic is the revelation of God and of the human self, through Christ, the transition from nothingness to the All.

It is worth noting that in our writing the peculiarly heretical traits of Gnosticism, such as the distinction between the Unknown God and the lower Demiurge or the enumeration of aeons, find no place. The writer is interested solely in Christ, Who is the discovery and revelation of Truth, and in the salvation which has been thus achieved. The sensitive language, the elevation of the thought, the powerful style would all seem to indicate that the author was none other than Valentinus himself, whose genius and eloquence were praised even by his bitter enemies. 'Et ingenio poterat et eloquio', said Tertullian. Does this heretical Gospel, which stands so very close to the orthodox conceptions of those days, purposely exclude all the more esoteric things that Valentinus had to utter? But this cannot be so, since it is clear that the book was intended only for initiates. Or is it that the writing is so near to orthodoxy because it was written at the time when Valentinus was still a member of the great Church of Rome and himself a serious candidate for the bishop's throne? That suggestion is more likely. In that case our Gospel must be dated even earlier than 150, say about 140. One thing is certain. If the author of the *Gospel of Truth* was not Valentinus himself, then he was one of Valentinus' contemporaries, a hearer or pupil of the first days, who had clearly grasped his thought.

3.   The Letter to Rheginos

The third writing of the Jung Codex, the short letter to Rheginos which was not previously known even by name, gives us valuable information about the Valentinian doctrine concerning man's resurrection-life. For the first time for many centuries it is now possible to read the heretical doctrines on this subject in the sources themselves. Hence the importance of this letter, despite its brevity. Moreover, it contains a surprise. To indicate this, we must look at the heretical teaching under discussion in a wider perspective.

From the very beginnings of Christianity there have been those who have held a spiritual conception about the resurrection of the faithful. They considered that 'the resurrection had already taken place', as did those mentioned in the Second Epistle to Timothy (ii. 18). Now over against the Hellenic idea of a more or less impersonal and automatic immortality the primitive Church held fast precisely to the conception of the resurrection, i.e. the belief that the whole man in the identity and historicity of his being is destined through the gate of death to share in the eschatological salvation. This conception of man, in his eternal perspective, obtained such pronounced accents in the conflict with Hellenism that certain more reserved utterances of the Apostle Paul did not wholly receive their due.

From our letter it now appears that the Valentinians consciously rejected the Greek conception and sought to believe in the resurrection, though they understood it in a spiritual sense. In this connexion they made their starting-point the Resurrection of Christ, the central verity of early Christianity. Our writing states:

The Redeemer has brought death to nought, but in no secret fashion so that we could not know it. For He did not remain in the perishable world: He passed over to the imperishable Aeon. And He was raised up after He had 'devoured' the visible through the invisible and He has opened for us the way for our immortality. Then, as the Apostle [Paul] said, we have suffered with Him and we have risen with Him and we have gone into Heaven with Him. But as we have come to manifestation in the world while we have put on the Christ we are rays of the Christ and we are borne by Him until we sink down. That is our death in this life. We are drawn up to heaven as rays by the sun, with nothing to hinder us. That is the spiritual resurrection which 'devours' the psychical and fleshly resurrection.

The reason why this passage is so remarkable is that the theme of the Pauline 'mysticism' here recurs: Death in life and the Resurrection-life with Christ. This is surprising because these influences of St. Paul are not to be found so definitely in the orthodox writers of the second century. It seems that it was just these heretics who allowed themselves to be influenced by the 'mysticism' of St. Paul. It naturally still remains an open question whether they properly understood St. Paul.

In a surprising way our author has conjoined with the themes of primitive Christian mysticism the speculations of a syncretistic sun-cult. According to him the faithful become sunbeams of Christ. Just like rays from the setting sun, the faithful at the moment of death are directly and of themselves brought back to this fountain of light which is their source. Such was also the way in which certain thinkers in Hellenism and the pagan Gnosis conceived the life after death.

The *Letter to Rheginos* is a systematic and comprehensive explanation of the conception we have just outlined, written in a flowing and excellent Greek which clearly penetrates the Coptic 'coat of varnish'. It is therefore a matter for great regret that the argument breaks off before the conclusion has been reached. This is to be regretted even more because certain inner pointers indicate that the letter must be very primitive. There are some pecularities of language that our letters shares with the fragments of Valentinus. And we may suppose, with even more confidence than in the case of the *Gospel of*

Truth, that it is by Valentinus himself. For this writing in many of its traits recalls the spirit and personal manner of the heresiarch. It is well put together, written in a supple and elegant Greek, as well as with the unction and warm enthusiasm which characterize the extant fragments of Valentinus.

Thanks to the new Codex we thus have a collection of three works put into our possession which, though different in style and content, are all of great importance for the history of early Christianity and the Gnostic heresy.

4. *The Treatise on the Three Natures*

The long and substantial writing which we have entitled *The Treatise on the Three Natures* and which shows close affinities with the conceptions of Heracleon, the leader of the Italian school of Valentinianism and the first commentator on the Fourth Gospel, begins with some elaborate speculations on the mysteries of the Godhead. In itself this it not surprising, for the Gnostic *Apocryphon Johannis* and the system of Basilides also open with a description of this kind. It is clear that this *theologia negativa* is an anticipation of certain speculations of the Church Fathers, especially of the mystics among them.

Our writing has the following passage:

No name that one can think or say or see or feel, none of these is given Him .... These names can be uttered to His glory and honour in accordance with the capacity of those who show Him honour. But Himself, in His essence and subsistence and being, no mind can understand Him, no word can express Him, no eye can see Him, no body can touch Him by reason of His unfathomable greatness and incomprehensible depth and immeasurable height and inaccessible will .... He is unknowable, i.e. unthinkable by any thought, invisible in any kind of way, unnameable by any word, untouchable by any hand: He is known to Himself alone.

These explanations, as I have already said, remind us in many respects of the *theologia negativa* of the mystics of every age. But notwithstanding this mystical *élan* the writer clearly shows us that he is not speaking of the undetermined Being after the manner of Plotinus. His Godhead is transcendent indeed but not unconscious, lifted up above all perception and all thought, yet a Being which is conscious and wills, which thinks Himself.

He is the only one who is known to Himself in His mode of existence, His form, His greatness and glory. He is capable of thinking, seeing, perceiving, comprehending Himself. He is for Himself consciousness, eye, mouth, structure, He who thinks Himself, sees, names, comprehends, this unthinkable, unnameable, incomprehensible, unchangeable.

In this passage the influence of Christianity, which lends personal traits to the mystic conception of the Unknown God, can perhaps be recognized. These Christian influences are to be seen even more clearly in the writer's speculations on the relation of the Father to the Son which foreshadow certain themes of the Origenist theology. It is striking, however, that he conceives of the Ecclesia as an eternal hypostasis, 'the Ecclesia of many men which existed before the aeons, which is rightly named the Aeon of aeons, the nature of the holy imperishable spirits'. This theology of the eternal Ecclesia is most remarkable.

After a long lacuna in which perhaps the coming into being of the Pleroma and the fall of the Sophia were recorded, the writing begins again with a cosmogony. This world is an image of a higher world and is so organized that the seeds of spirit, through their life in the world, are brought up, instructed and formed 'so that the small becomes gradually greater as by the image in a mirror'.

The author gives an allegorical explanation of the creation of Adam and his Fall and ensuing death, after which follows a description of the process of history. Three phases are distinguished: the hylic or Greek, the psychic or Jewish, and the pneumatic or Christian which forms the crowning of the world process. It is noteworthy how little sympathy the writer has for Greek culture. This is the more striking because various investigators, following in footsteps of Overbeck and von Harnack, have regarded the Gnostics as thinkers standing in the succession of Greek philosophy and Gnosis as an acute Hellenization of Christianity. It would now seem that at any rate the writer of this treatise stood consciously apart from Greek philosophy.

He writes of the Greek philosophers:

They did not possess the possibility of knowing the cause of existing things because this was not communicated to them. Therefore they introduced other explanations.
Some say that the things which happen take place according to a Providence; these are those who perceive the regularity and order of motion.
Others say that no Providence exists; these are those who take notice both of the irregularity and abnormality of the powers and of evil. Some say that what must happen happens .... Others say that what happens comes about according to nature. Others again say that the world is an automatism. But the great majority have turned to the visible elements, without knowing more than these.

Hence the writer sees in Greek philosophy only contradiction and demonic inspiration. He esteems at far higher worth the Hebrew prophets who did not contradict one another and announced the coming of Christ.

The Redeemer brings liberation from slavery and reveals the destiny of the three classes into which mankind is divided:

The pneumatic group, which is light from light and spirit from spirit, when its Head appears, has to hasten after Him and has a body formed for its Head, which has received Gnosis with eagerness at the revelation. But the psychic group, which is light from fire, has hesitated about receiving Gnosis, but hastened to Him in *faith* .... But the hylic group, which is wholly foreign [to Him], will be cut off as darkness by the brightness from the light.

The writer then gives us a long description of the eschatological destiny of these three classes.

Thus our writing includes an explanation of the origin of mankind and the world, of the course of history and the passage of the Spirit through the inferno of paganism, the purgatorio of religion and morality to the paradiso of pure spirituality when the Spirit shall have ascended above the steps from the Pleroma and live eternally in God.

And irresistibly we ask the question: Where do these ideas, myths and series of thoughts come from? Where are we to seek the origin of the Gnosis which is set out in this writing in a very Christianized form? And this leads us back again to the problem of the connexion which we raised in the beginning of this lecture.

C. THE CONNEXIONS

From the short summary given above it will no doubt have become clear that Heracleon, the Italian Gnostic who in our own judgement was the author of the *Treatise on the Three Natures,* is in many respects a precursor of Origen. The two writers have in common the *theologia negativa,* certain Trinitarian speculations, the transcendental Fall, the notion of the world as a *catharsis* and history as an education. Even more striking are the differences. Heracleon teaches a complete determinism of mankind and the world, a sort of *praedestinatio physica.* For Origen, on the other hand, man's freedom in his decision is essential. For freedom is the theme of Origen's every symphony. Indeed, in the perspective of the *Treatise on the Three Natures* it becomes clear that the main purpose of Origen's theology of freedom was to attack the determinism of the Gnostics. This concern for freedom was undoubtedly due to the influence of the Old Testament whose every page bears testimony to man's accountability and responsibility. Hence the 'true Gnosis' of Clement and Origen is to be regarded as in a certain sense a progressive Christianization of the 'Gnosis falsely so called' of the Valentinians.

Having thus established that this heretical Gnosis was already to a great extent Christianized in the Alexandrians, we now have to ask: What was Gnosis before it came into contact with Christianity? In other words, where are we to look for its origins?

It would seem as if the newly-found Codex can help us to answer this question [4]. The suggestions which follow are very provisional and can only be developed in full after the publication of the texts. Indeed, it may be that in the light of more extensive material the hypothesis which will be here propounded will prove unjustified.

On page 112 of the Codex, in the *Treatise on the Three Natures*, there occurs a passage dealing with heresies among the Jews, which will be read with close attention, now that documents on a Jewish heresy have been found by the Dead Sea:

They [sc. the Jews] have founded numerous heresies which exist down to the present day among the Jews. Some say that it is One God Who spoke by the Prophets; others say that there were many. Some say that God is one and singular in His being; others say that His acting is two-fold and the origin of both good and evil. Some say that He is the creator of what exists; others say that He created through His angels.

There is every reason to believe that these references accurately reflect an existing situation. The Talmud also frequently mentions a body of heretics, the Minim, who lived in Palestine in the first centuries of our era and were attacked by the orthodox Rabbis. It is, indeed, not always clear who are meant by these Minim and it is probable that the name covers many different groups. It would certainly be going much too far to regard all these Minim as Jewish Gnostics. Nor is it possible to connect all these passages with Christians, Jewish Christians or Christians Gnostics. In some passages it is beyond dispute that these heretics were neither Christians nor Jewish Christians, but heterodox Jews. At that date there existed in Palestine, side by side with official Judaism and Christianity, all kinds of sects which in varying degrees tended to unorthodoxy or could increasingly be regarded as unorthodox, as the orthodoxy of the Pharisees became consolidated and supplanted the original variety of religious teachings in Palestine. Among these 'heretical' groups were the Essenes, whose writings have now been found by the Dead Sea and prove beyond question the existence of a pre-Christian Jewish heterodoxy. It is therefore clear that all these streams in Palestine cannot be described simply as 'Gnostic' without more ado. More properly we should speak in some cases of a pre-Gnosis which incorporated certain opinions that were also congenial to Gnosticism.

It may well be that the passage cited above from the Codex has reference to these or similar unorthodoxies. And although a definitive judgment can hardly

---

[4] Discussed more fully in 'Der gnostische Anthropos und die jüdische Tradition' in *Eranos Jahrbuch* XXII, 1953 (Zürich, 1954), pp. 195-234. See below p. 173-195.

be possible before all the passages in the Talmud which relate to the Minim
have been severally investigated and the material made available by the
discoveries at the Dead Sea been compared with them, it may be permitted at
this stage to draw attention to some parallels.

In the *Manual of Discipline*, found at Qumran, we read that God endowed
man with a good and an evil spirit [5]. This statement should be brought into
connexion with the passage cited from the Codex referring to a Jewish heresy
which taught that God is the cause of good and evil. This was apparently also
the common conception of the Pharisees, though the Essenes known to the
Jewish philosopher Philo conceived of the Godhead as the cause of all good
things but not of the evil things. Similar conceptions were also found among
the Minim of Palestine. The expression current among some of them 'On
account of the good is Thy Name named' (not also 'On account of the evil')
was considered by the Rabbis to be heretical [6]. Certain Minim also criticized
the teaching of the Old Testament that God kills and makes alive: '[When
anyone says] that He cannot make alive and kill, that He cannot dispose of
evil and cannot do good then the Scripture teaches: "I kill and make alive" ' [7].
Hence it would appear that a difference of opinion actually existed among the
Minim on this matter, as our Codex indicates.

Another statement in the Codex is, perhaps, further confirmed when
Justin Martyr, the Apologist, who himself came from Shechem in Samaria and
was clearly well informed about the Jewish sects which he mentions in his
works, asserts that a Jewish heresy taught that the body of man was made
by angels [8]. Here again the information in the Talmud needs to be closely
studied before we can say with certainty how far certain Minim may have
thought that angels played a part in the creation of man and of the world.
But we can at least say that there were heretics who taught that angels were
concerned in creation. 'When Moses wrote the Torah, he described the work
of each several day. But when he reached the verse (*Gen.* i. 26) "Then spake
God, Let us make men", he said "Lord of the World! What an opportunity
Thou givest the heretics to open their mouths!" He answered, "Write! Who
wishes to go astray can go astray" ' [9]. It is possible that by the heretics here

---

[5] *Manual of Discipline*, iii, 18. A. H. Edelkoort, *De Handschriften van de Dode Zee*
(Baarn, n.d.), p. 88. A. Dupont Sommer, 'La "Règle" de la Communauté de la Nouvelle
Alliance' in *Revue de l'Histoire des Religions* 138 (1950), pp. 5-21.
[6] Philo, *Quod omnis probus liber* 458. Mishna, Megilla 4, 9 acc. to the interpretation of
H. L. Strack, *Jesus, die Häretiker und die Christen* (Leipzig, 1910), p. 48*.
[7] *Siphre Deut.* 32, 39.
[8] Justin Martyr, *Dialogus cum Tryphone* 62.
[9] *Gen. rabba* 1, 26.

referred to Christians are meant. But it is no less possible that there were non-Christian unorthodox Jews who gave a heretical interpretation to the view of certain Rabbis that the Biblical words: 'Let us make men' had reference to angels. The words were held to apply not only to the creation of men but also to creation in general. Indeed, R. Johanan went so far as to say that God does nothing without seeking counsel of the angels [10]. From this it becomes intelligible that, as our Codex says, the world, according to Jewish heretics, was created by angels. Provisionally we may thus accept the accuracy of the statement of Justin Martyr and of the Codex.

This fact is important when we seek to determine the influence of Judaism and Jewish heterodoxy on Gnosis [11]. For among the Gnostics we find similar conceptions about the work of the angels in creation. We meet with them, e.g. in the Samaritans, Simon Magus and Menander, in the Syrian Gnostic, Saturninus of Antioch, in the author of the *Apocryphon Johannis*, in Valentinus himself and in Heracleon, the probable author of the *Treatise on the Three Natures* of which we have already spoken. We can almost see this conception unfolding historically from Jewish heterodoxy *via* the Jewish Gnosis of Samaria down to our treatise. We can then understand how it is that some early Christian writers, notably the Jewish Christian Hegesippus c. A.D. 150, came to seek the origins of Gnosticism in heterodox Judaism [12]. It is quite possible that Justin Martyr intends by the Jewish heresy which taught that the body was created by angels the sects of Simon and Menander; but in this case, too, the origin of these Gnostic conceptions would have to be sought in the Jewish Gnosis of the first century. But our present information makes it more probable that Simon and Menander were themselves developing further an already existing Jewish heresy.

Our Codex makes the remarkable statement that according to some heretics there were many gods. It is hard to believe that in Palestine there were Jewish polytheists. It is possible indeed that this assertion is only a stylistic figure, a literary expression devoid of historical significance. But it must also be asked whether the intention of the passage is not to assert a multiplicity, i.e. a duality, in God. This would give us a good historical sense. For the Rabbis repeatedly reproached the Palestinian Minim with teaching two Divine 'Powers' or 'Principles' (*r'schujoth*). And even when only these two Principles were referred to, they were spoken of as 'many' Powers: 'For this reason a single man was created in order that the heretics could not say: "There are *many*

---

[10] *Sanhedrin* 38b.
[11] G. Quispel in *Eranos Jahrbuch* XXII (1954), p. 204. See below p. 180.
[12] Eusebius, *Hist. Eccl.* iv, 22, 5.

Powers in Heaven" ' 13. By this is meant that in certain cases these heretics, who were not Christians but unorthodox Jews, distinguished between God Himself, in His transcendence and hiddenness, and His 'Vicegerent', the Mediator of Revelation and the Lord of the Angels who was named the 'Little Jahweh' or 'Jaoel' or also, employing a *vox mystica,* 'Metatron'. In the Talmud two notable passages about this are to be found. '[The Rabbi] Aḥer saw that to Metatron was given the right *to be seated* (in Heaven) and to write down the merits of Israel. Then he said: "We are taught that above there is neither standing nor sitting, neither envy nor strife, neither separation nor union. Can there then be — which God forbid — two powers?" ' 14. The second passage is as follows: 'A heretic said to Rabbi Idi: "It is written: And to Moses He said, Go up to Jahweh (*Ex.* xxiv. 1). One expects, Go up to Me". Idi replied to him: "That is Metatron, whose Name is as the Name of his Lord, as it is written: For my Name is in him" (*Ex.* xxiii. 21). "As that is so, ought one not to serve him?" ' (asked the Minim who thus appeared to demand for Jaoel Divine worship) 15.

Thus the difference between the Rabbis and the Minim on the subject lies in the fact that while the Minim held fast to the divinity of this second 'hypostasis', the Rabbis, in a sense after the manner of the Arians, emphasized the creature-liness of the 'angel' Jaoel-Metatron. It may be asked whether these Minim, in their opposition to a growing orthodoxy, did not preserve in their own way the ancient doctrine that the Name of God was a representation and manifestation of the Godhead itself, the revelation of His Being 16. It is possible to follow the traces of this conception from the Apocalyptic period at the beginning of our era down to the writings of esoteric Judaism in later centuries. And it would appear to us that the attitude of Gnosis to Judaism would become clearer if more heed than hitherto was paid to this esoteric tradition which from the first century existed in Palestine as a lesser stream side by side with orthodoxy.

---

13   *Sanhedrin* 4, 5.

14   Bab. *Hagiga* 15a.

15   Bab. *Sanhedrin* 38b. The Karaïte author Qirqisani quotes the passage thus: 'This is Metatron Jahweh qaton'. With Scholem, I think it possible that the Name Jahweh qaton was deliberately eliminated from the Talmudic MSS. because of its heretical ring. Cf. G. Scholem, *Major Trends in Jewish Mysticism,* New York, 1946, p. 366, note 107.

16   H. Odeberg, *3 Enoch* (Cambridge, 1928), p. 144: 'The most important element or complex of elements which gave life and endurance to the conception in question [of Metatron in later Jewish mysticism] was the notion of the 'Angel of J H V H, who bears the Divine Name' and the 'Angel of the Face, the Divine Presence', called Yaoel, Yehoel, Yoel, the highest of the angels, *the Divine Name representing the Godhead.* Extensive speculations must have centred round this possessor of the Divine Name'.

In the *Ethiopic Book of Enoch,* a work referred to among the writings of the sect by the Dead Sea but not on that account to be regarded as specially representative of this sect, mention is made, if I correctly understand the text, of the 'hidden', Divine 'Name', by which the world was created:

This [angel] requested Michael to show him the hidden Name, that he might pronounce it in the Oath, so that they [sc. the fallen angels] might quake before that Name and Oath [by which] ... the heaven was made fast and suspended ... the earth was founded upon the water ... the sea was created ... and by which the stars complete their course [17].

This teaching is also not unknown to the Talmud. According to Rabbi Rabh, a prominent representative of the esoteric traditions at the beginning of the third century, the builder of the tabernacle knew the combination of letters whereby Heaven and earth were created [18]. These letters are the Name of God, the Tetragrammaton.

This conception was especially popular in the circles of esoteric Judaism. In the so-called *Hekkaloth Rabbati,* ch. ix, we read expressly: 'Great is the Name through which Heaven and earth have been created'. The *Third Book of Enoch,* a treatise put by Odeberg in the third century but by others dated later, also appears to be acquainted with this conception.

'He wrote with His finger with a flaming style upon the crown of my head the letters by which were created heaven and earth' [19]. 'Come and behold the letters, by which the heaven and the earth were created' [20].

Finally, in the 'Book of Creation', *Yezira,* written between the third and the sixth centuries, we have described at length and in a somewhat fantastic manner how the whole creation proceeds from one Name, the Name of God [21].

It thus seems clear that even in pre-Christian times the Name of God was considered as a cosmological principle, and thus in a certain sense as a distinct hypostasis. In the beginning was the Name and thereby everything was made [22].

---

[17] 1 Enoch 69, 14 ff.

[18] *Berakoth* IX, 55.

[19] 13, 1.

[20] 44, 1.

[21] For some of these references I am indebted to G. Scholem, 'Die Vorstellung vom Golem' in *Eranos Jahrbuch* XXII (1954), p. 246.

[22] The statement in the *Didache* x, 3: ἔκτισας τὰ πάντα ἕνεκεν τοῦ ὀνόματός σου needs closer study. The statement that the world was created *because of* the Name is unparalleled in early Christian literature. Whether or not the meaning here is: 'By the power of Thy Name', I will not venture to say.

But a related interpretation of the Name is also to be found in other conceptions of apocalyptic Judaism round about the beginning of the Christian era.

In the *Apocalypse of Abraham* we have a long account of the angel Jaoel to whom God gave His ineffable Name [23]. From the text it is quite clear that this figure is God's 'Vicegerent, second only to God Himself, the supreme figure in Jewish angelology' [24]. But it is also clear that this figure is the Mediator and Bringer of Revelation since He is in possession of the ineffable Name. Jaoel himself says in his revelation to Abraham: 'I am called Jaoel by Him Who moveth that which existeth with me on the seventh expanse upon the firmament, a power in virtue of the ineffable Name that is dwelling in me' (*Apocalypse of Abraham*, ch. x). It seems to me that the learned Dr. G. H. Box, who published the *Apocalypse of Abraham* for such a handful of readers, was right when he remarked that Jaoel is properly the Name itself [25].

This conjecture is apparently confirmed by the fact that in other places Jaoel is named 'Little Jahweh'. This must have happened at a very early date. For even though it is not quite certain that *III Enoch*, where this designation is found [26], comes from as early as the third century A.D., the designation 'Little Jao' is also found in the Gnostic *Pistis Sophia* [27] of the third century and must have been borrowed by the author of this writing from the esoteric Jewish traditions. Hence it is established that already in the second century Jaoel was termed the 'Little Jahweh'. This designation, which would be blasphemous for the orthodox, tells in favour of Box's view that Jaoel is a substitute for the Name itself.

This proves that the speculations in Judaism about the Name as a mediator of revelation were very ancient and pre-Christian.

Thus we have proved that at the beginning of our era there existed in more or less heterodox Judaism speculations about the Name as the 'mediator' of creation as well as others about the Name as the mediator of revelation.

Now it was already recognized, as we have said above, that third-century Gnosticism had taken over certain Jewish speculations about the Name. What is more, the Name Jao is to be found in a liturgical formula of the

---

[23] In the *Sepher ha-Qoma* ('Inyane Merkaba), Bodl. MS. Oppenheimer 467, fol. 61b, the *šem hammephoraš* is expressly identified with Metatron-Jaoel: 'The Explicit Name, which is Metatron the Youth' (cf. Odeberg *op. cit.* p. 33).

[24] G. H. Box, *The Apocalypse of Abraham* (S.P.C.K., 1919), p. xxv.

[25] 'The name Jaoel itself is evidently a substitute for the tetragrammaton, which was too sacred to be written out in full'. G. H. Box, *op. cit.*, p. xxv.

[26] Ch. 12, 5; ch. 48; ch. 7.

[27] Ch. 7.

Valentinians [28] which has hitherto given scholars many headaches but now, it would seem, can be satisfactorily interpreted [29]. Finally, in Valentinian documents, notably the *Excerpta ex Theodoto,* there occur a variety of allusions to the Name. But only now would it seem possible properly to understand what this Name meant for the Gnostics and to prove that these speculations about the Name go back *ultimately* to more or less heterodox Jewish conceptions which were taken over into Gnosis as early as the beginning of this second century.

For the *Gospel of Truth* contains very extensive comments on the Name of God, the 'Real Name' ($\kappa\acute{\upsilon}\rho\iota\upsilon\nu\ \acute{o}\nu\upsilon\mu\alpha$) which is not to be expressed in $\lambda\acute{\epsilon}\xi\epsilon\iota\varsigma$ and $\pi\rho\upsilon\sigma\eta\gamma\upsilon\rho\acute{\iota}\alpha\iota.$ This kind of language suggests the distinction which the Jews used to make between the *šem hammephoraš,* the secret ineffable Name of God, and the *kinnuj,* the utterable naming. This distinction made its way in a degenerate form into the Gnostic *Second Book of Jeû* which dates from the third century A.D., but it also appears to have been already known to Valentinus c. A.D. 140. It would thus seem that the conjecture of Prof. Scholem that in the Greek the pair of concepts $\kappa\acute{\upsilon}\rho\iota\upsilon\nu\ \acute{o}\nu\upsilon\mu\alpha$, properly 'Name', and $\pi\rho\upsilon\sigma\eta\gamma\upsilon\rho\iota\kappa\grave{o}\nu\ \acute{o}\nu\upsilon\mu\alpha,$ 'Naming', is used to indicate the *Tetragrammaton* and its synonyms, is confirmed by the latest discovery [30].

But in connexion with our argument about the Jewish speculations concerning the *šem* as a divine manifestation and independent hypostasis, it will be worth our while to reproduce the passage in the *Gospel of Truth* in its entirety:

And the end is the Taking-of-Gnosis about Him who is concealed. And this is the Father, He from whom proceeded the Beginning and to whom all who have proceeded from Him and who have been manifested for the Glory and for the Joy of His Name will return. And the Name of the Father is the Son. He it is who at the first gave the Name to him who proceeded from Him and who was Himself. And He has begotten him as Son, He has given him His Name which He possessed, He — the Father — to whom belong all things existing near Him. He has the Name, He has the Son, (and) it is possible for them [i.e. the Aeons] to see Him. But on the other hand the Name is invisible, for this alone is the mystery of the Invisible, who has reached to the very ears which are all filled with it by Him. For, in fact, they do not name the Father's Name. But He reveals Himself by a Son. Great, therefore, is the Name. Who then is there who could pronounce a Name for Him, the great Name, except He alone, to whom this Name belongs? And the Sons of the Name are those in whom the Name of the Father rests. And they for their part rest in His Name. Since the

---

[28] Iren. I, 21, 3.

[29] G. Quispel, 'Mandaeers en Valentinianen' in *Nederlands Theologisch Tijdschrift* viii. 3 (1954), pp. 144-8.

[30] G. Scholem, 'Ueber eine Formel in den koptisch-gnostischen Schriften' in *Z. N.T.W.* xxx (1931), p. 176.

Father is beyond being, only he whom He has begotten was (for Him) a Name before He had set in order the Aeons, in order that the Name of the Father might be on their head as the Real Name [tr. of κύριον ὄνομα]. Such is the authentic Name, steadfast in its authority and by its perfect power; for this Name does not belong to the words (λέξεις) nor is it from the designations (that) His Name (comes), for it is invisible. He has given a Name to him alone, while he it is who alone understands [lit. sees] it, while he alone is he to whom it is possible to give a Name. In truth, He, who is beyond being, has no Name. For what Name will one give to him who is not? On the other hand, he who has become in his being, he is also with his Name and he alone knows it and to give him a Name there was the Father alone. The Son is his Name; he has therefore not concealed it by this action; but as soon as the Son had come into being, He gave a Name to him alone. That is why [lit. 'therefore'] the Name (of the Son) was that of the Father, in the same way that the Name of the Father was (that of the) Son. This mercy, where shall it find a Name, if it be not that of the Father? But certainly someone will say to his neighbour: 'Who is it that will give a Name to Him before whom there was none, as in the case of the name which children receive from those who give them birth?' First of all, then, it is fitting for us to consider the mystery: What is the Name? For this [i.e. this Name] is the authentic Name. This, then, is the Name (which comes) from the Father, for this has become the Name in the true sense of the word. So he did not receive the Name as a loan, like the others, after the manner of each, by which he returns [prob. trans. of ὄνομα τῆς ἀποκαταστάσεως]. But this is the Real Name (κύριον ὄνομα). There is none other to whom He has given it; but He was Unnameable, He was Ineffable until the moment when He, He alone who is perfect, uttered it, and He it is who has the power to say his Name and to understand [lit. 'see'] it. When He then (wished), still existing in Himself, that His beloved[?] Name should become His Son and (when) He had given him the Name, (then) he who proceeded from the Depth spoke of the hidden things of Him, knowing that the Father is a Being without evil. Therefore He also sent this one that he might speak about the Topos[31] and His (place of) Rest, from whence he proceeded, in order that he might glorify in the Pleroma the Greatness of his Name and the Sweetness of the Father.

In this passage the Name is indeed a Divine Manifestation, an independent

---

[31] τόπος as a title of the Demiurge was already known from the *Excerpta ex Theodoto* 34, etc. This has long been regarded as the most decisive proof of Jewish influences upon Gnosis. For it is wholly inconceivable that the influences were the other way! We must observe that in our passage τόπος denotes not the Demiurge but God Himself. The separation of the highest God and the Demiurge does not yet occur in the *Gospel of Truth*. The astonishing thing is that the Unknown God of Gnosis is described as *maqōm* and termed *Jao*. Christ's Work and Function are understood as the revelation of the hidden Name. C. H. Dodd, *The Interpretation of the Fourth Gospel* (1953), p. 93, observed that according to Pinchas ben Jair the Jews do not yet known the *šem hammephoraš*, whereas God will reveal him in the Coming Age. This eschatology is realized in the Fourth Gospel and dehistoricized in the *Gospel of Truth*. But it is only to be understood from its Jewish origins.

hypostasis, which functions as a mediator of revelation. I am unable to see
how this passage can *not* ultimately go back to Jewish heterodox speculations
about the Name. We thus establish by another route that the speculations on
the Name, on Jahweh qaton, Jaoel and Metatron, which we meet with in the
writings of later Judaism somehow or other arose in the first century and
perhaps even earlier. It must be the object of a subsequent study to investigate
how far the Prologue of the Fourth Gospel and the Logos theology of
Justin Martyr and others must be seen in this perspective.

Finally it may well be the case that this passage throws some light on the
problem posed by Reitzenstein and Bultmann concerning the doctrine of a
pre-Christian Gnostic Redeemer, which is said to have influenced the Fourth
Gospel. This theory rests mainly on three pillars: 1. Reports in Iranian sources
of a late date concerning Gayomart. By the magic of a questionable *Quellenforschung* these sources are put back into the fourth century B.C. It should
also be noted that the oldest form of the Gnostic myth is concerned not with
Gayomart but with Sophia, Chokma, who brings forth the seven planets; and
this goes back not to Persia but to the ps.-Platonic *Epinomis*. 2. The doctrine
of the Anthropos, which was held captive in matter, mentioned in the
Poimandres. This is said to have been borrowed from a Persian source. But
Erik Peterson has proved that there was a Jewish tradition that Adam after
his Fall from the heavenly paradise returned to that paradise: the Anthropos
of the *Poimandres* seems to be not the Persian Gayomart but the Jewish
Adam [32]. 3. The Manichaean doctrine of the Primal Man (*Urmensch*) who
left the realm of light and is benumbed in darkness, but by the call from above
again comes to consciousness and, leaving his limbs behind, returns to the realm
of light. We are told that this, too, was borrowed by Mani, not from Gnostic
tradition, but from the Persian religion. So did Reitzenstein reconstruct an
Iranian 'mystery of redemption' which was said to have lain at the basis of
Christianity.

It would appear that the third pillar can now also be overthrown. In the Codex
we have so far found no traces of a so-called 'Iranian mystery of redemption'
or of a 'pre-Christian Gnostic redeemer'. Our Codex speaks, indeed, of the
'Perfect Man who is the All' and whose *members* are the *pneumatici*. And of
this Perfect Man we read in the Codex: 'When redemption was preached, the
perfect man received Gnosis into himself, so that he returned with haste to his
unity, to the place whence he had arisen, to the place whence he had come'.
His limbs, however, still remained behind to be transformed.

---

[32] E. Peterson, 'La Libération d'Adam de l' Ἀνάγκη' in *Revue Biblique* lv (1948), pp.
199-214.

This is the same conception as appears in Manichaeism. Thus the Manichaean Primal Man was borrowed not from the Persian religion but from the Gnostic tradition.

Now this tells us much about the origin of Gnosis. There would appear to be good grounds for supposing that is was from Christianity that the conception of redemption and the figure of the Redeemer were taken over into Gnosticism. A pre-Christian redeemer and an Iranian mystery of redemption perhaps never existed. And in so far as Gnosis is pre-Christian, it goes back to heterodox Jewish conceptions, e.g. about Adam and the Name.

In the light of these facts we can perhaps also understand better the real significance of the transition from primitive Christianity to early Catholicism. Late antiquity is a land of three streams in which Greek philosophy, Christian faith and Gnosticism flow side by side. In a fruitful confrontation Christian theology purged out rationalism and mysticism, while it integrated the Logos of the Hellenes and the Mythos of the Orient. The history of the Church is the Christianization of Greek thought and Eastern mysticism on the basis of the Gospel.

THE ORIGINAL DOCTRINE OF VALENTINUS

I

INTRODUCTION

The writings of Valentinus, the Christian gnostic who lived about 150 after Christ, are lost: only a few fragments remain. His pupils were divided into different schools, the so-called Italic school, of which Ptolemaeus and Heracleon were the leaders, and the Oriental school, to which among others Theodotus belonged. The antiheretic authors transmit ample and very contradictory accounts of their systems. How much of their opinions goes back to the founder of the sect, is still uncertain. Valentinianism therefore is generally considered to be "ein wüster Trümmerhaufen der sich zu einem verständlichen Bau nicht mehr zusammenfügen will" [1] .

This is a deplorable situation, because Valentinus seems to have been a person of some importance, who exercised a considerable influence on Christian theology. Moreover, the interpretation, translation and emendation of the *Refutatio* of Irenaeus, the *Panarion* of Epiphanius, the *Excerpta ex Theodoto* of Clemens Alexandrinus, the *Refutatio* of Hippolytus and the booklet of Tertullianus *adversus Valentinianos* are involved, if the information they contain cannot be understood. So Valentinianism offers a tempting problem to the puzzled mind. Are the antiheretic writers to be blamed for dishonesty to their opponents? Is there some evidence in our sources, which leads us to suppose that pupils changed the doctrine of their master? Will the outlines of the original system reappear when these additions have been removed? To these questions an answer, — if possible at all —, can only be given if the methods of modern criticism, based on philology, are applied. The various accounts we possess must be considered as reflecting different stages in the historical, and to a large extent comprehensible, evolution of the sect. When the sources of Irenaeus, our principal witness, have been determined and when the innovations and alterations introduced by Ptolemaeus into the myth of Valentinus, have been indicated with the aid of explicit testimonies and internal evidence, a new attempt to solve the Valentinian problem may be made in due course.

Much of the preliminary work has already been done: the achievements of research in this field of scholarship may be summed up in the following statements:

1. the brief sketch of the original system of Valentinus, Irenaeus 1, 11, 1, is trustworthy and valuable [2];

---

[1] E. Schwarz, Gött. Gel. Nachrichten 1908, p. 127.

[2] A. Hilgenfeld, *Ketzergesch. des Urchr.*, p. 52.

2. the opinions of the Oriental School, to which the *Excerpta ex Theodoto* partly refer, are very close to the conceptions of their master [3];

3. the description of the emanation of the aeons and the origin of evil (Iren. I, 1-1, 2, 3) contains no important deviations from the authentic theory;

4. the brief chapter Iren. I, 2, 3, beginning with the words: ἔνιοι δὲ αὐτῶν οὕτως τὸ πάθος τῆς Σοφίας κτλ. has much in common with the version of Hippolytus VI, 29 [4];

5. immediately afterwards (Iren. 1, 2, 4) we are told that Ὅρος emanates as as an image of the Father, who is conceived as a unity, whereas in the preceding chapters Ὅρος already existed and God was said to be a dyad (this very important hint of Heinrici has been neglected by later scholars; it means, that with the words of chapter I, 2, 4: Ὁ δὲ Πατήρ a new source begins;

6. Irenaeus (1, 4, 1-1, 6, 3) and Clement (Exc. 43-65) have received their information from a common source [5], which described the events outside the *pleroma*. This document was presumably written by Ptolemaeus himself [6];

7. the version transmitted by Hippolytus VI, 29 *seqq.* reflects a later development of the doctrine of the 'Italic' school [7];

8. almost complete agreement has been reached about the assignment of the different parts of the *Excerpta* to Theodotus, Ptolemaeus and Clement [8].

If these data are combined, a few inferences may be drawn concerning the historical development of the school.

VALENTINUS	PTOLEMAEUS	ITALIC SCHOOL
1. Deity is conceived as a *dyad* (Iren. 1, 11, 1).	A tendency to stress the unity of God (Iren. 1, 8, 5). Together with the Holy Spirit *Christ* emanates (Tert. adv. Valent. 11: munus enim his datur unum: procurare concinnationem Aeonum: et ab eius officii societate duae scholae, duae cathedrae, inauguratio quae-dam dividendae doctrinae Valentini).	God is one (Iren. I, 2, 4; Hippol. VI, 29). Together with the Holy Spirit Christ emanates (Iren. I, 2, 5; Hippol. VI, 31).
2. The inner life of God is a gradual emanation of the Son (aeons) and the Holy Spirit from the Father (Iren. 1, 11, 1).		

---

[3] Heinrici, *Die valentinianische Gnosis und die Heilige Schrift,* Berlin 1871.

[4] W. Foerster, *Von Valentin zu Herakleon,* Giessen 1928.

[5] O. Dibelius, Z. N. W. 1908, p. 230.

[6] C. Barth, *Die Interpretation des Neuen Testaments in der Valentinischen Gnosis,* T. und U. XXXVII, p. 11.

[7] Foerster, *o.c.* p. 100.

[8] R. P. Casey, *Excerpta,* London 1934, p. 5 sqq.

VALENTINUS	PTOLEMAEUS	ITALIC SCHOOL
3. *Horos* is a perpetual function of the Νοῦς (Iren. 1, 11, 1).		*Horos* emanates after the fall of *Sophia* (Iren. 1, 2, 4; Hippol. VI, 31).
4. One Sophia (Iren. 1, 11, 1).	A higher and a lower *Sophia* (ps. Tert. adv. omn. haeres. 4: et quod dicit Valentinus Aeonem tricesimum excessisse de pleromate, ut in defectionem, negant isti (Ptolemaeus et Secundus).	*Idem* Iren. I, 2, 4.
5. Preexistent Jesus, overcoming his deficiency, left his mother, Sophia, and ascended to the *pleroma* (Iren. I, 11).	This appalling conception will not be found in any document of 'Italic' source.	
6. The Demiurge is rather hostile (frag. I, Clem. Al. Strom. II 36, 2-4; Exc. 33, 4).	The Demiurge is rather friendly (*Epistola ad Floram*).	*Idem.*
7. Earth, water, fire, and air took their origin from the despair, sorrow, ignorance, and fear to which *Sophia* was subjected.	Moreover, the lower soul of man was made out of fear, the devil('s) out of sorrow (Iren. I, 4, 1 sqq.).	
8. Jesus was a *spiritual* human being (σάρξ) (Tert. *de Carne* 15: licuit et *Valentino* ex privilegio haeretico carnem Christi *spiritalem* comminisci. Ps. Tert. adv. omnes haereses 4: *spiritale* nescio quod *corpus* de caelo deferentem).	Jesus had a psychic body, a soul, and a spirit (Iren. 1, 6, 1).	

These conclusions are to a large extent confirmed by Iren. I, 14, a copy of a document written by Marcus, a pupil of Valentinus, who translated the latter's mysticism into the cryptic language of gematric occultism without interfering with the outlines of the system.

It is interesting to observe how Ptolemaeus managed to express difference of opinion within the limits of mythological categories. Valentinus was a visionary mystic, Ptolemaeus took a more reconciliatory attitude towards Christian orthodoxy. Living in the time after the attack of Marcion on Judaism and the

reaction of the apologists, he tried to mitigate the shocking speculations of his
master. Nevertheless, he preserved the main outlines and the terminology of
the system. This leads us to suppose that Ptolemaeus adopted an existing
manuscript by means of corrections, interpolations, and transpositions. The
author of this document can hardly have been anyone else than Valentinus
himself [9]. It may be taken for granted that Theodotus, who wrote during the
lifetime of Valentinus, did also possess this esoteric writing.

Since Theodotus lived in the East and Ptolemaeus in the West, the two
heretics must have had very few opportunities for exchanging their ideas: so
we are not jumping to conclusions assuming that, wherever the Theodotian
sources of the *Excerpta* and the Ptolemaic sources of Irenaeus agree, they both
preserve the tradition of Valentinus. The following reconstruction, which
depends largely on this suppositon, combines the evidence of the two above
mentioned sources with the data of Iren. 1, 11 and the fragments of the
master. It does not pretend to be complete: criticism by cross-examination and
insistant questioning may even reveal omissions, deliberate or inadvertent, and
smouldering contradictions beneath the surface. Our aim is to show that the
Valentinian doctrine was a systematic conception of the universe, poetical, but
not disorderly, heretic, but not confused.

The reader may need a provisional expedient to unravel this tangled tale.

If our hypothesis is to be accepted, the historical background and the person
of Valentinus will be somewhat less obscure. It is clear that the scheme of the
myth was borrowed from oriental gnostic sects as was already observed by
Irenaeus (Iren. I, 30). Philosophic and Hermetic influences may easily be
indicated: this reminds us of the fact that Valentinus was educated in
Alexandria. Johannine and Pauline ideas may be noticed.

But after all these influences are not very important. Hippolytus declares that
a vision of Christ was the impulse for the composition of the myth [10]. On the
whole this metaphysic poem seems inspired by vivid emotions and personal
experiences. Valentinus was not a philosopher, not a theologian, but a visionary
gnostic, who expressed his tragic conception of life in the symbols of creative
imagination.

---

[9]   abscesserunt enim < Ptolemaeus eiusque discipuli > a conditore < Valentino >, sed minime
origo deletur, et si forte mutatur; testatio est ipsa mutatio, as Tertullian rightly says (Adv.
Valent. 4).

[10] Hippol. VI, 42, 2: ἔπειτα προσθεὶς τραγικόν τινα μῦθον ἐκ τούτου συνιστᾶν βούλεται
τὴν ἐπικεχειρημένην αὐτῷ αἵρεσιν.

II

TRANSLATION

The generation of the Son

In invisible and ineffable heights the perfect Aeon, called Depth, was pre-existent. Incomprehensible and invisible, eternal and unbegotten, he was throughout endless ages in serenity and quiescence. And with him was Silence. And Depth conceived the idea to send forth from himself the origin of all and committed this emanation, as if it were a seed, to the womb of Silence. She than, having received this seed and becoming pregnant, gave birth to Νοῦς who was both similar and equal to him, who had produced him, and was alone capable of comprehending the greatness of the Father. Along with him Truth emanated.

Iren. 1, 1, 1

And Νοῦς perceiving for what purpose he had been produced, also himself sent forth Reason and Life, the father of all those who were to come after him and the origin and formative principle of the entire spiritual world. By the communion of Reason and Life were brought forth Man and Community. Each of these pairs is masculo-feminine.

These aeons having been produced to the glory of the Father and wishing to glorify him on their own account, set forth emanations in couples. Reason and Life, after producing Man and Community set forth ten other aeons, whose names are the following: Bythius and Mixis, Ageratus and Henosis, Autophyes and Hedone, Acinetus and Syncrasis, Monogenes and Macaria. Man too, along with Community, produced twelve aeons who have the following names: Paracletus and Pistis, Patricus and Elpis, Metricus and Agape, Aïnus and Synesis, Ecclesiasticus and Macariotes, Theletus and Sophia.

Iren. 1, 1, 2

The origin of evil

Depth was known to Νοῦς only, but to all the others he was invisible and incomprehensible: Νοῦς alone enjoyed the contemplation of the Father and reflected full of mirth on his immeasurable greatness, while he also had in mind to communicate to the other aeons the greatness of the Father, how lofty and vast he was, and how he was beyond origin and comprehension and understanding. But, according to the will of the Father, Silence withheld him, because it had been designed to lead them all to a thoughtful longing for God.

Iren. 1, 2, 1

And all the other aeons alike wished quietly to behold the author of their being and to contemplate their origin, which had no beginning.

Iren.
1, 2, 2
But forth rushed the very latest and youngest of the twelve, Wisdom, and suffered passion quite apart from her husband's embrace. This passion first arose among those who were connected with Νοῦς and Truth, but passed as by contagion to this aeon, who was led astray by professed love, which was actually hybris, because she did not, like Νοῦς, enjoy communion with the perfect Father. *Her passion was a desire to know the Father: for she craved to understand his greatness.* Not being able to realize her hope, because she aimed at the impossible, she became involved in extreme agonies because of the unfathomable depth and the Father's unsearchable nature and her love for him. Always reaching forward she would even have been absorbed by his sweetness and have dissolved into his infinite being, had she not met that power, which supports all things, the Limit, who exiled her from the spiritual world.

The emanation of the Holy Spirit

Iren.
1, 11, 1
When she had been expelled into the empty space devoid of knowledge which she had created by her trespass, she brought forth Jesus in remembrance of the higher world, but with a kind of shadow. And he, being masculine, severed the shadow of deficiency from himself and returned to the spiritual universe above.

Iren.
1, 4, 1
Left outside, alone, Sophia was subject to every sort of passion; *sorrow* she suffered because she did not obtain understanding; *fear,* lest life should leave her as enlightment had already done; moreover she was in *despair*; the root of all this suffering was *ignorance*. And being bereft of the reason that had been invisibly present with her, she strained herself to discover that light which had forsaken her, but could not achieve her purpose because she was prevented by the Limit. And as the Limit thus obstructed her further progress, he exclaimed: Iao.

Iren.
1, 4, 5
When she had passed through every state of suffering, she *raised herself* timidly and supplicated the light which had forsaken her, that is, Jesus.

Exc.
23, 2
And he, who had become unified with the ideal world, asked the aeons for help for Sophia, who remained outside.

Hipp.
VI, 31
And confusion arose in the spiritual world, for the aeons became overwhelmed with apprehension, imagining that likewise their own progenies should be form-less and incomplete, and that within a short time destruction should befall

them; all of them, therefore, betook themselves to supplication of the Father, that he would deliver Wisdom from sorrow; for she continued weeping and wailing on account of the abortion produced by her. The Father, then, full of compassion for the tears of Wisdom and accepting the supplication of the aeons, ordered a new emanation, the Holy Spirit, for the separation and fructification of the aeons, by entering invisibly into them.

Iren.
1, 11, 1

The emission of Christ

This one instructed them as to the nature of their conjunction, namely that being cognisant of their limited perception of the Unbegotten, they needed no higher knowledge. It also revealed to them the knowledge of the Father, that he is unfathomable and incomprehensible, invisible and inaudible, except in so far as he is known through <the Son>, Νοῦς, only. And that the origin of their eternal being is the Father, the incomprehensible part of the divine nature, but that the comprehensible part, the Son <or Νοῦς > is the origin of their becoming and formation.

Iren.
1, 2, 5

Then the Holy Spirit rendered all equal among themselves, taught them to offer thanksgiving and led them to a state of true repose. Thus all the aeons were constituted equal to each other in form and knowledge; all becoming Νοῦς and Reason and Man. The female aeons, too, all became Truth and Life and Community. After this, being thus established and brought into a state of perfect rest, they sang with great joy hymns in praise of the Father, who himself shared their lofty exaltation.

Iren.
1, 2, 6

And out of gratitude for the great benefit which had been conferred on them, the whole plenitude of the aeons with one design and desire — while the Spirit joined in and the Father set the seal of his approval on their conduct — brought together the most exquisite and flowery beauty each of them had in himself: and uniting all these contributions so as skilfully to blend the whole, they produced an emanation to the honour and glory of Depth, a being of perfect beauty, the very star of the spiritual world, its perfect fruit, Christ, who is also called Saviour and Reason and All and Paraclete; and he was sent forth along with his contemporary angels to the worldspirit in exile.

Iren.
1, 4, 5 and
Exc. 43

The spiritual background of matter

And Wisdom, filled with reverence, at first veiled herself through modesty, but by and by, when she had looked upon him with all his endowments, she ran forward to meet him, acquiring strength from his appearance. The Saviour immediately gave form to her essence and brought healing to her passions. For

Iren.
1, 4, 5

he separated them from her, put them apart, and condensed them, so as to transmute them from incorporeal passion into still unorganised matter.

Iren.
1, 4, 2

Iren.
1, 5, 4

This was the origin and essence of the matter from which this world was to be made: from her longing for the bliss of the ideal world the worldsoul derived its origin; earth arose from her state of despair; water from the agitation caused by her sorrow; air from the solidification of her fear; while fire, causing death and destruction, was inherent in all these elements, as ignorance lay at the root of the three other passions.

Iren.
1, 4, 5

After that the Saviour endowed the elements with affinity according to their nature, in order that they should be able later on to form concretions and corporeal structures.

Iren.
1, 4, 5

But when Wisdom was delivered from her suffering, she gazed with rapture on the dazzling vision of the angels that accompanied him; inflamed with love and conceiving from her imagination, she brought forth new beings after their image, a spiritual progeny after the image of the Saviour's attendants.

The formation of the visible world

Iren.
1, 5, 1

These three kinds of existence having come into being — matter from passion, soul from longing, spirit from imagination —, she next addressed herself to the task of giving these form. But she was not able to do this as regards the spirit, because this was of the same essence as herself. She therefore betook herself to give form to the psychic substance, which had proceeded from her longing, applying the revelations of the Saviour. She first formed out of psychic substance the Demiurge, a godly being, that is the image of the Father, who gave form to all things that came into existence after him, secretly impelled thereto by his Mother. For Wisdom, desirous of making all things to the honour of the aeons, made symbols of them <in the visible world>.

Exc.
47, 1

Iren.
1, 5, 2

The Demiurge separated the two substances hitherto confused and made them corporeal instead of incorporeal; then he fashioned things heavenly and earthly.

Iren.
1, 5, 3

And he imagined that he created all these things out of himself, although Wisdom was the productive power. So he made heaven, yet did not know what heaven really was; he fashioned man, yet ignorant of man, he brought to light earth, but had no acquaintance with the earth; generally speaking he was ignorant of the ideas of all he made, nay did not even know of the existence

of his Mother, Wisdom. She dwells in the intermediate abode above the
heavens, the demiurge dwells in heaven, which is the hebdomad, but the devil
in this sublunar world.

Iren.
1, 5, 4

Having thus formed the world, the Demiurge also created the earthy part of
man; into this he breathed the psychic part of his nature; but he was ignorant
of that spiritual offspring of his mother, which she had brought forth as a fruit
of her imagination, because it was of the same essence as Wisdom. Without his
knowledge it was deposited into him; so he was made the instrument of con-
veying the spirit into the soul and the material body of man, in order that it
should be carried as in a womb and should develop, until it had become fitted
for the reception of the perfect Logos, <which is Christ>. This spirit may be
called the Community of the Saints, an emblem of the Community, which is
above, and is the inner man. It is sent forth to the end that, being here united
with the soul, it may assume shape and be educated together with it in practical
life. For it needed psychic and sense training: on this account the world was
organised. And very often this spiritual seed has spoken through the prophets.

Iren.
1, 5, 5
1, 5, 6

As long, now, as we were children of the female, Wisdom, only, as if of a base
intercourse, incomplete and infants and senseless and weak and without form,
brought forth like abortions, we were only children of the female, but when we
have received form from the Saviour, we have become children of the
bridegroom and take part in the sacred marriage.

Exc. 68

Death vanquished

After the reign of Death, which had made a great and fair promise but had
nonetheless become a ministry of death, when every principality and divinity
had failed, Christ, the great hero, descended to assume as his body the
Ecclesia, symbolised by Jesus: thus he saved and bore aloft the human existence
of Jesus and thereby the whole of mankind, which is of the same essence with
Jesus. For "if the first fruits be holy, the lump will be also: if the root be holy,
then will also the shoots".

Exc.
58, sqq.

Nor was he separated from this human spirit which he assumed as a seed from
Wisdom, but contained it by power, so that it was given form little by little
through knowledge. Now the words: "Holy Spirit shall come upon thee" refer
to the spiritual essence of the body of the Saviour, and the words: "a Power of
the Most High small overshadow thee" indicate the fashioning of this body in
the Virgin by the Demiurge.

Jesus died at the departure of the spirit which had descended upon him in the river Jordan: it was not so much separated as withdrawn in order that death should also operate on him, for how could the body die when life was present in him? In that way Death would have prevailed over the Saviour himself, which is absurd. But Death was outgeneralled by guile. For when the body had died and Death had seized it, the Saviour sent forth the ray of power, which once descended upon Jesus at his baptism, destroyed Death, and raised up the mortal body, delivering it from suffering.

Exc. 38, 3   After his resurrection Christ sat down with the Demiurge, that the spirits might remain and not rise before him, and that he might subdue the Demiurge and provide the elect with a passage into the spiritual world.

The end of the worldprocess

Exc. 63, 1 <Iren. 1, 6, 1> Exc. 63, 1   The repose of the spiritual beings is in the intermediate abode with Wisdom, their Mother; and they keep their souls, the wedding garments, until the final consummation. But when every spiritual being has received absolute conscience, will take place the marriage feast, common to all who are saved, until all have become equal and know each other. Henceforth the spiritual beings, having put off their souls, together with their mother who leads the Bridegroom, also lead their bridegrooms, the angels of Christ who initiated them, and pass into the bridal chamber within the Limit. They attain to the vision of the Father — having become spiritual aeons — to the spiritual and eternal mystery of sacred marriage [1].

---

[1] For the Greek text and a commentary, see *Vigiliae Christianae*, 1, 1947, pp. 48-73.

LA CONCEPTION DE L'HOMME
DANS LA GNOSE VALENTINIENNE

I

L'homme se demande quelle est son essence, quelle est son origine, quel est le but de son existence. Cette question est de tous les temps. Elle se pose aussi dans le gnosticisme chrétien: "qui étions-nous, que sommes-nous devenus? Où étions-nous avant? Dans quel monde avons-nous été jetés? Vers quel but nous empressons-nous? De quoi sommes-nous délivrés? Qu'est-ce que la naissance? Qu'est-ce que la régénération" [1].

La réponse est donnée par la gnose, qui peut être définie comme une expérience immédiate de la révélation. C'est cette expérience qui a inspiré les mythes gnostiques, qui ne sont qu'une expression de cette émotion profonde. Ceci nous est clairement démontré par un passage très curieux d'un auteur anti-hérétique, qui s'exprime comme suit: "Valentin dit qu'il a vu dans une vision un enfant nouveau-né. Il lui demanda: "qui êtes-vous?". L'enfant répondit: "je suis le Logos". Ensuite il (Valentin) a exprimé cette expérience dans un mythe tragique (littér.: ayant ajouté, $\pi\rho\sigma\vartheta\varepsilon\iota\varsigma$). Depuis lors il a essayé de fonder l'hérésie introduite par lui" [2].

On peut être sûr que ces mots remontent à Valentin lui-même. Sans doute Hippolyte a-t-il formulé ce fragment à sa manière. Par exemple on doit soupçonner que l'expression "mythe tragique", qui nous semble rendre exactement le caractère de la pensée valentinienne, a été employée par l'auteur ecclésiastique dans un sens péjoratif. Cependant son témoignage est trop caractéristique pour qu'il soit inventé. L'auteur inconnu du Poimandre, l'écrit le plus important du *Corpus Hermeticum*, ne nous déclare-t-il pas que l'origine du monde qui est décrite dans ce document-là, lui a été révélée dans une vision? Ainsi pour Valentin c'était une vision du Sauveur qui a inspiré le mythe. Le mythe valentinien ne fait que rendre en images et en symboles la rencontre de l'homme et du Christ.

Si l'on se rend compte de ce fait, la doctrine valentinienne devient moins obscure. Elle ne contient pas de spéculations confuses sur une pré-histoire lointaine; elle est plutôt une expression poétique de la rédemption de l'homme par le Sauveur. L'homme et le Saveur sont les seuls protagonistes dans ce drame

---

[1] *Exc. ex Theodoto* 78, 1.
[2] Hippolyte, *Refutatio* VI, 42, 2.

sotériologique. C'est pourquoi on doit traiter toute la doctrine ésotérique, si l'on veut parler de la conception de l'homme dans la gnose valentinienne.

Voici en résumé ce qu'enseigne Valentin: "de la Profondeur et du Silence naît la Conscience, qui se forme des idées, $\alpha i \tilde{\omega} \nu \varepsilon \varsigma$. L'une d'elles, la Sagesse, $\Sigma o \phi i \alpha$, conçoit le désir hybride de comprendre la divinité et de pénétrer son essence impénétrable; mais, parvenue à la Limite posée devant tout esprit engendré ($^{''}O \rho o \varsigma$), elle est repoussée dans le néant ($\kappa \acute{\varepsilon} \nu \omega \mu \alpha$). Dans sa solitude elle est assaillie par l'angoisse, l'affolement, la douleur et l'ignorance. C'est là l'origine du monde perceptible: de ses larmes sont nées les mers, de son affolement est née la terre, de son ignorance le feu, mais de son sourire la lumière, l'âme du monde". L'essence de ce monde est donc la souffrance: combien terribles doivent avoir été les souffrances de l'homme pour qui cette conception du monde était une réalité vécue!

Et de même que la chûte est considérée comme la conséquence du désir de comprendre et non d'une transgression morale, de même la rédemption n'est pas considérée du point de vue éthique, mais du point de vue ontologique comme formation de la conscience spirituelle. Le Christ est l'incorporation de la pensée divine qui se révèle à l'esprit tombé, l'idée des idées, l'archétype des archétypes dans le sens platonique et philonien de ce mot. L'imagination poétique de Valentin voit ce mouvement intérieur en images grandioses: les éons apportent ce qu'il y a de plus beau et de plus sublime en eux et comme la fleur de leur substance pour former ensemble le Sauveur, le fruit le plus parfait du plérôme, du monde spirituel. Le devenir du monde trouvera sa fin quand tous les esprits seront doués de la gnose et retourneront vers leur patrie spirituelle. Alors l'homme glorifié acquerra la vision pure dans les noces sacrées de l'esprit avec l'époux, le Christ, $\tau \grave{o} \pi \tilde{\alpha} \nu$ de la pensée valentinienne [3].

Qu'est-ce qu'il faut penser de cette doctrine? Est-ce que la mystique orientale, si différente de la religiosité évangélique, a été introduite dans le christianisme, comme le veut Lietzmann? Ou est-ce plutôt la philosophie grecque qui a faussé la simplicité de la doctrine de Jésus, comme le pense Harnack?

Ce problème se pose de nouveau pour le savant de nos jours, parce que, grâce à une tendance qui se révèle dans tous les domaines de la science historique, le point de vue moderne est assez différente de celui de la génération précédente. Autrefois on s'efforçait surtout de découvrir l'origine d'une conception ou de déterminer les influences qu'un penseur ou un auteur avait subies; maintenant on voudrait saisir l'essence même d'une doctrine et l'originalité qu'un penseur

---

[3] Cf. G. Quispel, The Original Doctrine of Valentine, *Vigilae Christianae*, I, 1, 1947, pag. 43-73 (p. 27-36 de ce livre).

a apportée à disposer les éléments qu'il a empruntés à la tradition. Cette évolution générale s'est manifestée aussi dans l'étude du gnosticisme et elle a modifié nos conceptions. Nous voudrions savoir non seulement si le gnosticisme est d'origine grecque ou orientale, mais aussi ce qu'il est par lui-même.

Selon Harnack la gnose chrétienne était d'origine grecque. Tout le monde connaît sa définition fameuse selon laquelle le gnosticisme était l'hellénisation immédiate du christianisme. Par contre Bousset et Reitzenstein étaient d'un autre avis. Reitzenstein considérait le gnosticisme comme une partie du syncrétisme, dont il essayait de démontrer l'origine orientale. Bousset, à son tour, réduisait, dans son livre intitulé "Hauptprobleme der Gnosis", tous les éléments du gnosticisme à des mythologèmes, qu'il croyait retrouver un peu partout dans les religions du Proche Orient.

Ces points de vue, celui de Harnack autant que celui de ses adversaires, ne peuvent pas satisfaire Hans Jonas, qui fut le premier à appliquer la méthode phénoménologique à ce domaine de la science [4]. Il ne nie pas que le gnosticisme ait subi certaines influences de la part de la philosophie grecque, mais il se demande pourquoi Plotin, dans son livre contre les gnostiques, a réagi avec tant de véhémence contre le gnosticisme: c'est, croit-il, parce que ces gens-là rejetaient le monde visible, le κόσμος, qu'admiraient les Grecs. D'autre part, il veut bien admettre que les conceptions astrologiques qu'on retrouve dans le gnosticisme remontent à des spéculations babyloniennes, mais il remarque que ces divinités célestes ont subi, dans le gnosticisme, une certaine dégradation et sont devenues des démons hostiles.

C'est ce ressentiment contre le monde, cette conception que l'homme est un étranger dans un monde démoniaque, cet "acosmisme" qui ne se retrouve ni en Grèce ni dans l'Orient, qui est vraiment caractéristique pour le gnosticisme païen autant que chrétien. Ce qui est nouveau dans le gnosticisme, c'est, selon Jonas, la conception que l'homme, bien qu'étant dans ce monde, n'es pas de ce monde.

Il est sans conteste que M. Jonas a mis en évidence un trait caractéristique du gnosticisme: d'autre part il me semble qu'il a négligé les données de la philologie qui sont indispensables dans ce genre de recherches. La méthode phénoménologique est dangereuse en tant qu'elle perd de vue l'importance de la philologie qui interprète les textes, indique les sources dans lesquelles l'auteur a puisé et détermine les influences qu'il a subies. Tant qu'on ne sait pas exactement dans quelle mesure un auteur dépend de la tradition, il est impossible de saisir son originalité. Nos documents concernant le gnosticisme ont été si mal édités et si

---

[4] H. Jonas, Gnosis und spätantiker Geist, Goettingue 1934.

peu recherchés, notre connaissance est encore tellement limitée qu'il est presque impossible de tenter une synthèse.

Dans ces circonstances il est plus prudent de ne pas discuter la conception de l'homme dans le gnosticisme en général, mais de se limiter à l'anthropologie d'un seul gnostique, dans le cas particulier à celui de Valentin, de retracer les divers éléments de son anthropologie depuis leur source chrétienne, hellénistique ou bien gnostique et de constater comment Valentin a combiné ces données traditionnelles dans une synthèse nouvelle et originale. La justification de cette méthode nous a été fournie par quelques renseignements sur la vie de l'hérésiarque que nous a conservés la littérature anti-hérétique.

Valentin était né en Egypte. Il reçut à Alexandrie une éducation hellénique: il est très possible que sa préférence pour le platonisme, qui frappait déjà ses adversaires ecclésiastique et qu'on ne peut nier, date de sa jeunesse. Arrivé à Rome (environ 140), il fut un candidat sérieux pour la chaire épiscopale vacante, "quia et ingenio et eloquio poterat". On lui préféra toutefois un ancien martyr; il quitta alors l'église apostolique, entra en contact soit à Rome soit déjà en Egypte avec une secte gnostique et fonda une école. Ainsi l'histoire même de sa vie nous fait supposer que sa doctrine a subi l'influence du christianisme autant que du gnosticisme et de la philosophie grecque. C'est exactement ce que nous révèlent les fragments sur l'anthropologie qui nous ont été conservés.

Fragment 1: Un seul est bon, celui qui a parlé dans la révélation de Son Fils. C'est par Lui seul que le coeur pourrait devenir pur, tout esprit mauvais en étant chassé. Car dans son état actuel, une multitude de démons qui demeurent en lui l'empêchent d'être pur. Chacun d'eux produit les effets qui lui sont propres et le maltraite par de mauvais désirs. Et il me semble qu'il arrive au coeur à peu près ce qui arrive à une hôtellerie, lorsque des gens grossiers y séjournent: ils percent les murs, ils creusent des trous et souvent la remplissent d'ordures. Il en est de même du coeur, tant qu'il ne reçoit pas la grâce. Il reste impur, il est la demeure d'une foule de démons. Mais lorsque le Père, qui est seul bon, le regarde, il est sanctifié et rayonne de lumière. Bienheureux celui qui a un tel coeur, parce qu'il verra Dieu" (Clem. Alex., *Strom.* II, 114, 3).

A propos de ce fragment, Dölger a déclaré quelque part qu'il exprime exactement la conception de l'Eglise primitive sur les démons. On sait que la démonologie était une partie très importante de la religion chrétienne des premiers siècles. Les Chrétiens, devant les tribunaux, invitaient même leurs persécuteurs à amener des démoniaques, afin de les guérir et de prouver par là la vérité de leurs convictions. Valentin est donc en plein accord avec la foi ecclésiastique quand il insiste avec tant d'éloquence sur la démonie de l'existence humaine. Je voudrais souligner ce fait, parce qu'on croit souvent que le gnosticisme est un intellectualisme abstrait, qui existait plus ou moins en dehors de la communauté chrétienne. C'est là un préjugé qui ne tient pas compte des faits. Notre fragment montre clairement que la gnose se faisait plus d'une fois l'interprète des sentiments enracinés de la foi populaire. La gnose est plein d'un romantisme inconscient. D'autre part, le fragment nous révèle une mentalité qu'on cherche en vain dans la littérature catholique, de ce temps, bien entendu. On nous parle de la rédemption, de la lumière qui resplendit dans le coeur, de la contemplation de Dieu. C'est de la mystique, plus précisément c'est une mystique de la rédemption. Or, les savants de toutes les confessions sont d'accord que les apologistes de l'église ne mettent pas l'accent sur la sotériologie. En outre, les apologistes qui, ne l'oublions pas, étaient des contemporains de Valentin, n'appartenaient pas à ce type de religiosité qu'on appelle mystique. Si j'aimais le paradoxe, je pourrais donc dire que, d'un certain point de vue, Valentin est plus catholique que ses adversaires catholiques. Ajoutons que son anthropologie est profondément pessimiste: l'homme, selon lui, est possédé de démons. On ne saurait dire chose plus grave.

Tout ceci nous serait parfaitement compréhensible, si le fragment ne cachait pas, sous sa simplicité apparente, un problème très difficile. Ce problème s'entrevoit déjà, si l'on prend connaissance de la polémique que Clément d'Alexandrie a soulevée à propos des termes cités plus haut. Voici les paroles de Clément: "Qu'ils nous disent pour quelle raison une telle âme n'a pas reçu la grâce dès le commencement". Ceci est clair: Clément demande à Valentin ce que Tertullien demande à Marcion: cur tam sero revelatus est? Pourquoi la révélation est-elle venue si tard? En effet, les deux hérétiques admettaient que le Dieu inconnu n'a été révélé que par le Christ. Il s'ensuit qu'avant la descente du Christ le coeur humain ne pouvait être sauvé. Clément continue: "car ou bien elle n'était pas digne; comment peut elle alors après résipiscence recevoir la grâce?". (Clément semble faire allusion ici à des personnes qui ne sont pas dignes, c'est-à-dire qui ne sont pas spirituelles. Or, dit-il, si ces personnes sont privées d'esprit, il leur est impossible de venir à résipiscense et de recevoir la grâce, selon la théorie valentinienne, bien entendu.) "Ou bien", continue Clément, "elle (cette âme dont il est question dans le fragment) appartient à la classe des hommes qui sont sauvés ($\phi\acute{v}\sigma\iota\varsigma \ \sigma\omega\zeta o\mu\acute{\epsilon}\nu\eta$), comme il (Valentin) le veut; alors il est nécessaire qu'elle ait reçu la grâce dès le commencement à cause de sa parenté (avec le monde spirituel) et qu'elle n'admette pas les démons impurs, à moins qu'elle ne puisse être contrainte et se montrer faible". Clément s'étonne que l'homme spirituel, bien qu'apparenté au monde transcendant, puisse être dénué de connaissance et être la demeure des démons. (Nous apprenons de par sa réfutation que, selon Valentin, c'est bien l'homme spirituel dont il est question dans notre fragment.) Suivent, dans les Stromateis, ces mots énigmatiques: "Car s'il (Valentin) admet que l'âme humaine, étant venue à résipiscence ($\mu\varepsilon\tau\alpha\nuo\acute{\eta}\sigma\alpha\sigma\alpha\nu$) a choisi la partie la meilleure, il doit accepter malgré lui notre opinion (c'est-à-dire l'opinion des catholiques) que la rédemption arrive grâce au changement causé par une décision libre ($\grave{\varepsilon}\varkappa$ $\mu\varepsilon\tau\alpha\beta o\lambda\tilde{\eta}\varsigma$ $\pi\varepsilon\iota\vartheta\eta\nu\acute{\iota}ov$) et non à cause d'une disposition essentielle". Il est nécessaire de soumettre ces mots énigmatiques à une analyse plus détaillée. Il s'agit ici du libre arbitre. Que Clément préconise la liberté de la volonté, cela n'a rien d'étonnant. Clément et les Pères grecs de l'église exaltent la liberté humaine. Les savants catholiques aiment à souligner que cet enthousiasme ante-pélagien est surtout une réaction devant les spéculations gnostiques. Il nous serait difficile de nier cette constatation. Mais comme cette réaction a eu des conséquences assez importantes, il est nécessaire de bien connaître la position de l'adversaire qui a provoqué cette réaction. C'est pourquoi les mots de Clément, dans lesquelles la conception catholique du libre arbitre est nettement opposée à la conception contraire, méritent plus d'attention qu'elles n'en ont reçu jusqu'ici. Valentin admet que l'âme, ou plutôt l'esprit humain parvient à la résipiscence ($\mu\varepsilon\tau\acute{\alpha}\nuo\iota\alpha$) et choisit "la partie la meilleure". Néanmoins il ne veut pas admettre que ce changement soit causé par une décision libre. Il rejette donc le libre arbitre. Il croit plutôt que l'esprit est sauvé parce qu'il a une disposition essentielle à être sauvé.

La question se pose: quelle est cette $\mu\varepsilon\tau\acute{\alpha}\nuo\iota\alpha$, cette résipiscense; que veut dire cette rédemption $\grave{\varepsilon}\varkappa$ $\phi\acute{\upsilon}\sigma\varepsilon\omega\varsigma$, par une disposition essentielle?

Je n'ai pas hésité à traduire dans ce qui précède le mot $\mu\varepsilon\tau\acute{\alpha}\nuo\iota\alpha$ par "rési-piscence". Certes, dans la langue biblique ce terme a une signification différente: là il veut dire "le repentir" et évoque l'idée du péché et de la loi. Il me semble pourtant qu'on peut exclure par avance cette nuance de la significance, quand il s'agit de Valentin. Il semble que le mot "péché" ne se trouve pas dans son vocabulaire: dans tous les textes valentiniens, qui sont nombreux, on ne le trouve que rarement. Les termes qu'il a choisis pour exprimer sa pensée révèlent une préoccupation ontologique et existentielle, mais ils ont rarement une valeur éthique. Nous supposons donc que dans le texte auquel se rapporte Clément, $\mu\varepsilon\tau\acute{\alpha}\nuo\iota\alpha$ veut dire "la résipiscence", la prise de conscience du vrai Soi, et non "le repentir". "Comment donc", demande Clément, "peut-on accepter une "résipiscense" et rejeter le libre arbitre?".

Demandons-nous maintenant ce que signifie l'expression $\grave{\varepsilon}\varkappa$ $\phi\acute{\upsilon}\sigma\varepsilon\omega\varsigma$ $\sigma\acute{\omega}\zeta\varepsilon\sigma\vartheta\alpha\iota$, être sauvé par une disposition essentielle. Le contexte démontre clairement que l'homme spirituel est toujours sauvé et ne peut pas ne pas être sauvé, par le seul fait qu'il est esprit. Mais la question se pose si l'esprit est un attribut naturel de l'homme ou bien un don de la grâce. Dans le premier cas, le

Valentinianisme n'est en somme qu'une philosophie d'identité. Dans le second cas le Valentinianisme est une mystique de la rédemption, ce qui est autre chose. Or, je crois pouvoir démontrer que la gnose valentinienne est une mystique qui met l'accent sur la grâce et l'élection. Je veux pourtant déclarer que toute tentative de mettre en parallèle cette doctrine de l'élection qu'est le Valentinianisme avec le protestantisme moderne me semble erronée. Il y a des différences tellement essentielles qu'aucune comparaison ne saurait tenir. C'est surtout la conception de l'esprit qui semble être différente.

Les Valentiniens enseignent que l'esprit humain est apparenté au monde spirituel. L'esprit c'est, selon l'expression frappante d'Héracléon: "l'organe ($\delta\iota\alpha\vartheta\epsilon\sigma\iota\varsigma$) destiné à recevoir la vie, la réceptivité ($\check\epsilon\nu\nu o\iota\alpha$) pour la puissance qui émane du Seigneur, le vaisseau dans lequel (la Samaritaine) venait chercher l'eau vivante" (Fragment 27). Cette citation montre qu'il ne faut pas chercher des parallèles dans la théologie moderne. Il y a pourtant une autre solution, qui semble être plus raisonnable et plus vraisemblable. Mon compatriote et vénéré maître G. van der Leeuw a démontré dans son live: *La Phénoménologie de la Religion,* que l'idée de la grâce et de l'élection ne se retrouve pas seulement dans la mystique chrétienne, mais bien dans la mystique en général. Or, que le Valentinianisme soit dans ce sens une mystique de la grâce et de l'élection, c'est ce que nous tâcherons de prouver.

Que l'homme soit incapable d'être sauvé par ses propres forces, mais qu'il reçoive passivement la grâce, cela semble découler d'une conception valentinienne que l'on trouve souvent exprimée dans les fragments de la section orientale de cette école. C'est l'idée que l'homme est sauvé par un ange du Sauveur. Il semble que cette doctrine n'est qu'une application particulière d'une croyance fort répandue parmi les peuples de l'antiquité, selon laquelle chaque homme aurait son $\delta\alpha\acute\iota\mu\omega\nu$, son ange gardien, qui l'accompagne dès sa naissance, le guide et le protège. Cette croyance se retrouve un peu partout, chez les Grecs, chez les Juifs, et chez les peuples orientaux. Il semble que l'âme des peuples trouve spontanément cette image pour exprimer une dépendance absolue. Les valentiniens donnent à cette conception populaire une tournure très caractéristique pour leur doctrine. Ils croient que ces $\delta\alpha\acute\iota\mu o\nu\epsilon\varsigma$ sont les anges qui ont accompagné le Christ quand il descendait d'en haut: "Quand le Christ (litt. Jésus), notre lumière, s'est vidé de lui-même, comme dit l'apôtre, c'est-à-dire quand il est venu hors de la Limite (du monde spirituel) selon Théodote, il amenait à sa suite, étant l'ange du plérome, les anges de la semence transcendante. Et il possédait lui-même la rédemption parce qu'il provenait du plérome, mais il conduisait les anges *pour redresser le germe spirituel*" (*Exc. ex Théod.* 35). *Ce sont donc ces anges qui donnent la gnose à l'homme spirituel.*

Il y a encore un passage dans Clément qui semble être précieux pour nous faire connaître la fonction des anges du Christ. Il dit que selon Valentin "cette classe transcendante est venue d'en haut chez nous ici-bas pour *détruire la mort*" (Clém. Alex., *Strom.* IV, 89, I sqq.). Si je comprends bien ce passage qui se trouve dans un contexte assez obscur, Clément y fait allusion aux anges du Sauveur. Ce sont donc ces anges-là qui délivrent l'homme spirituel de la mort.

Il y a un parallélisme exact entre les anges et le Christ, car selon la doctrine valentinienne le Christ est descendu pour faire disparaître l'ignorance et anéantir la mort. Or, les anges ne sont pas autre chose que le Sauveur lui-même; l'ange est le Christ rapporté à l'existence individuelle de l'homme spirituel, c'est l'esprit du Christ dans chaque individu. Dans le baptême le Christ s'est divisé afin que les anges unissent les hommes spirituels. "Nos anges", disent-ils, "ont été émis dans l'unité, étant unis parce qu'ils provenaient de l'Un. Mais parce que nous existions nous-mêmes à l'état divisé, le Christ (litt. Jésus) se fit baptiser, de sorte que l'indivisé fut divisé, jusqu'à ce qu'il nous unisse aux anges dans le plérome, afin que nous, les multiples devenus un, nous nous confondions tous avec l'Un qui s'est divisé à cause de nous" (*Exc.* 36).

L'ange est donc le représentant du Christ dans la vie de l'homme spirituel, celui qui lui inspire la gnose et le délivre de la mort. La vie de l'initié est une imitation de la vie de Jésus.

Je n'insisterais pas sur ce trait quiétiste de l'anthropologie, s'il n'était pas caractéristique pour toute la doctrine. Valentin sait très bien que l'esprit humain se sent porté à s'élever et à monter vers le monde spirituel. Il a décrit dans le mythe le désir de Sophia de s'élever vers Dieu et de pénétrer jusqu'au fond de Son être, et il a condamné ce désir comme hybride ($\tau\acute{o}\lambda\mu\alpha$) et passionné ($\pi\acute{\alpha}\vartheta o\varsigma$). Quand Sophia a été reléguée à cause de cette transgression, elle éprouve à nouveau le désir de l'esprit qui l'a quittée. Les Valentiniens disent encore une fois que ce désir était une passion, une $\pi\acute{\alpha}\vartheta o\varsigma$ $\tau\tilde{\eta}\varsigma$ $\dot{\epsilon}\pi\iota\vartheta\upsilon\mu\acute{\iota}\alpha\varsigma$ (*Exc.* 33, 3). La gnose est révélée par le Saint-Esprit aux éons, par le Sauveur à Sophia, par l'ange à l'homme spirituel. Le Valentinianisme semble prêcher la passivité absolue.

Nous avons vu que l'homme spirituel ne se sauve pas lui-même, mais est sauvé par l'ange du Christ. D'où vient son esprit? Le germe spirituel est-il un attribut naturel ou un don de la grâce? Cette question trouvera une réponse quand nous aurons discuté un autre fragment, sur la création de l'homme.

Fragment 2: "Les anges du démiurge éprouvaient une sorte d'effroi pour l'homme créé, parce que son langage était plus sublime qu'on ne pouvait l'attendre d'une créature, grâce à Celui qui avait mis dans l'homme d'une façon mystérieuse le germe transcendant, de sorte qu'il parlait librement. C'est ainsi que pour les artistes les oeuvres d'art deviennent un objet d'effroi, les statues et les idoles, bref tout ce que les mains accomplissent au nom de Dieu. Car Adam, créé au nom de l'Homme, inspirait de l'effroi pour l'Homme préexistant, comme si celui-ci était représenté par lui. C'est pourquoi les anges furent épouvantés et se précipitèrent pour détruire leur oeuvre" (Clem. Alex. *Strom.* II, 36, 2-4).

Ce fragment est une paraphrase assez libre du récit biblique et contient deux éléments qui ne se trouvent pas dans la Génèse, à savoir la conception de l'homme archétypique et celle des anges hostiles. Il devient moins obscur quand on le compare avec le mythe ésotérique des Valentiniens. Ce mythe nous dépeint comment la Sophia, avant la création du monde, a produit des germes spirituels *d'après l'image des anges* du Sauveur [5]. Quand le démiurge a créé l'homme, c'est-à-dire son corps et son âme, un germe spirituel a été déposé dans l'homme sans que le démiurge s'en aperçoive. Ce germe, c'est l'homme spirituel au sens propre du mot, nommé aussi "*l'Eglise*", étant l'emblème (ἀντίτυπος) de l'Eglise idéale, et "l'homme intérieur" [6].

L'homme spirituel représente donc l'Eglise transcendante; on trouve en effet parmi les éons un couple qui est nommé *Anthropos* et *Ecclesia*. Les anges du démiurge éprouvent de l'effroi pour l'homme spirituel, parce qu'il est le représentant de l'homme archétypique: "l'effroi pour l'homme archétypique a rendu les anges agressifs vis à vis de l'oeuvre qu'ils avaient modélée à cause de la semence invisible de l'essence d'en haut insérée dans cette oeuvre" [7].

Qu'est-ce que l'homme archétypique? Quels rapports a-t-il avec le germe spirituel? Valentin était platonicien: les éons sont des idées, *sensus et affectus, motus divinitatis* [8]. Or, on trouve dans le platonisme de ce temps la conception que l'homme est une idée de Dieu: "*haec exemplaria rerum omnium deus intra se habet ... Itaque homines quidem pereunt, ipsa autem humanitas ad quam homo effingitur, permanet*" [9]: "Dieu contient en Lui-même les idées de toutes les choses. C'est pour cette raison que les hommes périssent, mais que l'idée de l'homme qui se réalise dans l'existence humaine est éternelle". Si donc Valentin dit qu'il y a dans le plérome un éon *Anthropos*, cela signifie qu'il y a une idée éternelle de l'homme, un "*homo sub ratione ideali*"; l'homme archétypique c'est l'idée de l'homme, telle qu'elle existe dans la conscience de Dieu.

Cette explication est confirmée par un passage dans Clément d'Alexandrie, qui est assez obscur et à la fois assez important. Clément, cela se comprend, ne

---

[5] Irén., *Adversus Haereses*, 1, 4, 5.
[6] Irén., *Adversus Haereses*, 1, 5, 6.
[7] Clem., *Strom.* II, 38, 3.
[8] Tert., adv. *Val.*, 4.
[9] Seneca, *Epist.* 65.

veut pas admettre que les anges fussent hostiles à l'homme qu'ils avaient créé et il essaie de démontrer que cela est impossible. Après avoir réfuté diverses explications du fragment, il conclut en supposant que les anges aient osé être hostiles à l'homme, parce qu'ils possédaient la gnose: "or", dit-il, "ceci est également impossible qu'ils (les anges) tendissent des pièges à l'homme tandis qu'ils connaissaient l'Homme transcendant dans le plérome, *et aussi le germe spirituel d'après l'image* ($\tau \grave{o}$ $\varkappa \alpha \tau$' $\varepsilon \grave{i} \varkappa \acute{o} \nu \alpha$) *dans lequel ils avaient reçu l'archétype et l'incorruptibilité avec le reste de la gnose*" [10]. Ce qui nous intéresse surtout, c'est la dernière partie de la phrase. Celui qui reçoit $\tau \grave{o}$ $\varkappa \alpha \tau$' $\varepsilon \grave{i} \varkappa \acute{o} \nu \alpha$ (apparemment le germe spirituel d'après l'image des anges du Sauveur), *reçoit l'archétype.* Le contexte nous démontre clairement que cela signifie l'*archétype* de l'homme. Le germe spirituel est donc aussi d'après ce passage un emblème ($\grave{\alpha} \nu \tau \acute{i} \tau \upsilon \pi o \varsigma$) de l'idée de l'homme. Mais on ne reçoit pas seulement l'archétype de l'homme, on reçoit aussi "le reste de la gnose". On a voulu changer ce texte. Ed. Schwarz propose: $\tau \tilde{\eta}$ τ' $\grave{\varepsilon} \varkappa \lambda o \gamma \tilde{\eta}$. Il me semble pourtant que ce n'est pas nécessaire. Il est possible qu'il veuille dire ceci: "celui qui possède le germe spirituel ne reçoit pas seulement la connaissance de l'archétype de l'homme, mais aussi le reste de la gnose, c'est-à-dire la connaissance des autres archétypes" ($\grave{\eta}$ $\gamma \nu \tilde{\omega} \sigma \iota \varsigma$ $\grave{\eta}$ $\lambda o \iota \pi \acute{\eta}$ = $\grave{\eta}$ $\gamma \nu \tilde{\omega} \sigma \iota \varsigma$ $\tau \tilde{\omega} \nu$ $\lambda o \iota \pi \tilde{\omega} \nu$ $\grave{\alpha} \rho \chi \varepsilon \tau \acute{\upsilon} \pi \omega \nu$). Le germe spirituel possède donc, bien que virtuellement, la connaissance des archétypes et surtout celle de l'idée de l'homme. Valentin veut donc dire que l'idée de l'homme doit et peut se réaliser dans l'existence humaine. C'est une conception assez simple et vraiment platonicienne.

Il a pourtant exprimé cette conception d'une manière qui n'est pas philosophique du tout et qui révèle l'influence du gnosticisme. Les anges du démiurge éprouvent de l'effroi pour l'homme spirituel: ils tendent des pièges à leur créature et font disparaître leur oeuvre. Cela nous rappelle l'opposition entre le Dieu de ce monde et le Dieu inconnu, opposition caractéristique pour le gnosticisme en général, je veux dire pour ces hérésies sans nombre qui ont existé dès les temps les plus reculés aux confins de l'église chrétienne, qui semblent être d'origine orientale et enseignent une mythologie assez compliquée. C'est dans ces milieux-là qu'on rencontre la conception que le démiurge est hostile envers le Dieu inconnu et envers l'homme spirituel. On constate que Valentin a subi l'influence de ces cercles hérétiques et il est nécessaire de déterminer sa source. Or il est presque toujours impossible d'indiquer l'auteur d'un mythologème gnostique, parce que le gnosticisme vulgaire tel que nous le décrivent les auteurs anti-hérétiques ressemble à une forêt vierge de l'Orient. Il semble pourtant que la fortune nous a été favorable et a conservé la mythologie gnostique qui a profondément influencé Valentin.

---

[10] Clem., *Strom.* II, 38, 5.

Irénée nous dit que le Valentinianisme est issu d'une certaine hérésie, qu'on appelle *ophitique*: "*tales quidem secundum eos sententiae sunt, a quibus, velut Lernea hydra, multiplex capitibus fera de Valentini schola generata est*" [11]. Valentin aurait "transformé les principes de la prétendue hérésie gnostique dans une école ayant un caractère propre" [12]. Les extraits qu'il fournit de cette hérésie semblent confirmer cette opinion de l'évêque de Lyon. Autant que nous sachions il n'y a pas d'autre système gnostique qui montre une ressemblance aussi frappante avec la doctrine valentinienne. En effet, il nous semble très probable que Valentin a connu ces conceptions "ophitiques": c'était peut-être l'hérésie dont il fit la connaissance soit en Egypte soit à Rome. Quoi qu'il en soit, on comprend beaucoup mieux en quoi consiste l'originalité de Valentin, quand on compare sa doctrine avec celle des "Ophites". On voit alors qu'il a employé les mythologèmes que lui fournit la tradition gnostique pour exprimer ses propres pensées. C'est ce que montre aussi l'anthropologie.

Les "Ophites" enseignent ceci: "quand le démiurge Ialdabaoth a soufflé l'esprit de vie dans l'homme, il a été privé, sans qu'il s'en aperçût, de la puissance (virtus). C'est de lui que les hommes reçoivent la conscience ($\nu o \tilde{\nu} \varsigma$) et la raison ($\dot{\varepsilon} \nu \vartheta \dot{\nu} \mu \eta \sigma \iota \varsigma$) (c'est cela qui est sauvé); immédiatement l'homme commença à rendre grâce au premier homme (c'est-à-dire au Dieu inconnu), sans prêter attention à ses créateurs. Mais Ialdabaoth, devenu jaloux, imagina de priver l'homme de sa puissance divine au moyen d'une femme" [13].

Quand on suppose que Valentin a connu cette anthropologie des "Ophites", il y a deux choses qui frappent le lecteur moderne. D'abord on ne trouve pas dans son anthropologie la doctrine bien connue, selon laquelle un être divin, nommé l'homme archétypique, est tombé dans la matière, doctrine qu'on retrouve entre autres dans le Poimandre et dans quelques apocryphes chrétiens. Selon Valentin l'Anthropos n'est qu'un éon. Le *mythologème de l'anthropos* est donc absent.

Puis il semble que les Ophites n'aient pas connu cette conception plus ou moins platonicienne selon laquelle l'homme spirituel représenterait l'archétype de l'homme. C'est apparemment une innovation de Valentin.

Il nous apparaît donc qu'on peut déterminer avec quelque vraisemblance les origines des éléments divers qui constituent l'anthropologie valentinienne: I. - l'homme nouveau est un ange du Christ, qui inspire la gnose et détruit la mort; *c'est l'élément chrétien*; II. - à l'insu d'un démiurge hostile un germe transcendant a été déposé dans l'homme; *c'est l'élément gnostique*; III. - ce

---

[11]   Irén., *Adv. Haereses*, I, 30, 14.
[12]   Irén., I, 11, 1.
[13]   Irén., *Adv. Haereses*, I, 30, 7.

germe spirituel contient virtuellement l'archétype de l'homme et les autres archétypes; *c'est l'élément platonicien.*

Valentin a donc hellénisé et christianisé l'anthropologie gnostique. On se demande si sa doctrine, contrairement à ce qu'en pense Harnack, n'a pas été *la christianisation et l'hellénisation de la gnose orientale.*

II

Qu'on ne s'imagine pas que Valentin ait automatiquement combiné ces composants divers comme par une sorte d'alchémie des idées. Ils n'ont été pour lui que des moyens pour exprimer une conception de l'homme qui me semble être très originale et très caractéristique pour la doctrine valentinienne, à savoir l'idée de la syzygie. Parce que l'anthropologie est dominée par cette conception de la syzygie, les éléments différents ont reçu une signification nouvelle. C'est pourquoi nous nous proposons de démontrer maintenant, comment Valentin a modifié les conceptions qu'il a empruntées à Platon.

Malheureusement nous ne disposons plus de fragments du maître lui-même. Ses disciples ont changé aussi l'anthropologie: les fragments de l'école orientale et de l'école occidentale, dans lesquelles la secte a été bientôt divisée, contiennent des données sur la nature de l'homme qui se contredisent et qui, nous l'avouons franchement, ne nous sont pas tous compréhensibles. On croit pourtant entrevoir la doctrine originale quand on lit, dans un écrit qui provient de l'école occidentale (l'école de Ptolémée) les spéculations suivantes: après avoir créé le monde, le démiurge "fabriqua une âme charnelle ($\gamma\epsilon\dot\omega\delta\eta\varsigma$) et matérielle, irrationnelle et de la même substance que l'âme des animaux" (*Exc. ex Theod.* 50). Il n'y a pas de doute que par ces mots les hérétiques veulent indiquer cette partie de l'âme que Platon a nommée l'$\dot\epsilon\pi\iota\vartheta\upsilon\mu\eta\tau\iota\kappa\dot\upsilon$, c'est-à-dire les passions et les instincts que les valentiniens appelaient $\tau\dot\upsilon$ $\dot\upsilon\lambda\iota\kappa\dot\upsilon$.

Dans cette âme instinctive le démiurge a insufflé l'âme au sens propre du mot, le $\vartheta\ddot\upsilon\mu\upsilon\varsigma$ platonicien, qui a pourtant reçu une autre fonction que chez Platon et est devenu le principe moral et conscient dans l'homme ($\tau\dot\upsilon$ $\psi\upsilon\chi\iota\kappa\dot\upsilon$) (*Exc.* 50).

A l'insu du démiurge un germe spirituel est déposé dans l'âme humaine ($\tau\dot\upsilon$ $\pi\nu\epsilon\upsilon\mu\alpha\tau\iota\kappa\dot\upsilon$); enfin l'homme reçoit un corps ($\tau\dot\upsilon$ $\chi\upsilon\iota\kappa\dot\upsilon$)[14]. Ceci, nous l'avons dit, est la théorie de l'école occidentale. Voici ce que déclare l'école orientale:

---

14   Irén., *Adv. Haereses,* 1, 5, 6 et I, 5, 5.

"Lorsque le corps physique eut été façonné, le Logos a déposé dans l'âme élue, pendant qu'elle sommeillait, un germe masculin .... Et ce germe opéra comme un ferment, unifiant ainsi les parties qui semblaient divisées, l'âme et la chair, lesquelles avaient été émises dans l'état de division par la Sophia" (*Exc.* 2, I).

Le passage cité plus haut, provenant de l'école occidentale, est plus détaillé, parce que cette école discerne clairement le corps de l'âme instinctive. Rappelons-nous toutefois que selon le mythe l'homme n'a reçu son corps qu'au moment où il est chassé du paradis: c'est pourquoi l'auteur du fragment "oriental", qui décrit la création, ne peut pas en faire mention. Il semble donc qu'il ait employé le mot σάρξ pour désigner l'âme instinctive.

Quoi qu'il en soit, il me semble certain que la version, qui discerne le corps de l'âme instinctive et qui divise l'âme en trois parties, est la plus ancienne. Car elle montre des analogies frappantes avec l'anthropologie platonicienne telle que le philosophe attique l'a décrite dans le Timée, qui était, ne l'oublions pas, le livre de chevet des hommes du temps de Valentin (Timée 69 sqq.). C'est donc Platon qui a divisé l'âme humaine en trois parties et ce doit être Valentin et non un de ses disciples qui a adapté cette conception au système valentinien.

Lorsque'on se rend compte de cette dépendance de la part de Valentin, on verra plus clairement à quel degré le gnostique a modifié la signification des conceptions qu'il a empruntées. Un philosophe comme Platon doit supposer que chaque homme peut penser s'il cultive certaines facultés de son esprit. La raison et l'esprit sont pour la philosophie des données naturelles de l'existence humaine. Or la gnose valentinienne nie que chaque homme possède de l'esprit: au contraire, les hommes spirituels forment une exception. L'âme instinctive est transmise par l'acte de la génération, mais l'âme psychique et l'esprit ne sont pas héréditaires. "Si Adam avait procréé son âme psychique (ἐκ ψυχικοῦ) et son esprit, comme il a procréé son âme instinctive, tous les hommes seraient égaux et justes et la vraie doctrine serait en tous. C'est pour cette raison que les hommes matériels sont nombreux, que les hommes psychiques sont peu nombreux, cependant que les hommes spirituels sont rares" (*Exc.* 56).

Il y a donc trois classes d'hommes: premièrement celle qui est matérielle et dominée par les passions et les instincts, secundo, celle qui est psychique et reconnaît la loi morale, et finalement une troisième qui est spirituelle. L'homme matériel et l'homme psychique ne peuvent pas accueillir la gnose: le seul qui en est capable c'est l'homme spirituel. Or, cet esprit est-il une donnée naturelle de l'home spirituel? Evidemment on ne peut pas être un homme spirituel sans avoir de l'esprit, mais on aimerait savoir quand l'esprit a été déposé dans l'âme. Certes, la Sophia sème les germes spirituels non seulement au moment de la création, mais continuellement jusqu'à ce jour: "les germes spirituels que sème l'Achamoth depuis ce temps-là (c'est-à-dire le temps de la création) jusqu'à maintenant dans les âmes justes" [15]. Malheureusement, non sources ne nous disent pas explicitement à quel moment de la vie l'esprit est déposé dans l'âme humaine. Néanmoins il me semble certain que les Valentiniens ont senti l'esprit qu'ils avaient reçu non comme une attribut naturel, mais comme un don de la grâce; c'est ce que déclare *totidem verbis* un passage assez inconnu, que j'ai trouvé chez Tertullien. Celui-ci rend de la manière suivante la doctrine valentinienne sur l'esprit: "*spiritalem ex Seth de obvenientia superducunt iam non naturam sed indulgentiam (= gratiam), ut quos Achamoth de superioribus in animas bonas depluat*" *(adv. Val. 29)*: "ils y ajoutent l'élément spirituel, symbolisé par Seth, qui provient de dehors et n'est pas (comme l'âme et le corps) un attribut naturel, mais un don de la grâce, parce que la Sagesse le fait descendre d'en haut sur les âmes bonnes". Il me semble que cette expression n'a pas été inventée par Tertullien, mais que celui-ci a puisé dans des sources valentiniennes que nous ne connaisons pas, peut-être dans la tradition orale. Quoi qu'il en soit, cette remarque est très importante: l'esprit n'est pas nature, mais grâce; non natura sed indulgentia. La conception philosophique de Platon est devenue une mystique de la grâce.

Ce germe spirituel sommeille dans l'âme et état d'inconscience. "L'esprit, qui est apparenté au Père, s'est perdu dans la matière profonde de l'erreur", dit Héracléon (frag. 23). C'est pourquoi avant la rédemption l'homme spirituel est un être débile et sujet à la tyrannie des démons: "l'homme, qui est l'enjeu de la lutte, étant un être débile, enclin au mal, est une proie facile pour les démons qui le haïssent" *(Exc. 73)*. C'est une conception très pessimiste de la condition humaine.

Un changement radical est causé par la descente du Christ: "Lorsque le Sauveur est venu, il a reveillé l'âme et enflammé l'étincelle de l'esprit: car les paroles du Seigneur sont puissance" *(Exc. 3)*.

En lisant ces mots enthousiastes on pense involontairement aux vers bien connus de Novalis:

> "Da kam ein Heiland, ein Erlöser,
> ein Menschensohn voll Liebe und Macht,
> und hat ein allbelebendes Feuer
> in unserm Innern angefacht".

Mais l'imagination poétique de ces hérétiques a trouvé encore d'autres symboles pour faire résonner dans nos coeurs leur expérience personnelle: le Christ est,

---

[15]   Irén., *Adv. Haereses*, I, 7, 5.

selon eux, "l'étoile étrangère et nouvelle, qui détruit l'ancienne constellation des astres et rayonne d'une lumière neuve qui n'est pas de ce monde"; ceci parce que "le Seigneur est descendu sur la terre, afin de transférer ceux qui croient en Christ de la sphère de la fatalité dans celle de la providence" (*Exc.* 74).

Ce n'est que depuis l'avènement du Christ que l'homme a reçu une personnalité idéale, l'ange du Sauveur qui le sauve de l'ignorance et de la mort. Dans l'école orientale de la secte valentinienne on souligne le contraste entre l'ange et l'esprit, entre l'homme nouveau et l'homme déchu: "nous sommes morts nous que l'existence ici-bas a introduits à un état de morts, mais les êtres masculins (les anges) sont vivants, parce qu'ils ne participent pas à l'existence dans ce monde" *(Exc.* 22). Cette dernière citation montre clairement en quoi consiste, selon les Valentiniens, la misère de l'homme: non pas dans le fait d'avoir péché, mais dans le fait d'être jeté dans ce monde, soumis à la tyrannie des astres, livré aux assauts des démons, à la mort. La rédemption délivre les hommes de la mort. "Celui qui est engendré par la Mère, est mis au monde et à mort, mais celui que le Christ régénère, est transféré à la vie, dans l'ogdoade. Et ils meurent au monde et vivent pour Dieu, afin que la mort soit anéantie par la mort et la corruption par la résurrection" (*Exc.* 80).

La vie dans ce monde et la vie nouvelle, c'est la mort et la vie, l'esclavage et la liberté, les ténèbres et la lumière, les démons et le Sauveur. Ceci ne veut pas dire que la vie dans le monde ne soit pas nécessaire à l'homme. On admet que la génération est nécessaire afin que s'accomplisse la rédemption des fidèles (*Exc.* 67); on ne rejette pas le mariage comme tant d'autres hérétiques de ce temps là; l'école occidentale, qui est moins radicale et moins pessimiste que l'autre école, déclare même que le monde fut créé pour former l'esprit et le préparer au salut (Irén., *Adv. Haer.*, I, 7, 5). Il est très possible que cette conception soit l'opinion de Valentin lui-même; la vie dans le monde a pour l'esprit une valeur préparatoire; l'esprit a besoin d'une éducation par les moeurs et les sens (cf. Origène). On ne doit pourtant pas perdre de vue que la vie dans le monde ne fait que donner forme à l'essence de l'homme spirituel, mais ne le rend pas conscient du monde transcendant: la vie dans le monde est, pour employer un terme technique de l'idiome valentinien, une μόρφωσις κατὰ οὐσίαν, une formation de l'essence, mais non une μόρφωσις κατὰ γνῶσιν, une formation de la conscience spirituelle: l'esprit est rendu conscient seulement par le Sauveur, qui éveille l'âme de l'homme et enflamme l'étincelle de son esprit. C'est là la différence principale entre la vie dans le monde et la vie nouvelle, entre l'homme déchu et son alter ego, entre le germe et l'ange du Sauveur: pendant la première période l'homme *est* spirituel sans le savoir lui-même; après la descente du Sauveur il reçoit la gnose et devient *conscient* de son origine transcendante. Il y a donc à la fois une identité et une différence entre ces deux états: l'ange

du Sauveur aussi bien que le germe sont spirituels, mais l'un révèle la gnose
dont l'autre est privé. Le Valentinianisme, qui est une "Brautmystik", a exprimé
cette relation entre l'ange du Sauveur et l'homme par le symbole du mariage
sacré: la Sophia est l'épouse mystique, le Christ est l'époux spirituel; de la
même manière le germe spirituel est considéré comme féminin, tandis que les
anges sont nommés les êtres masculins (οἱ ἄρρενες). Il est évident que ces
termes n'ont pas leur sens littéral, mais servent à désigner le principe masculin
et le principe féminin. Ceci nous est expliqué dans un passage se trouvant dans
un autre contexte, mais qui nous semble être assez significatif:

"Le principe féminin produit l'essence, le principe masculin forme l'essence que
le féminin a produite" [16].

Voilà une conception vraiment romantique qui rappelle les définitions d'un
Jakob Grimm. Le germe spirituel, étant féminin, est débile, imparfait et sans
forme; l'ange, étant masculin, est celui qui donne la révélation et forme
l'essence, il complète l'autre moitié du couple, il est le plérome (πλήρωμα)
de l'esprit déchu. "Tant que le germe spirituel est encore sans forme, il est
l'enfant de l'être féminin (Sophia), mais une fois formé il est transformé en
homme et devient un fils de l'Epoux" (*Exc.* 79). Il y a encore un autre fragment,
qui semble contenir toutes les nuances de l'anthropologie valentinienne: "Aussi
longtemps que nous étions des enfants de l'être féminin (Sophia), seulement,
comme d'une liaison honteuse, imparfaits et mineurs, sans raison, sans force,
sans forme, produits au dehors comme des avortons, nous étions des enfants
de la Femme; mais formés par le Sauveur nous sommes devenus des enfants
de l'Homme et de la chambre nuptiale" (*Exc.* 68).

La relation entre le germe et l'ange, entre le Sauveur et l'âme déchue est donc
celle du mariage sacré: l'ange et l'âme forment un couple, une συζυγία. C'est
nettement par cette conception-la que l'anthropologie est adaptée au système
valentinien. On sait que, selon les Valentiniens, même les éons étaient
engendrés en couples et que la divinité est conçue comme une polarité, *Bythos*
et *Sige*. Un savant américain, R. P. Casey, ose même dire que la doctrine
valentinienne en général n'est qu'une projection des conditions biologiques
dans la métaphysique [17]. Je crois que cette solution est un peu trop facile.
Néanmoins il est sans conteste que les Valentiniens ont employé l'image du
mariage pour exprimer la polarité des choses spirituelles.

Ce qui est vraiment très remarquable c'est que, d'une part, les passages des
sources dites "orientales" soulignent la faiblesse de l'esprit humain mais que,

---

[16]   Hippolyte, *Refutatio* VI, 30.
[17]   Dans son édition des *Excerpta ex Theodoto,* Londres 1934, p. 16.

d'autre part, ils déclarent que les anges du Sauveur ont besoin de l'homme: "car ils (les anges) prient pour nous comme pour leur autre moitié et plaident en faveur de nous, et retenus dans ce monde à cause de nous, alors qu'ils sont pressés de retourner dans le monde spirituel, ils demandent pour nous la rémission, afin que nous entrions avec eux. Car on peut presque dire qu'ils ont besoin de nous pour entrer dans le plérome, parce qu'il ne leur est pas permis de rentrer sans nous .... C'est pourquoi ils prient pour nous à juste titre" (*Exc.* 35).

L'homme spirituel ne peut pas se sauver lui-même: c'est l'ange du Christ qui lui révèle la gnose; d'autre part il est certain qu'il sera sauvé, il ne peut pas se perdre. D'où vient cette conviction inébranlable? Il me semble que le Valentinien ose dire franchement qu'il ne peut pas périr, parce que dans le fond même de son être il se sait élu. C'est pour cette raison que les Valentiniens se nommaient: "les élus", par opposition aux catholiques qui n'étaient que des "appelés" (*Exc.* 58). C'est encore pour cette raison qu'ils soulignent que dans l'âme élue seulement est déposé le germe spirituel (*Exc.* 2, 1). En outre, on nous déclare que l'église, c'est-à-dire les hommes spirituels, ont été élus avant la fondation du monde (*Exc.* 41). Il est évident que cette dernière phrase est une citation de l'apôtre St. Paul. Je n'oserais pas dire que les hérétiques s'autorisent à bon droit des mots de cet apôtre, parce que l'expérience m'a enseigné qu'un théologien hoche la tête quand un philologue classique commence à parler de St. Paul. Cependant je crois qu'il est assez significatif que les gnostiques s'efforcent de comprendre l'apôtre, car s'ils ont peut-être mal compris les conceptions fondamentales de la théologie paulinienne, il y en a, parmi leurs adversaires catholiques, qui ne les ont pas comprises du tout. J'admets pourtant que les valentiniens ont exprimé leur expérience de l'élection dans des symboles et des images qui sont très compliquées et très difficiles à interpréter.

C'est qu'on trouve dans nos sources valentiniennes la conception que non seulement les hommes spirituels, mais aussi Jésus, c'est-à-dire l'homme Jésus, a été élu: "Jésus fut adopté, parce qu'il a été élu parmi les êtres complets ($\tau\grave{\alpha}$ $\pi\lambda\eta\rho\acute{\omega}\mu\alpha\tau\alpha$) et qu'il a été le premier né des choses d'ici bas" (*Exc.* 33). Cette conception ne nous étonne pas: selon les valentiniens Jésus, bien qu'être spirituel, était dans ce monde, il était un fils de la Sophia; il est donc imparfait et a besoin du baptême et de la délivrance; au moment du baptême le Christ descend sur lui et lui inspire peu à peu la gnose. On comprend donc aisément que, selon les Valentiniens, Jésus fut élu.

Or il est sûr que cette idée remonte au fondateur de la secte, à Valentin lui-même. St. Irénée nous a conservé un abrégé de la doctrine primitive très précieux et digne de foi, qui contient le passage suivant: "Quand la Mère (Sophia) se trouvait hors du plérome, elle a produit en souvenir du monde meilleur Jésus

accompagné d'une ombre. Mais comme celui-ci état mâle (ἄρρην) il a retranché
l'ombre et s'est élancé vers le haut" (Irén. I, 11, I).

C'est de la mythologie. Cependant, on pourrait avec quelque effort comprendre
ces métaphores. Par l'ombre semblent être indiquées l'insuffisance, la défaillance
et la matérialité. Mais ce qui est vraiment très dificile à expliquer, c'est pourquoi
Jésus quitte sa mère et retourne au monde spirituel *avant la création du monde*.

J'avoue que ce problème me tourmente depuis longtemps et que je ne suis pas
sûr d'en avoir trouvé la solution définitive. En effet il est bien possible que
l'analyse historique ne dispose pas des moyens qui puissent résoudre un pareil
problème plutôt psychologique, mais "point n'est besoin d'espérer pour entre-
prendre ni de réussir pour persévérer". C'est pourquoi j'essaierai maintenant
de découvrir l'origine des éléments divers de ce symbole.

Or, on trouve dans le Poimandre une conception très curieuse qu'on peut
comparer à celle que nous présente la doctrine primitive de Valentin. On sait
que l'écrit hermétique dépeint la création du monde. Après que l'auteur a décrit
comment le ciel a été créé, il déclare: "aussitôt le Verbe de Dieu s'élança hors
des éléments qui se portent en bas vers cette pure région de la nature qui venait
d'être façonnée, et il s'unit au Νοῦς démiurge (car il était de même substance)"
(Poim. 10). Pourquoi donc le Logos quitte-t-il la matière? C'est parce que la
matière ne peut pas être matière, si elle reste, dans le chaos primitif, mêlée à
la raison. "De ce fait, les éléments inférieurs de la nature furent laissés à eux-
mêmes dépourvus de raison, de manière à n'être plus que simple matière"
(Poim. 10). Voici donc une explication plutôt physique, qui n'a rien à faire
avec l'anthropologie. La raison s'est élancée vers le haut: c'est pourquoi la
matière est dépourvue de raison.

On pourrait expliquer la conception valentinienne de la même manière. Les
sources nous disent que, Jésus ayant quitté la Mère, celle-ci était privée de la
substance spirituelle [18]. C'est alors qu'elle produit le démiurge, c'est-à-dire
l'âme du monde, et le diable, c'est-à-dire la matière. L'image de Jésus, qui
s'élance vers le plérome, servit donc entre autres à expliquer pourquoi la matière
et l'âme sont dénuées de spiritualité. L'analogie avec la conception contenue
dans le Poimandre est frappante [19].

Il y a pourtant un second élément. Valentin nous parle d'un souvenir du monde
spirituel, il nous décrit comment l'esprit se dégage de la matière et s'élance
vers les hauteurs spirituelles. Bien sûr, c'est de Jésus qu'il parle, mais Jésus
n'est-il pas le prototype de l'homme spirituel? C'est ainsi que ses disciples ont

---

[18]) Κεκενωμένη τῆς πνευματικῆς ὑποστάσεως, Irén., *Adv. Haereses*, I, 11, 1.
[19] Pour l'union avec le monde spirituel voir *Exc.* 32, 3, pour la consubstantialité *Exc.* 42, 2.

compris ce symbole. Ceci nous est indiqué par un fragment peu connu, mais d'une importance capitale pour le sujet que nous traitons, et qui se trouve chez Clément d'Alexandrie: "Ils(les Valentiniens) disent que le souvenir du monde spirituel est un dégagement de la matière (διυλισμός). Par dégagement de la matière ils entendent la séparation d'avec le monde inférieur à cause du souvenir du monde supérieur ... ils avouent que l'esprit lui-même, parvenu à résipiscence, s'élance vers le haut" (*Paed. 32, 1*).

"Le souvenir du monde spirituel, le dégagement de la matière, la séparation d'avec le mal, l'ascension". Certainement mes auditeurs s'en seront déjà aperçus que c'est la terminologie platonicienne dont se sert Valentin. Il semble que c'est surtout le mythe célèbre tiré de la République, "la comparaison de la grotte", qui a fait une grande impression sur notre gnostique [20]. C'est dans ce mythe que Platon a décrit le retour de l'homme au monde spirituel, sa μεταστροφή et sa ἐπάνοδος ἐπὶ τὰ θεῖα.

Le fragment que nous avons cité dit que l'esprit, parvenu à la résipiscence, s'élance vers le haut. C'est donc la μετάνοια, la prise de conscience du vrai Soi, que décrit le mythologème de Jésus. Ainsi nous sommes revenus à notre point de départ, c'est-à-dire à la remarque de Clément d'Alexandrie, qui se demandait comment Valentin pouvait admettre la μετάνοια, sans pourtant accepter le libre arbitre. Nous avons vu d'une part que l'homme ne peut pas être sauvé par ses propres forces et que d'autre part la μετάνοια était le commencement de l'ἀναδρομή, la "traversée" par laquelle l'esprit passe du monde visible au monde invisible. N'y a-t-il pas une certaine contradiction entre cette conception d'une passivité absolue et cette autre, selon laquelle l'esprit humain s'élance vers le plérome?

Je ne crois pas que ce soit le cas. C'est le Sauveur, nous l'avons vu, qui éveille l'âme sommeillante et enflamme l'étincelle de l'esprit: il forme peu à peu par la gnose l'esprit déchu (κατὰ μικρὸν μορφοῦται διὰ γνώσεως, *Exc.* 59, 1). On doit conclure que c'est le Sauveur qui éveille dans l'esprit la réminiscence du monde spirituel. La résipiscence est donc un effet de la révélation, la "traversée" est une conséquence de la grâce. Le gnostique exprime cette idée par une métaphore touchante: le Sauveur porte les élus sur ses épaules vers le plérome (*Exc.* 42, 1).

Si notre analyse du symbole de l'ἀναδρομή est correcte, cette conception est assez compliquée: d'une part elle rappelle la cosmologie du Poimandre, d'autre part elle contient des réminiscences de Platon, enfin elle sert à exprimer l'expérience très réelle de l'élection. Mais même si notre analyse n'explique pas tout, il est évident que l'homme spirituel n'est pas sauvé par une décision du

---

[20] *Rep. VII*, surtout ch. 4 et 13.

libre arbitre, mais parce que le Sauveur éveille en lui le souvenir du monde spirituel; dans cette anthropologie il n'y a pas de place pour la conception catholique d'une volonté libre.

Pour les hommes qui n'ont pas d'esprit, les hommes psychiques, la situation est différente. Ceux-ci vivent dans une autre sphère, la sphère morale: ils ne sont pas mauvais, ils vénèrent le démiurge et peuvent obéir à sa loi, ils peuvent se sauver à leur manière par les bonnes oeuvres, qui ont une valeur méritoire et sont récompensées dans l'au-delà; il est clair qu'ils possèdent le libre arbitre: "les hommes psychiques ont une volonté libre et sont aptes à la foi et à l'incorruptibilité autant qu'à l'infidélité et à la corruption selon leur propre choix" (*Exc.* 56). Pour mieux comprendre cette citation, on doit savoir que le mot "foi" (πίστις) a une signification toute spéciale dans la terminologie valentinienne. Une recherche lexicologique démontrerait que ce mot ne signifie pas "foi" dans le sens paulinien du mot, mais qu'il évoque plutôt l'idée du légalisme, de la justification par les oeuvres, du moralisme borné, de la "Werkheiligkeit". On comprend donc aisément que la religion juive de l'Ancien Testament est appelée "psychique" par ces disciples de l'apôtre Paul. Ce qui est beaucoup plus remarquable, c'est qu'aussi les catholiques de ce temps sont classés parmi les psychiques.

Ceci est rendu évident par un passage de St.-Irénée, le bon évêque lyonnais, qui déclare: "Les hommes psychiques étaient éduqués par des excercices moraux (litt. psychiques), c'est-à-dire les gens qui ont besoin de bonnes oeuvres et d'une foi nue et qui ne possèdent pas la gnose parfaite. Ils disent que c'est nous, les membres de l'église. C'est pourquoi, disent-ils, les bonnes oeuvres sont nécessaires pour nous (les catholiques), car il n'est pas possible que nous soyons sauvés autrement" [21].

Les Valentiniens ont vu clairement qu'il y a une différence fondamentale entre la justification par les oeuvres et la justification par la grâce: "Ils s'enorgueillissent d'eux-mêmes, en s'appelant parfaits et germes d'*élection*. Car nous (les catholiques), disent-ils, nous avons emprunté la grâce, mais eux, ils ont la grâce d'en haut de la syzygie ineffable et innommable en possession inaliénable" [22]. Pourtant les Valentiniens ne combattent pas cette conception de la justification par les oeuvres. Avec une tolérance qui n'est pas tout à fait dénuée d'ironie, ils admettent qu'elle est relativement vraie. Il y a selon eux certains hommes qui ont un libre arbitre: ceux-ci peuvent se sauver à leur manière par des bonnes oeuvres; il y a d'autres hommes qui ont reçu la grâce et ne peuvent pas se perdre, parce qu'ils sont élus. Entre ces deux classes d'hommes il y a une

---

[21] Irén., *Adv. Haereses*, I, 6, 2.
[22] Irén., *Adv. Haereses*, I, 6, 4.

différence essentielle. Or, si l'on compare la théologie d'un Clément ou d'un Origène à la mystique de Valentin, on découvrira qu'il existe entre ces deux doctrines non seulement des analogies frappantes, mais aussi des divergences fondamentales. Cependant mes recherches m'ont poussé vers la conviction que cette différence dans la conception du libre arbitre et de la grâce est essentielle. La solution de Clément et d'Origène prélude au principe catholique: *gratia non tollit naturam sed perficit*. C'est à mon avis une conception optimiste et harmonieuse du christianisme.

La mystique valentinienne oppose la nature à la grâce, la "*psyche*" immanent au "*pneuma*" transcendant, et le monde à Dieu. Elle est, en effet, un christianisme tragique [23].

---

[23] Pour le Valentinisme comme mystique de la grâce voir: W. D. Hauschild, *Gottes Geist und der Mensch*, München, 1972, p. 152; Elaine H. Pagels, *The Valentinian claim to esoteric exegesis of Romans as basis for anthropological theory*, Vigiliae Christianae, 26, 1972, pp. 241-250.

L'INSCRIPTION DE FLAVIA SOPHE

I

L'inscription de Flavia Sophè, poème funéraire trouvé à Rome il y a à peu près un siècle, offre un intérêt tout spécial au chercheur pour plusieurs raisons. L'épigramme n'est pas sans mérite littéraire; il provient certainement — chose assez exceptionnelle dans le domaine de l'archéologie chrétienne — d'un milieu hérétique; et surtout il semble porter quelque lumière sur le problème si contesté de la relation entre le baptême et l'onction. Récemment le père A. Ferrua a publié de nouveau le texte de ces vers fragmentaires, avec des photographies de la pierre [1]. Je me propose de donner une interprétation des lignes suivantes:

Φῶς πατρικὸν ποθέουσα, σύναιμε, σύνευνε Σόφη μου,
Λουτροῖς κρισαμένη Χριστοῦ μύρον ἄφθιτον, ἁγνόν,
Αἰώνων ἔσπευσας ἀθρῆσαι θεῖα πρόσωπα,
Βούλης τῆς μεγάλης μέγαν ἄγγελον, υἱὸν ἀληθῆ,
Ἰς νυμφῶνα μολοῦσα καὶ εἰς [κόλπ]ους ἀνοροῦσα
Ἀθάνατο]ς πατρικούς . . .

Il n'y a aucun doute que cet épigramme provient des cercles valentiniens de la capitale de l'Empire. M. Kirchhoff l'a déjà observé dans son commentaire, assez superficiel d'ailleurs, dans le *Corpus Inscriptionum Graecarum* [2]. Puisque ses arguments n'ont pas pu convaincre M. Dölger [3], il vaut la peine de donner quelque relief à ce fait évident.

A. Ce n'est pas par hasard que l'épigramme fait mention du "désir" de la défunte. Car les Valentiniens, bien qu'exaltant le silence comme un bien très précieux — *silentium maxima res est apud sapientes,* disaient-ils — deviennent éloquents, quand ils trouvent l'occasion d'exprimer leur nostalgie transcendante. Ce "désir" est, selon eux, "l'élan naturel d'un éon vers le Père infini", φυσικὴ αἰῶνος ὁρμή (*Irén.* I, 2, 4). Il est vrai que cette aspiration peut devenir une passion déchaînée et impétueuse, dépassant les limites imposées à tout esprit

---

[1] Estratto dalla *Rivista di Archeologia Christiana,* anno XXI-XXII (1945), nos. 1-4, p. 12-29. J'emploie dans cet article les traductions des textes valentiniens du père F. M. Sagnard (*La gnose valentinienne et le témoignage de saint Irénée,* Paris, 1947; *Extraits de Théodote,* Paris, 1948).

[2] *C. I. G.,* vol. IV, p. 594, n. 9595a.

[3] *Röm. Quartalschrift,* 1905, p. 9.

engendré. C'est la chute même du dernier éon, Sagesse. Elle ne peut pas, comme les autres, attendre la révélation, et elle tombe dans l'ignorance. Le πόθος est devenu un πάθος, *inquisitio magnitudinis patris fiebat passio perditionis*, dit S. Irénée (II, 20, 3). Et par conséquent, tous les hommes pneumatiques auront ce "désir" de contempler Dieu, mais obscurci par les passions. C'est pourquoi Héracléon peut dire que l'élément "parent du Père" s'est perdu "dans la profondeur de la matière d'erreur", mais qu'il a conservé néanmoins une disposition à recevoir la Vie et une "sensibilité" (ἔννοια) pour la puissance qui émane du Sauveur (*Hér.* fr. 23 et 27).

Le mot ἔννοια qu'Héracléon a choisi dans ce passage a la même tonalité que πόθος, ἐνθύμησις, ζήτησις τοῦ Πατρός, etc.: toutes ces expressions concernent dans la terminologie valentinienne ce "désir" de contempler la divinité, "désir" qui est le privilège douloureux des hommes pneumatiques, puisque les "psychiques" se sentent bien à leur aise dans le monde visible et n'éprouvent aucun besoin d'élever leurs âmes.

Le Sauveur, étant l'Ὅρος, impose son Logos à cette imagination désordonnée de l'esprit, purifie la nostalgie aveugle et passionnée, et lui révèle son but vrai: le Dieu inconnu. Dès lors le "désir" de Dieu des pneumatiques est pur et sincère, aspirant à la communion et à l'union avec le Père: *concupiscentia communicationis cum eo (Patre) et unitatis eis salutare fit* (ὁ πόθος ὁ τῆς κοινωνίας μετ' αὐτοῦ καὶ ἑνώσεως γίγνεται αὐτοῖς σωτήριος) (*Irén.* II, 18, 7). Le mythe ésotérique des Valentiniens décrit donc l'origine, la perversion et la purification du "désir" mystique.

On n'a pas encore observé que ces spéculations supposent chez l'auteur du mythe une certaine connaissance de la philosophie stoïcienne. C'est ce que montrent les mots mêmes qu'il a choisis pour exprimer sa pensée. Il sait que selon les sages du Portique, l'élan (ὁρμή) par soi est naturel et raisonnable, que la passion est un élan immodéré (πλεονάζουσα ὁρμή) et qu'enfin cette passion non naturelle et mauvaise trouve son origine dans la raison [4].

Quand on place les passages cités du mythe dans le cadre de la pensée stoïcienne, la conception valentinienne de l'origine du mal devient plus claire. Les textes eux-mêmes en effet nous laissent dans un certain embarras. Certes, nous voyons en quoi consiste l'originalité de Valentin comme penseur gnostique: dans la gnose vulgaire, qui le précède, une entité féminine tombe dans une

---

[4] *Stoic. Veter. Fragm.*, ed. I. von Arnim, *Index* s.v. ὁρμή. Sur la perspective philonienne du mythe voir mon article: *Philo und die altchristliche Häresie*, dans la *Theologische Zeitschrift*, Bâle, 1949, pp. 429-436.

matière préexistance, parce qu'elle se sent portée en bas vers les ténèbres [5], ou bien parce qu'elle veut rivaliser avec Dieu en créant le monde visible [6]: ces thèmes de la *curiositas* et de la *superbia* ne sont pas sans parallèles dans l'histoire des religions; selon Valentin, par contre, Sagesse crée un néant ($\varkappa\acute{\varepsilon}\nu\omega\mu\alpha$) puisqu'elle désire avec passion de comprendre Dieu et s'élance en haut pour pénétrer dans le mystère de son être [7]. Mais — et voici le problème — cette chute de Sagesse, la chute originelle, est-elle voulue, a-t-elle été préétablie par le Père? Alors, comme me le fit remarquer M. Martin Buber, le mal serait un moment nécessaire dans l'évolution de l'Univers, le mythe n'aurait pas un caractère tragique et l'on se tromperait donc en voulant retrouver dans la gnose valentienne une conception tragique de la vie.

Ou bien faut-il admettre que le mal commence déjà avec l'émanation et la différenciation des éons issus du Noῦς, qui ne peuvent pas contempler le Père et "désirent" Le voir? Alors, en dernière analyse, le "désir" de Dieu serait mauvais et le mal serait inhérent au principe d'individuation [8].

Il semble que la perspective stoïcienne de ces spéculations nous aide à résoudre cette question épineuse. Les autres éons ont le "désir", naturel et paisible, de contempler la Source de leur être ($\mathring{\eta}\sigma\upsilon\chi\mathring{\eta}\ \pi\omega\varsigma\ \grave{\varepsilon}\pi\varepsilon\pi\acute{o}\vartheta\sigma\upsilon\nu$, *Irén.* I, 1, 2). Cet élan ($\acute{o}\rho\mu\acute{\eta}$) subit une altération profonde dans Sagesse ($\grave{\varepsilon}\tau\varepsilon\rho\sigma\acute{\iota}\omega\sigma\iota\varsigma$, *Irén.* I, 4, 1) et devient une passion ($\pi\acute{\alpha}\vartheta\sigma\varsigma$). L'élan est naturel, mais c'est seulement la passion qui est mauvaise, elle qui trouve son origine dans Sagesse, entité spirituelle. Le mal n'est donc pas voulu par le Père, ni conséquence nécessaire de l'individuation, mais c'est une catastrophe, une neurose universelle pour ainsi dire, causée par la perversion inexpliquée de l'élan naturel de l'esprit vers Dieu.

Il est très possible que la version primitive du mythe laissait entrevoir l'influence stoïcienne d'une façon beaucoup plus claire que la recension de Ptolémée transmise par S. Irénée. Dans celle-ci il est décrit comment le Christ "a quitté Sagesse, afin qu'elle prît conscience de la passion qui était en elle à la suite

---

[5] Hegemonius, *Acta Archelai,* c. 67, 4-12. Ce fragment, transmis par Basilide, est le produit d'un gnosticisme naissant et encore préchrétien (comp. *La doctrine de Basilide,* dans les *Eranos Jahrbücher, 1948,* Zürich, 1949 = p. 103 ss. de ce livre.

[6] Dans l'*Apocryphon de Jean,* source de Valentin aussi bien que de saint Irénée (I, 29), il est dit: "sans l'$\varepsilon\mathring{\upsilon}\delta\sigma\varkappa\acute{\iota}\alpha$ du Pneuma et la connaissance de son propre $\sigma\acute{\upsilon}\mu\varphi\omega\nu\sigma\varsigma$, elle voulait agir" et elle s'élança au dehors, en s'étendant dans son *Prounikon*" (Carl Schmidt, *Philotesia.* p. 329, Berlin, 1907).

[7] Cfr. *The original doctrine of Valentine,* Vig. Chr., I, 1, p. 50.

[8] Si je le comprends bien, ceci est l'opinion de M. Sagnard, o.c., p. 400.

de son exclusion du Plérôme, et qu'ainsi elle *aspirât aux réalités transcendantes* (ὀρεχθῇ τῶν διαφερόντων)". Poussée par cette ὄρεξις, elle s'élance (ὁρμῆσαι) à la recherche de la Lumière qui l'avait abandonnée, mais elle tombe de nouveau dans les passions. Ce processus aboutit à la création du démiurge et du monde (*Irén.* I, 4, 2).

Il est manifeste que ce passage a été remanié par Ptolémée et ne transmet pas intégralement la doctrine authentique du fondateur de la secte [9]. On doit pourtant supposer que la version originale contenait un passage analogue, parce qu'un fragment provenant de l'école orientale nous déclare que Sagesse mit au jour le démiurge à l'image de ce Christ qui l'avait abandonnée, par suite du vif "désir" (ἐπιπόθησις) qu'elle éprouvait pour lui (*Excerpta ex Theodoto* 33). On dirait donc que cette ἐπιπόθησις et cette ὄρεξις sont à peu près synonymes et se rapportent à la même phase du mythe. Mais en même temps les Extraits nous déclarent que le démiurge résultait d'une "passion de désir" (πάθος τῆς ἐπιθυμίας). On doit conclure que selon Valentin lui-même, l'élan naturel (ὄρεξις) de Sagesse est devenu passion (ἐπιθυμία). Mais cette distinction se retrouve mot pour mot dans la philosophie stoïcienne:

ὄρεξιν οὖν ἐπιθυμίας διακρίνουσιν οἱ περὶ ταῦτα
δεινοί · καὶ τὴν μὲν ἐπὶ ἡδοναῖς καὶ ἀκολασίᾳ
τάττουσιν, ἄλογον οὖσαν · τὴν δὲ ὄρεξιν ἐπὶ τῶν
κατὰ φύσιν ἀναγκαίων, λογικὴν ὑπάρχουσαν κίνησιν.

Stoic. Veter. Fragm., éd. I. von Arnim, III, 10, 8.

Valentin a évidemment emprunté aux sages du Portique les notions qui lui semblaient indiquées pour exprimer les nuances de sa pensée, ou plutôt de son expérience religieuse. D'après ce que nous savons de l'instruction académique au second siècle après le Christ, le πόθος τῆς ζητήσεως τοῦ Πατρός, l'aspiration vers l'infini ne s'apprenait pas à l'école.

Mais ce que Valentin a appris à Alexandrie, où il recevait une éducation grecque, c'est à interpréter en homme cultivé, avec des paroles d'apparence philosophique, la nostalgie plus ou moins romantique qui était très vivante en lui. Le symbolisme de l'entité déchue fut emprunté à la tradition de la gnose vulgaire: la terminologie est d'origine stoïcienne; la conception du "désir" comme telle est l'apport personnel du maître lui-même.

Nous constatons donc que le πόθος est bien caractéristique pour Valentin et ses disciples, et il n'y a rien d'étonnant à ce que le verbe ποθεῖν se retrouve dans l'inscription de Flavia Sophè.

---

[9] Valentin ne connaît pas deux Sagesses ni l'émanation du Christ avec le Saint-Esprit (Tert., *adv. Val.*, 11).

B. L'expression "lumière paternelle" de l'épigramme n'est pas moins caractéristique. En effet, selon la définition bien connue de Ptolémée dans sa Lettre à Flora, le *Père* est "incorruptible et *lumière en soi,* simple et homogène" [10]. Et cette "lumière paternelle", *lumen paternum,* est telle, selon les Valentiniens, "qu'elle peut remplir tout ce qui est dans le Père et qu'elle peut tout illuminer" (*Irén.* II, 4, 3). Si les éons sont appelés des "Lumières", c'est parce qu'ils sont des flambeaux, des étoiles, des rayons qui empruntent leur éclat à cette Lumière archétypique: *paternum lumen est, ex quo omnia constituta sunt lumina* (*Irén.* II, 17, 5). On ne saurait pas dire si c'est à bon droit que S. Irénée attribue ce même titre au Sauveur, qui apparaît à la Sagesse déchue (II, 19, 4): dans les autres sources le Christ n'est nommé que "la Lumière" ou "notre Lumière" tout court. C'est pourquoi nous préférons croire que la "lumière paternelle", dans l'inscription, désigne la divinité suprême, le Dieu inconnu.

Dans les analyses rigoureuses, auxquelles il a soumis les spéculations hérétiques, l'évêque de Lyon parle presque toujours du *paternum lumen* IPSORUM: ceci semble indiquer qu'il s'agit d'un terme technique de la terminologie valentinienne. On est donc surpris de constater que S. Irénée lui-même n'a pas hésité à employer cette même expression dans certains passages du quatrième livre, où il exprime sa propre pensée: $\tau\grave{\alpha}$ $\dot{\alpha}\pi\text{οστ}\acute{\alpha}\nu\tau\alpha$ $\text{το}\tilde{\upsilon}$ $\pi\alpha\tau\rho\iota\text{κο}\tilde{\upsilon}$ $\phi\omega\tau\acute{ο}\varsigma$ (IV, 39, 3); *ut in carne domini nostri occurrat paterna lux* (IV, 20, 1). Il est possible qu'il ait emprunté cette désignation à ses adversaires, tout en lui attribuant une signification nouvelle.

C. L'auteur des Extraits de Théodote se demande, dans ce style de catéchisme fréquent dans les écrits philosophiques de l'époque, et avec un verbe cher aux auteurs syncrétistes [11]: "vers quel but nous empressons-nous?", $\pi\text{ο}\tilde{\upsilon}$ $\sigma\pi\varepsilon\acute{\upsilon}\delta\text{ομεν}$ (*Exc.* 78, 2); et c'est comme pour répondre à cette question que le poème funéraire déclare: "courant vers la Chambre Nuptiale et vous élançant immortelle vers le sein du Père, vous vous êtes empressée pour contempler les faces divines des éons". C'est à la contemplation du Père, à la communion et l'union avec le Fils que vise la gnose valentinienne. Ces vers, pourtant, ne nous apportent pas grand'chose de nouveau. Car, dans le mythe ésotérique, l'envol des pneumatiques est décrit de la manière suivante: "ils entrent dans la Chambre

---

[10]   Lettre de Ptolémée à Flora, VII, 7, p. 66, dans mon édition (*Sources Chrétiennes,* Éditions du Cerf, Paris, 1949).

[11]   Voir pour le style de catéchisme: R. Beutler, *Philosophie und Apologie bei Minucius Felix,* diss., Königsberg, 1936; A. J. Festugière, dans son commentaire sur *Hermetica,* VII, 5; pour $\sigma\pi\varepsilon\acute{\upsilon}\delta\varepsilon\iota\nu$ dans les *Oracles Chaldaïques:* W. Theiler, *Die Chaldäischen Orakel und die Hymnen des Synesios,* Halle, 1942, p. 35; dans les *écrits Hermétiques:* A. J. Festugière, ad IV, 5; en général E. Norden, *Agnostos Theos,* p. 107, n. 2.

Nuptiale (νυμφῶνα) à l'intérieur de la Limite et s'en vont vers la contemplation du Père" (*Exc.* 64). En effet, les lignes de l'épigramme semblent faire allusion à ce passage du mythe. La seule différence, peut-être, c'est que la perspective eschatologique, décalque du christianisme primitif que l'on trouve aussi bien dans les documents de l'école orientale que dans ceux de l'école de Ptolémée, a disparu: les initiés décédés ne doivent plus attendre dans l'Ogdoade jusqu'à ce que tous les élus prédestinés aient été formés par la gnose, mais ils entrent immédiatement après la mort dans le plérôme.

La "remontée" dé l'esprit est désignée par les participes μολοῦσα et ἀνοροῦσα. Il semble qu'on a choisi ces mots pour des convenances poétiques, car, en général, les Valentiniens préfèrent le verbe ἀνατρέχειν. Ainsi, Clément d'Alexandrie dit, dans un passage capital pour l'interprétation de la doctrine hérétique, qu'on cherche d'ailleurs en vain dans les manuels et dans les études spéciales: αὐτὸ γοῦν τὸ πνεῦμα ὁμολογοῦσιν μετανοῆσαν ἀναδραμεῖν; "ils décla-clarent que l'esprit même, étant venu à résipiscense, est remonté" (*Paed.* I, 6, 32, 1). De même les adversaires d'Irénée soulignent qu'ils remontent vers l'union: *et ipsi ad unitatem recurrere et omnes unum esse* (*Irén.* II, 12, 4). Cette phrase évoque la formule, dans laquelle Hippolyte résume toute la doctrine: "toutes choses remontent vers l'un selon Valentin": τὰ πάντα εἰς ἕνα ἀνατρέχει κατὰ Οὐαλεντῖνον (*Contra Noëtum* 11).

Il n'y a aucun doute que cette terminologie a été employée par le fondateur de la secte. Selon Valentin, le Christ, c'est-à-dire le prototype des pneumatiques, "retrancha de lui l'ombre et remonta (ἀναδραμεῖν) au Plérôme" (*Irén.* I, 11, 1).

Je n'hésite pas à déclarer que ce thème de la "remontée" a été, avec le thème de la "résipiscence" (μετάνοια), l'essentiel de la gnose valentinienne et je regrette que ce terme n'ait pas toujours reçu tout le relief qu'il mérite [12]. Car il se retrouve plus tard dans les écrits hermétiques, chez les philosophes néoplatoniciens et même chez les mystiques chrétiens d'époque postérieure [13]. La "remontée vers son vrai soi" était alors à l'ordre du jour. La conception des Valentiniens, cependant, comme nous le verrons dans la suite, avait pris des

---

[12] Sur la "résipiscence" voir *La conception de l'homme dans la gnose valentinienne*, dans les *Eranos Jahrbücher*, 1947, Zürich, 1948 (ici p. 103 ss.). Il faut bien se garder de confondre la "résipiscence", "prise de conscience de son vrai soi", avec le "repentir" qu'on trouve chez le gnostique Apelles (Tert. *de Carne*, 8 (ss.), où on doit lire, n'en déplaise à Waszink: *poenitentiam admiscuerit* (cfr. Ps.-Tert., *Adv. omn. haer.*, 19: *permiscuisse poenitentiam*). Apelles a emprunté cette conception du "repentir" à la gnose d'Égypte pendant son séjour à Alexandrie (cfr. *Ev. Eg.*, p. 59, *Vig. Ch.*, II, 3, p. 141).

[13] P. e. *Herm.*, X, 16, Porphyrius, *de abst.*, I, 29.

couleurs nettement mythologiques. Car cette "traversée" (qui est selon moi en même temps un processus d'intériorisation) était menacée par des démons et des divinités subalternes qui essayaient d'empêcher l'ascension de l'esprit vers le plérôme.

D.   L'épigramme est donc un poème savant, plein d'allusions dogmatiques, et résumant dans un coloris poétique et avec des termes plus ou moins philosophiques l'essence même de la doctrine valentinienne. Mais les réminiscences bibliques ne font pas défaut non plus. Il va de soi que l'expression "sein paternel" provient du prologue de l'Évangile de S. Jean, vénéré par ces hérétiques. Et il est bien important que la découverte d'un nouveau fragment de l'inscription par le père Ferrua a rendu sûre la leçon $\pi\alpha\tau\rho\iota\kappa o\acute{u}\varsigma$. Car nous voyons par cela que la Chambre Nuptiale, le plérôme et les éons étaient *dans* le sein du Père. Il n'est donc pas vrai que, dans l'école italique, les éons existaient "*extra deum*", comme nous voudrait la faire croire Tertullien [14].

Quant à la mention du "grand Ange du grand conseil", citation libre l'Isaïe 9, 6, elle est un peu surprenante, parce que l'Ancien Testament n'était certainement pas le livre de chevet des gnostiques. Il semble, pourtant, que cette citation peut nous aider à préciser l'origine de l'inscription. On sait que la secte valentinienne s'était divisée en plusieurs écoles, dont les divergences doctrinales étaient très considérables. L'école italique, par exemple, dont Ptolémée et Héracléon étaient les chefs, était beaucoup moins radicale que les autres écoles et affichait une certaine bienveillance envers le démiurge et son livre, l'Ancien Testament. C'est précisément dans un document provenant de cette école que se retrouve l'expression "Ange du Conseil" pour désigner le Sauveur: "Et quand le Père eut donné tout pouvoir, et le Plérôme, son consentement, "*l'Ange du Conseil*" est envoyé au dehors et devient "la Tête de toutes choses" après le Père" (*Exc. ex Theod.* 43, 2). Il est donc possible que Flavia Sophè appartenait à l'école italique, laquelle évidemment avait son centre à Rome, et qu'elle faisait partie de cette communauté fondée par Valentin après avoir quitté l'église orthodoxe de la capitale. L'inscription prouve que ce cercle hérétique existait encore vers la fin du troisième siècle et qu'il était resté fidèle aux principes qui l'avaient inspiré dès sa fondation. On se demande si c'est parmi les adhérents à cette école qu'il faut chercher les gnostiques combattus par Plotin.

Le terme "Fils vrai" n'est pas fréquent dans les documents valentiniens: je ne saurais citer qu'un seul passage: *initium quidem esse Monogenem, Logon autem*

---

[14]   *Adv. Val.* 4: *eam* (viam) *postmodum Ptolemaeus intravit, nominibus et numeris aeonum distinctis in personales substantias, sed extra deum determinatas, quas Valentinus in ipsa summa divinitatis ut sensus et affectus motus incluserat.*

VERUM FILIUM *Unigeniti* (*Irén.* III, 11, 1). Il semble pourtant que le "Fils vrai" de l'inscription ne désigne pas le Logos. Une autre interprétation fera comprendre plus justement les intentions de l'auteur.

Selon les Valentiniens la première émanation du Père est le Fils: le Père est cause de *l'être* de toutes choses, le Fils par contre de leur *devenir*: "La cause de la permanence éternelle de tous les éons est cette transcendance incompréhensible du Père. La cause de leur naissance et de leur formation est au contraire ce qui est compréhensible dans le Père, c'est-à-dire le Fils" (*Irén.* I, 2, 5). Pour cette conception, les hérétiques s'autorisent de l'Évangile de saint Jean: "Jean ... pose à la base un certain Principe, — premier-engendré de Dieu —, principe qu'il appelle encore *Fils*, Monogène, Dieu et dans lequel le Père a émis toutes choses en germe", dit Ptolémée (*Irén.* I, 8, 5).

Les éons ont été produits en couples: or, la conjointe du Fils est la Vérité: cela veut dire que la Vérité est l'aspect essentiel du Fils qui, à son tour, est le reflet vrai du Père. C'est pour cette raison que le poète de l'épigramme a pu désigner le Fils émané du Père par le terme "Fils vrai".

Nous retrouvons donc dans l'inscription de Flavia Sophè le Père de toutes choses (la lumière paternelle), le Fils ou le Νοῦς (le Fils vrai), les éons, et le Sauveur (l'Ange du grand conseil). Impossible de douter que l'épigramme ne provienne de l'école valentinienne.

II

L'inscription, nous dit-on, date de la fin du troisième siècle et dès sa découverte, on a supposé qu'elle constituait un témoignage très ancien sur le baptême. M. de Rossi fut le premier à l'observer [15]. M. Dölger, dont l'autorité dans cette matière est sans pareille, l'a répété [16]. Je ne puis accepter cette interprétation qu'avec certaines réserves. En effet, il semble que l'épigramme ne fait pas allusions au baptême dans le sens propre du mot, mais à la "rédemption" (ἀπολύτρωσις), sacrement gnostique des mourants.

Il nous dit: "ointe dans les bains du Christ avec l'onguent sacré, impérissable, vous vous êtes empressé de contempler les faces divines des éons, courant vers la Chambre Nuptiale et vous élançant, immortelle, vers le sein du Père". Ces mots nous font supposer qu'il y a une certaine relation entre le sacrement et la

---

[15] *Bulletino di Archeologia Cristiana*, 2, 1869, p. 30 seqq.: un antichissimo cenno della cresima data insieme al *battesimo*. Comp. d'ailleurs Brunengo, dans la *Civiltà Cattolica* III, X, 1858, pp. 357-359: Frase relativa al *battesimo* ed alla cresima.

[16] *Röm. Quartalschrift*, 1905, p. 1-41; *das Sakrament der Firmung*, 1906, p. 5 sqq.

"remontée": la défunte peut traverser ces mondes qui la séparent du plérôme grâce au sacrement qu'elle a reçu. En effet, le meilleur commentaire possible aux vers de l'inscription est fourni par un passage d'Irénée sur le sacrement des Valentiniens.

"D'autres, enfin, s'occupent des mourants. Ils leur versent sur la tête le mélange d'eau et d'huile — ou *l'onguent* mentionné plus haut, *mélangé à l'eau* — et font les invocations déjà dites, pour qu'ils deviennent insaissables et invisibles aux Archontes et aux Puissances; et *que leur Homme intérieur monte au-dessus des espaces invisibles*, abandonnant le corps à l'univers créé, et l'âme psychique au démiurge".   Irén. I, 21, 5

Pendant cette "remontée" l'initié doit adresser aux Puissances cosmiques et aux Puissances du démiurge des mots de passe magiques, qui lui ont été confiés lors du sacrement et qui lui permettront de continuer sans embarras son "voyage au bout de la nuit".

Il est infiniment probable que l'inscription de Flavia Sophè fait mention de cette "rédemption" gnostique plutôt que du baptême. De con côté elle nous aide à résoudre quelques problèmes qui se rapportent au passage cité. Irénée ne nous dit pas à quelle école de la secte valentinienne appartenaient les pratiquants de ce rite: il les nomme après les Marcosiens, mais dit seulement que c'étaient "d'autres". Épiphane, par contre, déclare que c'était parmi les adhérents d'Héracléon que ce rite existait [17]. Nous avons constaté que Flavia Sophè était vraisemblablement membre de l'école italique, dont Héracléon était un des chefs. Si elle a reçu la "rédemption" dans la forme transmise par S. Irénée, il est possible que, cette fois du moins, Épiphane a dit la vérité et que les "*alii*" de S. Irénée ont été des disciples d'Héracléon.

M. Holl, dans l'apparat critique de son édition d'Épiphane, s'est demandé si, dans le passage cité sur la rédemption, il s'agissait d'un sacrement des mourants ou bien d'un sacrement des morts; M. Hilgenfeld, par contre, suppose qu'il est question d'un baptême pour les morts, usage archaïque mentionné par saint Paul (1 *Cor.* 15, 29)[18]: en effet, la traduction latine d'Irénée contient la leçon: "*mortuos*", tandis qu'Épiphane parle des mourants ($\tau\varepsilon\lambda\varepsilon\upsilon\tau\tilde{\omega}\nu\tau\alpha\varsigma$). Cependant les savants allemands auraient pu trouver, l'un la réponse à sa question, l'autre la réfutation de son hypothèse, dans la *Réfutation* d'Hippolyte. Et c'est cet auteur qui nous apprend aussi l'origine de la "rédemption" gnostique: *ce rite a été dérivé du sacrement du baptême.*

---

17 *Panarion*, 36, 2 et 3. K. Müller, *Beiträge*, p. 195.
18 *Ketzergeschichte des Urchristentums*, p. 381 et p. 417.

Hippolyte a rencontré des Valentiniens, qui déclaraient que S. Irénée, en transmettant ces formules magiques, n'avait pas été exact. Alors l'auteur ecclésiastique a pris — toujours à Rome — des informations précises et délicates. Il s'est adressé à des adhérents de la secte qui lui ont confirmé la probité de l'évêque de Lyon; "leurs disciples les hérétiques *après* le baptême en promettent encore *un autre,* qu'ils nomment "rédemption". *Imposant la main* à celui qui reçoit la rédemption ils disent dans un langage ineffable quelque chose qu'on ne peut pas facilement proférer d'après eux s'il ne s'agit pas de quelqu'un de très éprouvé, ou *quand il est sur le point de mourir, l'évêque vient le lui dire dans l'oreille*" (Hipp., *Ref.* VI, 41).

La "rédemption" était donc un "second baptême", et elle consistait en la communication de certains mots de passe magiques, l'imposition des mains et l'"infusion" d'un mélange d'eau et d'onguent. On peut facilement s'imaginer comment Flavia Sophè a reçu le sacrement des mourants: quand elle agonisait, l'évêque l'a visitée, lui a versé quelques gouttes d'onguent et d'eau sur le front, et, en lui imposant la main, lui a susurré à demi-voix les mots énigmatiques et salutaires de la traversée.

On est fondé à supposer que ce rite de "rédemption" est issue du baptême gnostique. Autrement, comment Hippolyte pourrait-il le nommer: "autre <baptême>", comment pourrait-on parler des "bains du Christ", comme le fait l'inscription? Évidemment, la désignation $\lambda o \upsilon \tau \rho \dot{\alpha}$ pour l'infusion avec quelques gouttes, et l'emploi de l'eau en général, ne sont que des rudiments, mais ils trahissent qu'à l'origine, le baptême comprenait deux parties: 1) l'immersion dans l'eau et 2) la "*rédemption*" avec onction et imposition des mains.

Il est sûr que cette conception du baptême n'a pas été introduite par quelque épigone tardif: elle se retrouve dans les documents de l'école orientale. Ceci prouve que les deux ramifications de la secte ont emprunté cette doctrine au fondateur, à Valentin lui-même, qui, ne l'oublions pas, avait quitté l'église vers 140 après J.C. Selon Théodote, le baptême comporte un double aspect: ($\tau \dot{o} \ \beta \dot{\alpha} \pi \tau \iota \sigma \mu \alpha \ldots \ \delta \iota \pi \lambda o \tilde{\upsilon} \nu$): "l'un, sensible, *grâce à l'eau,* qui éteint le feu sensible; l'autre, intelligible, *grâce à l'Esprit,* qui protège du feu intelligible" (*Exc.* 81, 2). Ce passage nous enseigne deux choses: tout d'abord il démontre que le baptême gnostique est calqué sur le baptême chrétien orthodoxe. La distinction entre le baptême par l'eau et celui par l'Esprit a été empruntée à l'Évangile de Jean (I, 26; I, 33). Et si le baptême chrétien comportait tant le pardon des péchés que la communication du Saint-Esprit, c'est à ce deuxième aspect que se rapporte la "rédemption" (cfr. *Irén.* I, 21, 2). C'est pourquoi on ne saurait plus douter que "l'huile sanctifiée par la "dynamis" de Dieu" — simple équivalent de "l'onguent sacré" dans l'inscription de Flavia Sophè — que cette huile, dont il est question dans le numéro 82 des Extraits de

Théodote, est l'huile de l'onction baptismale. Et "l'imposition des mains", dont nous parle l'Extrait 82, appartient au même sacrement, comme le prouve le contexte même dans lequel se trouve cette expression aussi bien que le témoignage d'Hippolyte que nous avons cité. Or il est bien sûr que ces cérémonies se retrouvent dans l'Église du troisième siècle: *Exinde egressi de lavacro perungimur benedicta unctione ... Dehinc manus imponitur per benedictionem advocans et invitans spiritum sanctum*, dit Tertullien (*De Baptismo*, VII et VIII). Mais la combinaison des textes valentiniens nous permet de conclure que l'onction, l'imposition des mains et la communication du Saint-Esprit, considérées par les hérétiques comme faisant partie du baptême, existaient déjà dans l'Église avant 140 après le Christ, c'est-à-dire avant la crise gnostique dans l'église romaine, et doivent remontrer très haut.

D'autre part — et ceci est la deuxième considération suggérée par l'Extrait 81 cité plus haut — les hérétiques ont transformé la conception du baptême en la contaminant avec une conception tout autre, à savoir celle de la "remontée". Le baptême intelligible protège du feu invisible, parce que l'initié reçoit alors la "rédemption" qui assure l'immunité contre l'agression des Puissances capables d'empêcher la "remontée" de l'esprit vers le plérôme. Car par la "rédemption" l'homme reçoit le "Nom" <du Christ> qui le divinise (spéculation à base judaïque): un Ange vient pour le guider et le protéger pendant la "traversée" (un peu comme dans l'Ascension d'Isaïe). Par la possession de ce "Nom" et grâce à la protection de l'Ange, l'initié peut entrer dans le plérôme: "Et", disent-ils, "ceux qui se font baptiser pour les morts", ce sont les Anges, qui se font baptiser pour nous, afin que, possédant nous aussi le Nom, nous ne soyons pas arrêtés par la Limite et la Croix, et *empêchés* d'entrer au Plérôme. C'est pourquoi, dans "*l'imposition des mains*" ils disent à la fin: "*pour la Rédemption angélique*", c'est-à-dire pour celle que les anges ont aussi, afin que celui qui a obtenu la *Rédemption* se trouve *baptisé* dans le *Nom* même dans lequel son Ange aussi a été baptisé avant lui" (*Exc*. 22, 4). Ainsi, la "rédemption", transmise pendant le baptême, rend possible la "remontée". Le baptême marque la première phase de la "vie mystique".

Il n'est pas nécessaire de chercher très loin pour trouver la source de cette conception de Valentin. Ses adversaires nous déclarent qu'il a fait des emprunts à une gnose déjà existante avant lui, gnose qui affiche les noms les plus divers mais qui est essentiellement une et que l'on peut appeler: "gnose vulgaire d'Égypte". C'est précisément de tels gnostiques, appelés cette fois des Ophites, qu'Origène nous a transmis les mots de passe magiques (*C. Celsum*, VI, 31); c'est dans un document de ces mêmes gnostiques, à peine christianisé, sans doute antérieur à Valentin, qu'on retrouve les thèmes de la "résipiscence" et de la "remontée": *deligatam igitur hanc a corpore, quod erat a materia, et valde gravatam,* RESIPUISSE *aliquando et conatam esse fugere aquas et* ASCENDERE *ad matrem* (Irén., *Adv. Haer.,* I, 30, 3, comp. Valentin sur διυλισμός, μετάνοια et ἀναδρομή dans Clém. d'Alex., *Paed.* 32, 1).

Nous concluons donc que Valentin, en vrai penseur syncrétiste, a contaminé le baptême chrétien et la conception gnostique de la "remontée", ou, si l'on veut, que pour formuler sa mystique sacramentale, il a eu recours à certains thèmes inconnus à la tradition orthodoxe [19].

---

[19] Un passage de Tertullien, négligé jusqu'ici par les érudits, prouve que c'est bien à Valentin lui-même, et non à un épigone quelconque, que remonte le thème gnostique de la "remontée". Scorpiace 10: *cum animae de corporibus excesserint et per singula tabulata caelorum de receptu dispici coeperint et interrogari arcana illa haereticorum sacramenta, tunc confitendum apud veras potestates et veros homines. Theletos scilicet et Acinetos et Abascantos Valentini.* Il me semble superflu de citer la littérature bien connu sur la "Himmelsreise der Seele". En revanche je voudrais souligner que les spéculations sur le Nom et sur l'ange du baptême ont une base chrétienne très archaïque: l'homme reçoit son ange gardien non en naissant, mais à l'occasion du baptême.

LA LETTRE DE PTOLEMEE A FLORA

INTRODUCTION

L'Epître de Ptolémée à Flora est sans conteste un document important. Le problème qui y est traité, avec beaucoup de pénétration et de lucidité, à savoir la valeur de la loi juive pour la religion chrétienne, prête, même de nos jours, à de vives discussions. La lettre est, en outre, une des très rares oeuvres gnostiques qui nous aient été conservées par la tradition. Enfin, on a loué à juste titre la beauté de sa prose rythmique d'un art raffiné [1].

Certains savants ont mis naguère l'accent sur d'autres points intéressants. Ils voyaient en Ptolémée un précurseur de la critique biblique moderne. Ils pensaient que les "éléments progressifs" [2] de la gnose chrétienne contenus dans cette lettre, méritaient une attention plus grande que "les spéculations abstruses et confuses sur les éons" transmises par les auteurs antihérétiques. Et ils admiraient l'originalité supposé des conceptions de Ptolémée [3]

L'auteur de la présente étude ne cherche aucunement à insister sur l'actualité du sujet. Il préfère considérer les idées de Ptolémée en se plaçant, autant que possible, au point de vue de son temps, le deuxième siècle après Jésus-Christ, et de son milieu, l'école valentinienne.

C'est pourquoi il s'efforcera seulement:

1. d'indiquer les parallèles que peut offrir avec ce document la littérature chrétienne du second siècle;

2. d'établir les rapports qui relient les théories exprimées dans l'Epître aux idées fondamentales du système de Ptolémée et du système valentinien en général;

3. de marquer les différences qui, au sujet de l'Ancien Testament, distinguent de l'opinion catholique les idées de notre gnostique;

4. de signaler dans la pièce l'absence curieuse de certaines notions qui n'etaient pourtant pas inconnues à cette époque: celle, par exemple, de l'inter-

---

[1] Eduard Norden, *Die antike Kunstprosa*[2], Leipzig, 1909, II, p. 920.

[2] A. v. Harnack, *Sitzungsberichte Berliner Akademie*, 1902, p. 535: "Mögen die Kirchenhistoriker den Spuren jener "gnostischen Vereine" sorgfältiger nachgehen und dabei nicht nur auf die *krausen* Aeonennamen achten — als wäre das das Wichtigste, was sie uns lehren können — oder auf das Uralte, das sie bewahrt haben, sondern auf die *progressiven Elemente*, die sie als Schüler des Paulus und Plato entwickelt haben".

[3] A. v. Harnack, *o.c.*, p. 507 sqq.; E. Preuschen, *Real-Encycl. f. Prot. Theologie u. Kirche*, 20, p. 405 sqq.; C. Barth, *Die Interpretation des N. Testaments in der Valentinischen Gnosis*, dans *Texte und Untersuchungen* XXVII, p. 103: "Resultat, das auch einem *modernen Exegeten* Ehre machen würde".

pretation allégorique et d'une conception qui voit un développement dans l'histoire sainte.

Les résultats de cette investigation semblent permettre la conclusion que *chaque remarque de Ptolémée — ou peut s'en faut — peut être mise en parallèle avec un passage correspondant de la littérature chrétienne de son temps, mais que le choix et la disposition des arguments sont inspirés par un schème herméneutique qui est dérivé d'une doctrine ésotérique.*

TRADUCTION

(Pour la constitution du texte je dois renvoyer à mon édition commentariée, qui a été publiée dans la collection: "Sources Chrétiennes")[4].

Epiphanius, Panarion 33, 3, 1-33, 7, 10

3. 1. Que la loi promulgée par Moïse, ma bonne soeur Flora, n'ait pas été comprise jusqu'à maintenant par beaucoup de gens, parce qu'on n'avait acquis une connaissance exacte ni du législateur véritable ni de ses commandements, cela vous sera bien clair, je pense, quand vous aurez appris les opinions contradictoires qui ont cours sur elle.

2. Quelques-uns disent que cette loi a été donnée par Dieu le Père lui-même; d'autres, dans une direction diamétralement opposée, assurent qu'elle provient de l'Adversaire, du diable corrupteur, de la même manière qu'ils lui attribuent aussi la création du monde, affirmant que c'est lui qui est le père et le créateur de cet univers.

3. Les uns et les autres sont entièrement dans l'erreur; leurs contradictions se réfutent réciproquement; chacun de son côté n'a pas réussi à saisir la vérité du sujet.

4. Car il est évident que la loi n'a pas été donnée par le Dieu parfait qui est le Père, — elle qui est secondaire —, puisqu'elle est imparfaite et a besoin d'être complétée par un autre[5] et qu'elle contient des commandements qui ne peuvent pas s'accorder avec la nature et la pensée d'un tel Dieu.

---

[4] Notons toutefois les différences importantes avec l'édition de Karl Holl (H = Holl; Q = Quispel; V et M: les manuscrits).

III, 1 μαθούςη *H*, μαθούσης *V²*; 4 ἑπόμενον *H*, ἑπόμενος *VM*; 5 <τοῦτο γὰρ εἴη τῶν ἀσυνέτων> τῶν τε ἑξῆς τι... <κατὰ> *H*, τῶν τε ἑξῆς ἐστι *Q*. IV, 2 αὐτοί *H*, πρῶτον *V¹*; 2 καθὰ δι᾽ αὐτοῦ *H*, καθὰ αὐτὸς δι᾽ αὐτοῦ *Pet.*; V, 3 ἀναίρεσιν *H*, ἀπαγόρευσιν *Q*. (secundum *V₁*); 7†καταριθμεῖται *H*, καταρρυθμεῖται *Q*.; εἰπών *H*, εἶπεν *Q*.; VI, 6 διὰ τοῦ πάσχα... δείξας δι᾽ ἡμᾶς *H*, διὰ τοῦ πάσχα δι᾽ ἡμᾶς... *Q*.; VII, 2 ἡμῖν, τίς *H*, ἡμῖν εἰπεῖν, τίς *Q*. (secundum *V₁*).

[5] ὑπ᾽ ἄλλου, c. à. d. par le Christ.

5. A l'inverse ,il n'est pas permis d'imputer la loi à l'Adversaire injuste, parce qu'elle s'oppose à l'injustice: c'est là le fait de gens qui ne voient pas la conclusion nécessaire [6] qui se dégage des paroles du Sauveur: "car maison ou ville divisée contre elle-même ne peut subsister" a déclaré notre Sauveur.

6. De plus, l'apôtre (Jean), ruinant par avance l'inconsistante sagesse de ces menteurs, déclare que la création du monde Lui est propre, que tout a été fait par Lui et rien n'a été fait sans Lui, et que cette création est non l'oeuvre d'un dieu corrupteur, mais d'un dieu juste et qui hait le mal. De telles conceptions ne sont partagées que par des esprits bornés, qui perdent de vue la providence du créateur et qui sont aveugles non seulement au sens figuré mais aussi au sens littéral de ce mot.

7. Que ceux-ci n'aient pas réussi à découvrir la vérité, vous est évident d'après ce qui précédé. Cet échec a été subi par les représentants de ces deux partis chacun à sa façon: les uns, parce qu'ils n'avaient aucune connaissance du dieu de la justice; les autres parce qu'ils ignoraient le Père du Tout [7], que seul celui qui est venu et qui est le seul à le connaître, a révélé.

8. Ainsi il nous reste, à nous qui avons été gratifiés de la connaissance de ces deux dieux, la tâche de vous exposer avec exactitude l'origine de la loi et la nature du législateur [8] qui l'a promulguée. Les preuves de notre argumentation, nous les tirerons des paroles de notre Sauveur, les seules qui puissent nous mener sans le moindre faux-pas à l'intelligence de la vérité.

4. 1. Tout d'abord, il vous faut savoir que cette loi contenue dans le Pentateuque de Moïse n'a pas été promulguée dans son ensemble par un auteur unique, j'entends: non point par Dieu seulement, mais qu'elle contient aussi quelques commandements d'origine humaine. Les paroles du Sauveur nous enseignent que la loi se divise en trois parties.

2. La première partie doit être attribuée à Dieu lui-même et à son activité législatrice; le seconde à Moïse, non en ce sens qu'il fut inspiré par Dieu lui-même, mais en ce sens que, poussé par des considérations personnelles, il ajouta quelques commandements; la troisième aux Anciens du peuple, qui dès le début paraissent avoir introduit d'eux-mêmes quelques préceptes dans le corps de la loi.

3. Comment la vérité de cette conception peut être prouvée par les paroles du Sauveur, c'est ce que vous allez apprendre maintenant.

---

[6] Traduction incertaine.

[7] Terme technique (Πατὴρ τῶν ὅλων = Père des Eons).

[8] Littéralement: la loi elle même de quelle origine (ou: nature) elle est, et celui par qui elle a été promulguée, le législateur.

4.   Dans la discussion sur le divorce (lequel était permis par la loi), le Sauveur déclarait à ses adversaires: "C'est à cause de votre endurcissement que Moïse vous a permis de répudier votre femme: d'abord il n'en était pas ainsi. Car il est écrit: "Dieu a uni ce couple et ce que le Seigneur a uni", disait-il, "l'homme n'a pas le droit de le séparer".

5.   Par là il démontre qu'il y a une loi de Dieu qui défend de séparer une femme de son mari, et une autre de Moïse, qui, en raison de l'endurcissement des coeurs, autorise la rupture de l'union conjugale.

6.   Ainsi, à ce point de vue, Moïse donne un commandement qui est contraire à celui de Dieu: car "séparer", c'est l'opposé de "ne pas séparer". Si toutefois nous nous informons de l'intention qui inspira ce commandement, il apparaîtra que Moïse n'a pas fait cela de son propre chef, mais contraint par la faiblesse des hommes à qui la loi était destinée.

7.   Car ceux-ci n'étaient pas capables de s'en tenir à la volonté de Dieu, qui leur défendait de répudier leurs femmes, bien qu'il déplut à quelques-uns de cohabiter avec elles et qu'ils risquaient, en conséquence, d'aller de mal en pis et par là à leur perte.

8.   Alors Moïse, voulant porter remède à ce désagrément, qui menaçait de leur devenir fatal, a choisi dans ces circonstances de deux maux le moindre en promulguant en leur faveur, de sa propre initiative, une seconde loi, accordant le divorce;

9.   afin que, s'ils ne pouvaient pas observer la première, ils respectassent du moins l'autre et n'eussent pas recours à des procédés injustes et mauvais, qui auraient pour résultat leur complète ruine morale.

10.   Telle était l'intention qui inspirait ces prescriptions contraires à celles de Dieu. D'ailleurs, que nous ayons prouvé que cette loi vient de Moïse et est autre que la loi divine, voilà qui est hors de discussion, même si la présente démonstration ne s'appuie que sur un seul exemple.

11.   Qu'il y ait aussi, mêlé à la loi, quelques traditions qui proviennent des Anciens du peuple, c'est une chose qui a été également démontrée par le Sauveur. "Car Dieu", a-t-il dit,

12.   "a ordonné: honorez votre père et votre mère, afin que vous prospériez. Mais vous", a-t-il ajouté, en s'adressant aux Anciens du peuple, "vous avez déclaré: "L'aide que vous

13.   auriez pu recevoir de moi, est une offrande à Dieu", et vous avez annulé la loi de Dieu en faveur de la tradition qui est la vôtre, Anciens du peuple. Isaïe l'a déjà proclamé: "ce peuple m'honore des lèvres, mais son coeur est loin de moi. C'est en vain qu'ils m'honorent, parce qu'ils enseignent des préceptes qui sont des commandements d'hommes".

14. Il ressort clairement de là que la loi, dans son ensemble, se compose de trois parties: car nous y avons rencontré des préceptes de Moïse, des préceptes des Anciens du peuple et des préceptes de Dieu lui-même. Cette division de la loi, prise dans son ensemble, ainsi établie par nous, a mis en lumière l'élément authentique que renferme la loi.

5. 1. Cette partie, la loi de Dieu lui-même, se laisse, à son tour, diviser en trois parties: *la législation pure*, qui n'était pas mélangée de mal, la Loi dans le sens propre du mot, que le Sauveur n'est pas venu abolir, mais accomplir (car celle qu'il a complétée ne lui était pas étrangère, mais avait besoin d'être perfectionnée, ne possédant pas la perfection); puis *la partie mêlée de mal*, que le Sauveur a abolie, parce qu'elle ne s'accordait pas avec sa nature.

2. Enfin, on peut distinguer *une partie typique et symbolique*, destinée à représenter le spirituel et le transcendant, qui a été transposée par le Sauveur du sensible et du visible au spirituel et à l'invisible.

3. Et la loi de Dieu, pure et franche de tout alliage inférieur, c'est le décalogue, ces dix commandements gravés sur deux tables, qui interdisent ce qu'on ne doit pas faire et ordonnent ce qu'on doit faire, commandements purs mais imparfaits qui avaient besoin d'être complétés par le Sauveur.

4. A côté de la loi de Dieu, il y a une loi qui est accompagnée d'injustice, celle du talion et du châtiment d'un crime commis, celle qui ordonne de crever oeil pour oeil, de briser dent pour dent et de rendre mort pour mort. Car qui commet une injustice en second lieu n'est pas moins coupable que qui l'a commise en premier lieu: l'ordre est différent, le fait reste le même.

5. Il faut du reste admettre que ce commandement était juste et l'est encore, donnée qu'elle est à cause de la faiblesse de ceux à qui la loi était destinée et au cas où il y aurait transgression de la Loi pure. Néanmoins, on ne peut pas concilier ce commandement avec la nature et la bonté du Père du Tout.

6. Sans doute était-il le résultat d'une adaptation aux circonstances, mais plutôt d'une nécessité. Car celui qui ne veut pas que se commette un seul meurtre en édictant: "tu ne tueras pas" et qui ensuite a ordonné que le meurtrier soit tué à son tour, a donné une deuxième loi, et étant ainsi au principe de deux meurtres, lui qui avait défendu d'en accomplir un seul, a été, évidemment, à son insu la victime de la nécessité.

7. C'est pourquoi son Fils, à son arrivée, a annulé cette partie de la loi, tout en avouant qu'elle aussi venait de Dieu: entre autres choses, sa reconnaissance de l'Ancien Testament [9] se manifeste par les mots suivants: "*Dieu a déclaré: celui qui maudit son père ou sa mère, doit mourir*".

---

[9] Litt.: de l'ancienne αἵρεσις.

8. Enfin, il y a la partie symbolique, qui représente le spirituel et le transcendant, je veux dire: les prescriptions relatives aux sacrifies, à la circoncision, au sabbat, aux jeûnes, à l'agneau pascal, aux pains sans levain, etc. ....

9. Tous ces rites, n'étant que symboles et images, ont une signification différente après la révélation de la Vérité. Quant à leur forme extérieure et quant à leur application littérale, ils ont été abolis, mais, dans leur sens spirituel, leur signification est devenue plus profonde, parce que les vieux termes ont reçu un contenu nouveau.

10. Ainsi le Sauveur nous a ordonné de faire des sacrifices, non au moyen de bêtes privées de raison ou au moyen d'offrandes de parfum, mais par des hymnes, des glorifications, des actions de grâce spirituelles, par la charité et la bienfaisance envers le prochain.

11. De même, il demande de nous la circoncision, non du prépuce corporel, mais de notre coeur spirituel.

12. D'observer le sabbat, car il veut que nous nous reposions à l'égard des oeuvres mauvaises.

13. Aussi de jeûner. Pourtant ce ne sont pas les jeûnes corporels qu'il désire de nous, mais plutôt les jeûnes spirituels, qui consistent dans l'abstention de tout mal. Néanmoins, on reste aussi chez nous attaché aux jeûnes ordinaires, parce que la vie de l'âme en peut tirer profit, quand on le fait avec discernement et non pour imiter les autres ou par habitude ou encore parce qu'un certain jour a été fixé pour cela.

14. En même temps on y reste attaché en rappel des jeûnes véritables, afin que ceux qui ne peuvent pas encore pratiquer ces derniers en aient en eux, par le truchement des jeûnes ordinaires, la réminiscence.

15. Et que l'agneau pascal et les pains sans levain étaient de même des symboles, c'est ce que montre aussi l'Apôtre Paul par ces paroles: "notre agneau pascal a été immolé, le Christ" et: "afin que vous soyez sans levain, ne participant pas au levain (il appelle ici la méchanceté levain), mais que vous soyez une nouvelle pâte".

6. 1. Ainsi donc la partie de la loi qui sans aucun doute est de Dieu se laisse également diviser en trois parties: une partie a été accomplie par le Sauveur (car les commandements: "tu ne tueras point, tu ne commettras pas d'adultère, tu ne feras pas de faux serments" sont compris dans l'interdiction de se mettre en colère, de convoiter ou d'affirmer par serment).

2. Une autre partie est entièrement abolie. Car le commandement: "oeil pour oeil et dent pour dent", qui est accompagné d'injustice, parce qu'il a pour

conséquence un acte inique, a été remplacé par le Sauveur par un commandement contraire. Car des antithèses absolues s'annulent.

3. "Mais, moi, je vous dis: ne résistez absolument pas au méchant. Mais si quelqu'un vous frappe sur la joue droite, présentez-lui aussi l'autre".

4. Enfin, il y a une partie de la loi qui est transportée et changée du sens littéral en un sens spirituel; la partie symbolique, qui est donnée en image du transcendant.

5. Car les images et les symboles, qui représentaient d'autres choses, étaient bons, aussi longtemps que la Vérité n'était pas apparue. Mais maintenant que la Vérité s'est révélée, on doit faire les oeuvres de la Vérité, non celles de l'allégorie.

6. De ces trois parties, les disciples de Jésus ont parlé aussi bien que l'apôtre Paul: de la partie symbolique, comme nous l'avons déjà dit, en parlant de l'agneau pascal, qui a été immolé pour nous, et des pains sans levain; de la partie accompagnée d'injustice, en disant que "la loi des commandements est devenue sans effet par un nouvel enseignement"; de la partie de la loi qui est pure de toute injustice par ces paroles: "la loi est sainte et le commandement est saint, juste et bon".

7. 1. Pour autant que cela est possible dans un court espace, je crois avoir suffisamment prouvé l'adjonction de prescriptions d'origine humaine dans la loi et la division de la loi de Dieu lui-même en trois parties.

2. Il nous reste à dire quel est bien ce dieu qui a donné la loi. Mais je pense que ce point aussi est déjà devenu clair pour vous d'après ce qui précède, si vous m'avez accordé toute votre attention.

3. Car si la loi n'a pas été donnée par le Dieu parfait lui-même, comme nous l'avons déjà dit, et certainement pas par le diable (ce qu'il n'est même pas permis de dire), ce législateur doit être un autre dieu qui existe à côté des deux autres.

4. Ce législateur est le démiurge et le créateur du monde et de tout ce qui fait partie de ce monde. Parce qu'il est, en son essence, différent des deux autres et se tient au milieu d'eux, on pourrait l'appeler à bon droit la "médiation".

5. Si le Dieu parfait est bon en son essence, comme il l'est effectivement (car notre Sauveur a dit qu'il n'y avait qu'un seul bon Dieu, son Père, qu'il a révélé), et si l'être qui est par nature Adversaire est mauvais et méchant, caractérisé par l'injustice, alors le dieu qui se tient entre le Dieu parfait et le diable, et qui n'est pas bon, mais qui n'est pas non plus certainement mauvais ou injuste, peut avec raison être appelé juste, parce qu'à sa manière, il maintient le droit.

6. Ce dieu est inférieur au Dieu parfait et sa justice, parce qu'il est engendré

et non pas inengendré (car un seul est inengendré, le Père, de qui viennent toutes choses, parce que toutes choses, à leur manière, dépendent de Lui), mais il sera plus élevé et plus puissant que l'Adversaire, différent en essence et en nature de ces deux.

7. L'essence de l'Adversaire est corruption et ténèbres (car il est matériel et multiple). Du Père qui est inengendré, du Père du Tout, l'essence est d'être incorruption et lumière en soi, simple, homogène. Par contre le démiurge, bien que donnant l'existence à une puissance double, est pourtant un symbole du Dieu suprême.

8. Maintenant vous n'avez pas besoin de vous inquiéter de ceci de savoir comment il a été possible que d'un principe de toutes choses, qui est simple, que nous confessons, auquel nous croyons, d'un principe qui est inengendré, incorruptible et bon, aient pu sortir ces autres natures, celle de la corruption et celle de la médiation, qui sont d'essence différente, quoique le bien ait la propriété d'engendrer seulement des êtres semblables et consubstantiels à lui.

9. Car, si Dieu le permet, vous recevrez plus tard des éclaircissements plus précis sur leur principe et leur naissance, quand tu auras été jugée digne de connaître la tradition des apôtres, que nous aussi, nous avons reçue par voie de succession; en ce cas aussi nous confirmerons nos conceptions par les paroles du Sauveur.

10. Je ne suis pas lassé de vous avoir dit cela en peu de mots, ma soeur Flora. Bien que dans ce qui précède j'aie été bref, j'ai cependant traité le sujet d'une manière décisive. Ces observations pourront, quand le temps en sera venu, vous aider beaucoup, si, après avoir reçu comme une bonne et belle terre des semences fécondes, tu en fasses le fruit.

ANALYSE

1. *Sujet et caractère de l'écrit* (Ch. 3, 1)

Les sources nous apprennent que Ptolémée était un des chefs de la section "italique" de l'école valentinienne. Il est probable qu'il résidait à Rome. Flora n'est connue que par cette lettre. C'était une de ses auditrices auxquelles les maîtres gnostiques s'adressaient de préférence. Elle était certainement chrétienne, puisqu'elle est supposée connaître la Bible. Peut-être était-elle aussi membre de l'église catholique, mais, à coup sûr, une fidèle peu satisfaite de la doctrine enseignée par cette église. Elle désire recevoir des informations sur la question brûlante de la Loi juive, radicalement attaquée par Marcion et défendue sans doute par le catholique Justin dans son *Syntagma*, aujourd'hui perdu.

La réponse du maître fameux fait preuve de dons pédagogiques très remarquables et a été adaptée à la tournure d'esprit d'une profane. Ptolémée aurait pu répondre brièvement que la Loi et l'Ancien Testament tout entier étaient "psychiques" comme le dieu judaïque lui-même, mais que tout ce qui est "psychique" ($\tau \grave{o}$ $\psi v \chi \iota \varkappa \acute{o} v$) était un symbole du monde spirituel ($\tau \grave{o}$ $\pi v \varepsilon v \mu \alpha \tau \iota \varkappa \acute{o} v$). Or, il est frappant que le terme: "$\psi v \chi \iota \varkappa \acute{o} \varsigma$", si adéquat et si caractéristique de la terminologie valentinienne, ne figure pas dans la lettre. L'auteur préfère user de désignations éthiques, plus familières à sa correspondante, pour paraphraser cette idée ontologique. Ce procédé était fort utilisé dans les cercles valentiniens. On le voit grâce à cette déclaration très significative de Tertullien sur leur propagande: "même à leurs disciples", dit-il, "ils ne confient pas leur doctrine avant de les avoir gagnés totalement. Ils ont une méthode qui ne manque pas d'habilité: ils persuadent avant d'instruire" (*Adv. Val. 1*).

C'est pourquoi notre lettre n'est pas un document gnostique dans le vrai sens du mot, mais plutôt une introduction au gnosticisme. Il ne faut donc pas s'étonner, comme le fait E. Preuschen (l.c.), de ne pas trouver dans un tel écrit, qui est exotérique, des spéculations métaphysiques qui étaient exclues par la loi du genre.

2. *L'opinion des catholiques et de Marcion* (Ch. 3, 2-6)

Il y a un parti qui attribue la loi à Dieu le Père. Harnack a supposé que c'étaient les Juifs, quoique la qualification même de Dieu comme Père fasse plutôt penser aux chrétiens. Un autre parti imputait la loi au diable. Il est possible que ce parti fût la secte des Carpocratiens (Iren. I, 25, 4).

Mais si l'on se rend compte du fait que Ptolémée vivait probablement à Rome, et si l'on se souvient qu'à cette époque la communauté chrétienne de la ville était déchirée par le violent conflit qui opposait Marcion aux orthodoxes, il semble plus vraisemblable que Ptolémée ait pensé à cette situation concrète plutôt qu'à des contradictions imaginaires.

Quelle est l'erreur des orthodoxes? Selon Ptolémée, ils ont tort de supposer que la Loi, qui n'est que secondaire ($\dot{\varepsilon} \pi \acute{o} \mu \varepsilon v o \varsigma$ V.M., non $\dot{\varepsilon} \pi \acute{o} \mu \varepsilon v o v$, correction de Pétau qu'acceptent les éditeurs modernes), a été donnée par un dieu parfait, alors qu'elle est imparfaite.

Cette objection est fondamentale: si l'on jette un coup d'oeil général sur la polémique véhémente alors dirigée contre l'Ancien Testament, on s'apercevra que cette opinion de Ptolémée se trouve à la base de toute la critique hérétique.

Les catholiques ne tardèrent pas à formuler une réponse solide: pourquoi un dieu parfait ne pouvait-il pas donner une Loi imparfaite et sévère pour élever, à un niveau plus haut, un peuple encore "rude"? Irénée et Tertullien admettent que la révélation du Christ est d'un ordre plus élevé que la doctrine de l'Ancien Testament. Ils acceptent même un certain progrès de la moralité dans l'histoire religieuse d'Israël; la conception de la responsabilité personnelle, prêchée par les prophètes, est supérieure à celle de la culpabilité collective que connaît la Loi [10]. Les attaques des hérétiques ont poussé les auteurs catholiques à développer, à leur manière, l'idée d'un *développement dans la révélation divine*. On cherchera en vain ce point de vue dans notre lettre, pour des raisons diverses, mais surtout parce que la mystique gnostique, en tant que mystique, tend à nier l'histoire, et, tant que gnosticisme, est saturée de ressentiment contre la réalité spatiale et temporelle [11]. A cet égard, notre document est encore moins "moderne" que les oeuvres des Pères.

Marcion et ses disciples sont condamnés dans des termes sévères pour avoir attribué la Loi au diable. Même si ces mots voulaient indiquer d'une manière fort insuffisante que Yahweh, qui a créé le monde et donné la Loi, était mauvais selon Marcion, on ne peut pas nier que Ptolémée a très inexactement rendu l'opinion du grand hérétique. Marcion, en effet, ne niait pas, mais méconnaissait la justice de Yahweh: il la trouvait mesquine, vindicative et voisine du mal ("mali adfinis") [12]. Nous rencontrons ici la même simplification, erronée et fâcheuse, que chez Hippolyte (*Elenchos* VII, 29) et Irénée (*Adv. Haer.* III, 12, 12), lorsqu'ils veulent insinuer que Marcion concevait Yahweh comme le principe du mal.

Pourquoi cette altération? Dans la suite, Ptolémée déclarera que le démiurge, qui a donné la Loi, n'est ni bon ni mauvais, mais juste. C'est-à-dire que Ptolémée accepte plus ou moins la conception de Marcion qu'il a passée sous silence. Bien sûr, son appréciation de la justice était beaucoup plus favorable. Si Marcion a découvert la relativité de la justice, c'est Ptolémée qui a accentué sa grandeur relative. Cela n'empêche pas qu'entre sa conception et celle de Marcion il n'y a qu'une variation de degré, non, comme il veut le faire croire, une différence fondamentale.

Cette représentation défectueuse de la théorie marcionite a deux grands avantages pour notre auteur:

1. Tout d'abord, elle lui permet de formuler un argument assez ingénieux: la Loi ne peut pas être mauvaise, puisqu'elle défend les actes mauvais. La même réponse a été donnée par Clément d'Alexandrie à certains critiques de l'Ancien

---

[10] Tertullien, *Adv. Marcionem* II, 15; *id.,* II, 18; W. Bousset, *Kyrios Christos,* Göttingen, 1913, p. 438; G. Quispel, *De bronnen van Tertullianus' Adversus Marcionem,* Leiden, 1943, p. 39.

[11] Même si on trouve chez Héracléon (fr. 20) la conception qu'une période "hylique" et païenne a été suivie par la période "psychique" et juive, à laquelle a succédé une période "pneumatique" et chrétienne, il y a là succession, non évolution.

[12] Tert., *Adv. Marc.* II, 11.

Testament: "si le commandement, qui défend presque toutes les actions mauvaises, était mauvais, le mal donnerait des lois contre lui-même, ce qui est impossible" (*Strom.* III, 35, 3). Victoire illusoire sur un adversaire qui n'existe pas! Marcion n'a jamais dit que la Loi était mauvaise.

2.   Grâce à cette représentation, Ptolémée peut appliquer à une situation historique une idée preconçue, Convaincu que la Loi n'était ni donnée par le Dieu parfait ni d'origine hylique et diabolique, il a prêté ces points de vue à deux de ses adversaires contemporains, les catholiques et les marcionites. D'où la grande clarté et l'actualité qui caractérisent cette lettre.

3.   *La sympathie pour le catholicisme* (Ch. 3, 7)

Le point de vue des deux partis en lutte est erroné, parce que les orthodoxes ne connaissent pas le Dieu supérieur et que Marcion ne connaît pas Yahweh. On doit conclure de cette observation que Marcion avait bien, comme Ptolémée lui-même, une certaine connaissance du Dieu Inconnu, du Père du Christ, tandis que les simples croyants de l'Eglise ignoraient son existence, ce qui semble pire. Nous constatons de nouveau que Ptolémée avait avec Marcion beaucoup plus d'idées en common qu'il ne voulait l'admettre, et nettement l'idée de Dieu. Aussi est-il surprenant de constater que l'auteur réagit avec une grande vigueur contre les conceptions marcionites, alors qu'il parle d'une manière décisive, mais avec modération, quand il discute les erreurs des catholiques. Comment une telle contradiction apparente peut-elle être expliquée? Est-ce, peut-être, un procédé de propagande à bon marché pour tromper quelques agneaux imprudents du grand bercail? Ou cette inconséquence provient-elle d'une conviction sincère?

Comme l'appréciation de notre lettre dépend plus ou moins de la réponse qu'on donne à cette question, il me paraît nécessaire d'esquisser ici brièvement l'évolution de l'école valentinienne. Valentin et Marcion étaient des contemporains; à la même époque (± 140), ils vivaient à Rome, tâchant en vain de gagner à leurs idées la communauté chrétienne de la ville; ils doivent certainement avoir fait connaissance. On ne saurait dire si l'un a eu une influence sur l'autre. Tous deux portent l'empreinte de l'esprit du siècle, tous deux semblent être nés chrétiens et avoir été profondément influencés par les conceptions pauliniennes, l'un et l'autre s'appuient sur la même tradition, mi-chrétienne, mi-gnostique. De plus, les principes essentiels d'une doctrine aussi importante que celle de Marcion ou de Valentin semblent moins inspirés par une influence extérieure que par une expérience personnelle, faite à un moment décisif dans la vie des très grands esprits, expérience intérieure qui n'admet aucune analyse scientifique.

Il n'en est pas moins vrai que les conceptions des deux hérétiques sont beaucoup plus apparentées que certains savants ne le croient.

Ils insistaient, l'un comme l'autre, sur la transcendance de Dieu en tant qu'opposée au "monde" et révélée seulement par le Sauveur (cet accord entre les idées de Valentin et de Marcion devient encore plus remarquable si on les compare aux vues de leurs contemporains, les apologistes grecs, qui exaltaient la beauté de la nature et la sagesse de la Providence, mais passaient à peu près sous silence le salut). Tous deux considéraient Yahweh comme une divinité inférieure, comme un créateur et un législateur sans bonté, une personnification symbolique du monde extérieur.

Mais, à côté de cette affinité très prononcée, il y avait des différences caractéristiques: tandis que Marcion, en penseur qui argumente dialectiquement, développait l'antithèse de la grâce et de la création jusqu'à ses conséquences extrêmes, Valentin, qui était un mystique et un platonicien, distinguait entre la nature inférieure, τὸ ὑλικόν, mauvaise sous tous les rapports, et la nature supérieure, τὸ ψυχικόν, qui, malgré tout, était symbole du monde spirituel.

Cela ne l'empêchait pas de montrer un certain ressentiment à l'égard du démiurge, de souligner son infériorité et de l'accuser d'être cause de la mort (Clém. d'Alex., *Strom.* IV, 89, 1 sqq.). Les fragments de Théodote, fidèles à la doctrine primitive, osent même parler de sa sévérité odieuse (*Exc.* 33, 3). Il est clair que, si Valentin a pu vaincre, grâce au platonisme, le sentiment tragique qu'il avait de la vie, et qui se reflète dans sa mythologie, il en reste toujours chez lui quelques traces.

Cette ambiguïté dans la conception de Yahweh a donné lieu à des interprétations divergentes. Certains disciples, évidemment influencés par Marcion ou par des gnostiques vulgaires, ont accentué les traits négatifs dans l'image qu'ils se formaient du démiurge: ils l'appelaient même: μῶρος "stupide" (Hippol., *Refutatio* VI, 35).

On peut constater une évolution en sens contraire chez Ptolémée. L'attitude assez sympathique envers Yahweh, la Loi et l'Eglise catholique, qu'on observe dans la lettre à Flora, est en plein accord avec l'appréciation plus favorable de l'élément "psychique" en général, qui est caractéristique de sa doctrine. On trouve dans quelques pages issues de son école une admirable exaltation de l'âme "divine, logique et céleste" (*Exc.* 51 sqq.). En revanche, on chercherait en vain dans les fragments sortis de l'école de Ptolémée des remarques hautaines et dénigrantes sur Yahweh. On nous dit même, que Yahweh s'est converti au Christ et protège l'église (Iren. I, 7, 4). Cette conception ne peut pas remonter au fondateur de la secte: dans les *Excerpta ex Theodoto* (38) Yahweh menace les élus, qui veulent lui échapper (ce changement devait avoir de graves

conséquences pour le mythe calentinien). Et l'exaltation de tout ce qui est
"psychique" n'est pas un fait isolé. De plus, le docétisme est atténué. La
distance entre Dieu et l'esprit déchu est accentuée grâce à l'introduction d'une
deuxième Sophia. La doctrine du Jésus préexistant a disparu. Bref, tout le
système a été renouvelé avec l'intention, semble-t-il, de se rapprocher de la
doctrine de l'Eglise [13].

Pourquoi ce changement? Sant doute la réaction catholique contre les théories
audacieuses de Valentin y est-elle pour quelque chose. Mais si Ptolémée a été
influencé par les critiques des orthodoxes, c'est qu'il était plus enclin que son
maître à prendre en considération ces objections. Tout en apportant des idées
nouvelles, il suivait les tendances de con coeur imbu de religiosité.

Cette sympathie pour le catholicisme, exprimée tant dans l'épître à Flora que
dans ses écrits ésotériques, était donc bien sincère.

4. *La méthode d'interprétation* (Ch. 3, 8)

Ptolémée, lui, peut interpréter la Loi mosaïque, parce qu'il a reçu la gnose,
tandis que ses adversaires ont échoué parce qu'ils ne la possédaient pas.

Qu'est ce principe épistémologique qui, seul, garantit une interprétation
authentique? On craint de devenir banal quand on constate que cette
"connaissance" n'a rien à faire avec le bon sens philologique qui semble suffire
aux modernes interprètes de la Bible. A cette époque, le mot "gnose" évoquait
l'idée de la révélation et du mystère. Il est extrêmement difficile de définir d'une
façon précise ce que les valentiniens entendaient par ce terme technique, plein
de nuances subtiles. On peut dire néanmoins que la "gnose" n'est pas innée et
humaine, mais divine et "charismatique", étroitement liée au *pneuma* transcendant. Or les valentiniens distinguaient entre le *pneuma* humain, d'origin
céleste, incapable de retourner par ses propres forces dans sa patrie spirituelle
et sommeillant dans quelques hommes, et le *pneuma* divin, le Christ et ses
anges, qui révélait la "gnose" à l'esprit élu. Même le *pneuma* imparfait n'est
pas une donnée naturelle, mais un don de la grâce: *spiritalem ex Seth de
obvenientia superducunt iam non naturam sed indulgentiam* (= gratiam)
(Tert., *adv. Val.* 29). A plus forte raison la "gnose" est-elle de nature
"charismatique".

Ptolémée ne s'étend pas sur la nature de la "gnose", mais observe qu'elle se
rapporte au Dieu Inconnu et au démiurge. Ces mots deviennent plus clairs,
comparés avec un autre passage de notre lettre (ch. 7, 9), où l'auteur déclare

---

[13] G. Quispel, *The original doctrine of Valentine*, dans *Vigiliae Christianae*, I, 1, 1947, p. 46
(= p. 29 de ce livre).

qu'il peut expliquer la naissance de Yahweh et l'origine du diable, parce qu'il a reçu la tradition apostolique. Nous savons exactement ce qu'il entend par là. C'est une tradition secrète, exclusivement révélée aux initiés, et qui remonte au fondateur de l'école. Elle s'appelle apostolique parce que Valentin l'aurait héritée de Theudas, disciple de Paul (Clém. d'Alex., *Strom.* VII, 106). Du fait que, selon Ptolémée, cette tradition traitait de la Cosmologie et de la chute originelle, il faut conclure qu'elle est à peu près identique au mythe ésotérique. L'auteur de notre lettre semble donc dire dans ce passage (ch. 3, 8) qu'on doit connaître la doctrine métaphysique pour pouvoir interpréter la Loi mosaïque.

Par là, il ne fait qu'appliquer une règle générale à un cas spécial. Les valentiniens ne croyaient-ils pas qu'il était impossible de trouver la vérité dans la Bible à ceux qui ne connaissaient pas la tradition (Irén. III, 2, 2)? Il faut donc s'attendre à trouver quelques renvois au système ésotérique dans la lettre à Flora.

Cette conception d'une tradition secrète est bien curieuse. D'une part, il est évident que la doctrine ésotérique de Valentin est très différente de l'enseignement apostolique tel que le Nouveau Testament et la hiérarchie épiscopale l'ont conservé. La "tradition apostolique" était même l'arme la plus redoutable des évêques contre les hérésies. D'autre part, un Clément d'Alexandrie s'appuie également sur une tradition secrète qui lui a fait connaître sa "gnose" spéciale: "cette gnose", dit-il, "vient des apôtres pas succession". Elle a été transmise à quelques uns par une tradition non écrite (Clém. d'Alex., *Strom.* VI, 7, 61). Une question se pose: Valentin et Clément ont-ils menti?

Sans vouloir trancher ce problème très complexe, je crois pouvoir affirmer qu'il n'est pas impossible que quelques érudits chrétiens du deuxième siècle aient conservé quelques détails d'origine fort ancienne. Mais on a peine à croire que ces traditions aient été *secrètes*. On a plutôt l'impression que cette tradition apostolique des hérétiques a été calquée sur la tradition des évêques, qu'elle a été plus ou moins inventée en réponse à la "praescriptio" [14]. Les valentiniens ont, semble-t-il, adopté des termes respectables comme $\pi\alpha\rho\acute{\alpha}\delta o\sigma\iota\varsigma$ $\dot{\alpha}\pi o\sigma\tau o\lambda\iota\kappa\acute{\eta}$ et $\pi\alpha\rho\alpha\lambda\alpha\mu\beta\acute{\alpha}\nu\epsilon\iota\nu$, en leur donnant un sens secret qu'ils n'avaient pas à l'origine. Même cette méthode de Ptolémée qui consiste à citer des passages scripturaires pour confirmer la tradition pourrait être empruntée à l'Eglise. Il est vrai que Tertullien ne formule le principe que quelques années plus tard: "etiam in traditionis obtentu exigenda est auctoritas scripta" (Tert., *de Cor.* 3). Il est

---

[14] On sait que la conception d'une tradition secrète se trouve aussi chez les platoniciens et les ébionites de ce temps.

pourtant très possible que la coutume remonte beaucoup plus haut. Mais, nous objectera-t-on, il y a toujours cette grande différence que Ptolémée s'autorise, non de toute la Bible, mais des paroles du Sauveur pour déterminer son attitude envers l'Ancien Testament, et c'est là le point le plus important. Je me demande si ce principe a été inventé par Ptolémée. On lit dans une source très ancienne des Homélies pseudo-Clémentines, le célèbre Κήρυγμα Πέτρου, d'origine judéo-chrétienne, les mots suivants: "En se fondant sur la doctrine de Jésus on pourra distinguer ce qu'il y a de vrai et ce qu'il y a de faux dans les écrits de l'Ancien Testament" (ps. Clém., *Hom.* III, 50). C'est exactement la conception de Ptolémée. Bien sûr, le parallèle ne suffit pas, à lui seul, à prouver une dépendance de la part de notre auteur; elle est pourtant assez frappante pour attirer notre attention sur ce problème [15].

5. *Les interpolations dans l'Ancien Testament* (Ch. 4, 1, 4)

Ptolémée nous déclare que la Loi contient des additions humaines. Il serait erroné de croire que cette observation est le résultat d'une recherche objective et spéciale, faite à cette occasion et limitée à la Loi. Si l'auteur avait traité d'une autre partie de la Bible, il aurait probablement dit la même chose. "Les valentiniens formulent une accusation contre les Ecritures Saintes en disant que certains passages ne sont pas corrects ou n'ont pas d'autorité ou se contredisent, de sorte qu'il est impossible à ceux qui ne connaissent pas la tradition secrète de trouver la vérité dans la Bible" (Irén. III, 2, 1). Ce texte semble signifier que toute la Bible contient des passages inauthentiques et que, pour distinguer les passages faux des passages authentiques, on doit connaître la tradition secrète et être initié à la doctrine ésotérique.

On aimerait donc savoir si les valentiniens traitaient le reste de la Bible de la même manière que la Loi et s'ils distinguaient aussi dans le Nouveau Testament, comme le fait la Lettre à Flora, *les additions qui peuvent être justifiées des interpolations qui sont absolument à condamner.* Malheureusement les données de nos sources touchant l'Evangile son trop peu nombreuses pour permettre une conclusion certaine. On nous dit que "les apôtres ont ajouté des éléments "légaux" (legalia) aux paroles du Sauveur" (Irén. III, 2, 2), en d'autres termes qu'il y a des additions humaines dans le Nouveau Testament. Puis on déclare que "les apôtres, non sans hypocrisie, ont adapté leur enseignement au niveau de leurs auditeurs" (Irén. III, 5, 1). Une telle attitude présente une certaine ressemblance avec la conception de la lettre à Flora: Moïse a adapté ses prescriptions à la dureté de coeur de ses compatriotes. — Il faut ajouter que les

---

[15] En suivant un *obiter dictum* de A. Hilgenfeld, dans *Zeitschrift für wissenschaftliche Theologie*, XXIV, 1881, p. 214 sqq.

valentiniens rejetaient, non seulement, comme le montre notre Epître, la tradition des Anciens israëlites, mais aussi la tradition des Presbytres ecclésiastiques. "Quand on les attaque au nom de la tradition apostolique, *transmise par les Anciens* et conservée dans l'Eglise, ils s'opposent à cette tradition, en disant qu'ils sont *plus sages que les Anciens* et même que les apôtres, parce que, eux, ils ont découvert la pure vérité" (Irén. III, 2, 2). Nos sources ne nous autorisent pas à supposer que, selon les valentiniens, les Presbytres ecclésiastiques ont interpolé le Nouveau Testament, bien que nous avions là un parallèle exact avec la lettre à Flora. Il est certes fort possible que telle était l'opinion des hérétiques, mais nous sommes incapables de le prouver.

Cependant, les passages cités sont autrement significatifs pour l'interprétation de notre texte: c'est toujours cette "gnose" mystérieuse qui permet à l'initié de s'élever au-dessus des autorités, d'un Moïse ou des apôtres, aussi bien qu'au-dessus de la tradition des Presbytres. Seulement, on ne voit pas clairement comment cette doctrine ésotérique se rapporte à l'interprétation de la Bible.

Mais, par une heureuse coïncidence, la tradition nous a conservé une indication très précieuse, qui nous permettra peut-être de résoudre le problème. Elle est contenue dans le compte rendu que fait Irénée des conceptions de l'école de Ptolémée relatives à l'inspiration de la Bible.

Les hérétiques admettaient que les prophéties renfermaient des passages "pneumatiques", qui n'ont pas été compris par le démiurge: "Le démiurge, ignorant le monde transcendant, fut bien touché par ces paroles "spirituelles". Néanmoins il les négligea en les attribuant à des causes diverses, tantôt à l'esprit prophétique, qui possédait une certaine spontanéité, tantôt à l'homme, tantôt à l'interpolation d'êtres inférieurs προσπλοκὴ τῶν χειρόνων)" (Irén. I, 7, 4).

Si la conception que Ptolémée prête à Yahweh est vraie (et si l'on excepte les passages pneumatiques) il y a trois composants de la prophétie: 1) l'esprit prophétique, sans doute de la même substance que Yahweh; 2) le prophète lui-même, en tant qu'humain et non inspiré; 3) les interpolations [16].

On peut observer une certaine gradation dans cette série: ces êtres inférieurs ne sont pas seulement plus mauvais que le prophète: ils sont mauvais tout court. Ces interpolations semblent être d'origine et d'essence hyliques (χειρόνων est un terme technique). Le prophète, tout humain qu'il soit, est sans doute meilleur; mais, s'il est distingué de l'esprit prophétique, c'est qu'il n'a pas atteint ou ne peut pas atteindre à la même perfection. L'esprit prophétique, évidemment, n'est ni pneumatique ni hylique, mais psychique, comme le Créateur.

---

[16] Voir la note de l'éditeur d'Irénée, Harvey, *ad locum*.

Cette gradation semble s'accorder avec la théorie de l'école de Ptolémée: ceux-ci divisaient les psychiques en deux classes, une de tendance bonne, l'autre d'inclination mauvaise. Il y a donc le "hylique", le "psychique" inférieur et le "psychique supérieur" (Irén. I, 7, 5).

C'est pourquoi il est presque impossible que ces idées aient été attribuées à Yahweh par quelque caprice. Est-il hasardeux de soupçonner que l'école de Ptolémée ait, à cette occasion, prêté à Yahweh leur conception de l'inspiration des écritures prophétiques? Il me paraît à peu près impossible d'expliquer d'une autre manière l'énumération systématique des origines diverses des prophéties donnée dans le passage cité plus haut (Irén. I, 7, 4).

Concluons donc des mots énigmatiques d'Irénée que l'école de Ptolémée distinguait dans les prophéties de l'Ancien Testament à côté des éléments pneumatiques, un composant hylique, un composant humain et un composant divin, inspiré par l'esprit prophétique.

Il semble que l'on retrouve la même division dans l'épître de Ptolémée à Flora: y sont distinguées les interpolations des Anciens, les additions humaines de Moïse, les parties divines et démiurgiques. Il s'agit là vraisemblablement de la même gradation: Ptolémée a donc appliqué le même schème herméneutique aux prophètes et à la Loi (peut-être même a-t-il considéré Moïse comme un prophète).

On peut supposer que cette gradation repose sur un fondement identique. C'est ainsi qu'on croit entrevoir comment la gnose se rapporte à l'interprétation de la Bible [17].

Si l'école de Ptolémée affirme que toute la Bible contient des interpolations humaines, il faut reconnaître que ce point de vue ne se retrouve pas ailleurs. Marcion, tout en rejetant l'Ancien Testament, ne doutait pas qu'il fût entier inspiré, tout en attribuant son inspiration au démiurge. En revanche, c'était le Nouveau Testament qu'il supposait plein d'additions parasitaires et qu'il soumettait à une épuration radicale. De son côté, le Pierre "ébionite" du Κήρυγμα Πέτρου n'admettait des interpolations — très nombreuses, du reste — que dans les livres de l'Ancien Testament. C'est une différence qu'on ne doit pas perdre de vue.

6. *Les additions de Moïse* (Ch. 4, 4-11)

Il est toutefois possible que Ptolémée s'appuie sur les traditions judéo-

---

[17] Notre thèse, dont nous soulignons le caractère hypothétique, deviendra plus vraisemblable quand nous aurons prouvé que la division des trois parties de la loi divine s'appuie, elle aussi, sur la tradition secrète.

chrétiennes quand il déclare que la Loi sur le divorce n'est pas d'origine divine. Voici ce qu'on lit dans une discussion très ancienne sur la valeur à accorder aux paroles de Jésus dans la découverte des passages authentiques de l'Ancien Testament. La discussion est rapportée ici encore dans le Κήρυγμα Πέτρου: "c'est pourquoi il est impossible sans sa doctrine (celle de Jésus) de trouver cette vérité libératrice (sur l'inauthenticité de passages choquants de l'Ancien Testament), même si l'on cherche jusqu'à la fin du monde là où elle ne peut pas être trouvée. Elle était et est dans les paroles de notre Jésus. Ainsi, *comme connaissant les passages vrais de la Loi,* il répondit aux Sadducéens qui lui demandaient: "comment est-il possible que Moïse ait permis de se marier sept fois successivement?": "C'est bien Moïse qui, à cause de votre endurcissement, vous a permis cela. Il n'en était pas ainsi dès le commencement. Car Celui qui a créé dans le commencement a fait l'homme en être masculin et féminin" (ps. Clém., *Hom.* III, 54). Il est clair que ce passage contient exactement la même pensée que celui de Ptolémée. On hésite pourtant à accepter une dépendance de la part du gnostique, si l'on compare l'explication qu'Irénée donne du même texte évangélique.

Il semble en conclure: "et praecepta quaedam *a Moyse* posita eis propter duritiam illorum", comme l'ont fait *aussi* les apôtres dans le Nouveau Testament quand ils disent: "haec ego dico, non dominus" (Irén. IV, 15, 1-2).

Irénée est un *saint* et un champion de l'orthodoxie. Il est presque incroyable qu'il ait admis que la Loi sur le divorce soit d'origine humaine. C'est pourquoi nous avouerons volontiers notre erreur, si on démontrera que notre interprétation du passage cité est erronée. Entre temps, nous croyons qu'Irénée, ne fut-ce que pour un moment, a joué avec l'idée qu'énonce avec tant de vigueur l'hérétique Ptolémée (avec cette seule différence qu'il observe quelques lignes plus bas que "Dieu a voulu que ce fît quelque chose de tel"). Irénée n'a pas connu les écrits pseudo-clémentins ou leurs sources. Ceci nous avertit qu'une telle conception peut naître spontanément. Il n'est donc pas nécessaire que Ptolémée l'ait empruntée aux traditions judéo-chrétiennes.

7. *La Mischna dans l'Ancien Testament* (Ch. 4, 11 sqq.)

Si nous croyons cependant que cette dépendance existe, c'est surtout à cause du passage sur la tradition des Anciens. Ces Anciens ne sont pas seulement les chefs du peuple juif à l'époque de Jésus: ils ont, *dès le début* introduit des passages faussés dans la Loi ($\pi\rho\tilde{\omega}\tau o\nu$ V$_1$ (ch. 4, 2), non cité par Holl dans son édition d'Epiphane, est extrêmement significatif). De plus, le prophète Isaïe aurait fait allusion à leurs opinions pernicieuses.

Il est vrai que la parole de Jésus sur le "Corban" n'a pas la signification que lui prête Ptolémée. D'abord, les mots: "δῶρον τῷ θεῷ" ne se trouvent pas dans l'Ancien Testament, comme veut nous le faire croire l'hérétique. Puis, Jésus condamne une tradition existante sans déclarer qu'elle était primitive (λέγετε dans le texte de l'évangile, non εἰρήκατε, comme écrit notre auteur). Enfin, Isaïe a prédit, mais non observé dans son temps de telles coutumes (ἐπροφήτευσεν, non ἐξεφώνησεν). Ptolémée a dû fausser le texte sacré afin d'appuyer sa thèse sur l'autorité des Ecritures. C'est, en effet, l'argument le plus faible de toute la lettre.

Mais si l'on néglige le résultat et si l'on recherche l'intention de l'auteur, c'est ce passage qui révèle l'origine de ses idées. Il veut démontrer que certaines traditions se sont glissées dans la Loi. Or, déjà Epiphane, avec une perspicacité dont on ne le croirait pas capable, a aperçu que Ptolémée entendait par ces traditions les δευτερώσεις, c'est-à-dire la Mischna (Epiph., *Pan.* 33, 9, 2). Puis Ptolémée est assez au courant des conceptions judéo-chrétiennes pour croire que ces δευτερώσεις remontent jusqu'au début de la religion mosaïque. Tout ceci répond nettement au point de vue où se placent les auteurs des écrits pseudo-Clémentins: "bon nombre de péricopes faussées, contraires à Dieu, ont été glissées dans les écrits de l'Ancien Testament de la manière suivante: quand le prophète Moïse, avec l'approbation de Dieu, a transmis la Loi avec les explications nécessaires à soixante-dix "Anciens" élus, *peu de temps après*, quand la Loi fut fixée par l'écriture, ont été aussi incorporées dans la Loi quelques péricopes faussées, inspirées, à juste titre d'ailleurs, par le diable (ps. Clém., Homél. III, 38).

On pourrait soupçonner que l'auteur du Κήρυγμα Πέτρου a introduit cette théorie des péricopes faussées afin de défendre l'Ancien Testament contre les attaques de Marcion et qu'il serait plutôt question ici d'une influence venant du gnosticisme hellénique. Cette conjecture serait très mal fondée. J'ai cherché en vain dans la littérature gnostique des parallèles aux conceptions tant de l'épître à Flora que du Κήρυγμα Πέτρου. Par contre, cette théorie que la Mischna aurait été insérée dans le texte sacré, doit être d'origine juive. On la trouve combattue dans le livre d'Henoch [18]. Cullmann dit dans son remarquable ouvrage sur les écrits pseudo-Clémentins: "L'attitude des *Prédications de Pierre*, qui, malgré leurs tendances judaïsantes, se permettent tant de libertés à l'égard

---

[18] O. Cullmann, *Le problème littéraire et historique du roman Pseudo-Clémentin*, Paris, 1930, p. 175. Cf. H. Waitz, *Die Pseudo-Clementinen*, Eine quellenkritische Untersuchung, *T. u. U.*, N.F. X, 4, Leipzig, 1904. Carl Schmidt, *Studien zu den Pseudo-Clementinen*, *T. u. U.*, IV, 1, Leipzig, 1930.

de l'Ancien Testament, ne nous étonne plus, lorsque *nous plaçons cet écrit dans le cadre du gnosticisme juif*" [19].

Nous supposons donc que *Ptolémée a connu, directement ou indirectement, les conceptions des cercles judéo-chrétiens sur l'Ancien Testament* que nous avons citées plus haut. Ce résultat ne laisse pas de surprendre: la conception des péricopes faussées, loin d'être l'invention fantasque et éphémère de quelque gnostique, remonte jusqu'aux milieux juifs qui ont vu naître le christianisme.

Signalons l'extrême modération et le bon goût qui ont guidé Ptolémée dans le choix de ses emprunts. Le Κήρυγμα Πέτρου rejette plusieurs passages narratifs de la Génèse et élimine toutes les parties qui traitent du culte et des sacrifices ainsi que tous les Livres Prophétiques. Le valentinien se borne à quelques péricopes d'une importance limitée. Les mots qu'il a su trouver pour exprimer sa pensée démontrent qu'il n'a pas seulement fait quelques emprunts, mais qu'il a vécu le problème.

8. *Les trois composants de la Loi divine* (Ch. 5, 1-3)

Ptolémée étudie ensuite la Loi divine. Elle contient trois parties de valeur inégale: la loi inférieure, la loi symbolique, la loi pure. On retrouve une division en trois parties à peu près identique dans le dialogue de Justin avec le rabbi Trypho (ch. 44).

La chose n'a rien d'étonnant. Nous avons soupçonné que Ptolémée résidait à Rome. Pourquoi n'aurait-il pas connu le livre de Justin? Ou, peut-être, la thèse de Justin est-elle un lieu commun de l'apologétique chrétienne? Quoi qu'il en soit, il est très probable que Ptolémée s'appuie sur la tradition catholique.

Mais, de nouveau, nous constatons qu'il a adapté cette conception à un schème herméneutique. Cette conclusion est inévitable, si l'on compare les remarques de notre auteur avec les données sur l'inspiration de la Bible que nous offrent nos sources valentiniennes. Comme dans la Loi, les hérétiques distinguaient dans les livres prophétiques trois éléments divers (nous l'avons dit déjà: peut-être considéraient-ils Moïse comme un prophète). Mais quelle différence avec Justin! Ces éléments ne sont pas seulement de valeur inégale, mais aussi d'origine diverse. Les valentiniens attribuaient un de ces composants au σπέρμα, un autre à Sophia, un troisième au démiurge (Irén. I, 7, 3). Il faut connaître le mythe valentinien pour pouvoir apprécier une telle conception. Selon les valentiniens, le monde a été créé par trois personnes: le Christ, la Sophia et le

---

[19] O. Cullmann, *o.c.*, p. 187.

démiurge. Le Christ montre les idées transcendantes; la Sophia produit la
matière brute; le démiurge arrange et gouverne le monde visible. Dès le
commencement, un germe spirituel a été déposé dans l'homme. Nous avons vu
plus haut que ce germe parlait par la bouche des prophètes. Il y a donc une
étroite cohérence entre la conception de l'inspiration des prophéties et le mythe
cosmologique ou, plutôt, sotériologique.

On fait la même constatation quand on étudie les données de nos sources sur
l'inspiration de l'Evangile. Les paroles de Jésus elles-mêmes ne sont pas tenues
pour homogènes mais contiennent des passages provenant du Sauveur, ou de
la Sophia ou bien de Yahweh (Irén. I, 7, 3). L'assertion se comprend. L'homme
Jésus, sur qui le Christ descendait, n'avait-il pas une âme (nommée "le Christ
psychique", ce qui veut dire: le Messie juif) et un esprit imparfait, dérivé de la
Sophia (Irén. I, 6, 1)? C'était donc tantôt son âme qui parlait, tantôt son esprit,
tantôt le principe divin. Il est clair que l'école de Ptolémée a appliqué le même
schème herméneutique tant aux paroles de Jésus qu'aux prophéties. N'est-il pas
vraisemblable que le même principe tripartite se retrouve dans la lettre de
Ptolémée à Flora? Car on peut présumer à bon droit que ces trois lois, pure,
symbolique et inférieure, doivent être attribuées aux trois "Causes premières",
le germe spirituel, la Sophia et le démiurge.

Cette hypothèse, qui est d'une grande importance pour l'interprétation de notre
lettre, est si simple qu'on se demande comment il se fait qu'aucun savant, à
notre connaissance, ne l'ait encore énoncée. Nous nous efforcerons de confirmer
cette hypothèse dans les chapitres suivants.

9. *Le Décalogue* (Ch. 5, 3)

La Loi pure est le décalogue, c'est-à-dire, cette partie qui a été complétée par
le Sauveur. On nous dit qu'elle ne lui était pas étrangère. L'affirmation nous
étonne. Un peu plus haut (ch. 3, 4) l'auteur n'a-t-il pas déclaré qu'elle avait
besoin d'être complétée par un autre que le démiurge? Ce qui semble impliquer
que, dans son état imparfait, elle provient de Yahweh. En outre, elle est
considérée ici comme faisant partie de la loi de Yahweh. On se demande, en
désespoir de cause, ce que cela peut signifier. Quelle relation le décalogue
a-t-il avec le démiurge et avec le Christ?

Ce problème se résout, si l'on reconnaît que la Loi pure a été inspirée par le
"germe spirituel". Ce σπέρμα n'est pas étranger au Sauveur, parce qu'il est
spirituel comme Lui, mais peut avoir inspiré le décalogue de Yahweh, parce
qu'il a été mis dans l'âme du démiurge. Examinons donc, pour prouver cette
thèse, l'origine de la doctrine du σπέρμα et son rapport avec la conception de
l'inspiration.

Il est sûr que la théorie du "germe spirituel" remonte au fondateur de l'école. En vrai poète, Valentin nous raconte que "les anges du démiurge éprouvaient une sorte d'effroi pour l'homme créé, parce que son langage était plus sublime qu'on ne pouvait l'attendre d'une créature, grâce à Celui qui avait mis dans l'homme d'une façon mystérieuse le germe transcendant, de sorte qu'il parlait librement. C'est ainsi que pour les artistes les oeuvres d'art des hommes mondains deviennent un objet d'effroi, les statues et les idoles, bref tout ce que des hommes créent εἰς ὄνομα θεοῦ. Car Adam, créé au nom de l'Homme, inspirait de l'effroi pour l'Homme préexistant, comme si celui-ci était représenté par lui. C'est pourquoi les anges furent épouvantés et se précipitèrent pour détruire leur oeuvre" (Clém. d'Alex., *Strom.* II, 36, 2-4). Ces mots aussi beaux qu'énigmatiques de l'hérésiarque me semblent montrer clairement qu'il est impossible de comprendre les fragments existants sans avoir recours au système de Valentin. Car c'est précisément le mythe qui nous explique ce que c'est que le σπέρμα. Quand le Sauveur, accompagné de ses anges, apparut à l'esprit déchu, la Sophia, ravie par leur aspect, engendra une postérité spirituelle d'après leur image (Irén. I, 4, 5). Ces germes portent le nom d'"Homme" ou bien d'"Eglise, emblême de l'Eglise transcendante. Lorsque le monde fut créé, ces germes furent déposés dans Yahweh d'une façon mystérieuse sans qu'il se doutât de rien, afin qu'ils fussent insufflés par lui avec l'âme dans le corps humain. *Dans l'âme du démiurge sommeillent, en état d'inconscience, des germes de spiritualité* (cf. *Exc. ex. Théod.* 53, 5).

Par sa nature, ce σπέρμα, bien que spirituel et, par là, apparenté à l'esprit pur, au Christ, est défectueux. L'homme n'est qu'"un dieu tombé qui se souvient des cieux" et a besoin de la grâce pour être sauvé par le Christ. C'est de nouveau Valentin lui-même qui le dit en des paroles d'une extraordinaire beauté: "Un seul est bon, celui qui a parlé dans la révélation de son Fils. C'est par lui seul que le coeur (= le germe spirituel) pourrait devenir pur, tout esprit mauvais en étant chassé. Car dans son état actuel, une multitude de démons qui demeurent en lui l'empêchent d'être pur. Chacun d'eux produit les effets qui lui sont propres et le maltraite par de mauvais désirs. Et il me semble qu'il arrive au coeur à peu près ce qui arrive à une hôtellerie, lorsque des gens grossiers y séjournent: ils percent les murs, ils creusent des trous et souvent la remplissent d'ordures. Il en est de même du coeur, tant qu'il ne reçoit pas la grâce. Il reste impur, il est la demeure d'une foule de démons. Mais lorsque le Père, qui est seul bon, le regarde, il est sanctifié et rayonne de lumière. Bienheureux celui qui a un tel coeur, parce qu'il verra Dieu" (Clém. d'Alex., *Strom.* II, 114, 3)[20].

---

[20] Traduction d'après Simone Pétrement, *Le dualisme chez Platon,* etc., Paris, 1947, p. 251.

On ne peut pas imaginer une illustration plus expressive de la théorie ésotérique
selon laquelle ces germes spirituels sont en soi *"imparfaits,* puérils, absurdes,
faibles et sans forme, mais, formés par le Sauveur ils deviennent des enfants de
l'époux céleste et participent au mariage sacré" (Exc. 68). Soulignons que le
germe, comme le décalogue, est imparfait et se rapporte toujours au Christ: Lui
et ses anges, ils sont le complément, le πλήρωμα de l'esprit déchu [21].

Voyons maintenant comment l'école de Ptolémée applique cette conception du
σπέρμα à l'inspiration de la Bible. Ils soutiennent *que le germe spirituel a
beaucoup parlé par les prophètes.* En outre, la Sophia a parlé maintes fois, tant
par le moyen du démiurge que par le moyen des âmes qu'il avait créées
(Irén. I, 5, 6). A parler rigoureusement, on ne dit pas *totidem verbis* que le
germe spirituel a employé non seulement les âmes humaines mais aussi le
démiurge comme porte-parole. Nous nous permettons pourtant d'émettre cette
hypothèse qui nous paraît assez bien fondée. Pourquoi, en effet, ce germe, qui
sommeille dans l'âme du démiurge comme enveloppé dans un vêtement
(Héracléon, frag. 1), n'aurait-il pas parlé quelque fois? Et certes, le σπέρμα
a parlé par la bouche du démiurge, non seulement dans les livres prophétiques
de l'Ancien Testament, mais aussi *dans la Loi.*

Ptolémée a-t-il inventé cette doctrine de l'inspiration? Ou l'a-t-il plutôt
empruntée à Valentin? On peut résoudre ce problème si l'on accepte d'interpréter un des fragments du maître d'après son système: "Beaucoup", dit-il,
"de ce qui est écrit dans les livres profanes, on le retrouve écrit dans l'Eglise
de Dieu. Ce qui est commun, ce sont les mots qui proviennent du coeur, la Loi
écrite dans le coeur. C'est là le peuple de l'Aimé, les bienaimés qui l'aiment"
(Clém. d'Alex., *Strom.* VI, 42, 3-4).

Du fait que les interprétations proposées de ce passage par des savants très
célèbres sont divergentes, on n'ose pas avancer une explication nouvelle sans
quelques réserves méthodiques [22]. Je crois, cependant, pouvoir affirmer que
Hilgenfeld avait raison, lorsque, se fondant sur quelques données d'Origène
et des Homélies pseudo-Clémentines, il identifiait les "écrits profanes"

---

[21] Cf. Héracléon, fr. 1, 18.

[22] Th. Zahn, *Geschichte des Neutestamentlichen Kanons,* Erlangen, 1888, t. I, p. 720:
"Während die kirchlichen "Gnostiker" es liebten, in der heidnischen Literatur Anklänge an
die Offenbarung aufzuspüren und diese als Zeugnisse für die christliche Wahrheit anzuführen,
macht Valentin die umgekehrte Beobachtung, dass viele in der ausserchristlichen Literatur
bezeugte Wahrheiten auch in der Bibel zu finden seien, und erklärt gerade diese Aussagen der
natürlichen Gotteserkenntnis und des *algemein menschlichen* Sittengesetzes für das Wesentlichste
und Wichtigste auch in den christlichen Offenbarungsurkunden". Pour ma part, je crois que
Valentin, en vrai gnostique, ne reconnaissait pas la connaissance de Dieu et la morale naturelle,
parce qu'il croyait que le Dieu inconnu avait été révélé seulement par le Christ.

(δημοσίαι βίβλοι) dont il est question dans ce fragment, avec l'Ancien Testament [23]. L'Eglise de Dieu, c'est évidemment la communauté des vrais chrétiens, ou, dans un sens moins général, les valentiniens eux-mêmes. Les mots qui proviennent du coeur, siège du pneuma (Ptolémée ne dira-t-il pas (5 ,11): καρδία πνευματική? Comparez aussi le deuxième fragment de Valentin), doivent être les paroles inspirées par le germe spirituel. Ce germe est nommé dans le système *Ecclesia*. Valentin, plein d'onction, préfère dans ce fragment le terme "peuple de l'Aimé", ce qui revient au même. Si le maître identifie d'une façon assez curieuse la Loi écrite au "peuple de l'Aimé", c'est parce que le germe spirituel, qui a inspiré ces passages, est lui-même l'*Ecclesia*. Enfin, ce qui est commun à l'Ancien Testament et à l'Eglise du Christ, c'est "*la Loi qui est écrite dans le coeur*", l'élément spirituel de la Loi. *Valentin reconnaissait donc une certaine partie de la Loi juive, et de l'Ancien Testament en général, en tant qu'inspirée par l'esprit.*

Est-il donc téméraire d'attribuer le décalogue, que Ptolémée considère comme Loi pure, au "germe spirituel"? Le disciple ne semble-t-il pas suivre la route que son maître lui a montrée?

Quoi qu'il en soit, il est certain que, selon Ptolémée, dans l'âme du créateur sommeillent des germes imparfaits, qui ont inspiré certains passages de l'Ancien Testament et ont été complétés par le Sauveur. *Ce sont là les présuppositions nécessaires à la conception de l'épitre à Flora, selon laquelle le décalogue, donné par le démiurge, et qui pourtant n'est pas étranger au Sauveur, était imparfait et a été complété par le Christ.*

Il est évident que ces spéculations se fondent sur une interprétation toute spéciale d'un texte évangélique, le verset bien connu: οὐκ ἦλθον καταλῦσαι (τὸν νόμον) ἀλλὰ πληρῶσαι (Matth. 4, 17). Laissons les savants discuter sur le sens original de ces mots très controversés. Il suffit, à notre propos, de savoir que certains auteurs catholiques appliquaient, comme Ptolémée, ces paroles au seul décalogue, qu'ils séparaient du reste de la Loi. Ces lois dures et sévères, devenues nécessaires après l'adoration du Veau d'or, ont été abolies, mais les dix commandements sont restés, supplées et complétés par le Sermon sur la montagne. Il n'y a pas là de quoi s'étonner: ce sont les préceptes même de la nature, l'éthique naturelle si chère aux stoïciens (Irén. IV, 15, 1 et IV, 16, 4). (Il faut souligner l'importance de cette identification. On y voit même une première annonce du principe thomiste: "gratia non tollit naturam sed perficit") [24].

---

[23] A. Hilgenfeld, *Ketzergeschichte der Urchristentums*, Leipzig, 1884, p. 290 sqq.
[24] A. v. Harnack, *Geschichte eines programmatischen Worts Jesu*, dans *Sitzungsber. Berliner Akad.*, 1912, p. 205.

Ptolémée, lui aussi, a employé la terminologie stoïcienne. Si notre conjecture, d'après la leçon originale du *Codex Vaticanus* que nous avons découverte, est exacte, l'auteur déclare que le décalogue sert εἰς τε ἀπαγόρευσιν τῶν ἀφεκτέων καὶ εἰς πρόσταξιν τῶν ποιητέων (*Vat. corrector, Marc., editores*: ἀναίρεσιν, *Vat.* (*erasus*): ἀ.α.ωρευσιν). C'est la définition stoïcienne qu'on rencontre un peu partout (p.e. Stobée, *Eclogae* II, 96, 10 Wachsmuth) et qu'emploie particulièrement Clément d'Alexandrie pour désigner la Loi (par ex. *Strom* III, 84, 1). Mais le choix de mots de Ptolémée n'a aucune signification fondamentale, comme c'est le cas chez Irénée, parce que le germe spirituel, qui a inspiré ces commandements n'est pas une donnée naturelle, mais un don de la grâce. On ne nous dit nulle part comme le font les apologistes, que les philosophes grecs ont participé au Verbe. Le germe spirituel a parlé seulement dans l'Ancien Testament. La doctrine valentinienne, qui précède la théologie d'un Irénée et d'un Clément d'Alexandrie, oppose la nature à la grâce et à la transcendance et n'admet point une théologie naturelle.

Nous croyons avoir prouvé que, selon Ptolémée, le germe spirituel a inspiré le décalogue et certaines autres parties de l'Ancien Testament. Ce résultat n'est pas sans importance, puisqu'il nous permet de préciser la différence qui existait entre l'Ancien Testament et le Nouveau d'après cet hérétique, différence que les savants modernes ne semblent pas avoir observée. Tandis que la loi pure et certains passages des prophètes ont été inspirés par un germe spirituel mais imparfait, c'est le Sauveur lui-même qui a parlé dans les parties les plus sublimes de l'Evangile. *Il y a donc une différence de niveau spirituel*: la connaissance absolue de Dieu ne se manifeste que dans les paroles du Christ. Pourtant, l'estime qu'on a pour l'Ancien Testament est très grande. Non seulement il a été inspiré par ce Yahweh, qui, bien que tout à fait "psychique", est l'image du Dieu Inconnu, mais encore il contient des passages spirituels, dont les paroles du Christ sont le complément.

10. *La Loi du talion* (Ch. 5, 4-9)

La deuxième partie de la Loi (qui doit, selon notre hypothèse, être attribuée à Yahweh tout seul), c'est la loi de la vengeance. Les paroles que Ptolémée consacre à ce sujet nous mettent à nouveau au milieu des débats acharnés entre marcionites et catholiques. Selon Marcion, le Dieu bon ne punit pas. L'idée de de la vengeance lui répugne. Dans son oeuvre perdue, les Antithèses, Marcion citait expressément le passage: "oeil pour oeil, dent pour dent", pour prouver l'opposition absolue qu'il mettait entre le Dieu juste et le Dieu bon (Adamantius, *Dialogus de recta fide*, 814d, p. 32 Bakh.). Les orthodoxes, par contre, ne se lassaient pas de défendre le droit que Dieu a de punir. La sévérité de la loi était excusée par la dureté d'un peuple encore "rude", c'est-à-dire, par les

circonstances historiques (par ex. Tert., *adv. Marc.* II, 15). Quant au commandement: "oeil pour oeil, dent pour dent", il servait de frein; il effrayait celui
qui avait un penchant au crime en lui inspirant la peur d'une rétribution. Il avait
donc plutôt une intention préventive (par ex. Tert., *adv. Marc.* II, 18). Enfin,
les auteurs orthodoxes aimaient à souligner que Jésus lui-même avait reconnu
l'Ancien Testament et son auteur divin. On sait que Tertullien, dans les deux
derniers livres de son oeuvre contre Marcion, n'a pas de peine à démontrer que
cet hérétique, malgré l'épuration radicale à laquelle il soumettait le Nouveau
Testament, n'avait pas réussi à faire disparaître cette évidente vérité.

Ptolémée examine ces trois arguments. Il est possible qu'il ait anticipé sur les
solutions présentées par des écrivains postérieurs. Ceux qui se souviennent
qu'au temps de Ptolémée il existait toute une littérature antimarcionite,
aujourd'hui perdue, et qui se rendent compte de la ténacité de la tradition dans
ce genre de littérature [25], supposeront plutôt que le valentinien conserve l'écho
de certaines discussions entre marcionites et catholiques, auxquels il a été
présent.

L'auteur constate que la loi du talion est toujours accompagnée d'injustice,
parce que celui qui commet un acte mauvais en deuxième lieu, ne diffère de
celui qui le commet en premier lieu que par l'ordre de succession, mais en réalité
fait la même chose. Remarque particulièrement pénible pour les croyants de
l'Eglise. Ceux-ci ne rejetaient-ils pas, à l'aide de la même argumentation, la
rétribution comme principe éthique? N'est-il pas d'une ironie singulière que nous
retrouvions un parallèle presque littéral de notre passage dans les Homélies
pseudo-Clémentines (XII, 30) et même chez le féroce Tertullien? (de Pat. 10).
Seulement, ceux-ci parlaient de la vie des chrétiens. Faut-il donc supposer que
le niveau moral de Dieu est moins élevé que celui de ses fidèles? Ptolémée,
indifférent à la politique comme les autres chrétiens de son temps, ne connaît
pas une différence de principe entre un crime contre la loi et la vindicte
publique. — Cependant la loi du talion est juste, parce qu'elle a été donnée en
vue de la faiblesse de l'homme. La punition de Dieu n'est donc pas vindicative,
mais préventive. Concession trop magnanime aux apologistes de l'orthodoxie,
qui semble méconnaître un trait très essentiel de la religiosité israëlite: l'idée de
la vengeance divine. Ptolémée ne discute pas le principe du talion, mais ses
conséquences plus au moins violentes. Il semble supposer, sans le prouver, que
la violence est toujours *mauvaise.* C'est pour cette raison que la loi du talion,
bien que juste, ne peut pas s'accorder avec la nature du Dieu suprême, qui
est *bon* par essence (cf. Héracléon, frag. 48: le dieu punissant est le serviteur

---

[25] G. Quispel, *De Bronnen,* etc., passim.

subalterne du Dieu bon; la punition est donc bien nécessaire et très utile, quoiqu'indigne de Dieu).

Il est possible, continue Ptolémée, en résumant une autre réplique des orthodoxes, qu'un tel précepte fût nécessaire dans une situation historique donnée (les philosophes contemporains l'auraient nommé περιστατικός). Mais que penser d'un Dieu qui devient, malgré lui, la victime de la contrainte des circonstances, qui d'abord défend de tuer, puis, dans une seconde loi, commande de tuer un meurtrier à son tour, qui fait valoir sa justice aux frais de deux meurtres? Un lecteur moderne observera à cet égard que le décalogue ne défend pas de tuer, mais de commettre un meurtre, ce qui est autre chose. La contradiction que Ptolémée a soulignée n'existe donc pas. Erreur sublime, qui fait honneur à notre hérétique, car c'est l'horreur de la violence qui l'a inspirée!

Selon Ptolémée, même la loi du talion était divine. C'est ce que prouve la parole de Jésus; quand il dit que c'est *Dieu* qui a ordonné la peine de mort pour celui qui maudit ses parents, il admet que même cette partie vindicative de la loi doit être d'origine divine. Il semble que Ptolémée, cette fois, donne raison aux catholiques. Irénée ne dit-il pas exactement la même chose, en s'autorisant du même texte évangélique? (Irén. IV, 9, 3). Mais quelle différence dans la conception se cache sous cette ressemblance superficielle! Irénée conclut que le Dieu de l'Ancien Testament est le même que le Père du Christ. On dirait presque que Ptolémée, dans des termes sagement déguisés, donne une seconde réplique à cet argument catholique. Car, s'il est vrai que "son Fils, à son arrivée" en ce monde, ou, littéralement, "le Fils qui est venu de chez lui (le démiurge)", reconnaît l'Ancien Testament, (καταρυθμεῖται d'après notre conjecture pour la *crux interpretum*: καταριθμεῖται des manuscrits), il est encore plus vrai que ce fils de Yahweh n'est pas identique au Christ qui est descendu du Plérôme. Si nous consultons les données du système, il apparaît que ce fils du démiurge était plutôt le Messie juif. Ce ne peut être notre but d'exposer ici la christologie de Ptolémée avec toute l'ampleur qu'elle mériterait. Elle se résume dans la conception assez simple que le Christ divin est descendu sur l'homme Jésus, qui avait un corps, une âme et un esprit, tous trois de qualité extraordinaire. L'âme était le ψυχικὸς Χριστός, prédit par les prophètes, c'est-à-dire, le Messie juif (*Exc. ex Theod.* 59, 2). C'est lui, semble-t-il, qui, selon la lettre à Flora, a reconnu et aboli la loi du talion.

Autant que nous puissions le savoir, cette théorie du "Christ psychique" ne remonte pas à Valentin. Celui-ci, plus docète que son disciple, enseignait que Jésus était un "corps" spirituel que le Christ avait adopté [26]. Or, si Valentin

---

[26]   G. Quispel, dans *Vigilae Cristianae*, I, 1, 1947, p. 46 (= p. 29 de ce livre).

n'a pas encore connu la conception du "Christ psychique", il est impossible qu'il lui ait attribué une signification quant à l'appréciation et à l'abolition de la loi. Cette pensée est bien la propriété de Ptolémée lui-même (influencé par Marcion? cf. Tert., *adv. Marc.* III, 21). D'autre part, il est très probable que Valentin attribuait certains passages de la Loi au démiurge.

Tout ce passage sur la vengeance nous paraît extrêmement significatif pour la méthode de notre auteur. Il connaît les arguments des catholiques (ou, du moins, anticipe sur ces arguments) et les considère avec une grande impartialité. D'autre part, il a appris beaucoup de Marcion, mais parce qu'il limite sa critique à la loi du talion, sa critique est devenue beaucoup plus honnête et plus sage. Contrairement à Marcion, qui aime les solutions radicales, Ptolémée les évite et a le souci d'être objectif.

11. *La Loi symbolique* (Ch. 5, 8 sqq.)

La conception de Ptolémée concernant les cérémonies et les rites liturgiques du peuple juif ne semble pas différer de celle des auteurs catholiques qui ont polémisé contre la synagogue. C'est, en effet, chez eux surtout que l'on retrouve cette interprétation plutôt éthique du sacrifice, de la circoncision et du sabbat (par ex. Tertullien, *adv. Judaeos* c. 5, c. 3 et c. 4; on sait que la tradition de ces "testimonia" est très ancienne). La remarque que les jeûnes consistent dans l'abstention des actes mauvais, mais que l'observation littérale du commandement peut aider l'âme à se libérer de la matière, trouve son parallèle exact dans les *Eclogae Propheticae* (Clemens Alex., *Ecl. Proph.*, 14, 1). On constate de nouveau que Ptolémée, en bon théologien, est capable d'apprécier les opinions des orthodoxes et de s'exprimer dans leur langage.

Il est plus difficile de comprendre comment l'auteur peut s'autoriser ici des paroles du Sauveur. Les mots mêmes qu'il a choisis trahissent l'origine ultérieure de ces idées, c'est-à-dire les Psaumes (Ps. 49, 14), ou les prophètes israélites, Isaïe (58, 6), Jérémie (4, 4). Par contre, on ne trouvera aucun texte évangélique qui paraisse appuyer les assertions de Ptolémée. Faut-il donc supposer que l'auteur se réfère à quelque texte apocryphe? C'est ce qu'a fait Th. Zahn (avec quelque réserve d'ailleurs)[27]. Cette hypothèse est devenue beaucoup plus séduisante depuis qu'on a retrouvé les *Logia Jesu*. Car ceux-ci contiennent le texte suivant: "Jésus dit: si vous ne *jeûnez* pas par rapport *au monde*, vous ne trouverez pas le royaume de Dieu. Si vous ne *célébrez pas le sabbat*, vous ne trouverez pas le Père" (White, *The Sayings of Jesus*, p. 26)[28]. A ceci on peut ajouter que certains hérétiques, les Masbothéens, déclaraient que c'était Jésus

---

[27] Th. Zahn, o.c., p. 745.

[28] [C'est, comme il s'est avéré plus tard, le logion 27 de l'Évangile selon Thomas].

lui-même qui leur avait commandé de "*sabbatizare ab omni re*" (Ps. Hier., *Index de Haeres.*, dans *Corpus haeres.*, éd. Oehler, I, p. 283). Il reste donc possible que Ptolémée se réfère à quelque parole inconnue ou apocryphe de Jésus, conformément à son usage de s'autoriser d'une parole du Sauveur.

La partie rituelle de la Loi, déclare l'auteur, symbolise les choses spirituelles et transcendantes (διαφερόντων est un terme technique du vocabulaire valentinien). On s'attend donc, non sans quelque inquiétude, à une allégorisation des détails liturgiques, qui représenteraient *les événements dramatiques survenus dans le Plérôme*. C'est ainsi, en effet, que les disciples de Valentin interprétaient la Bible, en général, et la loi rituelle, en particulier. A cet égard, cette remarque d'Origène est extrêmement significative. Il dit: "Héracléon et ses disciples devraient démontrer à propos de chaque cérémonie de la Loi, la façon dont elle peut être un symbole des événements du monde spirituel (πῶς ἐστιν εἰκὼν τῶν ἐν τῷ πληρώματι) (Orig. *in Joh.* XIII, 19, § 116, éd. Preuschen p. 243; cf. Irén. I, 18, 2; Tert., *adv. Val.* 4).

Mais comment expliquer ce symbolisme ésotérique à une femme qui n'est pas encore initiée? Elle comprendra que ces commandements doivent être spiritualisés: le sacrifice, c'est l'intimité de la conviction et la bienfaisance envers le prochain; la circoncision, la pureté du coeur; les jeûnes vrais consistent dans l'abstention des actes mauvais; le sabbat signifie qu'on laisse reposer le mal. Bref, les cérémonies extérieures ont été remplacées par une attitude morale sincère et profonde. Flora avait appris tout cela déjà dans l'Eglise. Mais si l'on y regarde de plus près, on doit admettre que cette interprétation de la Loi n'est ni allégorique ni typologique, mais plutôt *éthique*.

Du reste, Ptolémée connaît aussi cette méthode qu'on appelle aujourd'hui "typologique": l'agneau pascal est bien pour lui un τύπος de la souffrance du Christ. On peut comparer cette conception avec un développement d'Héracléon à propos du même agneau (frag. 12), qui nous montre que celui-ci s'accordait avec son collègue pour accepter sur ce point les résultats de l'exégèse catholique (cf. Tert., *adv. Jud.* 14). Les méthodes herméneutiques de l'école valentinienne, tout en étant "spirituelles", étaient donc assez complexes. Mais si, dans notre lettre, Ptolémée évite l'allégorisation, assez suspecte dans les milieux ecclésiastique, et ne donne que des explications éthiques et typologiques, *il doit avoir fait une certaine distinction entre ces diverses méthodes herméneutiques*. De même, Héracléon donne *trois* explications d'un passage évangélique, la première "simple", la deuxième "plus élevée", la troisième "encore plus élevée" (frag. 8). Ces passages ne sont pas sans intérêt pour celui qui étudie l'évolution de l'herméneutique qui aboutit à Origène. Il faut être d'ailleurs reconnaissant à Ptolémée de s'être limité à ce point de vue moins "élevé", parce qu'il nous permet de constater que la morale tant décriée des valentiniens ne méritait

aucun reproche. Notre lettre montre clairement que Tertullien commet une
généralisation abusive, quand il déclare: "ideoque nec operationes necessarias
sibi existimant *nec ulla disciplinae munia observant*" (*Adv. Val.* 30; cf. Irén. I,
6, 2). Sans doute n'attribuaient-ils aux bonnes oeuvres aucune valeur méritoire,
ce qui ne veut pas dire qu'ils les rejetaient. Le système de Ptolémée nous
enseigne que le "psychique" (les bonnes oeuvres et le comportement moral)
était, non pas la cause, mais bien *la condition de la grâce* pour les hommes
spirituels (Irén. I, 5, 6). Cette mystique suppose un fond de moralité et de
religiosité.

C'est sans doute en raison de scrupules pédagogiques plus que par une fâcheuse
réticence, que l'auteur ne nous dit pas qui a inspiré la loi symbolique. Les
fragments que nous a conservés Irénée s'expriment plus franchement. C'est la
Sophia qui a parlé maintes fois, tant par le canal du démiurge que par le
truchement des âmes qu'il avait créées (Irén. I, 5, 6). Certes, on ne nous
explique pas quels passages de l'Ancien Testament ont été inspirés par cette
entité. Mais Irénée nous fournit une donnée très précieuse, qui semble prouver
que c'est la loi rituelle qui doit être attribuée à la Sagesse. Il nous déclare: "Car
c'est aussi *à la Loi* qu'ils se réfèrent pour prouver leur thèse d'une manière
forcée, tout en choisissant ce qui leur convient par le nombre. Mais si *leur Mère*
(la Sophia), ou bien le Sauveur, s'était proposé de *montrer* (*dans la Loi*) *des
symboles* ("*typos*") *du Plérôme par le moyen du démiurge*, ils les auraient
représentés dans des choses plus vraies et plus saintes" (*Irén.* II, 24, 3). Il est
évident qu'Irénée combat dans ce passage l'opinion de certains valentiniens,
suivant laquelle la Sophia a montré dans la Loi des symboles du monde
transcendant et spirituel [29]. C'est précisément la conception que notre analyse
de la lettre à Flora nous suggérait de proposer. Il est vraie qu'il semble
qu'Irénée s'adresse plutôt aux marcosiens, autre secte des valentiniens; mais
rien n'empêche de supposer que Ptolémée a accepté, lui aussi, ce principe. Nous
avons vu qu'Héracléon enseignait que la loi rituelle contenait des symboles *du
Plérôme*; les marcosiens ne disaient pas autre chose, et Ptolémée a choisi le mot
διαφερόντων pour suggérer la même conception. Or, c'est toujours la Sophia
qui, selon les valentiniens, produit les images d'après les idées du Plérôme
(Irén. I, 5, 3). En expliquant un fragment assez obscur du maître, Clément
d'Alexandrie nous transmet un principe valentinien d'une extrême importance:
"Tout ce qui provient d'un couple est plénitude (πληρώματα); tout ce qui
provient d'un seul (la Sophia) n'est qu'une image (εἰκόνες)" (Clem. Alex.,

---

[29] Si Irénée nomme en second lieu le Sauveur comme l'auteur de la loi symbolique, c'est parce
qu'il inspirait, selon Ptolémée et ses disciples, la Sophia (*Adv. Haereses,* I. 5, 1).

Strom. IV, 89, 6). Il est vraisemblable qu'on peut dire aussi que *tout ce qui est* "image" doit remonter à la Sophia. C'est que la Sophia est l'intermédiaire entre l'âme du monde (le démiurge) et les idées (le Plérôme). Cette gradation est essentielle pour tout le système et doit remonter à Valentin lui-même. Si l'on se souvient que l'interprétation allégorique de la Loi est reconnue par toute l'école valentinienne, et que la conception selon laquelle les symboles de la Loi sont inspirés par Sophia se rencontre chez deux disciples de Valentin, Marc et Ptolémée, dont l'un résidait en Asie Mineure et l'autre à Rome (ce qui rend invraisemblable une influence mutuelle), il apparaît probable que cette conception remonte au fondateur même de la secte.

12. *Résumé* (Ch. 6)

Voici le résumé de la doctrine de Ptolémée: le décalogue a été complété par certains passages du Sermon sur la Montagne; la loi du talion a été abolie; la loi symbolique a reçu une signification plus spirituelle et plus intime. Ce qui revient à dire que toute la Loi de Moïse n'est plus valable.

Ce résultat n'a rien de très étonnant, si on le compare avec l'opinion d'un auteur qui a combattu les hétérodoxes avec une passion acharnée, Tertullien (*de Pudicitia*, 6). La différence ne paraît pas ici bien grande.

Mais sous cette ressemblance apparente, se cache une différence fondamentale, qui est, à vrai dire, beaucoup plus intéressante. Aucun auteur orthodoxe n'aurait admis que le décalogue ait été inspiré par le "germe spirituel"; que le dieu, qui a donné la loi du talion, n'était qu'une divinité inférieure; que la loi symbolique provient de l'esprit déchu. Nous croyons avoir néanmoins prouvé que c'est là la doctrine que la lettre à Flora laisse entrevoir. Cette conception n'était pas originale; il est très probable qu'elle remonte à Valentin lui-même. En revanche, les données de nos sources ne nous permettent pas de supposer que Valentin a enseigné que la Loi contenait des éléments humains. C'est possible, mais on ne peut en fournir la preuve. Nous avons vu que, peut-être, Ptolémée a emprunté sa doctrine des péricopes faussées aux cercles judéo-chrétiens d'où proviennent les écrits pseudo-clémentins. Le mérite de Ptolémée est d'avoir confronté méthodiquement les conceptions de son maître avec les opinions des marcionites et des catholiques. Il n'est pas impossible qu'il soit plus indépendant à cet égard que nous ne l'avons supposé. Mais, même s'il s'est appuyé moins qu'il ne semble sur la tradition littéraire de l'Eglise et a anticipé les réponses des orthodoxes à la synagogue et aux marcionites, il n'en reste pas moins vrai que chaque remarque de Ptolémée — ou peut s'en faut — peut être mise en parallèle avec un passage correspondant de la littérature chrétienne de son temps.

13. *Conclusion* (Ch. 7)[30]

La conclusion qui se dégage des chapîtres précédents va de soi: le législateur n'est pas bon et n'est pas mauvais; il est juste. Ptolémée ne fait aucun effort pour estomper la contradiction qu'il met entre Rédemption et Création. Il est sincère. Cependant, en bon pédagogue, il choisit avec soin ses mots. C'est une femme religieuse, à qui la lettre est adressée. Elle sait que le diable est mauvais et que Dieu est bon. A un esprit de cette sorte la doctrine de Marcion est compréhensible: Loi opposée à Evangile, Justice opposée à Bonté. Mais il est plus difficile et plus troublant de penser que Dieu est "Abîme" et "Silence", pur esprit au delà des idées et que le démiurge et le diable, personnifications symboliques de la nature supérieure et de la nature inférieure, naissent de la souffrance de la Sophia. Il est vrai que les valentiniens disent également que Dieu est bon et que le diable est mauvais. Mais de pareilles catégories éthiques n'expriment pas complètement la doctrine valentinienne, qui est une mystique ontologique, non une éthique. C'est pourquoi le dessein de l'auteur doit être d'employer la distinction marcioniste de la bonté et de la justice pour indiquer la différence entre le Dieu suprême et le créateur du monde extérieur. Et, à ce propos, il convient de remarquer que notre auteur, contrairement à Marcion, distingue nettement la justice du mal, en même temps qu'il apprécie beaucoup la justice dans sa relativité.

Et cependant, Ptolémée vit en pensée dans la doctrine ésotérique qu'il s'efforce avec tant de soin de passer sous silence. C'est pour cette raison que ses paroles deviennent obscures. Il déclare que le démiurge donna naissance à une διττὴ δύναμις, mais était lui-même une image du Dieu suprême. Comment Flora qui n'était pas encore initiée, pouvait-elle comprendre cela? Des savants modernes, eux-mêmes, qui avaient à leur disposition les écrits ésotériques de l'école de Ptolémée, se sont trompés à ce sujet. Stieren et Harnack ont admis l'existence d'une lacune, ce qui est un moyen commode pour résoudre une difficulté. Holl dit que cette διττὴ δύναμις est: "ein zwischen Licht und Finsternis geteilter,

---

[30] A. Stieren a essayé de prouver (dans un livre intitulé: *De Ptolemaei Valentiniani ad Floram epistula*, Pars I, Jena, 1843, que je n'ai pas pu consulter) que cette dernière partie de notre épître n'était pas authentique. Dans son édition d'Irénée (p. 933) le savant allemand déclare: "Parte priore usque ad verba τριχῇ διαιρούμενον (c. 7, 1) et posteriore inde a vocibus Ταῦτά σοι — ἀναδείξῃς, quas partes genuinas esse in commentatione mea probavi, auctor finem epistolae facit ... *Falsarius* vero exponit, *quis sit deus legislator*". Que cette opinion doit être erronée, est prouvé par la considération suivante: Ptolémée, qui a écrit sa lettre selon les règles de l'ancienne rhétorique, a annoncé dans une vraie *propositio* (ch. 3, 8) qu'il allait traîter: primo "l'origine de la loi", secundo "la nature du législateur". Après avoir discuté la première partie de son sujet (ch. 4, 1-ch. 6, 6), il aborde maintenant la seconde question, la nature du législateur, qu'il s'avait proposée de traîter ensuite. C'est pourquoi ce passage doit être authentique.

das heisst der μεσότης". Mais qu'est-ce que la lumière et les ténèbres ont à faire ici? Pourtant, Ptolémée ne fait que citer sa propre doctrine. Celle-ci enseigne que "le démiurge est une image du Père et que le ciel et la terre ont été créés par lui, c'est-à-dire les choses célestes (psychiques) et les choses terrestres (hyliques)" (*Exc.* 47, 1). La διττὴ δύναμις est donc la nature supérieure et la nature inférieure.

Il importe d'examiner de plus près ce passage. La remarque que Yahweh est une image du Dieu suprême, nous donne sur l'attitude des valentiniens touchant l'Ancien Testament plus de renseignements que tout le reste de la lettre à Flora. Soulignons que cette remarque se retrouve dans le cinquième fragment de Valentin.

Dans tout le cours de l'histoire, ce symbolisme platonicien a été le moyen d'expression employé principalement par les mystiques chrétiens, pour s'approcher à nouveau, en partant de l'extase, du monde qu'ils avaient abandonné. Valentin, en sa qualité de platonicien alexandrin, est le premier qui se soit engagé dans ce chemin. Ce qui est particulier chez lui, c'est que ce symbolisme est appliqué au dieu juif. C'est, en fait, une solution très originale, bien qu'inacceptable pour nous, du problème que pose l'Ancien Testament. Il n'y a pas seulement une différence de niveau entre le dieu de l'Ancien Testament, d'une part, et le dieu du Nouveau Testament, d'autre part, parce que l'un est psychique et que l'autre est spirituel, mais encore l'un est une image de l'autre.

Si l'on veut comprendre ces métaphores, on doit se rendre compte du fait que pour la mentalité mythologique des valentiniens la différence entre l'Ancien et le Nouveau Testament s'est personnifiée et est devenue une différence dans la nature des dieux (c.à.d. de Yahweh et du dieu inconnu). Alors on voit que la conception valentinienne, selon laquelle le démiurge, quoique "psychique", est une image du Père du Christ, est une synthèse: la différence entre l'Ancien et le Nouveau Testament, sur laquelle Marcion mettait l'accent, et l'accord entre ces deux documents, sur lequel les catholiques attiraient continuellement l'attention, sont reconnus au même degré.

GNOSTIC MAN: THE DOCTRINE OF BASILIDES

1. INTRODUCTION

The great Christian Gnostics, Valentinus, Basilides, et al. were mystics: they seem to have had an inner experience which we must assume to have been, I shall not say true, but sincere and authentic. If even in our most meticulous researches we keep in mind this fundamental truth, Christian Gnosticism will appear to us in a new and unexpected light. For the mysticism of all times and all nations has its source in the same spiritual attitude and reveals the same trends. And that is why it often arrives at similar conclusions. Hence it should not surprise us to hear of a scholar who was able to find striking analogies between Basilides, for example, and the Buddhist religion of distant India [1]. This scholar, writing in the first years of the present century, tried to explain these parallelisms on the basis of a dependence: according to his hypothesis, Basilides, living in Alexandria in the second century A.D., borrowed his conceptions from a Buddhism propagated by Indian merchants visiting the great city at the crossroads of the world. The arguments on which this theory is based are none too substantial. We hope, indeed, to show in the course of this essay that Basilides was not influenced by the religions of the Far East. But that makes the problem all the more interesting, for we must then conclude that within the Greek world of the second century, within the Christian church of Alexandria, a mysticism comparable to the religions of India was born of an original and living inspiration which was the very foundation of the Gnostic doctrine.

When we consider the documents concerning Basilides in this perspective, which is that of the phenomenology of religions, we soon perceive that these texts have not always been studied with the respect due to all religious phenomena. And disrespect is indeed the offense with which we might reproach certain scholars who have concerned themselves in their way with the Gnosis of Basilides: having discovered that certain phrases of Basilides quoted by Hippolytus showed some resemblance to passages from other Gnostics transmitted by the same author, they presumed that all these texts were mere forgeries, ephemeral and fantastic inventions of a Roman Gnostic determined to make a little money and deceive the good Hippolytus. This would make a forgery of Hippolytus' whole collection, which contains the most varied documents, sometimes bearing the distinct imprints of a personal and individual

---

[1] J. Kennedy, "Buddhist Gnosticism, the System of Basilides", *Journal of the Royal Asiatic Society* (London, 1902), 377-415.

experience [2]. What the proponents of this thesis forget is that such a forger would have had to be a religious genius. Hypotheses of this sort merely demonstrate the dullness of their author and clearly show that in philology, as in other fields, *akribeia* for its own sake is fatal.

However, the critical study of our sources for the doctrine of Basilides is not a simple matter. Clement of Alexandria has transmitted a number of fragments revealing a subtle mind, attentive to the message of the Gospel and concerned with the radical character of original sin; and Irenaeus gives an account of his system, representing it unmistakably as a theory of emanation. Hence it was a great surprise when in 1852 a young Greek discovered in a monastery on Mount Athos a book hitherto unknown, the *Elenchos* (*Refutatio*) of Hippolytus, which created a sensation among scholars and contains among other things a so-called Basilidian system irreconcilable with that described by Irenaeus, because it is clearly monist and evolutionist. Finally, we find in a Latin manuscript a fragment of Basilides in which he speaks of two eternal principles, light and darkness, and which can only be called dualistic.

Emanation, evolution, monism, dualism: what confusion, what contradiction! It is understandable that certain critics should have presumed that the doctrine transmitted by Hippolytus was not that of Basilides. What is less understandable is that these same scholars should have failed to recognize the importance of this document for the knowledge of Christian gnosis. Actually, it is a matter of relative indifference whether the *Elenchos* reflects the original doctrine of Basilides himself or of an unknown Gnostic master. Even in anonymity, greatness remains greatness. De Faye, however, believes that the author of this document, which he believes to be of much later date than the era of the great Gnostics, was a man of little originality, whose sole merit was to take up again the ideas of the old masters and compound them into a new system foreshadowing the decadence and degenerescence of gnosis as embodied in the *Pistis Sophia* and the *Book of Jeu* [3]. But if, as is becoming increasingly evident, Hippolytus' note is authentic and reflects the original doctrine of Basilides, and if on the other hand, as recent discoveries demonstrate, the distance between the vulgar gnosis represented by such works as the *Apokryphon Johannis* and learned gnosis is much smaller than a de Faye or a Harnack would like to admit, why have these adherents of the school of the history of dogmas, who considered the Christian Gnostics as philosophers and theologians — why, I say, have these scholars fallen into such radical error? Is it perhaps because they approached the texts with a preconceived idea, which led them to

---

[2] H. Stählin, *Die gnostischen Quellen Hippolyts* (Leipzig, 1890).
[3] Eugène de Faye, *Gnostiques et Gnosticisme* (Paris, 1913), p. 215.

reject and misunderstand everything that did not suit them? Is it because they wished to find their own rational, enlightened idealism in texts of an entirely different character?

And certain adepts of the school of the history of religions can also be reproached with disrespect for the texts. Bousset would like at all costs to find Iranian dualism in the Gnostic texts [4]. In a fragment of Basilides he finds the following words:

Let us renounce this vain and curious eclecticism and rather examine the questions which the barbarians themselves propounded concerning goods and evils, and the opinions at which they arrived on all these matters. For there are some who have said that the principles of all things are two, to which goods and evils attach, and that these principles themselves are without principle and unengendered. That is to say, there was at the beginning light and darkness, which issued only from themselves and from nothing other. When each of these principles was in itself, each one led its own life, the life it wished and the life which was appropriate to it. For each thing loves that which is appropriate to it and nothing appears evil to itself. But after each principle had attained knowledge of the other, after darkness had contemplated light and recognized it as a better thing, it coveted the light and pursued it, desiring to join and participate in it. Such was the action of darkness. As for the light, it accepted nothing from darkness, nor desired it, but it did also feel impelled to contemplate it. And so it regarded darkness as in a mirror. And thus a reflection, that is to say, a certain color of light, arose in the darkness; but the light itself merely looked and withdrew, having taken no particle of darkness. The darkness, on the contrary, seized the regard of the light and the reflection or color that matter had received from it in the moment when it inspired horror in the light. As the most evil beings had taken from the best not the true light, but a certain appearance and reflection of it, it acquired a certain good by a rape which changed the nature of that good. This is why there is no perfect good in this world and why what good there is is exceedingly weak, since that which was conceived in the beginning was already weak. Nevertheless, thanks to this little light, or rather thanks to this appearance of light, creatures have had the strength to engender a semblance of this mixture of light that they had received. And that is the creature which we see [5].

According to Bousset there is no doubt that this fragment reveals the true thinking of Basilides, that it shows the influence of Persian religion, and that it is one of the most important documents of Gnosticism. The notes of Hippolytus and Irenaeus (still according to Bousset) merely represent later developments and are not authentic.

But what does a rigorous analysis of this text in its context show? The author

4 W. Bousset, *Hauptprobleme der Gnosis* (Göttingen, 1907), pp. 93-96, based on a passage in Hegemonius's *Acta Archelai,* LXVII, ed. C. H. Beeson (Leipzig, 1906), p. 95.
5 *Acta Archelai,* LXVII, 7-11; ed. Beeson, pp. 96-97.

of the *Acta Archelai* wished to consider Basilides as a precursor and teacher of Mani. Accordingly, he wishes us to believe that Basilides taught the same dualism as the Persian Mani, and that he preached in Persia, not that he was influenced by Persian religion. Of this the *Acta Archelai* do not say a word. On the contrary, they tell us that Basilides borrowed the principle of dualism from a certain Scythianus, an apprentice in Egyptian and Pythagorean wisdom, who invented dualism in the course of his sojourn in Egypt.

We need not say that these fantasies are without historic value. It may seem curious, however, that the author, like modern scholars, believes that Manichaeism grew out of a Christianized gnosis. What is important, however, is that he nowhere mentions an Iranian influence.

If in this fragment Basilides cites the authority of certain barbarian writings, this does not mean that the content of these writings was Iranian. We know from other sources that the same Gnostic referred to the prophets Barcabbas and Barcoph and other more or less imaginary barbarians (Eusebius, *Historia Ecclesiastica*, IV, 7, 7, Mommsen) with names which do not seem particularly Persian. The syncretist writers of this period often affect exotic and mysterious pseudonyms, but in general they reflect the eclectic and vulgar philosophy of the Greek world. And this seems to be the case with the work which Basilides has quoted in this passage.

Here are the principal motifs of the text: the light is desired, the light is curious, hence it must be a woman, the Virgin of Light or a similar personage; this woman becomes a victim of her curiosity, like Psyche, who in the learned allegory of Apuleius wished to see the face of Eros. Basilides' contemporaries would surely have recognized this motif: the woman whose curiosity causes her to fall into the darkness of matter, they would have said, is a Platonic myth on the fall of the human soul. And indeed, Clement of Alexandria remarks that a certain Gnostic supposes, like a true Platonist, that the divine soul descended from on high into the world of generation and corruption because of its amorous desire (*Stromateis*, III, 13). The consequence of this catastrophe is that the visible world is an image of the luminous world, a conception close to that of Plato. Our fragment would seem, then, to reflect the pleasant, fragrant atmosphere of the syncretism then in vogue. But, to continue: darkness, the power which later created the world, is quite hostile to the light. Repelled by the darkness, the light departs. This reminds us of the Gnostic myths of the creation, of the hostile angels and Wisdom's disgust in the system of Valentinus (*Excerpta ex Theodoto*, 33, 4) and in the *Apokryphon Johannis*. Finally, the absolute dualism of matter-darkness and spiritual world-light is found in various Gnostic documents. If we compare the fragment cited by Basilides with the oldest Gnostic document known up to now, Chapters I, 29-30 of Irenaeus, we find almost the same motifs. It would seem, then, that this exotic book, the authority of which is cited by Basilides, is merely a product of an early, pre-Christian gnosis.

But this fragment does not contain the Basilidian doctrine in the stricter sense. It is clear that the Gnostic quotes these lines with a certain sympathy: doubtless because they contain the doctrine of an original confusion, a chaotic state in which all things were intermingled. We know through Clement of Alexandria that Basilides accepted this conception (*Strom.* II, 20), which, moreover, recurs in the account of Hippolytus. But, as we shall see, he modified it in a highly original way. Thus, the most we can say is that Basilides cited a Gnostic document and Hellenized and Christianized its content. In this case Bouset's hypothesis becomes highly improbable.

After this orientation we see clearly with what attitude a seeker after truth will approach these texts. He will have but one aim: to seize the original inspiration which animates the doctrine, whose depth and authenticity he recognizes. However, his method will be rigorously inductive: he will seek patiently to discover and determine the elements borrowed from the tradition, because he knows that there is no other means of distilling the original emotion. For this reason we have divided our essay into three parts, the first of which, rather technical in character, is an attempt to determine the Platonist influence, while the second stresses the Christian elements of the doctrine. These preliminary investigations will at length enable us to penetrate to the core of Basilidian gnosis.

2. THE FRAME: PLATONIST PHILOSOPHY

Basilides is the oldest Gnostic thinker known to us. Consequently, students of the origins of Christian Gnosticism have given very special attention to his doctrine. Some scholars have thought it to be of Oriental origin. Hilgenfeld and Bousset believed the Basilidian theory to be an offshoot of Iranian dualism. Kennedy, on the other hand, asserted that Basilides borrowed most of his ideas from Buddhism. But these interpretations assuredly go too far. Basilides was an Alexandrian Christian living in the second century A.D. We may be justified in presuming a priori that he was primarily influenced by the spiritual currents of his era and of his native city. Recent studies and discoveries make it increasingly clear that the main currents to be considered are Egyptian Christianity, vulgar gnosis, and contemporary Platonism.

True, the orthodox church of Egypt has left us no literary documents, but the polemics of Valentinus and Clement of Alexandria against the *simpliciores* prove that such a church existed. Next, we may presume that the vulgar, or, if you prefer, pure, gnosis, which seems to have been imported to Egypt from the Near East and which in the course of the years assimilated certain Christian elements, goes further back than Basilides and Valentinus. Finally, the Platonism of the period, whose initiator is held to have been Antiochus of Ascalon, was in vogue in Alexandria, and it is this Platonism which contributed more than any other school to the philosophical formation of the great heresiarchs.

If I stress the influence of the *schools* on the Alexandrian Gnostics, it is in order to make it clear that in my opinion the Gnostics did not, as the "historians of dogma" like to believe, have a profound knowledge of classical philosophy. The period in which they lived owed most of its rather superficial philosophical notions to little manuals and arid doxographies. This is also true of Valentinus and Basilides. It even seems to me that Hippolytus' thesis that Basilides was inspired by Aristotelian doctrine rests upon rather dubious arguments. It is true that this hypothesis, energetically defended by a highly suspect witness, has been accepted by several modern scholars and has led them to doubt the authenticity of the account transmitted by Hippolytus, our principal source for the Basilidian gnosis [6]. But on close inspection we perceive that this presentation of the matter is schematic, artificial, and inexact. If we disregard certain conceptions which were accepted in that period by the most divergent schools and which had long been current in certain semi-civilized circles, the doctrine of Basilides, as transmitted by Hippolytus, shows no influence of the esoteric writings of the great Stagirite.

Nor can we consider the Gnostics as direct disciples of Plato, even if they had read some of his better-known works. For, considered as a whole, the electic Platonism of the epoch, and particularly its conception of the spiritual world, was far removed from the original doctrine of Plato. The truth is that this late Platonism taught certain opinions which are not to be found in the books of the master. The most important of these are the following:

a) The ideas are God's ideas but they serve as patterns solely for the things of nature [7].

b) The spiritual world has been divided into two parts: on the one hand we have ideas residing as patterns in the mind of God; these are designated by the technical term "paradigmatic" ($\tau\grave{o}\ \pi\alpha\rho\alpha\delta\epsilon\iota\gamma\mu\alpha\tau\iota\kappa\acute{o}\nu$); and on the other hand we have the ideas which served as an instrument for the creation of the world; these are called "organic" ($\tau\grave{o}\ \acute{o}\rho\gamma\alpha\nu\iota\kappa\acute{o}\nu$); this conception is already found in the early works of Philo Judaeus of Alexandria [8].

---

[6] C. Schmidt, *Religion in Geschichte und Gegenwart*, I, 790.
[7] Willy Theiler, *Die Vorbereitung des Neuplatonismus* (Berlin, 1930), pp. 10, 15-19; Tertullian, *De anima*, xviii, 3 (Migne, *PL*, II, 678). It does not seem to have been observed thus far that this rather important modification of original Platonism is also found in Tertullian.
[8] Theiler, pp. 19 ff.

These Platonist concepts occur in all the texts of the Valentinian gnosis and are exceedingly important for their interpretation. Thus, for example, the relation between the Savior, who descends from the pleroma, and the Aeons becomes infinitely clearer if it is studied against the background of late Platonism: the Aeons are in certain respects ideas remaining in the consciousness of God (our sources tell us so quite categorically and no one has yet denied it); these ideas are the patterns for the things of nature; the demiurge (without knowing it) fashions the heavens after the ideal heavens, man after the archetypal man, and the earth after the ideal earth (Irenaeus, *Adversus haereses*, I, 5, 3). The influence of Platonism is evident [9]. And it is tempting to give the same explanation of the conception of the Savior, formed by the union of all the Aeons and sent down from the pleroma to show the ideas to Wisdom and induce her to create the visible world. Beneath its mythological appearance does not this division of the ideas reflect the Platonist distinction between the "paradigmatic" and the "organic" which we have just noted? Are not the Aeons contained in the Νοῦς the archetypal ideas, and does not the descending Savior represent in certain respects the instrumental ideas? It must indeed be admitted that the Valentinian notions, which at first sight seemed so complicated and confused, become quite simple and limpid when examined in the perspective of the Platonism of their time.

What is truly astonishing — and we frankly own that we did not expect this result from our researches — is that the same division of ideas recurs in the doctrine of Basilides as transmitted by Hippolytus. This is all the more surprising when we consider that the general view of things is quite different from that which we find in the documents of the Valentinian school. This would seem to exclude a mutual influence and suggest a common source.

Actually the two men lived at approximately the same time in the same city, Alexandria, where they received a Greek education; they must have been familiar with the same brand of Platonism, from which they both seem to have borrowed this conception of a division of ideas. To prove this thesis we shall have to outline the Basilidian conception of the world as we find it in the account of Hippolytus, *Elenchos*, VII, 20-27.

We know that according to Basilides the universal seed produced in the beginning by God contained a triple filiality which was in all things consubstantial with God. The first of these, as soon as it was produced, detached itself from the cosmic seed and rose up to God. Then the second was raised and placed below the first. It was only the third filiality, the spiritual man, who remained here below in the great mound of the universal seed.

---

[9] See Pseudo-Justin, *Cohortatio ad Graecos*, 30 (Migne, *PG*, VI, 295-98).

Basilides, then, conceived the spiritual world as a hierarchy, composed of a God, two filialities, and the human spirit.

Though his conception of the spiritual world is quite remarkable, his view of the external world is rather simplistic. The visible world includes a zone of pneuma, a zone of ether, and finally a zone of air, beneath which is the earth. The origin of these zones is described in mythological images. The second filiality, we are told, was raised up by the "intermediate pneuma" ($\mu\varepsilon\theta\acute{o}\rho\iota o\nu$ $\pi\nu\varepsilon\tilde{\upsilon}\mu\alpha$). But when these two reached the first filiality and God, the inter-

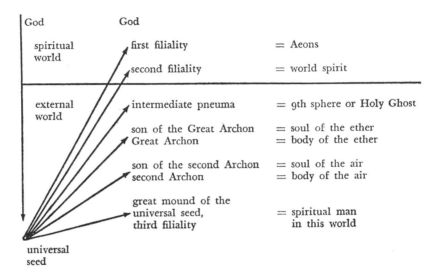

God	God	
spiritual world	first filiality	= Aeons
	second filiality	= world spirit
external world	intermediate pneuma	= 9th sphere or Holy Ghost
	son of the Great Archon	= soul of the ether
	Great Archon	= body of the ether
	son of the second Archon	= soul of the air
	second Archon	= body of the air
	great mound of the universal seed, third filiality	= spiritual man in this world
universal seed		

BASILIDES' WORLD CONCEPTION

mediate pneuma was compelled to remain behind, because it was not of the same substance and nature as the transcendent entities. That is why the intermediate pneuma is in the immediate vicinity, but not within the confines of this blessed zone; it is the firmament ($\sigma\tau\varepsilon\rho\acute{\varepsilon}\omega\mu\alpha$) between the visible world and the transcendent world and is situated beyond the sky ($\grave{\upsilon}\pi\varepsilon\rho\acute{\alpha}\nu\omega$ $\tauo\tilde{\upsilon}$ $o\grave{\upsilon}\rho\alpha\nuo\tilde{\upsilon}$).

It is clear that this demarcation line, this iron curtain, as it were, between the two worlds, designates the sphere outside the visible world. Like a true syncretist thinker, Basilides identified this entity with the Holy Ghost of the Christians. All this is comprehensible. But how shall we conceive of an "intermediate pneuma" which, though belonging to the perceptible world, is beyond the heavens? For by heavens the Gnostic seems to mean the Ogdoad, the heaven of the fixed stars, which is the dwelling of another entity and is below the demarcation line (Hippolytus, *Elenchos*, VII, 23, 7). There is, then, according to Basilides, still another region beyond the fixed stars. Greek astronomy knew the conception of a ninth sphere. We might then suppose that the intermediate pneuma, which is at the same time the Holy Ghost, was localized by Basilides in the ninth sphere, posited by the Greek astronomy of that time and adopted by Ptolemy the Alexandrian astronomer in his geocentric system. Be that as it may, the intermediate pneuma constitutes the highest part of the perceptible world.

After the ascent of the Holy Ghost, the Great Archon rises from the formless mound of the universal seed to the demarcation line. He then produces a son far wiser and better than himself, whom he places at his right hand. After this, inspired by his son, he forms the region of the ether (23).

It is evident that in certain respects this Archon is the Jewish God; the son whom he sets at his right hand is the pre-existent Messiah. But why is this son wiser and better than his father? Why is the father subordinated to his son? Hippolytus believed that he knew. This son, he said, "is the entelechy of an organic physical body, he is the soul acting upon the body .... Basilides conceived the relation between the Great Archon and his son as Aristotle before him conceived the relation between body and soul" (24, 1).

Hippolytus cannot be said to have found all this in his source. However, it is possible that the heretic conceived the relation between son and father as that between soul and body. For Hippolytus seems to be rendering the doctrine of Basilides and not his own invention when he describes the action of the Son on his Father in these words: "as the entelechy directs the body, so does the son, *according to Basilides*, direct the God who is more ineffable than all ineffable things. But all ethereal things as far as the moon are animated and directed by the entelechy of the Great Archon" (24, 2, 3).

It is possible that a philosophical conception is concealed beneath this mythologem. For we do in that period encounter the belief that according to Aristotle God was the soul and body of the ether.

Aristotle and his disciples, introducing a being analogous to a composite living creature, say that God is constituted by a soul and a body. They think that *his body* is the *ether* with the planets and fixed stars, all of which revolves; that his soul is the reason presiding over the movement of the body, being itself motionless and the cause of this movement [10].

It is not impossible that Basilides combined this philosophical conception, which he may have found in any doxography, with mythologems having nothing to

---

[10]   Athenagoras, *Supplicatio*, VI. French tr. by G. Bardy (Paris, 1943), p. 85.

do with Greek wisdom: for in his version the Ogdoad, the dwelling place of the Great Archon and the son who inspires him, includes the ethereal region of the fixed stars and planets. Nevertheless, the opinion of Hippolytus is erroneous. For the doctrine described in the *Supplicatio* of Athenagoras is not, as Hippolytus would have us believe, to be found in the preserved writings of Aristotle, but presumably goes back to the young Aristotle of the lost dialogues [11].

After the intermediate pneuma and the Great Archon of the ether another Archon rises from the great mound and also produces a son: this lower Archon reigns over the sublunar world: his domain is the air (24). It is not certain that this lower Archon should be identified with de devil.

If we disregard certain mythological amplifications and certain philosophical emendations, it would seem that fundamentally this conception of the external world is a variation on a well-known theme: the sensory world includes a pneumatic region, an ethereal region, and an aerial region which surround the earth; in this there is nothing astonishing. Moreover, the philosophers and syncretists of that period liked to describe how the elements, one after another, detached themselves from brute, chaotic matter and rose up to occupy the place befitting their greater or lesser subtlety. Accordingly, this conception of Basilides, which perhaps reveals a Stoic or Peripatetic influence, might be that of an eclectic Platonist. On the other hand, the Stoics and Peripatetics would never have recognized the existence of a spiritual world composed of God, two filialities, and man. It is not the Portico or the Academy which could have inspired this doctrine, for the simple reason that those schools did not know of a transcendent world. Moreover, though it is probable that Christianity suggested the term "filiality", since the pre-existent Christ is the son of God and the elect are the sons of God, it is impossible to see how this Christian conception could have led to the doubling of the transcendent filiality. Finally, the vulgar gnosis preceding Basilides knows of a pleroma populated by innumerable entities such as Aeons, Ogdoads, lights, angels, and powers, but not this relatively simple conception of a double, transcendent filiality.

What then can be the significance of the triple filiality? In the literature on Basilides, and even in the monograph of Hendrix [12], we search in vain for a serious interpretation of this mythologem. De Faye even goes so far as to say that it is "indubitably a most curious conception, but an absurd one even for a speculative thinker of that time". We shall see, however, that this conception

---

[11] Luigi Alfonsi, "Traces du jeune Aristote dans la *Cohortatio ad Gentiles*", *Vigiliae Christianae* (Amsterdam), II (1948), 80 ff.

[12] P. J. G. A. Hendrix, *De alexandrijnsche Haeresiarch Basilides* (Amsterdam, 1926).

cannot have been invented by Basilides because several texts of the imperial period show striking analogies to it. And what shall we say of Kennedy's theory of a Buddhist Basilides? In the triple filiality he finds the three *gunas*, i.e. *sattva* (the intellectual, light principle), *rajas* (the emotional principle), and *tamas* (the heavy, dark principle); his interpretation would place the second filiality in the region of the passions - *rajas*. But it is hardly sound methodology to elucidate an obscure conception by a very remote analogy, and we are not justified in ignoring the facts of the text even in order to obtain such alluring conclusions. And this is just what Kennedy does when he situates the second filiality in the region of the passions, when the texts place it in the transcendent world above the line of demarcation dividing it from the visible world.

Such adventurous and unsubtle interpretations cannot be sustained in the presence of the facts: the conception of a triple filiality is neither absurd nor exotic, but finds exact parallels in the texts of Hellenistic syncretism.

In this connection we must extend our researches to a passage in Arnobius which has hitherto escaped the attention of students of Basilides. It is true that editors of Arnobius have wished to correct the transmitted text. But it has long been recognized that the manuscript is excellent and requires no conjectures. On the subject of the human soul, the Christian rhetorician questions his adversaries: "Is this, then, the soul which you call learned, immortal, perfect divine, which after God who is the cause of things and after the twin Intellects occupies fourth place?" [13].

This passage presents a striking analogy with the conception of Basilides. The God who is the "cause of things" can be regarded as a parallel to the God whom Basilides names αἴτιος τῶν πάντων. The "learned, immortal, divine soul" is none other than the spiritual man (the third filiality): and the "twin intellects", *mentes geminae,* correspond to the two filialities situated between God and man. One question arises, however: in what period did the conception mentioned by Arnobius originate, and what is its significance? The adversaries of Arnobius seem to have been Gnostics of various schools and sects, who invoked the authority of Plato among others and lived in the third century A.D. [14]. It seems certain, however, that the doctrine of a double divine mind goes further back than Porphyry and even Plotinus, because it occurs in two documents which do not seem to have undergone the influence of Neoplatonism, namely the Hermetic book of *Asclepius* and the *Chaldaean Oracles.*

---

[13] Arnobius, II, 25: "Haecine est anima docta illa quam dicitis, immortalis perfecta divina, post deum principem rerum et post mentes geminas locum optinens quartum?".

[14] See A.-J. Festugière, "La Doctrine des *Viri novi* ... d'après Arnobe", *Memorial Lagrange,* ed. L. H. Vincent (Paris, 1940), pp. 97-132.

The *Asclepius* contains a passage whose meaning has been well brought out by Father Festugière's translation:

The total intellect (*omnis sensus*, ὁ πᾶς νοῦς) which resembles the godhead, is without motion of its own but moves in its stability: it is holy, incorruptible, eternal, and possessed of any superior attribute there may be, since it is the eternity of the supreme God, subsisting in absolute truth. It is infinitely filled with all sensible forms (*sensibilium*, or, better: νοητῶν = intelligible things); it is universal, coexistent, as it were, with God. The intellect of the world (*sensus mundanus*, ὁ ἐγκόσμιος νοῦς) is the receptacle of all sensible forms and particular orders. Finally, the human intellect depends on the retentive power proper to the memory, thanks to which it preserves the recollection of all its past experiences. The divine intellect does not descend beyond the human animal [15].

In this passage the author distinguishes four divine intellectual entities: the godhead, the total intellect, the intellect of the world, and the intellect of man. Clearly this presents a striking analogy to the passage in Arnobius quoted above. And it is only on the basis of the Hermetic work that we can understand the meaning of the *mentes geminae* of Arnobius. These are the introspective intuition of the godhead and the intellect of the world, which is directed largely toward externals. If our hypothesis that the *sensibilia* of which this passage speaks should be identified with the νοητά, or ideas, is sound, we may conclude that the conception is Platonic.

These two divine intellects, immediately followed by the soul, seem to occur also in the *Chaldaean Oracles,* which mention a Heavenly Father, a paternal intellect, and a second intellect. Kroll supposes God and the paternal intellect to be identical [16].

It would seem, however, that the excellent editor of the *Oracles* was too skeptical in this respect. For Pletho tells us categorically that the *Oracles* designate the paternal intellect as a second God (δεύτερος θεός) [17].

This explains the following verses (Kroll, p. 14):

δυὰς παρὰ τῷδε κάθηται·
ἀμφότερον γὰρ ἔχει, νῷ μὲν κατέχειν τὰ νοητά
αἴσθησιν δ' ἐπάγειν κόσμοις·

---

[15] *Asclepius,* 32. French tr. by Festugière in A. D. Nock and A.-J. Festugière, *Hermès Trismégiste* (Paris, 1945), II, 340. [Cf. W. Scott, ed., *Hermetica* (4 vols., Oxford, 1924-36), I, 355.]

[16] W. Kroll, "De Oraculis Chaldaicis", *Breslauer Philologische Abhandlungen,* VII (1894), 14.

[17] Quoted by W. Theiler, *Die Chaldäischen Orakel und die Hymnen des Synesius,* Schriften der Königsberger Gelehrten Gesellschaft, 18, 1 (Halle, 1942), p. 7.

(A dyad is seated before him;
for he has this double aspect: he contains the ideas
in his mind and brings perception to the worlds.)

Our surprise becomes still greater when we read (Kroll, p. 28):

μετὰ δὴ πατρίκας διανοίας
ψυχὴ ἐγὼ ναίω θερμῇ ψυχοῦσα τὰ πάντα.

(After the paternal intellects
I, the soul, remain, animating the universe with my warmth.)

We believe, then, that we are justified in saying that the *Chaldaean Oracles*, which seem to date from the second century A.D. and reveal a Platonist influence, presuppose a triad consisting of a supreme God and two intellects and followed by the soul [18]. We may presume the Gnostics of Arnobius to have held the same conceptions as we find in the *Asclepius*. All these passages contain indications that these two divine intellects signify on the one hand the introspective intuition of the godhead (or else the archetypes in the mind of God) and on the other hand the "extraverted" mind of God, turned principally toward the outward world. Basilides' doctrine of the triple filiality shows an unmistakable analogy to these speculations. Furthermore, the atmosphere of the Basilidian gnosis is much closer to Hermeticism and the Chaldaean system than to the pedantic and arid Platonism of the first centuries of the Roman empire. We might then be tempted to suppose that Basilides borrowed his conception from the syncretistic systems of Hellenistic gnosis. Alluring as it is, this hypothesis encounters an objection which is more than a matter of detail. For we do not know whether these Hellenistic systems, or at least the conception we have been discussing, existed at the time of Basilides. All the documents we have just quoted are of a later date. The most that can be said today is that the documents of the vulgar Egyptian gnosis, which have preserved a number of doctrines anterior to Basilides, do not mention any conception analogous to that of the triple filiality. Hence it is more prudent to assume that the pagan Gnostics and the Christian Gnostic drew on a common source. Seen in this perspective, the speculation on God's two intellects as well as the mythologem of the triple filiality would be merely an adaptation and mystical development of the Platonic doctrine which distinguished the archetypal (paradigmatic) ideas from the instrumental (organic) ideas. Since this doctrine was accepted by Philo of Alexandria and Valentinus of Alexandria, it seems quite possible that Basilides should also have adopted it.

---

[18] See E. R. Dodds, "Theurgy and its Relation to Neoplatonism", *Journal of Roman Studies* (London), XXXVII (1947), 55 ff.

But was Basilides a Platonist?

The fragments preserved by Clement as well as the account of Hippolytus show that Basilides was influenced by Platonism. True, the fundamental experience of gnosis in general and of the Basilidian gnosis in particular is far from being either Christian or Platonist; it is nonetheless true that Basilides expressed this experience in Platonic terms and more than once modified the conceptions he found in the Gnostic tradition in a manner consonant with his philosophical education. Platonist influence can be found both in the fragments and in the system.

A. D. Nock was therefore right in saying: "An explanation in terms of Platonism and independent thought fits the general accusation against Basilides and Valentinus, that they followed Greek philosophy rather than revealed truth" [19].

Consequently, the Platonist conception of a division of ideas can help us to explain the doctrine of the triple filiality in Basilides. Hippolytus' account declares: Basilides divides being ($\tau \grave{\alpha}$ $\emph{ὄντα}$) into two main, contiguous parts, one of which he calls the world ($\varkappa \acute{o} \sigma \mu o \varsigma$) and the other the transcendent world ($\tau \grave{\alpha}$ $\emph{ὑπερκόσμια}$; *Elenchos*, 23, 2). It is quite possible that these terms refer to the sensory world and the spiritual world of the Platonists. In this same document there is an allusion to a time before the creation of the world, when there were as yet neither sensory nor spiritual things ($\delta \iota$' $\emph{αἰσθήσεως λαμβανομένων ἢ νοητῶν πραγμάτων}$; 21, 1); this seems to indicate that after the creation there were $\emph{νοητά}$, ideas, as well as perceptible things. Finally, we read — and this is especially significant — of the "ideas of the filiality ($\tau \grave{\alpha}$ $\emph{νοήματα τῆς υἱότητος}$), which are communicated to us in the visible world (25, 7). These passages permit us to conclude that the two filialities must be conceived as $\tau \grave{o}$ $\emph{παραδειγματικόν}$, the introspective intuition of God and the seat of the ideas, and $\tau \acute{o}$ $\emph{ὀργανικόν}$, the "extraverted" mind of God, in the sense employed by the syncretist authors we have quoted.

True, these "ideas of the filiality" in Basilides are not exactly Platonic ideas. This we must conclude from a fragment transmitted to us by Clement. This fragment speaks of two "hypostases", Justice and her daughter Peace, which remained in the Ogdoad. The context of this fragment in Clement *(Strom., IV,*

---

[19] Arthur Darby Nock in *Classical Philology* (Chicago), XXXVII: 4 (1942), 450, n. 12 (review of Konstantin Vilhelmson, *Laktanz und die Kosmogonie des spätantiken Synkretismus*, Tartu, 1940).

25, 162) suggests that this Ogdoad is not situated in the sensible world but is the superior Ogdoad [20].

If this is true, the brief fragment on "Justice and her daughter Peace" is extremely important. For it then shows that Basilides conceived these "ideas of the filiality", these archetypes remaining in the mind of God, not as ulterior objects of rational thought, but as Aeons, powers, and hypostatic personifications revealed by initiation.

3. CHRISTIAN INFLUENCE

Platonist philosophy provides the frame of Basilides' thought. But the movement of his thinking is not in the least Platonist. To appreciate this contrast we need only compare those sublime pages of the *Phaedrus* or *Symposium* in which the noble Athenian describes with inspired enthusiasm the ascent of the human soul, raised by the love of beauty to the spiritual heights where it rediscovers its home and contemplates the pure ideas of eternal being. This theme was developed by the Platonists of the second century (Maximus of Tyre 143, 11 Th. 57). We may reasonably presume that Basilides was familiar with it. Yet, what a contrast! For Basilides, it is not man who rises up to seek God, but God who descends to reveal himself to man. Revelation moves downward from on high, ἄνωθεν κάτω, to use his own words. For him this descent was not a metaphor without content, as it is for a modern man who can no longer accept the geocentric conception of the world. Basilides visualizes this descent in a striking image: the strange new light spreads through the dark, ignorant worlds, illumining all the terrifying demoniacal powers which people this universe, and finally descends on Jesus at the moment of his baptism. The conception concealed beneath mythological details is a simple one: only Christ reveals the unknown God. Yet this is the fundamental experience of the great heretics of the second century. And this is not the subjective impression of a modern student: it is the explicit testimony of the sources themselves. The conception is found in Marcion as well as in Basilides and Valentinus. Their sole preoccupation was salvation, their only hope Christ. Despite differences in detail, all three believed, each in his own way, that man by himself cannot know God (and it should be stressed that, according to Basilides and Valentinus, even the spiritual man could not know God before the coming of Christ), that Christ was alone in revealing him, that man receives the gnosis of an unknown, transcendent God through Christ, i.e. indirectly.

---

[20] Actually, Basilides did not deprecate justice as did Marcion and Valentinus: according to him the supreme God is just (*Strom.*, IV, 11, 83: δίκαιον δὲ τὸν θεόν).

Each of these heretics expressed these conceptions in his own way. Basilides expresses them as follows: Before the coming of Christ everything was veiled in a mysterious silence. This was the mystery which, in the words of the apostle, was not made known to the sons of men in other ages (*Elenchos*, VII, 25, 3). For "God is so great and such is His nature, that creation cannot express Him or conceive Him in thought" (22, 1). Consequently "the third filiality, spiritual man, is abandoned like an abortion in the formlessness [of our sublunar world]. The mystery which in other ages was not made known to the sons of men must be revealed to him" in accordance with the words of Scripture: "How that by revelation he made known to me the mystery" and "I heard unspeakable words which it is not lawful for a man to utter".

This ardent aspiration, this unquenched thirst of the spiritual man assumes cosmic dimensions: the entire universe suffers with him, suffers because of him. And here Basilides invokes St. Paul, alluding to the profound words of the Epistle to the Romans: "When it was needful that we be manifested, we the children of God, for whom the creature sighed in the pangs of childbirth while awaiting revelation, then it was that the Gospel came into the world and entered into every principle and every power and every thing that can be named" (25, 5).

"This light of the Gospel descended upon Jesus, son of Mary, and he was illumined, set aflame by the light that cast its brightness upon him" (26, 8). This Jesus, who must be distinguished from the divine Christ which descended on him, was the spiritual man *par excellence*. "He is the inner spiritual man in the natural man ($\psi\upsilon\chi\iota\kappa\acute{o}\varsigma$) according to their conception", who was predestined from all eternity ($\pi\rho o\lambda\epsilon\lambda o\gamma\iota\sigma\mu\acute{e}\nu o\varsigma$) to receive the Christ (27, 6, 7).

This union of the Christ and Jesus determines the course of history. For now the spiritual power of the sons of God is confirmed according to their nature by this light which has projected its brightness downward from on high (26, 10); the third filiality has been purified by the Christ (27, 11).

For Basilides, as for the other heretics, the coming of Christ was the decisive moment in human history, the moment in which eternity traverses and intersects all the "*Seinsschichten die sich überlagern*". And this "revelation of transcendent things" is the goal of all human history.

Less radical than the other heretics, Basilides could not accept the notion that history is meaningless and has fallen into absurdity. To him God is the absolute and transcendent cause of all things ($\alpha\H{\iota}\tau\iota o\varsigma$ $\pi\acute{a}\nu\tau\omega\nu$; 27, 7); his plan is carried out in the course of time. Before the beginning of the cosmic process, God established in his mind which things should happen when and how (24, 5). It may seem, to be sure, that a great Archon, a god of this world, has put himself forward to dominate the visible world: all this is necessary, everything in its time, nothing is unforeseen: "for all these events were predestined by God", the transcendent, unknown God who acts behind the scenes and carries out his plan conceived in the beginning. God's plan, however, the goal of history, is the salvation of man, who must be manifested and then restored to the spiritual world when the time has come (25, 1). And the salvation of man does not signify primarily the personal salvation of any individual, but rather the deliverance of the entire human race. It might be argued that according to Basilides not all the living creatures called men are saved. But these men without spirit, who feel so thoroughly at home in the immanent world and know no transcendental nostalgia — are they men in the true sense of the word? Basilides categorically denies this: "We are men", he declares, "all the others are pigs and dogs" [21]. Man is purely and simply the spiritual man. In this perspective, the coming of Christ, prepared for by all preceding history according to God's plan, is the spiritual freedom of all humanity.

If the descent of Christ is the center of history, toward which the preceding development moves and which determines the subsequent development, history must have a beginning and an end. Thus the strictly Christocentric conception implies a true philosophy of history which is quite remarkable and in certain respects suggests that of Hegel. Basilides applies the notion of evolution to the history of the universe and finds instructive comparisons to elucidate his thought. Let us, he tells us, observe the development of a human being: the teeth appear only several months after birth; the spermatic vein does not function before the fourteenth year [22]; the intelligence develops only after a certain number of years — in short the growing man gradually becomes what he was not before: however, all his faculties were virtually present in the newborn babe. The same is true of the universe: "All the things which we can enumerate and all the things of which we can say nothing because they have not yet been discovered, which were to belong to the future universe that has been developed progressively, all in its appointed time, by God ... were heaped up within the original germ" (*Elenchos*, VII, 22, 1). This germ is a potential world, comparable to a mustard seed which contains a whole plant, a world in which everything was present in an undifferentiated state.

In the beginning, then, there was confusion. From this great mound issued one after another the personifications representing the strata of the universe: the ideal world, the world spirit, the pneuma, the ether, the air. The invisible and external world were formed in successive stages. Everything is perfect: nothing

---

[21] Epiphanius, *Panarion*, 24, 5, 2; ed. Holl, *GCS*, I, 262.

[22] This is my interpretation of the enigmatic words on the child's $\pi\alpha\tau\rho\iota\kappa\dot{\eta}$ $o\dot{\nu}\sigma\dot{\iota}\alpha$.

is missing. However, "the third filiality still remains in the great mound of the universal seed". This is man, who is in this world but does not belong to it; from the very beginning he is consubstantial with God, because he is spiritual, but he does not yet know this. The aim of history, the *raison d'être* of the universe, is to "manifest man and to restore him" to his spiritual home (25, 1). True, history requires centuries to arrive at this aim: for hundreds of years the Archons reign, who are quite different from God and do not know God. But without knowing it they carry out the pre-established plan of God, who directs the historical process.

If it is permissible to transpose the mythological terminology of Basilides into better-known categories and to interpret so obscure a text with a certain boldness, we may divide the history of the world into three periods: that of paganism, dominated by the devil; that of Judaism, in which Yahweh ruled; and that of Christianity, inaugurated by Jesus. Thus the history of religions, represented by the gods men worship, culminates in Christianity, which is the absolute religion. The Gospel, which is nothing other than the revelation of the transcendent world, has spoken through the mouth of Jesus. This was the decisive moment in the history of the universe: for it was then that, thanks to revelation, man for the first time became aware of his kinship with God. And this determines the whole subsequent course of history: like Jesus, the elect among men can remember their divine essence and return to God. Through Christ, the spiritual man is freed from matter and purified, the spiritual element is released from the great and formless mound of the immanent world, the great differentiation begins. And that is why Jesus is called "the initiator of the differentiation of confounded things".

Ever since the decisive moment of Christ's coming, the last period of history has been in progress: the spirit can take form, now that "its total power has been confirmed according to its nature by the light that has descended from on high". The spirit returns to its proper dwelling place. This process will be continued until the filiality has fully purified itself and has crossed the limit of the spiritual world. That is the moment of restitution, when everything finds the place assigned to it by nature. Then there will be no more nostalgia, no more tears, but absolute repose, the consummation of the historic process. "And such will be the restitution of all the things that were heaped up in the germ of the universe at the beginning; at the proper moment they will be restored to the place befitting them".

This conception of history is both simple and grandiose: history has a beginning, confusion or σύγχυσις; a center, the φυλοκρίνησις, or election of the chosen people; and an end, the restitution or ἀποκατάστασις. "Their whole doctrine is summed up in the confusion of the universal germ, and in the selection and restitution to their proper place of the things that are now confounded" (27, 11). This historic process is determined by God's pre-established plan, which is progressively carried out in the course of the centuries. This plan, it goes without saying, does not change in accordance with the arbitrary will of this God. It is an unalterable law, fixed and eternal, given in the beginning of the world as an immanent force which directs evolution. "Do not seek to know whence have issued the things of which I say that they appeared later, after the planting of the cosmic seed. For [this cosmic germ] contains piled up within it all the [particular] seeds, not yet existing and destined to come into being by a God who is not" (22, 6). This doctrine, so original and characteristic, is found in a fragment preserved by Clement (irrefutably proving the authenticity of Hippolytus' account): "Providence was inseminated in the substances by the God of man's salvation at the very moment of their genesis [in the universal germ] by the God of all things" (*Strom.*, IV, 13, 90). The purpose of this plan is man's salvation; history is the history of salvation which is accomplished when Jesus teaches men that God is their Father. Now man can be free; the elect can purify themselves and leave the world to regain the spiritual dwelling places to which they were destined.

It is clear that this conception of history cannot be of Greek origin, for the simple reason that the Greeks conceived no philosophy of history, excepting for Poseidonius, whose idea of it was very different. True, Basilides expresses himself as a learned man and sometimes uses philosophical terms, but the meaning he ascribes to them is new and original. In this connection it is interesting to consider one of the terms he borrowed: the "restitution of all things" ($\dot{\alpha}\pi o\varkappa\alpha\tau\dot{\alpha}\sigma\tau\alpha\sigma\iota\varsigma\ \tau\tilde{\omega}\nu\ \pi\dot{\alpha}\nu\tau\omega\nu$) was of Stoic origin. But how changed is its content! For the Stoics, the apocatastasis was the return of things to their primitive state in the course of the successive and aimless cycles of the cosmic process. For Basilides, on the other hand, the apocatastasis is the realization of the aim of history; in it things regain the place which was appointed to them by nature but which they never occupied before. The same term designates two very different conceptions.

The same is true of the term "original confusion". Basilides seems to have found this expression in the work (a Gnostic work, in our opinion) which he quotes in his commentary on the Gospel. It is interesting to note how he modified this conception. In the Gnostic work the confusion of things, the chaotic state at the beginning of the world, was the consequence of a fall. The Virgin of Light fell into pre-existing matter. Basilides does not accept these ideas. These conceptions, dear to gnosis, are not adopted in his system and are not to be found in his fragments: "Basilides absolutely avoids, and fears to speak of, an *emanation*. For how would it be possible for God to require an emanation or a pre-existing matter to make the cosmos, in the manner of a spider spinning its web or of a mortal man taking copper or wood or any other material to fashion it" (22, 2). Even the primitive germ from which the universe issued is not an emanation; indeed, it is nothing other than the creative word God uttered when he said: "Let there be light". There is no emanation and no pre-existing matter: "He spoke and it came to pass". We find — and this is absolutely startling — that Basilides attempted to introduce into gnosis the conception of a *creatio ex nihilo*, and that for this reason he eliminated the mythologems of a fallen Wisdom or of an archetypal man.

It seems that it was also Christian influence which gave the system of Basilides an eschatological tendency. The early Christians awaited the end of the world and believed that it would come as soon as the number of the elect was complete. These believers had been elected before the creation of the world, and all history, the entire universe in fact, awaited their deliverance. Basilides' account of the genesis of the world is not very unusual. Quite a number of philosophical and syncretist documents of the time offer similar cosmogonies. What is truly extraordinary is his idea of historical evolution, culminating in the coming of Christ and the end of the historic process. I shall not go so far to say that this idea is to be found in the Bible, but it is certain that in reading the Bible the ancient Christians formed the idea of a historic evolution, beginning with creation, having as its center the coming of Christ, and culminating in the liberation of the elect from the *massa perditionis*. I think it safe to say that Basilides' conception is a development, though a very free one, of these Christian conceptions. It is certain that the clearly predestinationist theology of St. Paul made a profound impression on him: the idea of election, fundamental in Basilides as well as Valentinus, was borrowed from the apostle, though the Gnostic assuredly distorted it [23].

All in all, the Gnostic election is, as it were, a *mystification* of the Biblical conception. It remains none the less true that the mere adoption of this doctrine shows the enormous influence of Christianity on Basilides [24].

---

[23] When the apostle speaks of the chosen people, he has in mind the historic people of Israel, of which the Christian Church is a continuation, while Basilides applies this term to the people, transcendent, i.e. nonhistorical, spirit. Furthermore, St. Paul would never have identified God's predestination with astrological fatality in the manner of the Gnostic master.

[24] It should not be forgotten that this man wished most of all to be a Christian. He wrote innumerable commentaries on the Bible. It is even probable that he was a member of the Church: we have no indication that he was excommunicated. Egyptian Christianity seems to have been rather peculiar and extremely tolerant. It was in Rome that bold, unsubmissive thinkers were excommunicated.

Let us add that this conception of history cannot have been borrowed from Gnosticism. For gnosis is essentially a revolt against time; it aspires to an eternity which negates and annuls

This Christian influence is not a matter of detail, but gives an eschatological perspective to the entire system. If Basilides saw the history of the world from an evolutionist point of view, it is because the historical process is directed toward an end. "All things below strive upward".

True, this eschatology is different from that of primitive Christianity, which liked to paint the end of the world in the most garish colors. For Basilides the end of the historic process is the end of the impulse which animates the universe: everything is in its place, imbalance has been done away with, disorder has ceased. The regions of being succeed one another in perfect harmony. The spirit has arrived at its end. "When the entire filiality has come together and risen beyond the limit, then the world will find mercy. For up until now it sighs and suffers and awaits the manifestation of the sons of God, in order that all men belonging to the filiality may rise from this world. When that occurs, God will bring *the great ignorance* over the whole world in order that all things may remain in their place and nothing may desire anything contrary to its nature" (*Elenchos*, VII, 27, 3). These are words of infinite melancholy; imagine, if you will, this great merciful oblivion descending upon the earth and covering all things like snow.

And those who have remained here below must not attempt to pass the limit imposed on them. They cannot attain to the things of the spirit. The psychic man does not accept the things of the spirit. A time will come when no knowledge of the spiritual world will be left in this world. No one will know that there is a beyond; all men will content themselves with the given world. Happily so, for if they aspired to the impossible they would be as ridiculous as a fish wishing to graze on the mountainside along with the sheep. "For all the things that remain in their place are incorruptible, but they can perish when they seek to surpass the natural order".

Thus the great ignorance will spread through the universe and its being. There will be no more pain or suffering; there will be no more desire, but neither will there be any spirit. It would be hard to say which prophecy is more frightening and more timely: the destruction of the universe announced by primitive Christianity, or the heretic's vision of a world in eternal repose, without nostalgia.

4. THE INSPIRATION OF THE SYSTEM: THE GNOSTIC EXPERIENCE

We have attempted to show that the Basilidian conception of the world, hidden

---

the flow of time. *Time must have a stop*. If a Gnostic recognizes that historical evolution is necessary for salvation, he does so in spite of himself, because Christianity has opened his eyes to this truth.

beneath its Christian aspect and very personal terminology, is essentially Platonist: the framework is Greek. The central place occupied by Christ in the system, the ideas of predestination and election, the conceptions of a *creatio ex nihilo*, of cosmic salvation, eschatology, and evolution reveal the influence of the New Testament and particularly of St. Paul: the movement of thought is Christian. These analyses may help us to understand the mythologems of Basilides. But when we read and reread the account of Hippolytus and find ourselves still baffled by its rich, strange content, we cannot help feeling that our investigations, whose findings, it must be owned, remain more or less uncertain, have not led us to the true essence of the doctrine. These bold, profound speculations, these furtive flights of the imagination, this remarkable combination of the most abstract thought with an authentic mythology cannot be explained on the basis of Christianity alone. We must go farther and penetrate to the true core of the theory: the Gnostic experience which animates the whole and gives it its characteristic imprint.

It seems to me that for Basilides the world and history were merely symbols referring to an inner process. I am well aware that in putting forward this point of view a writer must exercise the greatest circumspection to avoid being confused with those simpletons who seek to explain the phenomena of religion without recognizing the autonomy of religious experience.

For this reason I shall call upon a witness who is above all suspicion, Father J. Daniélou, a subtle critic, who remarks in connection with the mysticism of St. Gregory of Nyssa:

All cosmological expressions are allegorical in Gregory. They are the symbols of the stages in an inner ascent that is profoundly real, that leads the soul through distinct, objective worlds which however cannot be localized in space. In this sense we have in Gregory the same interiorization of the concept of the soul's return through the cosmic spheres as in Plotinus or Augustine [25].

What is highly remarkable is that St. Augustine was perfectly well aware that this return of the soul to God is not a voyage through the spheres of the external world. This is revealed by the words with which he described the experience he had in common with Monica, his mother, at Ostia:

We, raising ourselves with a more glowing affection toward the "self-same", did by degrees pass through all things bodily, even the heaven whence sun and moon and stars shine upon the earth; yea, we were soaring higher yet, by inward musing, and discourse, and admiring of Thy works; and we came to our own minds, and went beyond them, that we might arrive at that region of never-failing plenty, where Thou feedest Israel for ever ...[26].

---

[25] Jean Daniélou, *Platonisme et théologie mystique* (Paris, 1944), p. 157.
[26] *Confessions*, IX, 25; tr. William Benham (New York, 1909).

I own that I am struck by the great profundity of these words: "et ad hoc *ascendebamus* interius cogitando et loquendo et mirando opera tua et *venimus in mentes nostras et transcendimus eas*".

But what Daniélou says is true also of the Gnostics. The center of their doctrine is man with his anxieties, his wretchedness, his transports, and his joy. The Valentinian myth, as I have said before, merely states in images and symbols the encounter between man and Christ. Father Sagnard has remarked in speaking of Valentinianism: "The point of departure is always *man*: it is of man that we must think unremittingly. The center of gravity of this system is *our salvation*" [27].

But the mythologems of Basilides also reflect the Gnostic's states of mind rather than objective contemplations [28]. Accordingly, we shall venture to

---

[27] F. M. M. Sagnard, *La Gnose valentinienne et le témoignage de St. Irénée* (Paris, 1947), p. 591.

[28] This is clearly brought out by a passage on the Great Archon: This Archon, the God of the world, persisted, like a true Gnostic demiurge, in believing that he was the sole existing God in this world; he knew nothing of the spiritual things above him. We have seen that this Great Archon represented the ether and that he was identified with the Jewish God. However, the following words show that he had still another aspect which might well have been the most important of all. When the Gospel descended into the world,

"the Archon understood that he was not the God of all things but that he had been engendered and had above him the treasure set in place by the nonexistent "God" who is ineffable and unnamable, and by the filiality. And he repented and was afraid, understanding in what ignorance he had been: and therefore it is written: "The beginning of wisdom is the fear of the Lord"; for he began to be wise when he was catechized by the Christ (the Messiah) who was seated beside him, when he learned who was the nonexistent "God", who the filiality, who the Holy Ghost, and what had been the disposition of the universe to which these things will be restored. This is wisdom spoken in a mystery, of which the Bible says, "not in words taught by human wisdom but in 'words' taught by the spirit". When the Archon had been catechized and instructed, and when he had grown afraid, he confessed the sin he had committed in glorifying himself" (*Elenchos*, 26, 1, 2).

This passage, absurd from the philosophical point of view and blasphemous from a Christian point of view, reveals the heart of Basilides' thinking. The Gnostic would never have opposed the human wisdom of the Archon to the spiritual wisdom of the Gospel if this Archon had not been the symbol of man, that is to say, of that short-sighted man who contents himself with the visible world. Light and gnosis are revealed to him. A student of mysticism might suppose that Basilides is here alluding to illumination as an indispensable phase in mystical life. Though I have no wish to oppose this hypothesis, I believe we can go into greater detail. The light that is diffused through the world is the Gospel, the gnosis of transcendent things which illumines the man Jesus at the time of his baptism in the Jordan. What relation is there between this light and baptism? An old interpolation in the Gospel's account of the baptism declares: "Et cum baptizaretur, lumen ingens circumfulsit de aqua, ita ut timerent omnes qui advenerunt" (When he was baptized, a vast light arose from the water and shone round him). But still more important for our subject is the circumstance that the baptism of the faithful in the Christian Church was called φωτισμός, illumination. This ceremony was preceded by the confession of sins, instruction in the form of catechism, and the *traditio symboli*, the communic-

reconstruct, after the account of Hippolytus, the various stages of mystical life as Basilides saw it: the origin in ignorance, the illumination which marks the beginning of the ascension, and the final return to God.

The Origin in Ignorance

The spiritual man's life begins in ignorance and despair. It is in himself that the Gnostic finds this confusion, this disorder, this primitive chaos. The human spirit is not pure and simple but weighed down by passions, possessed by demons, obsessed by evil. Why? Because man is in this world but does not belong to it. This is the fundamental experience of the Gnostic, who knows that he is an alien in this world and that the world is alien to him; who cannot content himself with the immanent world, because he feels at the very bottom of his being a yearning for eternity. "The elect are strangers in this world, because they are transcendent by nature" (*Strom.*, IV, 26). Thus there is a kind of original guilt (*Urschuld*), which is the immediate consequence of being in the world. "Anguish and misery accompany existence as rust covers iron" (*Strom.*, IV, 12).

This human experience of being a stranger in the world is readily expressed in Platonist conceptions. Confusion and disorder, according to Basilides, have enabled the passions, which in essence are spirits (demons), to fasten on to the rational soul. The passions are "appendages" (ἀπαρτήματα). Later, probably in the course of successive reincarnations, other components of the human beast were added: the natures of the wolf, the monkey, the lion, and the ram. Diverse reincarnations have left the characteristics of animals in the lower strata of the soul; they appear to the soul and inspire it with bestial desires (*Strom.*, II, 20, 112).

Clement of Alexandria ridicules this conception, declaring that this Basilidian man, who takes a horde of diverse demons into his body, rather resembles the famous Trojan Horse. But does not this charming pleasantry of a learned, well-balanced man conceal an inability to sound the depths of man's miserable condition? The Gospel says that the name of the demons is Legion, and the

---

ation of the rule of the faith. A passage from the *Excerpts from Theodotus* tells us that the Gnostic catechism dealt with important questions of esoteric gnosis: "But it is not only the washing that is liberating but the knowledge of who we were and what we have become, where we were or where we were placed, whither we hasten, from what we are redeemed, what birth is and what rebirth" (*Excerpta ex Theodoto*, 78; ed. and tr. R. P. Casey, 1934, pp. 88-89).
It is plain that the passage on the catechizing of the Archon reflects the impression made on the neophyte by the Gnostic baptism. Basilides has projected this inner experience into space and time. Such details give us an indication of how we should interpret the Gnostic myths, which are above all human documents.

heretic would seem to have understood this better than certain lovers of gilded mediocrity.

Thus it should not surprise us that Basilides prized the Christian doctrine of original sin. He echoes the words of Scripture: "No one is pure of taint". Even if a man has not committed a sin, he remains inclined toward sin, because the sins exist in him virtually. Such a man resembles a child who has not yet found occasion to sin but carries within him the disposition to sin [29]. "Thus the perfect man, who has never sinned in effect, still carries within him the disposition to sin, but he has not yet found the material to sin upon: it is for this reason alone that he has not committed sin. Hence it is not permissible to call him impeccable" (*Strom.*, IV, 82).

No doubt the Gnostic conception of man's alien condition in this world, the Platonist conception of the passions as appendages to the rational soul, and the Christian doctrine of original sin are confounded in Basilides. Actually, they resemble one another considerably, and we must take care not to place the accent on their divergences by an excess of intellectualism. Beyond any doubt, the very Gnostic antithesis between spirit and soul lies at the base of all these speculations. The transcendent pneuma is attached to an immanent psyche; there is a ψυχὴ προσφύης and an ἀντίμιμον πνεῦμα.

This antithesis was not invented by Basilides: it is characteristic of all gnosis and cannot be mechanically identified with the banal dualism of good and evil, or of spirit and matter.

The pneuma feels nostalgia for the transcendent world; the psyche remains by nature in this world (Hippolytus, *Elenchos*, VII, 27, 6).

> Two souls, alas, are housed within my breast,
> And each will wrestle for the mastery there,
> The one has passion's craving crude for love,
> And hugs a world where sweet the senses rage;
> The other longs for pastures fair above,
> Leaving the murk for lofty heritage [30].

Consequently, the aim of the mystical life can be none other than that of the historic process: purification, catharsis. The third filiality which has remained in the great mound of this world, requires purification (ἀποκαθάρσεως δεόμενον; 22, 7).

But why does the spirit find itself in these tragic circumstances? Why is the spirit attached to this soul? Not because it was exiled from the heavens, as

---

[29] We see, then, that Basilides, like St. Augustine and the psychologists of our time, did not look upon the child as innocent.

[30] Goethe, *Faust, Part One*, tr. Philip Wayne (Harmondsworth and Baltimore, 1960), p. 67.

Plato believed: indeed, Basilides does not mention any fall into matter. Nor are these passions which darken the spirit a consequence of the first man's sin. In this Basilides differs from Tertullian. The essential difference between their two conceptions is that according to Tertullian the union of a divine soul with another nature results from a moral transgression on the part of the first man. Basilides makes no mention of this conception. True, men expiate the crimes they have committed in their earlier existences; but from the very beginning the spirit is bound to the passions. Why then was man placed in the world, to which he does not belong, if he did not fall into matter and did not commit this original sin?

Basilides reflected on this central problem. He declares that "the filiality is abandoned in formlessness in order that it may perfect ($εὐεργετεῖν$) the souls and be perfected itself" (26, 9). In short, the task of the spirit is to work upon the soul: "and the sons of God", he says, "are ourselves, the spiritual men, who have been abandoned here that they may order, form, correct and perfect the souls which have a natural tendency to remain in this region of the world" (25, 2).

But how does the spirit, or, as it is called, "the internal man in his psychic envelopment" (27, 6), profit from its association with the soul? It is intimated that the spirit needs the soul (27, 6 and 22, 11): just as a bird cannot rise without wings, so does the spirit ascend, thanks to the soul. In less figurative language, this means that the spiritual ascent to God is not possible unless the soul frees itself from matter by submitting to an ascetic regime and abstaining from marriage [31].

Illumination

This spiritual life is, of course, unknown before the coming of Christ. Man is in a state of unconsciousness and his spirit still slumbers; it is an abortion ($ἔκτρωμα$) without form; the phantom self obscures the true self; man is already the son of God, but he does not yet know it. That is why the universe groans and suffers, awaiting the deliverance of the sons of God. But when Christ enters into the existence of the elect he reveals to them their real self and

---

[31] The libertinism of which Irenaeus accuses the Basilidians is unknown to Basilides. He advises abstention from the marriage tie not because it is bad but because of the numerous cares it involves. And his son Isidore declares: "Beware of a passionate woman". This accent on $ἐγκράτεια$ does not suggest a pedantic, pitiless moralism. "But a man is young or poor or sensual and he does not wish to marry in accordance with reason. He does not leave his brothers. Let him say to himself: 'I have entered into the sanctuary; nothing can happen to me'" (*Strom.* III, 1, 2). Nevertheless, the mores of the Basilidians were strict and austere.

makes them aware of their consubstantiality with God. This event, as we might suppose, takes place at the moment of baptism. It is then that "the filiality which is abandoned in formlessness to perfect the souls and be made perfect is formed; it follows Jesus and rises up and is purified and subtilized to the point where it can rise by itself: for it has confirmed all its power in accordance with nature by virtue of the light which casts its beams downward from on high". The initiation of the elect is only the beginning of this process; the selection of the spiritual people begins with the coming of Christ. Illumination is the first stage in the mystical ascension. At this moment Christ reveals the gnosis of transcendent things. And the initiate discovers that he is sensible to the grandeur of the unprecedented words which are addressed to him and which respond to his most profound aspirations. For "it is by an essential disposition (φύσει) that we know God" (*Strom.*, V, 1, 3): the faith of the elect finds insights through a spiritual intuition (καταλήψει νοητικῇ; *Strom.*, II, 3, 10).

From the moment of his initiation man knows that he is "believing and elect by virtue of his essential disposition"; he seeks to overcome the passions which trouble the purity of his spirit and to expiate the faults he has committed. In this connection Basilides is particularly severe: "Not all sins can be pardoned, but only those that have been committed involuntarily and from ignorance" (*Strom.*, IV, 24, 135). But God's goodness has given the elect the mean of expiating this original sin, of purifying themselves from their hereditary guilt. God has given man the grace of suffering.

Basilides' strange speculations on human suffering have their origin in the problem which martyrdom presented to Christians. The Christian martyrs were condemned by Roman judges for merely confessing to the name of Christians. It is true that in the popular faith these martyrs rose immediately to heaven, while the other dead had to await the Last Judgment. Nevertheless, the problem of the martyr was vexatious: did God permit innocent men to be tortured? To this Basilides could not assent: "I shall say anything rather than admit the malice of providence". There are no innocent men. All have sinned even if no one knew it. Accordingly, martyrdom is a grace, a good (ἀγαθόν), granted by the goodness of God who directs the historical process (τοῦ περιά_γοντος), who enables the elect to expiate their crimes and rise to their celestial dwelling place.

I maintain that all those who become victims of persecution are led to this good by the goodness of Him who directs the world, because, though no one is aware of it, they have sinned through other transgressions; they are accused of offenses other than those which they have committed in reality, in order that they may not suffer for confessed crimes or be covered with opprobrium for such offenses as adultery and murder, but for the sole fact that they are

Christians, which so comforts them that they do not believe that they are suffering at all (*Strom.*, IV, 81, 1).

The same is stated in similar terms in another fragment: "The soul, having sinned in another, previous existence, suffers punishment here below; the elect soul is privileged by martyrdom, while the other is purified by his own punishment" (*Strom.*, IV, 12, 83). This process is called an "economy of catharsis". Through martyrdom the elect soul is totally purified of its sins [32].

Not only martyrdom, but suffering in general is a grace: "If the child, not having previously sinned or having effectively sinned, but having sin within him, is subjected to pain, he benefits, drawing profit from his numerous sufferings" (IV, 82).

Here we begin to see how the elect benefits by his sojourn in the world. Suffering is a good because it purifies the spirit, liberates the soul from matter, and accelerates the rise of inner man: suffering leads man to God.

The Final Return

The documents tell us that the life of the initiate is characterized by severe asceticism and acceptance of suffering. But when the spirit has been freed from matter by asceticism and suffering, it will rise upward. It will leave behind it the soul that has enveloped it and traverse the "real but interior spheres", it will traverse the Limit that separates the visible world from the spiritual world and will arrive at the summit of happiness, because it will be close to God. The mystic ascent, which is at the same time the most radical internalization, has reached its end. The spirit is close to God.

Though this motif is discernible in the account of Hippolytus, it might pass unnoticed if it were not confirmed by a passage in Clement — a passage of paramount importance which has scarcely been mentioned in studies on Basilides.

For if a man knows God by essential disposition ($\phi \acute{u} \sigma \epsilon \iota$), as is believed by Basilides, who regards the faith of the elect as an "intuition" ($\nu \acute{o} \eta \sigma \iota \varsigma$) as well as a "royal dignity", a "beautiful creature", and an "essence worthy of being with its creator", then he will call faith an "essence", but not a freedom, he

---

[32] On the one hand, this reflects the Christian conception according to which the martyr rises immediately to God. But, on the other hand, we are given to understand that martyrdom is a good, because it expiates transgressions and purifies the soul. This is almost word for word what Basilides may have found in a Platonist doxography: "For to suffer a punishment is not an evil but a good ($\mathring{\alpha} \gamma \alpha \theta \acute{o} \nu$) because it will be a purification from crimes committed" (Hippolytus, *Elenchos*, I, 19, 22: τὸ γὰρ κόλασιν ὑποσχεῖν οὐ κακὸν εἶναι ἀλλὰ ἀγαθόν, εἴπερ μέλλει κάθαρσις τῶν κακῶν γίνεσθαι).

will call it a nature and a substance, an "infinite beauty of the most sublime creature", but not the logical adherence of a soul gifted with free will (*Strom.*, V, 1, 3).

The human spirit, Basilides means to say, is a substance worthy of being with its creator. And Hippolytus' account tells us that the third filiality is situated close to the other filialities, above the Limit (*Elenchos*, VII, 27, 11 and 27, 1). The spirit, Clement's fragment continues, is "an infinite beauty of the highest creature". And Hippolytus explains this by recording that the spirit has become "the most subtle of things, so subtle that it can rise of itself, like the first filiality" (26, 10). The spirit is, in the terms employed by Basilides' "an intuition", "a royal dignity". However, it is not confused with God. Why not? Because it is a creature — true, a beautiful creature ($\varkappa\alpha\lambda\grave{\eta}$ $\varkappa\tau\acute{\iota}\sigma\iota\varsigma$), but still a "creature". These words, it might be said in passing, prove the authenticity of Hippolytus' account, which declares that the germ was not an emanation but a creation out of nothingness, and that the filiality, though in all things consubstantial with God, had issued from nothingness (22, 7). And it might also be remarked that the conception of a creation of the spiritual world reveals a profound Christian influence. What is more important is that for Basilides there is always this difference between God and the spirit: God is unengendered, while the spirit is engendered. And that is why the spirit is not confused with God and is not dissolved into the absolute being but keeps a certain distance.

All this is highly significant, for the same conception is found in Valentinus, who condemns the striving of the spirit to penetrate to the very depths of God and taste his sweetness. Thus the Christian gnosis is a mystique of Christ and not a mystique of God. Though on the one hand it stresses the consubstantiality of man with God, on the other hand it does not forget that God is "entirely different", and it describes God in purely negative terms. Valentinus says that God is "abyss and silence". Basilides is more eloquent in this respect. In striking paradoxes and with a sobriety betraying the profoundest emotion he makes it clear that God escapes all human definition.

His passage about God before the creation of the world is rightly famous and merits the greatest attention because it shows the nature of the God whom Basilides encountered in the profoundest depths of his being.

Once upon a time there was nothing, nor was that nothing any kind of entity, but in plain, unequivocal, and unsophisticated language there was nothing at all. When I say "was" I don't assert that "there was", but merely to indicate my intention I declare that there was nothing at all. For if we would call that about which I am speaking "transcendent" ($\mathring{\alpha}\rho\rho\eta\tau o\varsigma$, uneffable), it would not be absolutely transcendent, because we give it this name. But it is beyond transcendency: for what is beyond transcendency cannot be predicated, not

even as transcendent, but is above every possible name. That this must be true appears from the fact that there are not even names enough to predicate the things of the visible world, so complicated this is. And I don't undertake to find proper names for everything, but one must grasp the properties of the things not by spoken words, but by silent intuition ....
Now when there was nothing, neither matter, nor substance, nor nonentity, nor simple nor compound, nor perceptible nor imperceptible, nor man nor angel nor god, nor anything that can be named or perceived by sense or by thought, but when in this and in a still more subtle way everything was simply designed, then not being God, without consciousness or perception, without plan, without purpose, without affection, without desire, willed to make a world. I only say "willed" to express my feeling, but I mean an act involuntary, irrational, unconscious. Likewise, by "the world" I don't mean the world of time and space, which came into being afterwards, but the germ of a world. And this seed of the world contained all things within itself, just as a grain of mustard-seed collects into the smallest body all things at once (potentially), the roots, the trunk, the numberless leaves, the seeds begotten by the plant, that are cast off as germs of innumerable other plants in an endless process. Thus not being God made a not being world out of nothing (*Elenchos*, VII, 20, 2-21, 4).

This God whom Basilides encountered in his most secret heart is the Gnostic God, a nothingness beyond thought and will, unconscious, and containing within it the future universe in a state of unconsciousness. God is transcendence of transcendence.

It is clear that this passage reflects a personal experience of Basilides. However, it would be a mistake to suppose that such descriptions of God are an exception in Gnostic literature and unknown to the Gnostic masters who preceded Valentinus and Basilides. This is, indeed, the great error of the adherents of the history-of-dogmas school, who believed that a gulf separated learned gnosis from vulgar gnosis. Now it is true that Irenaeus does not breathe a word about any such description of God in his account of the Gnostic system of the predecessors of Valentinus, who were also the predecessors of Basilides, i.e. representatives of the vulgar gnosis of Egypt: he merely says a few words about a "certain unnamable Father" (*patrem quendam innominabilem;* Iren., *Adv. haer.,* I, 29, 1). But, thanks to a discovery of Carl Schmidt, we know today that Irenaeus, in his extract from the *Apokryphon Johannis,* his source for this chapter, omitted a highly remarkable description of a God transcending transcendence - a description worthy to be considered on a plane with that of Basilides [33].

Thus, we can say that the conceptions of God in learned gnosis and vulgar gnosis were fundamentally the same. We can even go further and declare that, in the phenomenological sense at least, the God of Basilides, this God who

---

[33] See Sagnard, *La gnose valentinienne,* p. 588.

is actually nothing and potentially everything, is the God of mysticism pure and simple. For the phenomenology of religion has very well demonstrated that the conception of God in ontological mysticism is everywhere the same, in all times and in all religions.

The problem then arises: Is this Gnostic God, this mystical God different from the God of the Bible? Is he another God! This problem is delicate, terrifying in fact, but it does not belong to the field of philological research. All we can say is that the Gnostic conception differs from the Biblical conception. It is most significant, for example, that Valentinus and Basilides, who wished to be Christians, who were well acquainted with the Bible and in particular with the Gospel of St. John, never said that God is love. The Valentinians themselves noticed this later and attempted to introduce the notion of love into their conception of God. This is the best proof that Christian Gnosis was a premature attempt to Christianize a pre-Christian gnosticism and did not succeed in adopting the characteristic trait of the Christian religion. Later, Gregory of Nyssa, though recognizing the Neoplatonic conception of divine transcendence, made it clear that the very essence of God is love. This he did because he was a mystic more penetrated by grace than Basilides, knowing not only the night of the senses but also the night of the spirit in the ecstasy of love.

"ANIMA NATURALITER CHRISTIANA"

La plage d'Ostie. A l'horizon les contours fins des monts Albains. Des gosses font des ricochets sur les ondes paisibles de la mer et dans ce paysage deux hommes en conversation .... Mais pourquoi évoquer l'atmosphère du petit dialogue qui s'intitule *Octavius* et est attribué à Minucius Felix? Tout le monde connaît cette dispute entre un païen sceptique et un chrétien stoïcien sur l'existence d'un Dieu providentiel et la vérité de la religion chrétienne. Écoutons donc ce que ce chrétien stoïcien, vrai contemporain d'un Marc Aurèle, nous enseigne sur la preuve psychologique de Dieu, sur ce sens commun des âmes chrétiennes par nature. Après avoir prononcé un éloge inspiré de la Providence, qui se manifeste par la finalité de l'Univers, Octavius fait suivre une preuve de l'existence de Dieu fondée sur l'accord de tous. D'après ce que je sais, on n'a pas jusqu'à maintenant observé à quel point ce passage est intéressant et caractéristique. On lit dans l'*Octavius*: "Que dire du fait que je puis m'autoriser du consentement de tous sur l'existence de Dieu: ... j'entends le peuple ..., j'entends les poètes ...; demandons l'opinion des philosophes" [1].

Le résultat de cette enquête c'est que tous les philosophes, aussi bien que les poètes et le peuple, s'accordent à admettre l'existence d'un Dieu unique. Cette formulation est remarquable, car on cherche en vain telle tripartition dans les oeuvres philosophiques de Cicéron. En effet, il faut se dégager du préjugé si répandu que Minucius en fin de compte n'a fait que copier Cicéron et Sénèque: il vaut mieux découvrir quelle est l'originalité de Minucius Felix. Et, comme il arrive presque toujours dans le domaine de la philologie latine, il faut aller en Grèce pour retrouver les parallèles, qui nous permettront de reconstruire l'archétype, dont les opinions émises par Minucius Felix ne sont qu'un remaniement. Pour couper court, la tripartition signalée dans l'Octavius se retrouve chez plusieurs auteurs grecs antérieurs à Minucius, et il est incompréhensible qu'on ait omis de faire ces rapprochements. Dans un débat entre des sceptiques et des stoïciens, transmis par Sextus Empiricus [2], un Stoïcien défend le dogme d'un commun accord sur l'existence du Divin de la manière suivante: "même s'il fallait laisser à part *la foi populaire,* ... il y a la religion des *poètes,* il y a la masse des *philosophes* qui s'accorde avec la conception des poètes". C'est exactement la même tripartition, dans la même succession et sur le même sujet que chez Minucius. Et il apparaît dès maintenant que le Stoïcien de Sextus emploie une distinction bien connue: c'est la division des religions en

---

[1] *Octavius,* XVIII, 11 sq. — Pour les textes grecs et latins des citations, je renvoie à mon commentaire sur Minucius Felix (Leyde, 1949).
[2] Sextus Empiricus, *Adv. Phys.,* I, 62.

trois classes, à savoir la religion populaire, fondée par les législateurs, la religion poétique et la religion des philosophes. Tout lecteur de la *Civitas Dei* de saint Augustin sait que cette tripartition nous a été transmise par la bouche de Scévola, disciple de Panétius aussi bien que de Posidonius, et que l'ancien Portique ne la connaissait guère. Mais pour pouvoir comprendre pour quelles raisons ces trois types de religiosité s'accordent à admettre l'existence de Dieu, bien qu'ils soient si différents, il faut pénétrer plus avant dans les sources qui nous transmettent les doctrines du Portique moyen sur l'origine et l'évolution de la religion. C'est Dion Chrysostome qui nous fournit dans son *Oraison olympique* la solution de ce problème: toutes les religions s'accordent en ceci qu'elles sont issues d'un monothéisme primitif et ont conservé cette conception vraie malgré toutes les déformations subies. Le discours de Dion nous transpose dans les temps les plus reculés, vrai printemps du monde, à la naissance de l'humanité. Quand ces hommes récemment surgis de la terre contemplaient le mouvement ordonné des cieux, ils apercevaient, spontanément, avec une intuition certaine, qu'il y avait un Être divin. L'univers était le temple d'initiation, les astres dansaient leur choeur mystique autour de l'homme et lui suggéraient l'existence d'un "régisseur, qui mettait en scène ce spectacle et dirigeait le ciel et l'univers tout entier", considéré par Dion comme "un Père premier et immortel que nous autres Grecs appelons le Zeus paternel". Le monothéisme cosmique était la religion naturelle des primitifs.

Cependant cette pureté naïve n'a pas duré. Dans le cours des temps les religions positives ont été introduites, à savoir la religion des législateurs, qui n'est que conventionnelle et autoritaire, celle des poètes, qui s'exprime par des mythes, et enfin la religion des philosophes qui se fonde sur la raison. Évidemment ces législateurs et ces poètes ont introduit beaucoup d'éléments secondaires et arbitraires. C'est pourquoi les religions du monde sont tellement différentes. Malgré cela tous tombent d'accord pour reconnaître le Dieu cosmique. Ceci parce que toutes les religions ont hérité et conservé l'essentiel du monothéisme primitif qui est à la base de toutes les religions positives, lesquelles n'auraient pu s'épanouir sans ce fondement.

On admire la hardiesse et la profondeur d'une théorie qui veut expliquer dans une synthèse grandiose l'origine de la religion naturelle, le développement des superstitions positives, leurs différences historiques, leur unité fondamentale et leur justification devant le tribunal de la raison. Tous les savants, qui se sont occupés de ce problème, ont supposé, avec des arguments très solides, que le discours de Dion reflète les grandes lignes de la philosophie religieuse de Posidonius. Et c'est dans cette perspective que la conception de Minucius Felix, selon laquelle le peuple, les poètes et les philosophes sont unanimes à admettre l'existence d'un Dieu unique, prend tout son relief.

Dans ces circonstances il vaut la peine de regarder de près les examples qu'apporte Minucius, sans toutefois s'étendre trop. Que le peuple, bien que païen, admette l'existence de Dieu, Minucius Felix le dit nettement: "J'entends le peuple: tandis qu'ils lèvent les mains au ciel, ils ne disent que *Deus*" [3]. Or ceci est un malentendu. Le vocatif *deus* n'a jamais existé dans le latin des païens et c'est M. Löfstedt qui l'a prouvé. C'est un hébraïsme emprunté par les chrétiens romains au grec de la Bible. Le peuple disait évidemment: o *Juppiter*, ὦ Ζεῦ. C'est pourquoi on a supposé que le passage de Minucius remonte en dernière analyse à Démocrite [4], qui, selon une interprétation probable, a dit: "Quelques sages, levant les mains vers cet endroit que nous autres Grecs appelons l'air, ne disaient que ὦ Ζεῦ". Il est en effet infiniment probable que ce fragment a été cité par un Stoïcien pour prouver que l'homme avait un sens commun de l'existence d'un Dieu cosmique. Minucius, lui, considère ces exclamations comme le langage naturel du peuple. Évidemment, si les superstitions positives n'ont pas pu corrompre le monothéisme primitif, alors la prière avec les mains levées et l'invocation du Dieu cosmique prouvent que la religiosité naturelle s'exprime grâce à une réminiscence et une prise de conscience du vrai soi. Tout ceci cadre excellemment avec la pensée posidonienne et c'est pour cette raison que l'auteur anonyme du *De Mundo* [5] et Maxime de Tyr [6] s'autorisent de la prière avec les mains levées et du témoignage de l'âme parlante pour prouver l'accord commun sur Dieu.

Pour prouver que les poètes eux aussi étaient des monothéistes, Minucius cite quelques vers de Virgile et d'Ennius. Ce passage ne semble être qu'une adaptation latine d'une conception stoïcienne. En effet, Sextus Empiricus se rapporte à Homère pour prouver l'existence d'un dieu tout-puissant. Ceci devient encore plus frappant quand on se souvient que ce parallèle se trouve dans le même cadre: tous les deux renvoient d'abord à la foi populaire, puis s'autorisent des poètes et enfin affirment l'unanimité des philosophes.

Car Minucius apporte une longue liste doxographique, empruntée à Cicéron, pour prouver que presque tous les philosophes, y compris Épicure, ont admis l'existence d'un Dieu unique. C'est précisément cette conception, absurde du reste, que l'on cherche en vain dans le passage de Cicéron (*De nat. deorum*,

---

[3] *Octavius*, XVIII, 11.
[4] Chez Clément d'Alexandrie, *Protr.*, 6, p. 52, 19. Interprétation selon Q. Cataudella dans *Atene e Roma*, III (1941), 9, 2 et *Studi Italiani di Filologia Classica*, N.S., XVII (1940), fasc. 4.
[5] *De Mundo*, éd. Lorimer, p. 400a, 16.
[6] Maxime de Tyr, *Dial.*, II, 2b.

I, 25) utilisé par Minucius et que l'on retrouve chez le stoïcien cité par Sextus [7].

Nous concluons donc que les idées de Minucius sur l'accord commun de tous concernant l'existence de Dieu, sa distinction de trois catégories, peuples, poètes, philosophes et l'accent mis sur leur accord parfait ne sont qu'un remaniement de vues stoïciennes, conservées par Sextus Empiricus et d'autres auteurs grecs, et que cette conception reçoit tout son relief quand on la replace dans le cadre de la philosophie posidonienne, telle que Dion l'a décrite. Ainsi on entrevoit derrière les mots de l'apologiste chrétien l'essentiel de cette conception de l'homme, qu'on trouve aussi bien chez Minucius que chez Tertullien et qui a été défendue jusqu'à nos jours, selon laquelle l'âme est chrétienne par nature. Bref c'est une anthropologie bien connue dont il est question.

Pour apprécier cet état des choses, il est nécessaire de rechercher par quel intermédiaire Minucius a reçu ces arguments stoïciens et quelles étaient les intentions qui dominaient sa pensée quand il les insérait dans son oeuvre. Quel est le genre littéraire auquel appartient l'*Octavius*? L'auteur l'indique nettement: c'est une discussion. Pour préciser, c'est en premier lieu une *disputatio in utramque partem* entre un sceptique et un stoïcien sur la providence. Or, il est avéré que les rhéteurs de l'Empire avaient coutume de faire prononcer par leurs élèves une thèse sur la providence. Sans doute il ne s'agit ici que d'un exercice d'éloquence, pour préparer les forces juvéniles aux grands plaidoyers, où il faut être à même de défendre n'importe quel point de vue. C'est pourquoi l'élève de l'école de rhétorique composait d'abord un discours dans lequel il démontrait qu'il n'existait aucune providence et ensuite un autre pour prouver que le monde est gouverné par une providence divine. C'est Quintilien qui avance tout ceci: il nous apprend que parmi les sujets possibles à défendre comme thèse théorique la providence constituait un thème favori [8]. Comment composer une telle thèse? Le professeur de rhétorique donnait à ce propos des indications détaillées, comme le montrent les *Progymnastiques* de Théon [9]. En ce qui concerne la thèse pratique, il faut d'abord prouver qu'elle est possible.

En second lieu, qu'elle s'accorde avec la nature et avec les us et coutumes communs à tous les hommes. Voilà la preuve *ex consensu omnium,* dont nous parlions plus haut. Comment diviser une telle preuve? Il faut apporter pour chaque affirmation les "témoignages des hommes célèbres, c'est-à-dire les poètes, les hommes d'état, les philosophes". A un autre endroit ce trio est

---

[7] Sextus Empiricus, *o.c.,* I, 64.
[8] Quintilien, *Inst. Or.,* III, 5, 5.
[9] Théon., *Progymnastica* 12, Rhet. Graeci, II, p. 121.

composé comme suit: "… les législateurs, les poètes, les sages" [10]. Pas de doute, nous retrouvons la tripartition stoïcienne signalée tout à l'heure aussi bien chez Minucius que chez Sextus et Dion.

Que contenait la thèse sur la providence? Théon nous le dit. Une description inspirée de l'ordre cosmique, la succession des saisons, la comparaison avec une maison bien ordonnée y trouvaient une place. Puis la preuve e *consensu*: les Grecs, les barbares, les sages comme Platon, Aristote, Zénon, les législateurs, tous admettent qu'il existe une providence [11].

Il appert donc que Minucius, en donnant une description de la providence et la faisant suivre par le témoignage du peuple, des poètes et des philosophes, reflète les prescriptions des rhéteurs sur la composition d'une thèse. Et ceci nous éclaire sur l'intention de ces arguments stoïciens. Ils sont, certes, d'origine philosophique, mais ont reçu une fonction rhétorique, ayant pour but de parler à un intellectuel dans un langage qu'il comprenait. Et c'est précisément dans ce désir d'incarner une parole transcendante dans une littérature sécularisée, c'est dans cette alchimie de la foi, dans ces réticences psychagogiques que consiste l'actualité de Minucius.

Si les sources de Minucius ont pu être indiquées, s'il n'y a presque pas un mot dans ce passage qu'on ne retrouve chez des auteurs antérieurs, si l'auteur a gardé intégralement la tripartition stoïcienne en liaison avec la description de la finalité cosmique, s'il a été prouvé que les arguments stoïciens sont parvenus à Minucius par l'intermédiaire d'une thèse rhétorique, il n'est pas nécessaire de supposer qu'il ait puisé à une autre source encore. Par contre Tertullien, dans son *Apologétique*, n'a pas gardé le schème stoïcien, il ne parle pas de l'accord commun du peuple, des poètes et des philosophes, il ne dit rien de la providence dans la nature; enfin le système posidonien, qu'on entrevoit derrière les mots de Minucius, a disparu chez cet apologiste. Tout ce qu'il apporte, c'est un développement magnifique sur le christianisme de l'âme qui s'exprime d'une manière spontanée. Nous croyons qu'une comparaison détaillée des deux passages, comparaison qui doit évidemment être faite ailleurs, apportera aux chercheurs la conviction que c'est Minucius qui a introduit la doctrine de l'âme chrétienne par nature et que Tertullien, qui lui est postérieur, l'a adopté, modifié et utilisé pour ses propres buts, d'abord dans l'*Apologétique*, puis, d'une manière encore plus géniale, dans son ouvrage sur le témoignage de l'âme. Il apparaîtra alors que cette anthropologie fameuse, dont Tertullien est censé être l'initiateur, a une préhistoire.

---

[10] *O.c.,* p. 108.
[11] *O.c.,* p. 126.

Ces recherches jettent une lumière nouvelle et inattendue sur la genèse de la conception de l'homme par les apologistes. Quand on y regarde de près, Tertullien est beaucoup plus chrétien que Minucius. Selon lui l'âme ne connaît pas seulement Dieu, mais aussi son jugement, non moins que le Diable, l'Enfer et la Vie éternelle. On aperçoit le progrès lent et patient d'un processus grandiose, la christianisation de l'hellénisme, d'abord avec prudence chez Minucius, puis avec plus de décision chez Tertullien. Un temple est démoli pour édifier une église. Et comme en Sicile on trouve dans certaines cathédrales des colonnes antiques qui soutiennent les voûtes médiévales, ainsi l'anthropologie tertullianiste contient certains éléments dont nous ne connaîtrions ni l'origine ni la fonction, si on ne les considérait pas dans leur perspective historique. En se répandant dans le monde antique, le christianisme a trouvé sur sa route deux grandes puissances, la philosophie grecque du Portique et la mystique orientale de la Gnose. Avec les tâtonnements d'une première rencontre, on a essayé de christianiser la Gnose, puis dans un effort plus prudent et plus réfléchi, on a accepté les conceptions gnostiques qu'on pouvait assimiler sans nuire trop à la structure phénoménologique de sa propre religion. Ce sont les noms prestigieux d'un Valentin et d'un Origène qui marquent les étapes de la route parcourue. Dans le domaine romain on observe un processus analogue: c'est la ligne stoïcienne qui, ayant traversé l'école rhétorique, mène de Minucius jusqu'à Tertullien. Les deux phénomènes s'unissent dans un mode d'expression qui semble résumer l'histoire même de l'église ancienne; la littérature chrétienne primitive nous montre comment fut opérée la christianisation de l'hellénisme et de la mystique orientale.

DAS EWIGE EBENBILD DES MENSCHEN
ZUR BEGEGNUNG MIT DEM SELBST IN DER GNOSIS

Die Begegnung mit dem Selbst in der Gnosis ist ein Thema, das in den letzten zwanzig Jahren von verschiedenen Forschern auf der Eranos-Tagung behandelt wurde. Als 1947 der Verfasser dieses Beitrages zum ersten Male nach Ascona kam und über die Auffassung des Menschen in der valentinianischen Gnosis sprach, wies er darauf hin, dass die Begegnung mit dem höheren Selbst das eigentliche Zentrum des tragischen Mythos Valentins war. Nach den Quellen dieser Gnosis, vor allem den *Excerpta ex Theodoto*, ist mit Christus der Engel jedes einzelnen Menschen herabgekommen, welcher mit Christus wesensgleich ist. Es ist dieser Engel, welcher dem Menschen zugeordnet ist und ihm während seines Lebens die Gnosis schenkt. Beim Sterben aber besiegt er den Tod und führt den Menschen, zu dem er gehört, hinauf. Er ist schicksalhaft mit diesem Menschen verbunden, weil es dem Engel nicht gestattet ist, ohne diesen Menschen in das Pleroma zurückzukehren: so braucht der Engel den Menschen, wie der Mensch den Engel braucht. So sind Mensch und Engel gegenseitig aufeinander angewiesen, gleich wie Mann und Frau in der Ehe, und feiern am Ende der Zeiten die heilige Hochzeit im Brautgemach des Pleroma. Und der Redner zweifelte schon damals nicht daran, dass dieser Engel das eigentliche und transzendente Selbst des Menschen versinnbildliche, den Geist Christi in jedem Einzelnen. 1947 hat Henry Corbin dieses Thema aufgegriffen und näher beleuchtet. Sein Ausgangspunkt war die Lehre des islamitischen Theologen Sohrawardî. Corbin hatte einige von diesem sehr bedeutenden Denker verfasste Abhandlungen in Dialogform entdeckt. Der Dialog wird zwischen dem Verfasser und dem Engel der Menschheit geführt, und dieser Engel wird mit Recht von dem französischen Gelehrten als der persönliche Engel des einzelnen Menschen aufgefasst. Gewiss ist es sehr auffallend bei einem islamitischen Theologen, dass der Mensch nicht mit dem einen Gott, sondern mit einem Engel konfrontiert wird. Das kann in seinem Ursprung nicht islamitisch sein. Deshalb nimmt Corbin an, dass diese Vorstellung ein *survival* der gnostischen Religiosität ist, wofür er auf die erwähnte Vorstellung der valentinianischen Gnosis und die noch zu erwähnenden manichäischen Parallelen wie auch auf die altiranische Auffassung der Daēnā verweist.

In einer vollendeten Sprache macht Corbin deutlich, dass es hier um eine eigene Struktur der religiösen Erfahrung geht, für welche er den Terminus *kathénothéisme* bildet. Es geht hier um die Zweisamkeit des Menschen, seine *dualitudo*, das *mysterium conjunctionis* des menschlichen Ichs mit dem göttlichen Selbst, worin die Gottheit Gestalt annimmt.

In seinem Buch „Von der mystischen Gestalt der Gottheit" hat Gershom Scholem dann ausgeführt, dass auch das esoterische Judentum des Mittelalters die Begegnung mit dem Selbst gekannt hat, obwohl man nur selten und nicht gerne davon sprach: „Der verstorbene tiefgelehrte Rabbi Nathan hat mir gesagt: 'Wisse, dass das vollkommene Geheimnis der Prophetie für den Propheten darin besteht, dass er plötzlich die Gestalt seines Selbst vor sich stehen sieht und sein Selbst vergisst, und es von ihm entrückt wird, und er die Gestalt seines Selbst vor sich sieht, wie sie mit ihm spricht und ihm das Zukünftige verkündet ...'. Und abermals ein anderer Gelehrter schreibt folgendes: '... und doch rufe ich Himmel und Erde zu Zeugen an, im Himmel ist mein Zeuge und mein Bürge in den Höhen, dass ich eines Tages sass und ein kabbalistisches Geheimnis niederschrieb, und plötzlich sah ich die Gestalt meines Selbst mir gegenüberstehen und mein Selbst von mir entrückt, und war genötigt und gezwungen, mit Schreiben aufzuhören'. ". Kommentar von Scholem: „Was hier als Selbst bezeichnet wird, bleibt in bezug auf die traditionellen Einteilungen der Grade der Seele undefiniert. Ja, es lässt sich mit gutem Grund argumentieren, dass dieses Selbst ein mit der wesentlichen Natur des Menschen verbundenes, engelgleiches Selbst sei, der zum Menschen wesensmässig gehörende persönliche Engel, der ihm hier sichtbar wird" (o.c., S. 252).

Immerhin bleibt es auffallend, dass es im Judentum wie im Islam, trotz der streng monotheistischen Fassung des Glaubens, wirklich die Offenheit für eine Begegnung mit dem Selbst gegeben hat. Die Religionshistoriker haben also in den letzten zwanzig Jahren diese für das religiöse Erleben charakteristische Grunderscheinung, welche auch als *mysterium conjunctionis* bezeichnet werden kann, an den verschiedensten Orten aufgezeigt. Und eigentlich fanden diese Entdeckungen statt in Gebieten, wo man es nicht erwartet hätte, nämlich in der Geschichte des Judentums und des Islams. Inzwischen sind noch neue gnostische Texte bekannt geworden, welche diese typisch gnostische Vorstellung ausführlicher darstellen und besser beleuchten. Vor allem müssen hier das Philippusevangelium und das Thomasevangelium, beide 1945/46 bei Nag Hammadi in Oberägypten gefunden, erwähnt werden. Das Philippusevangelium, das der valentinianischen Gnosis entstammt, bringt neues Material zu der schon bekannten valentinianischen Vorstellung von der heiligen Hochzeit zwischen dem Engel und dem Menschen. Das Thomasevangelium, um 140 nach Christus in Edessa geschrieben, enthüllt, dass das syrische Christentum schon sehr früh die Vorstellung gekannt hat, dass der Schutzengel des Menschen, das heisst sein wahres Selbst, das Ebenbild (εἰκών) des Menschen darstellt. Es ist an der Zeit, nach den vielen Vorarbeiten auf Grund des neuen Materials zu versuchen, den historischen Ursprung dieser Vorstellung festzustellen und ihre genetische Entwicklung zu verfolgen.

Das wollen wir in diesem Vortrag tun. Dabei sei es gestattet, das Resultat unserer Untersuchungen schon jetzt vorwegzunehmen: die Auffassung, dass der persönliche Schutzengel des Menschen sein Ebenbild darstellt, stammt aus dem Griechentum und ist vom Judentum in der hellenistischen Zeit übernommen worden.

Auf dieser Grundlage beruht das gnostische *mysterium conjunctionis*, sowohl in der Schule Valentins wie in der Religion Manis.

*   *   *

Die Griechen sagten, dass jeder Mensch seinen eigenen Daimon habe. Oder besser: dass der Daimon den Menschen habe. Allerdings hat die Vorstellung des Daimons bei den Griechen eine Entwicklung durchgemacht, als der griechische Weg vom Mythos zum Logos führte.

Die ursprüngliche und noch lange volkstümliche Auffassung wird vom Dichter Menander zum Ausdruck gebracht:

„Jedem Menschen gesellt sich ein Daimon gleich bei der Geburt als Führer in die Geheimnisse des Lebens" (Frg. 550 Kock).

Allerdings waren die Anschauungen über den Sitz des Bewusstseins und des Lebens anfänglich noch sehr primitiv. In seinem mutigen, in Einzelheiten umstrittenen, aber doch sehr anregenden Buch über die Ursprünge des europäischen Denkens zeichnet R. B. Onians folgendes Bild: Sitz des Bewusst-seins seien in alten Zeiten für die Griechen die Lungen, die $\varphi\rho\acute{e}\nu\epsilon\varsigma$, gewesen, mit welchen man den Atem, den $\vartheta\upsilon\mu\acute{o}\varsigma$, einholt und wieder ausatmet. Man dachte damals mit den Lungen. Die Psyche dagegen, das heisst der unbewusste Lebensgeist und die Erzeugungskraft, sei im Haupte lokalisiert worden. Und darum wurde auch Athena aus dem Haupte des Zeus geboren. Das steht allerdings vollkommen in Widerspruch mit der späteren philosophischen Anschauung, dass das Haupt Sitz des Denkens, die Brust Sitz des Gemütes und der Unterleib Sitz der Begierde sei. Aber es spricht manches dafür, dass ein Homer und seine Zeitgenossen so primitiv über die Seele, ihren Sitz und ihre Funktionen gedacht haben. So waren auch die Vorstellungen vom Genius bei den Römern und vom Daimon bei den Griechen sehr handfest und konkret. Der Genius hatte Verbindungen mit der sexuellen Zeugungskraft. Man trank Wein, um den Genius zu stärken (*genio indulgere*); man versorgte den Genius (*curare genium*). Und doch wurde der Genius auch wieder als Schutzgeist aufgefasst. Nur dieser unbewusste Genius war unsterblich und wurde nach dem Tode göttlich, weshalb man auch vom verstorbenen Kaiser als *divus Augustus* sprach. Daimon und Genius sind später miteinander identifiziert worden, waren sich aber ursprünglich nicht genau gleich. Der vornehmste

Unterschied scheint zu sein, dass der Daimon keine Verbindung mit der Zeugungskraft des Mannes hatte. Dennoch lassen sich beide Vorstellungen vergleichen. Auch vom Daimon gilt, was Onians vom Genius sagt: er sei eine innere Quelle der Inspiration, welche das Leben und Handeln des Menschen beeinflusst, abgesehen von und sogar trotz seinem bewussten Denken (o.c., S. 162).

Ursprünglich war also der Daimon eine Gestalt im Innern des Menschen; er war nicht das Bewusstsein oder die Intelligenz, sondern vielmehr die Lebenskraft selbst.

Der Weg vom Mythos zum Logos der griechischen Philosophen, welcher entscheidend gewesen ist für unsere Kultur, führte nun notwendig auch dazu, dass diese irrationale Sicht eliminiert wurde. Das tut vor allem Platon. Als konservativer Politiker und frommer Mann bewahrt er scheinbar die altertümlichen Worte und Vorstellungen. Der Daimon wird dargestellt als der Geist, der den Menschen nach dem Tode zum Orte des Gerichts führt (*Phaedon* 107d); der Daimon gilt auch als Schutzgeist, „Hüter des Lebens" (*Respublica* 620d).

Trotzdem ist der Mythos im Prinzip überwunden, und zwar gerade dann, wenn Platon in Mythen spricht.

Er beschreibt in seinem *Staat,* wie ein gewisser Armenier, Er genannt, das Jenseits erschaut. Dort sagt die Lachesis, die Schicksalsgöttin, zu den Seelen, welche in das wiederholte Erdenleben zurückkehren: „Nicht wird euch der Daimon wählen, sondern ihr werdet euch eueren eigenen Daimon wählen" (*Respublica* 617d). Gewiss sagt Platon das, um dem Menschen die Schuld an allem Bösen zu geben, das ihm widerfährt, und die Schuldlosigkeit Gottes, das heisst der Idee des Guten, am Menschenelend darzustellen. Aber das sind eben rationale Überlegungen, welche dem Mythos fremd sind. Platon meint, dass der Mensch, der Verstand des Menschen, seine Existenz beherrschen und sein Leben bestimmen kann. Das ist die Grundlage jedes Rationalismus bis zum heutigen Tage. Der Mythos vom Daimon besagte aber im Gegenteil, dass der bewusste Mensch eben nicht sein Leben bestimmt, sondern Glück (Eudaimonie) und Unglück (Kakodaimonie) einem irrationalen Faktor in seinem Leben, eben dem Daimon, zu verdanken hat.

Mit Recht hat Ernst Cassirer in seiner „Philosophie der symbolischen Formen" die epochale Bedeutung dieser platonischen Stelle hervorgehoben, weil hier das mythische Weltbild vom wissenschaftlichen Weltbild abgelöst wird. Für Platon ist mithin der Daimon mit der Vernunft identisch (*Timaeus* 90a).

Bei dem einflussreichen stoischen Denker aus dem ersten vorchristlichen Jahrhundert, Posidonius von Apameia, ist es nicht anders. Auch für ihn ist der Daimon dasselbe wie die Vernunft. Diesem Daimon gilt es, in allem zu folgen, weil er verwandt und wesensgleich mit der Gottheit ist, welche das All durchwaltet. Gewiss, Posidonius hatte eine Ahnung davon, mit welcher Macht die irrationalen Teile der Seele sich gegen die Vernunft auflehnen können. Und fromm und warm spricht er von der Sympathie aller Dinge, welche Mensch und Gottheit verbindet. Wenn man aber genauer zuschaut, bemerkt man, dass letztlich doch wieder der Mensch als Vernunft und die Wirklichkeit als vernünftig aufgefasst werden. Der hochgerühmte und emphatisch verkündete Vitalismus des Posidonius ist doch wieder nur ein mit Begeisterung vorgetragener Rationalismus.

Es ist klar, dass zu seiner Zeit der Logos die Griechen nicht mehr ganz befriedigte. Der Weg führte ja nicht nur vom Mythos zum Logos, aber auch vom Logos zum Mysterion; und Posidonius stand auf der Schwelle. Die philosophische Auffassung vom Daimon ist aber nicht die Vorstufe gewesen, welche zu der von uns untersuchten Struktur der Zweisamkeit des Menschen geführt hat. Und doch ist diese bei den Griechen zu finden, wie ich im folgenden noch näher zeigen möchte.

Nur ganz beiläufig und zufällig hören wir, dass die Pythagoräer den Daimon des Menschen mit seinem Eidolon identifizierten. Das erzählt uns Plutarch in seinem Buch *De Genio Socratis* (583B und 585E); er beschreibt dort ein Gespräch thebanischer Flüchtlinge aus dem 4. Jahrhundert, welche Pythagoräer sind. Da wird berichtet, dass die Mitglieder dieses Mysterienbundes durch ein gewisses Zeichen wissen, ob das Eidolon eines Menschen, das ihnen im Traum erscheint, einem Gestorbenen oder einem noch Lebenden angehört. Dieses Zeichen besteht darin, dass die Toten im Traume keinen Schatten haben und nicht mit den Augenlidern zwinkern. So erkennt dann einer der Pythagoräer, dass ein Freund, dessen Daimon ihm im Traum erscheint, schon gestorben ist. Also ist der Daimon nach den Pythagoräern mit dem Eidolon identisch.

Man fragt sich unwillkürlich, ob das eine primitive Vorstellung ist, hat man doch in letzter Zeit die archaischen Grundlagen der pythagoräischen Vorstellungen herausgearbeitet und sogar zu den ekstatischen Erfahrungen der Schamanen gegriffen, um ihre Auffassung der Seele zu verdeutlichen. So weit werden wir nicht gehen. Wir fragen nur, was dann eigentlich ein Eidolon ist.

Das Eidolon ist nach Homer die Schattenseele, welche im Hades fortlebt. Diese wird mit dem Kopf in Verbindung gebracht: „der Schatten kraftlose Köpfe", sagt Homer. Sie hat durchaus die Gestalt des Leibes des Gestorbenen und kann dadurch wiedererkannt werden. Das sieht man auch auf zahllosen Vasenbildern, wo das Eidolon in der Gestalt des Gestorbenen entflieht. So ist das

Eidolon eigentlich die Seele selbst, soweit sie das Bewusstsein verloren hat und als beinahe erschöpfte Lebenskraft weitervegetiert. Wenn also unsere Auffassung des Daimons richtig ist, nach welcher er die unbewusste Lebenskraft darstellt, wäre schon für homerische Zeiten eine Identität des Daimons und des Eidolon zu postulieren. Dann hätten die Pythagoräer in späteren Zeiten die archaische Vorstellung treu bewahrt. Allerdings gab es doch einen Unterschied; denn nach den Pythagoräern wäre der Daimon oder das Eidolon prä-existent und himmlischen Ursprungs. So sagt der Dichter Pindarus, wie so oft pythagoräische Auffassungen wiedergebend:

„Es besteht, ganz lebendig, ein Bild unseres Lebens, $\alpha i \tilde{\omega} v o \varsigma$ $\varepsilon i \delta \omega \lambda o v$, denn dies allein stammt von den Göttern" (Frg. Schroeder 131).

Der Daimon war also nach den Pythagoräern das Ebenbild des Menschen. Und diese Vorstellung hat sich dann in hellenistischer Zeit auch ausserhalb der pythagoräischen Kreise gehalten. So erzählt Plutarch, dass einem Vater das Bildnis eines Jünglings erschienen sei, das seinem gestorbenen Sohn in Alter und Gestalt vollkommen ähnlich war. Darauf fragt der Vater: „Wer ist das?". Und die Antwort lautet: „Es ist der Daimon deines Sohnes".

Der Daimon ist also der körperlichen Gestalt des Menschen vollkommen gleich. Die Juden in Palästina, welche sich jahrhundertelang mit dem Hellenismus auseinandergesetzt haben und gerade in ihrem Widerstand gegen den Geist der Griechen so oft von ihnen beeinflusst worden sind, haben diese Vorstellung des Ebenbildes übernommen. Sie glaubten, jeder Mensch habe einen Schutzengel; und nicht selten wird dieser als das „Bild" (iqōnin) bezeichnet. Es ist dies ein Lehnwort aus dem Griechischen, Eikon oder Ebenbild. Und diese Tatsache genügt, um zu beweisen, dass die Vorstellung den Griechen entnommen ist und nicht anderswo ihren Ursprung hat.

Dieses Ebenbild des Menschen schützt ihn, wenn er von den bösen Dämonen bedrängt wird. So wird in einer Exegese von Psalm 55, 19, gesagt:

„Er erlöst in Frieden meine Seele im Kampfe gegen mich" … Wann? Wenn viele mit mir sind. Und wer sind diese? Die Engel, welche den Menschen behüten. R. Josua ben Levi sagte: „Das Ebenbild geht vor dem Menschen einher, und Herolde rufen vor ihm aus. Was sprechen sie? Machet Platz für das Ebenbild Gottes!" (*Deuteronomium Rabba* 4 [201d]; Wünsche, S. 57, 58).

Es kommt also das Ebenbild des Menschen aus der Engelwelt zu dem Menschen auf die Erde, welcher von den Dämonen umringt und bedrängt wird. Da rufen andere Engel zu diesen Dämonen: „Machet Platz dem Ebenbilde Gottes". Eine sehr bemerkenswerte Stelle: der Schutzengel lebt im Himmel und ist der Doppelgänger des Menschen, zu dem er gehört. Wenn der Mensch in Not ist und so wohl auch in der Stunde des Todes, rettet er den Menschen.

Er ist gewissermassen der Erlöser des Menschen. Und auf ihn bezieht sich eigentlich das Wort der Genesis (I, 27), nach dem Gott den Menschen nach seinem Bilde (hebr. *zelem*, gr. εἰϰών) geschaffen hat. Der Schutzengel ist zugleich das Ebenbild des Menschen und das eigentliche Gottesbild.
R. Josua ben Levi lebte um 250 nach Christus. Diese Ansicht muss aber schon viel früher bei den Juden in Palästinas bestanden haben. Das zeigt das Neue Testament.

In den Apostelakten, Kapitel 12, wird erzählt, wie der Apostel Petrus in Jerusalem gefangengenommen und im Gefängnis verwahrt wurde. Auf wunderbare Weise wird er gerettet und geht zum Hause der Maria, der Mutter des Johannes Markus, wo viele Mitglieder der christlichen Gemeinde versammelt waren und beteten. Als er an die Türe des Vorhofes klopfte, kam eine Magd mit Namen Rhode herbei, um zu öffnen. Und als sie die Stimme des Petrus erkannte, tat sie in ihrer Freude das Tor nicht auf, sondern lief hinein und meldete, Petrus stehe vor dem Tore. Sie aber sagten zu ihr: „Du bist von Sinnen". Doch sie versicherte, es sei so. Da sagten sie: „Es ist (nur) sein (Schutz)engel" (12, 15).

Die letzten Worte setzen voraus, dass Petrus einen Schutzengel hat, der ihm an Stimme und auch an äusserer Gestalt ganz ähnlich ist. Der Schutzengel ist als Ebenbild des Petrus gedacht, er ist, hebräisch gesagt, sein Iqōnin. Die jüdische *couleur locale* der Erzählung zeigt, dass der Autor der Apostelakten, Lukas, hier wie sonst Traditionen der Jerusalemer Gemeinde verarbeitet. Also kannten die Mitglieder der Urgemeinde, welche zu dieser Zeit ausschliesslich aus „Hebräern", das heisst aus aramäisch sprechenden Juden aus Palästina bestand, die Vorstellung des Schutzengels als eines Ebenbildes. So sehr war diese ursprünglich griechische Vorstellung „eingejudet", dass sogar die Aramäischsprachigen Jerusalems sie ganz spontan voraussetzten. Das führt uns zu einer wichtigen Schlussfolgerung: der Glaube, dass der Mensch mit einem himmlischen Doppelgänger verbunden ist, gehört zum ältesten, aramäischen Bestand der christlichen Überlieferung und geht auf die Urgemeinde Jerusalems zurück.

Kann man noch weiter zurückgehen? In Matthäus 18, 10 wird folgendes Jesuswort überliefert:

„Sehet zu, dass ihr keinen dieser Kleinen verachtet! Denn ich sage euch: Ihre Engel in den Himmeln schauen allezeit das Angesicht meines Vaters in den Himmeln".

Das ist eine Sondertradition des Matthäus, welche sich weder bei Markus noch bei Lukas findet. Es ist durchaus möglich, dass Matthäus hier, wie so oft, judenchristliche Tradition aufgenommen hat. Was ist mit diesem Wort gemeint? Die Formgeschichte hat uns gelehrt, zu unterscheiden zwischen dem, was Jesus sagen wollte, und dem, was die Gemeinde verstanden hat.

Jesus hat hier wohl die Ehrfurcht für das Kind einschärfen wollen. *Maxima debetur puero reverentia.* Diese wird damit begründet, dass die Kinder einen speziellen Schutzengel haben. Dieser befindet sich im Himmel und schaut „allezeit" das Anlitz Gottes. Dass dieser Engel auch das Ebenbild des Kindes sei, wird nicht gesagt, kann aber sehr wohl vorausgesetzt sein. Alle Kinder haben solch einen Schutzengel, nicht nur jüdische oder christliche, beschnittene oder getaufte Kinder.

Es ist ein schönes und eindrucksvolles, aber doch auch melancholisches Wort.

Denn wird hier doch nicht auch implizite gesagt, dass nur den Engeln der Kinder die Möglichkeit zur Gottesschau geboten ist? Muss man nicht hinzufügen, dass aus irgendwelchen Gründen die Engel der Erwachsenen diese Gottesschau nicht mehr erlangen? Ist da etwas passiert, hat sich irgendeine tragische Entwicklung vollzogen, wodurch die Erwachsenen diese indirekte und unbewusste, aber reale Gottesschau nicht mehr kennen? Die Frage kann man stellen, aber man bekommt keine Antwort.

Immerhin hat nach Jesus jedes Kind einen speziellen und personalen Schutzengel, welchem das Schauen Gottes geschenkt wird. Und das geschieht διὰ παντός, „allezeit". Parallelen aus späterer Zeit legen es nahe, dass auch diese Worte eine besondere Bedeutung haben.

Das ursprüngliche griechisch geschriebene, in syrischer Übersetzung bewahrte, im 5. Jahrhundert in Syrien entstandene *Testamentum Domini* (S. 97) sagt vom Schutzengel:

„Denn von jeder Seele steht das Ebenbild [syr. *zalma* = hebr. *zelem*) oder der Typus vor dem Angesicht Gottes vor der Grundlegung der Welt".

Das ist verständlich. Nach jüdischer und christlicher Auffassung sind die Engel, also auch die Schutzengel, vor der Schöpfung der Welt geschaffen worden. Also lebt auch der Schutzengel nach dem Tode des Menschen, zu dem er gehört, im Himmel weiter fort. Dieses transzendente Ebenbild des Menschen ist ewig. So mag auch das „allezeit" im Jesuswort zu verstehen sein. Die Gemeinde und auch der Evangelist haben das Wort wahrscheinlich aufgegriffen, weil sie es ganz anders verstanden haben.

Sie haben „die Kleinen" nicht als die Kinder, sondern als die Christen aufgefasst. Das zeigt der Anfang dieser Perikope (18, 6): „Wer aber einen dieser Kleinen, die an mich glauben, zur Sünde verführt, für den wäre es besser, dass ihm ein Mühlstein um den Hals gehängt und er in die Tiefe des Meeres versenkt würde". Die „Kleinen" sind also in diesem Kontext „diejenigen, welche an Christus glauben, die Gläubigen". Man muss diese Exegese der Gemeinde ganz ernst nehmen. Das Wort bedeutet dann etwa folgendes: „Passet auf, dass ihr keinen Christen, auch nicht den niedrigsten und geringsten, verachtet. Denn sie haben jeder für sich einen Schutzengel, welcher im Himmel das Antlitz Gottes schaut". Das setzt voraus, dass nicht jedermann so einen Schutzengel hat: das ist ein besonderes Privileg der Christen. Christ wird man, indem man sich taufen lässt. Nicht selten findet man in den Quellen, dass der Christ erst bei der Taufe seinen Schutzengel bekommt.

So spiegelt das Jesuswort in der Fassung des Matthäus in seinem heutigen Kontext wahrscheinlich eine liturgische Auffassung der Gemeinde: erst wenn der Christ der Welt entsagt und die Taufe empfängt, wird ihm sein Schutzengel zugeordnet, der ihn dann vor Gott vertritt. Erst während des Lebens kommt die Verbindung mit dem Ebenbild zustande. Ob dieses Verhältnis nach dem Tode aufgelöst wird oder bestehen bleibt, wird nicht gesagt. Es ist aber deutlich, dass man auf Grund dieses Wortes sehr leicht zu der Auffassung kommen könnte, dass eine ewige Verbindung zwischen dem Menschen und seinem ewigen Ebenbilde bestehe.

Unsere Untersuchung hat uns zu unerwarteten Resultaten geführt. Die Vorstellung von der Zweisamkeit des Menschen, von der intimen Verbindung zwischen dem Erdenwesen und seinem transzendenten Ebenbild, geht auf die palästinensische Urgemeinde zurück und findet sich möglicherweise auch bei Jesus selbst.

Es ist hier der Ort zu bedenken, dass es schon sehr früh in der Geschichte eine gewisse Spannung zwischen der Gemeinde Antiochiens und Jerusalems gegeben hat. Man kann die eine der Parteien die Judenchristen und die andere die Heidenchristen nennen, weil der Streit darum geht, wieweit das jüdische Gesetz auch für die Christen, die vom Heidentum hergekommen sind, verbindlich sei.

Paulus, ein Missionar der antiochenischen Gemeinde, vertrat die Auffassung, dass Heidenchristen nichts mehr mit dem mosaischen Gesetze zu tun hätten. Die Judenchristen von Jerusalem hatten verschiedene Meinungen: keiner von ihnen aber ging so weit wie Paulus.

Der Streit wurde schiedlich-friedlich beigelegt, indem entschieden wurde, dass die Antiochener unter den Heiden, die Jerusalemer unter den Juden Mission treiben sollten (Gal. 2, 9). Und Lukas hat uns in seiner Apostelgeschichte dargestellt, welche glänzenden Erfolge Paulus als Apostel der Heiden gehabt hat. Lukas berichtet nicht, wie das Christentum nach Ägypten oder nach Mesopotamien gekommen ist; auch über den Ursprung des Christentums in Rom teilt er nichts mit. Es ist uns nun in der letzten Zeit klar geworden, dass das palästinensische Christentum viel wichtiger gewesen ist und zur Ausbreitung des Christentums viel mehr beigetragen hat, als man früher meinte. Gerade in den Gegenden, wo viele Juden wohnten, scheinen judenchristliche Missionare tätig gewesen zu sein. Es steht heute wohl fest, dass Edessa, das dauernde Zentrum des syrischen Christentums, sein Christentum aus Palästina empfangen hat. Die Ursprünge des Christentums in Ägypten sind ungewiss; man hat aber mit guten Gründen vermutet, dass auch hier zuerst Judenchristen aus dem so nahen Jerusalem als Missionare tätig gewesen sind. Und nach einer Überlieferung sollen auch in Rom Judenchristen schon vor der Ankunft Pauli tätig gewesen sein.

Die Belege für die Auffassung, dass der Mensch ein himmliches Ebenbild hat, finden sich vor allem im *Pastor Hermae,* in Schriften der valentinianischen Schule und im Thomas-Evangelium.

Hermas war ein römischer Christ des 2. Jahrhunderts. Valentinus war ein christlicher Gnostiker, der in Ägypten geboren worden ist; das Thomasevangelium ist 140 nach Christus in Edessa geschrieben worden. Man fragt sich, ob in diesen drei Fällen nicht ein Erbe des palästinensischen Judenchristentums vorliegt.

*   *   *

Die manichäische Religion ist in diesem Jahrhundert durch die Funde unbekannter Handschriften besser bekannt geworden. Seit 1903 werden regelmässig ausführliche Fragmente von Übersetzungen ins Parthische, Mittelpersische und in andere orientalische Sprachen veröffentlicht, welche man seinerzeit in Turfan (Chinesisch-Turkestan) gefunden hat. 1931 wurden in Medinet Madi koptische Schriften der manichäischen Religion gefunden, die bis heute nur zum Teil herausgegeben sind.

Ich würde nicht sagen, dass dadurch die manichäische Dogmatik oder der manichäische Mythus viel besser bekannt geworden sei: die Lehre hat man schon ziemlich gut aus den Streitschriften christlicher oder islamitischer Bekämpfer des Manichäismus gekannt. Überraschend war aber, dass diese Lehre sehr eng mit der Liturgie, also mit dem Leben zusammenhing und als Ausdruck davon gelten darf. Vor allem die sogenannte Totenmesse scheint der eigentliche Kern dieser Religion zu sein. Im koptischen Psalmenbuch werden viele Hymnen der Totenmesse überliefert, die unter den „Psalmen für Jesus" und den „Psalmen von Herakleides" zu finden sind. Die parthischen Fragmente der Totenlieder wurden 1954 von Mary Boyce herausgegeben und zeigen mit den koptischen Psalmen in Stil und Inhalt grosse Übereinstimmung. Es ist deutlich, dass diese koptischen und parthischen Totenlieder einem literarischen Genus angehören, das bis in die Frühzeit des Manichäismus zurückgeht. Man vermutet, dass die parthischen Hymnuszyklen auf Mar Ammo, Manis eigenen

Apostel der Parthen, zurückgehen. Auch die koptischen Psalmen dieser Art
können von einem Schüler Manis, welcher nach dem Westen ausgesandt
wurde, verfasst sein.

Das sind meistens sehr schöne, sehr eindrucksvolle Gedichte. Es wird dargestellt, wie die Seele in der Todesstunde von allen Seiten durch Dämonen
bedrängt wird und ihren Erlöser um Hilfe fleht, dann aber auch erhört wird,
indem der Erlöser ihr erscheint und sie in das „Brautgemach" führt. Dieser
Erlöser hat verschiedene Namen: Jesus, oder Mani, oder Geist, Nous; und
damit ist der so komplizierte manichäische Hymnus auf seine einfachste Formel
zurückgebracht: der Geist rettet die Seele aus der Materie.

Es scheint mir, dass diese Liturgie der Totenmesse nun wieder etwas zum
Ausdruck bringt, was der Stifter des Manichäismus selber erlebt hat. Dann
wäre diese Liturgie eigentlich die Institutionalisierung eines einmaligen
Erlebnisses, das als exemplarisch und massgebend für jeden Anhänger oder
wenigstens jeden Erwählten betrachtet wird.

Über dieses Erlebnis des Mani sind wir gut unterrichtet. Es berichtet der
arabische Schriftsteller An Nadim in seinem *Fihrist*, Mani habe schon als
Knabe weise Worte gesprochen. Als er das zwölfte Jahr vollendet hatte, habe
ihm Gott einen Engel geschickt, von dem er Eingebungen erhielt. Dieser Engel
hiess at-Taum. Er befahl ihm, die asketische Glaubensgemeinde, welcher sein
Vater angehörte, zu verlassen. Als er das vierundzwanzigste Jahr vollendet
hatte, kam der Engel at-Taum abermals zu ihm und sprach: „Die Zeit ist nun
für dich da, dass du öffentlich hervortrittst und deine eigene Lehre verkündest".

Dieser Bericht wird von den gefundenen Originalschriften bestätigt. So heisst
es in einem mitteliranischen Fragment, M. 49:

„Und auch jetzt noch begleitet er selbst mich, und er selbst hält und schützt
mich … Und den Weg der Weisen ergriff ich, und diese Dinge, die der
Zwilling mich gelehrt hatte, begann ich dann meinem Vater und den Ältesten
meiner Familie mitzuteilen und sie zu lehren".

Mani betrachtet also seine Lehre als eine von einem Engel geschenkte
Offenbarung. Seitdem begleitete und schützte ihn dieser Engel: er war also
Manis Schutzengel. Aber er war auch mehr: er war die fortwährende Quelle
seiner Inspiration, er gab ihm die Gnosis ein. Und der Name dieses Engels
war: „Zwilling".

In den koptischen manichäischen Schriften, wo diese Gestalt sehr oft erwähnt
wird, heisst er allerdings nicht „Zwilling", aber „Paargenosse" (*saiš*), was dem
griechischen σύζυγος entspricht. Dort hören wir auch, dass diese Lichtgestalt
Mani noch in den Bedrängnissen der Todesstunde beigestanden habe.

„Ich schaute auf meinen Paargenossen mit meinen Lichtaugen, betrachtend meinen herrlichen Vater, der allezeit mich erwartet(?) und vor mir die Türe nach oben öffnet" (*Man. Psalmbuch,* Allberry, S. 19, 22-24).

Der Paargenosse erlöst Mani also auch vom Tode, führt ihn hinauf und öffnet für ihn die Türe des himmlischen Paradieses.

Es ist deutlich, dass diese Auffassung der valentinianischen sehr ähnlich ist. Mani hat einen personalen Engel, der ihm die Gnosis schenkt und ihn vom Tode rettet.

Nun wissen wir leider nicht, ob die valentinianische Gnosis Mani bekannt gewesen ist. An sich wäre es möglich, denn Valentinus lebte im 2. und Mani im 3. Jahrhundert. Weiter muss Mani gewisse gnostische Vorstellungen gekannt haben; dass zum Beispiel einer der dämonischen Mächte nach ihm Ashaqlun heisst, geht zurück auf Saklas, „Tor", eine Bezeichnung für den Demiurgen im Apokryphon des Johannes, das dem 2. Jahrhundert entstammt.

Aber das Verhältnis des Mani zur Gnosis des 2. Jahrhunderts ist noch nicht sorgfältig untersucht worden. Bei der heutigen Lage der Forschung dürfen wir nicht ohne weiteres annehmen, dass er die valentinianische Vorstellung vom *mysterium conjunctionis* zwischen Engel und Mensch gekannt hat.

Und doch ist der Vergleich sinnvoll. Denn dann sieht man, dass das eigentliche Anliegen des Mani nicht so sehr der Dualismus als die *dualitudo* war. Er lehrt zwar den absoluten Gegensatz von Gott und Teufel, Geist und Stoff, Licht und Finsternis; aber das ist nur eine Begleiterscheinung seines eigentlichen Erlebnisses, der Verbundenheit und Polarität von Mensch und Engel, Ich und Selbst. Weder Gott noch die Materie haben damit viel zu tun.

Man kann nun sagen, dass dieses Erlebnis durchaus einmalig sei und damit die Originalität des Mani als Stifter einer Weltreligion herauszustellen versuchen. Aber dann ignoriert man wohl absichtlich, dass sich die Forschung seit zwanzig Jahren eingehend mit dieser religiösen Struktur der *dualitudo* beschäftigt und auch manches entdeckt hat, was das Erlebnis des Mani besser verstehen lässt. Wir verzichten darauf, diesen Weg einer angeblichen Phänomenologie auf Kosten der historischen Wissenschaft zu gehen, und suchen die Perspektive, welche es ermöglicht, Manis Begegnung mit dem Engel, und so den Manichäismus überhaupt, besser zu verstehen.

Mani hat das syrische Christentum gekannt. Und zwar scheint er hauptsächlich mit der Fassung der christlichen Religion in Berührung gekommen zu sein, welche sich durch einen weitgehenden Enkratismus und eine strenge Askese — kein Weib, kein Fleisch, keinen Wein — von anderen Richtungen unterschied.

Er kannte und benutzte das Thomasevangelium, eine enkratitische Schrift. Er scheint auch das Evangelium hauptsächlich aus der Evangelienharmonie des syrischen Enkratiten Tatian zur Kenntnis genommen zu haben. Und man muss sich fragen, ob die strenge Askese der Manichäer nicht hauptsächlich dem Einfluss dieses enkratitischen Christentums zu verdanken ist. Im syrischen Christentum finden sich nun auch die Vorstufen und Vorformen, welche es verständlich machen, dass Mani seinen Engel „Zwilling" und „Paargenosse" genannt hat.

„Thomas" ist aramäisch und bedeutet „Zwilling". Es ist überhaupt kein Eigenname. Das wussten die syrischen Christen, welche aramäisch sprachen. Deshalb nannten sie den Apostel Thomas auch „Judas Thomas". Dabei wurde vorausgesetzt, dass Judas, der im Evangelium als Bruder von Jesus erwähnt wird, mit dem Apostel Thomas identisch sei. Ein amerikanischer Gelehrter hat neuerdings die Vermutung ausgesprochen, dass das auch wirklich so gewesen sei und dass Jesus einen Zwillingsbruder namens Judas Thomas gehabt habe. So weit braucht man nicht zu gehen; aber es steht fest, dass die syrischen Christen Judas Thomas als Herrenbruder betrachteten.

Dieser Judas Thomas war nun für die syrischen, enkratitischen Christen der grosse Apostel. Was Petrus für Rom war und Johannes für Ephesus und Jakobus für Jerusalem, das war Thomas für Edessa.

In den Thomasakten, welche um 225 nach Christus in Edessa entstanden sind und die Reise dieses Apostels nach Indien darstellen, wird Thomas als Zwilling Christi bezeichnet: „du Zwilling Christi, Apostel des Allerhöchsten" (c. 39). Christus erscheint auch in den Thomasakten in der Gestalt des Apostels, und zwar als Lichterscheinung bei einer Taufe. — Man muss, wenn man diese Darstellung liest, vor Augen haben, dass Zwillinge einander meistens zum Verwechseln ähnlich sind. Christus ist als Zwillingbruder des Thomas sein Ebenbild, sein himmliches und ewiges Ebenbild.

Das war in diesem Fall möglich, weil die edessener Christen annahmen, Christus sei der Zwllingsbruder des Judas Thomas. Aber es ist schon so, dass nach hellenistischen Vorstellungen jedermann seinen Zwillingsbruder haben kann.

Beim griechischen Schriftsteller Lucian finden wir eine lustige Geschichte. Da begegnet der Zyniker Diogenes in der Unterwelt dem Schatten des Herakles. Es ist dies das Eidolon des Helden. Das Lustige dieser Erzählung besteht darin, dass Herakles selbst körperlich in den Himmel aufgenommen ist, während sein Eidolon im Hades verbleibt. Lucian verspottet hier die landläufige Vorstellung, dass die sterbliche Hülle hier auf der Erde verbleibt, während der Geist in die himmlische Unsterblichkeit eingeht. Das Verhältnis vom Eidolon des Herakles zu seinem Körper wird nun so dargestellt, dass das Eidolon die εἰκών des Herakles sei, also sein Ebenbild, das ihm genau gleicht: Eidolon und Mensch sind Zwillinge (*Dial. Mortuorum* 16).

Da versteht man, dass es auf Grund von hellenistischen Vorstellungen sehr gut möglich war, die Lichtgestalt des himmlischen Christus als Zwilling und Ebenbild des irdischen Judas Thomas darzustellen. Erik Peterson hat schon vor zwanzig Jahren festgestellt, dass das religiöse Erlebnis des Mani diese Auffassung der syrischen Christen voraussetzt, ist doch der Name des Engels, der sich dem Mani offenbart, at-Taum, genau derselbe wie der des Apostels Thomas [1].

Das heisst: die Form des religiösen Erlebnisses des Mani ist von syrisch-christlichen Vorstellungen bestimmt. Mani hat sich später nicht ohne Grund einen Apostel von Jesus Christus genannt, offenbarte sich ihm doch dieselbe Zwillingsgestalt, die sich einst mit dem Apostel Thomas verbunden hatte.

Nun darf man nicht fragen, ob die Lichtgestalt entweder Christus oder der Heilige Geist war. Die syrischen christlichen Quellen lassen eine solche Differenzierung nicht zu. Dort erscheint der Geist mit seinem Licht in der Gestalt Christi, weil er der Geist Christi ist. Wahrscheinlich aber hat Mani seinen Zwilling als den Geist betrachtet; es wird berichtet, er habe sich darauf berufen, von seinem Zwilling, das heisst vom Heiligen Geist, angenommen zu sein.

Das führt uns nun zu der Frage, wie der Ausdruck „Paargenosse" aufzufassen sei. Wiederum Erik Peterson hat dafür auf die Theologie des Syrers Tatian verwiesen. Dieser gibt einmal eine sehr merkwürdige Interpretation des Bibelwortes: „Und das Licht leuchtet in der Finsternis und die Finsternis hat es nicht erfasst". Diese Worte beziehen sich nach ihm auf den Geist, der zu der Seele kommt, sie erleuchtet und hinaufführt. Geist und Seele bilden eine Syzygie. Der Geist wäre also der Paargenosse, der Syzygos, der Seele.

So bietet uns das syrische Christentum manche wertvolle Parallele zum Erlebnis des Mani. Von jeher hat man auch das Perlenlied zum Vergleich herangezogen und sogar vermutet, dass der Prinz, der in diesem Gedicht nach Ägypten zieht, um die Perle zu holen, und auf der Rückkehr seinem eigenen Selbst in der Form seines himmlischen Kleides begegnet, eigentlich Mani selbst war. Denn Mani war königlicher Herkunft und hatte seine Begegnung mit dem Zwilling.

Es ist aber mit volkomener Sicherheit festgestellt worden, dass das Lied von der Perle vormanichäisch ist und die geistige Welt zeigt, in die Mani eingetreten ist. Das Perlenlied ist aber in einem christlichen Buch enthalten, das, wie gesagt, um 225 nach Christus in Edessa erschienen ist; es ist auch selbst ein

---

[1] E. Peterson, *Frühkirche, Judentum und Gnosis*, Rom, 1959, p. 205.

christliches Gedicht, das die Geschichte der Seele und die Begegnung mit dem Ebenbilde erzählt:

> „Doch plötzlich, als ich es mir gegenüber sah, wurde das
> Strahlenkleid ähnlich meinem Spiegelbild mir gleich;
> Ich sah es ganz in mir,
> und in ihm sah ich mich auch mir ganz gegenüber,
> so dass wir Zwei waren in Geschiedenheit
> und wieder Eins in einer Gestalt".

Das himmlische Kleid ist das Kleid des Geistes; als solches ist es das himmlische Ebenbild, der Eikon, das eigentliche Selbst des Menschen. Das kann man nur verstehen, wenn man weiss, dass die Juden sich den Schutzengel als himmlisches Ebenbild vorgestellt haben und dass die syrischen Christen dies durch Vermittlung des Judenchristentums übernommen haben.

Es ist aber deutlich, dass das eine sehr schöne Parallele für das religiöse Erlebnis von Mani ist.

Andererseits muss nun auch beachtet werden, dass im Perlenlied der Mantel nicht nur Ebenbild des Menschen, sondern zugleich *imago Dei* ist:

> „Und das Bild des Königs der Könige
> War ihm vollständig überall aufgemalt".

Diese Terminologie setzt die Auffassung der Genesis voraus, dass der Mensch nach dem Bilde Gottes geschaffen ist, allerdings dann nicht der empirische Mensch, das Ich, sondern der himmlische Doppelgänger, das Selbst. Das Selbst ist die eigentliche *imago Dei* und Einfallspforte für das Göttliche in das Menschenleben. Wir haben diese Auffassung schon im Judentum und im syrischen Christentum gefunden.

Sie scheint mir grundlegend für den Manichäismus zu sein: Gott spricht zu Mani durch den Zwilling, das Ebenbild; er spricht zu den Manichäern durch die Lichtgestalt. Das ist vom Judentum und vom syrischen Christentum her zu verstehen. Man streit darüber, ob der Manichäismus eine iranische oder eine hellenistische Religion ist. Mir scheint es, der Manichäismus sei eher eine christliche Gnosis, allerdings mit iranischen und hellenistischen Elementen. Aber um das religiöse Erlebnis des Mani zu verstehen, reichen die Dokumente des syrischen Christentums aus: dort fand er die Auffassung, dass der Erlöser sein Zwilling, dass der Geist sein Paargenosse sei.

Und obwohl natürlich nicht zu bezweifeln ist, dass Mani ein echtes, authentisches Erlebnis gehabt hat, das ihn zu seiner gewaltigen Tätigkeit in Asien inspiriert hat, kann man andererseits sagen, dass er dieses Erlebnis in christlichen Kategorien ausgedrückt hat.

Die Auffassung der Erlösung im Manichäismus läuft nun mit dem Erlebnis des Mani parallel.

Darüber berichtet An-Nadim im *Fihrist:*

„Wenn der Tod", lehrt Mani, „einem Wahrhaftigen naht, sendet der Urmensch einen Lichtgott in der Gestalt des leitenden Weisen und mit ihm drei Götter und zugleich mit diesen den Sieg(espreis), das Kleid, die Kopfbinde, die Krone und den Lichtkranz.
Mit ihnen kommt die Jungfrau, ähnlich der Seele dieses Wahrhaftigen.
Auch erscheint ihm der Teufel der Habgier und der Sinnenlust mit anderen Teufeln. Sobald der Wahrhaftige diese erblickt, ruft er die Hilfe des Gottes(?), welcher(?) die Gestalt des Weisen angenommen hat, und der anderen drei Götter an, und diese nähern sich ihm.
Sobald die Teufel sie gewahr werden, wenden sie sich fliehend um. Jene aber nehmen diesen Wahrhaftigen, bekleiden ihn mit der Krone, dem Kranze und dem Kleide, geben ihm den Sieg(espreis) in die Hand und steigen mit ihm auf der Säule des Lobpreises zu der Sphäre des Mondes, zu dem Urmenschen und zu der strahlenden Mutter der Lebendigen bis zu dem Zustand, in dem er zuerst im Paradiese des Lichtes war".

Die Totenlieder der koptischen und parthischen Manichaica bestätigen diesen Bericht im grossen und ganzen. Allerdings besteht ein gewisser Unterschied zwischen beiden: in den koptischen Schriften wird der Erlöser dann und wann als Nous, Geist, oder als Mani, der Paraklet, bezeichnet, meistens aber als Jesus; in den parthischen Schriften wird der Erlöser nur „dein Geist" oder „dein Grosser Geist" genannt. Die Lage ist bei diesen Totenmesseliedern komplizierter als bei der Darstellung des Erlebnisses von Mani. Man sieht ganz deutlich, dass Mani ein synkretistischer Denker war, der Elemente aus verschiedenen Religionen übernommen hat.

Der Lichtgott in der Gestalt des leitenden Weisen wäre dann das Ebenbild. Daneben findet sich die Vorstellung eines Mädchens, das der Seele der Verstorbenen ähnlich ist.

In einer sogdischen Erzählung der Manichäer ist dieses Mädchen das Werk des Verstorbenen, eine wunderbare, göttliche Prinzessin, eine Magd. Durch seine guten Werke hat der Mensch auf Erden diese Gestalt im Himmel aufgebaut. Es ist zweifellos die Daēnā der iranischen Religion.

Davon muss nun aber die göttliche Lichtgestalt in der Gestalt des Weisen unterschieden werden. Dieser ist nicht ein Erzeugnis des Menschen, der neue Mensch, sondern eine ewige, göttliche Gestalt. Er ist, wie die koptischen Kephalaia ausführen, eine Gestalt, die eine parallele Funktion hat wie der Paargenosse von Mani.

„Die zweite ist der Paargenosse, der zum Apostel kommt und sich ihm offenbart, indem er ihm Wohngenosse ist und ihn überallhin begleitet und ihm zu jeder Zeit aus allen Bedrängnissen und Gefahren hilft. Die dritte ist die Lichtgestalt, welche die Electi und die Katechumenen annehmen, wenn sie der Welt entsagen".

Die Lichtgestalt kommt also nicht erst beim Tode zum Gläubigen, sie tritt schon während des Lebens in die Existenz hinein, und zwar dann, wenn der Mensch in die manichäische Kirche eintritt. Wie in der christlichen Kirche der Schutzengel und der Geist bei der Taufe zum Menschen kommen, so tritt auch die Lichtgestalt bei dem Eintritt in die Gemeinde der Manichäer in Erscheinung.

Die „Lichtgestalt" tut im Leben des einzelnen, was „der Zwilling" im Leben Manis tat: sie gibt ihm die Gnosis und rettet vom Tode.

In einem koptischen Psalm des manichäischen Psalmbuches wird der Seele ein Paargenosse zugesprochen (*Pesaiš n̄atouine*). Das setzt natürlich voraus, dass jede einzelne Seele einen Paargenossen und Doppelgänger hat. Es ist dies meiner Ansicht nach die Lichtgestalt.

Das Eigentliche scheint mir aber zum Ausdruck gebracht zu sein, wenn die Lichtgestalt „das zweite Selbst" oder auch „das lebendige Ich" oder „die Seele oben" genannt wird. In all diesen Fällen wäre es wohl möglich, mit „Selbst" zu übersetzen. Und das Merkwürdige ist nun, dass dieser Erlöser, dieses Selbst, dann doch auch wieder vom Menschen, zu dem er gehört, erlöst wird. Wie in der valentinianischen Gnosis nicht nur der Mensch auf seinen persönlichen Engel angewiesen ist, sondern der Engel auch unbedingt den Menschen braucht, weil er ohne ihn unvollständig ist und nicht in das Pleroma zurückkehren kann, so ist auch im Manichäismus das Selbst vom Ich abhängig und benötigt es.

Darum sagt in einem parthischen Hymnus das Selbst zu der Seele: „And I am the Light of thy whole structure, thy soul (*gryv*) above and base of life".

Und in einem parthischen Hymnus der Elekten auf das Lebendige Ich heisst es:

> „Dich, o Ich, wollen wir preisen, unsrer Seele Leben.
> Dich wollen wir lobpreisen, Jesus Messias,
> verzeihender Beleber, sieh auf mich!
> Würdig bist du der Verehrung, erlöstes Licht-Ich.
> Heil sei über dich, o Ich, und auch über uns sei Heil.
> Würdig bist du des Licht-Ichs, glänzendes, strahlendes Glied.
> Gekommen bist du mit Heil, der Götter Licht-Ich, das im
>   Finstern leuchtet,
> Preist, ihr Söhne der Wahrheit, das Ich, das unser Leben ist.
> Gekommen bist du mit Heil, du teures
> Ich, geschickter und kampfsuchender Gott,
> Gekommen ist dieses verehrte Ich, (befreit) aus aller
>   Umklammerung".

Auch das Leben des einzelnen Manichäers beruht auf der *dualitudo*, der Spannung und der Verbundenheit der menschlichen Seele mit ihrem Selbst, worin die Gottheit sich vergegenwärtigt.

Das heisst: Mani hat sein eigenes religiöses Erlebnis, die Begegnung mit dem Zwilling, institutionalisiert und für die Mitglieder seiner Religion verbindlich gemacht. Es ist dies aber mehr als die Verbundenheit mit dem Schutzengel oder auch dem Geist, welche sich im syrischen Christentum findet. Grundlegend ist die Ansicht, dass die Gottheit sich durch Vermittlung dieser *dualitudo* verwirklicht und erlöst. Jeder einzelne Manichäer kann durch sein Leben und seine Taten dazu beitragen, dass die göttliche Tragödie ihrer Vollendung zugeführt wird. Die Gottheit hat durchaus ein Interesse daran, dass der Mensch seine Aufgabe erfüllt, weil sie dadurch selbst aus der Umklammerung mit der Materie erlöst wird.

Das ist gnostische Religion. Es setzt voraus, dass es einen tragischen Bruch innerhalb der Gottheit gegeben hat. In der älteren Gnosis wird das so ausgedrückt, dass die Sophia gefallen ist und durch die Welt hindurchgehen muss, um zu ihrem Ursprung zurückzukehren. Im Manichäismus wird eigentlich dasselbe gesagt, wenn es heisst, dass der Urmensch vor Bestehen der Welt im Kampf gegen die bösen Dämonen besiegt worden ist und seine Seele oder auch seine Glieder in der Materie hinterlassen hat: jede Seele des einzelnen Menschen ist ein Teil davon; deshalb hilft auch die Seele der Gottheit in ihrem Kampf gegen die Finsternis und ermöglicht es ihr, sich ganz vom Reiche der Materie zu trennen. So kann darum der Lichtgeist zu der Seele in einem parthischen Hymnus sagen: „Thou art my word and my panoply of war, which saved me fully from the fight, and from all sinners".

Auf dem Hintergrund der göttlichen Tragödie erhält das Leben des Einzelnen seine volle Bedeutsamkeit. Das göttliche Selbst wird vom menschlichen Ich erlöst, weil im Selbst die werdende Gottheit um ihre Befreiung ringt. Es ist dies eine abgründige Sicht, welche in anderer Form bei den deutschen Idealisten Schelling und Hegel wiederkehrt.

Bei den Manichäern beruht sie auf der Erfahrung, dass Bild und Ebenbild, Mensch und Zwillingsbruder, Seele und Geist, Ich und Selbst eine ewig bleibende Polarität und Verbindung der Gegensätze bilden.

FROM MYTHOS TO LOGOS

Valentinus lived in the second century A.D., whereas Plotinus and Origen were contemporaries in the third century A.D. Plotinus was a philosopher, in fact the greatest Greek philosopher after Plato and Aristotle. He profoundly influenced the philosophers of the Italian Renaissance, as well as Hegel and Bergson, and indeed all true philosophers of our time.

Origen was a theologian and a dogmatician. His work, *De Principiis* (About the Beginnings), was the first systematic Christian dogmatics. Through his disciples, such as Gregory of Nyssa, he exerted a decisive influence on the development and finalization of the dogma of the Trinity at the oecumenical Council of 381 A.D. and his influence on the Eastern Churches, as well as the Roman Catholic Church, can be felt even today.

Of the three — Plotinus, Origen and Valentinus — one was thus a philosopher, the other a dogmatician, and the third a Gnostic. It is hardly possible to conceive of three more different worlds. Yet, in a daring move, Hans Jonas tried to bring these three persons under one hat in his much quoted and influential book, entitled *Gnosis und spätantiker Geist* (Gnosis and the Spirit of Late Antiquity)[1]. According to him, Valentinus, Origen and Plotinus, each in his own way, represented some form of Gnosis. In fact, he claimed that not only Valentinus but also Origen and Plotinus were actually Gnostics. Gnosis *and* Late Antiquity? No, Gnosis *was* Late Antiquity. I must point out immediately that Hans Jonas' arguments met with strong opposition both from philosophers and theologians. Just at the time Jonas published his book, the classical philologists were busy discovering that Plotinus fitted perfectly into the traditional mould of Greek philosophy, i.e., Greek rationalism. Whereas it is true that he took up the ontological problems of Plato and Aristotle, excellent research work carried out in the last decade showed that he also incorporated the tradition of so-called Middle Platonism, as, for instance, that of Albinus, or of Antiochus of Ascalon[2]. In looking, for instance, at Plotinus' differentiation between intuitive and discursive reasoning, which was basic for his thinking, we find that it was already part of the middle Platonist tradition at the beginning of the Christian era. Therefore, the classical philologists claimed that Plotinus should be understood strictly in terms of the classical

---

[1] H. Jonas, *Gnosis und spätantiker Geist,* I, II, 2nd ed., Göttingen, 1954.

[2] P. Merlan, *From Platonism to Neoplatonism,* The Hague, 1953 (2nd ed. 1960); A. H. Armstrong, *Plotinus,* in *The Cambridge History of Later Greek and Early Medieval Philosophy,* Cambridge, 1967, pp. 195-268.

tradition and Plotinus' doctrine of the sympathy of all things should be traced to the middle Stoa of Posidonius.

On the whole, the classical philologists wanted nothing to do with Jonas' thesis. But even the theologians did not exactly welcome it. After the second world-war, the French *Nouvelle Théologie*, under the leadership of Henri de Lubac and Jean Daniélou, rediscovered Origen as a Christian theologian. They wrote many excellent books in order to show that in actual fact Origen had little in common with philosophy or Gnosis, but that he had been a biblical theologian, who lived and was caught up in the world of biblical ideas, as only Luther was after him [3].

In the meantime we have come to know more about Valentinus. Until recently, we had only a few meagre fragments of his works. However, the situation changed completely with the acquisition of the *Jung Codex*, which contains the *Gospel of Truth* [4]. This document may have been written by Valentinus or one of his disciples. In any event, it belongs to Valentinian Gnosis and clearly shows that this Gnosis was based on an experience. Later, another document from the *Jung Codex* was published, *De Resurrectione*, which may very well have been written either by Valentinus or one of his disciples. It is concerned with resurrection and is a beautiful illustration of Goethe's verse:

> Until you have grasped this,
> Die and be transformed!
> You will be nothing
> But a sorry guest on the sombre earth. (*Selige Sehnsucht*)

A third text from the *Jung Codex*, the *Epistula Jacobi Apocrypha* [5] (the Apocryphal Letter of James), which is definitely Gnostic and possibly belongs to Valentinian Gnosis, was published in 1969. In addition the findings at Nag Hammadi gave rise to the publication of another document, entitled *The Gospel of Philip*, and two *Apocalypses of James*, all belonging to Valentinian Gnosis [6]. A whole new field of studies was opened up by these discoveries in Egypt. Finally, mention should be made of a fourth text from the *Jung Codex*. It was

---

[3] J. Daniélou, *Origène*, Paris, 1948; H. de Lubac, *Histoire et Esprit. L'Intelligence de l'Écriture d'après Origène*, Paris, 1950.

[4] *Evangelium Veritatis*, ed. M. Malinine, H.-Ch. Puech, G. Quispel, Zürich, 1956; *Evangelium Veritatis (Supplementum)*, ed. M. Malinine, H.-Ch. Puech, G. Quispel, W. Till, Zürich-Stuttgart, 1961.

[5] *Epistula Jacobi Apocrypha*, ed. M. Malinine, H.-Ch. Puech, G. Quispel, *et al.*, Zürich-Stuttgart, 1968.

[6] J. E. Ménard, *L'Évangile selon Philippe*, Paris, 1967; A. Böhlig and P. Labib, *Koptisch-gnostische Apokalypsen aus Codex V von Nag Hammadi im Koptischen Museum zu Alt-Kairo*, Halle-Wittenberg, 1963.

given the title of *Tractatus Tripartitus* and should probably be attributed to one of Valentinus' disciples, a certain Heracleon, who lived in Rome [7].

It seems to me that the time has come to have another look at Jonas' thesis, a hypothesis which, however, seems to me pregnant with possibilities from a different point of view. Actually, Plotinus, Valentinus and Origen do not represent the same spirit of late Antiquity phenomenologically speaking, but both Origen and Plotinus were historically influenced by Valentinian Gnosis. It has always been said that in his writings, Plotinus had been opposed to the Gnostics. This is indeed true. However, at times one is opposed to just those people, for whom one has a particular feeling of affinity. We are reminded of Pascal, for instance, who fought against Calvin. Before Plotinus wrote *Against the Gnostics*, he had tolerated Gnostics in his school for many years. As Porphyry pointed out in his biography, Plotinus had even been close friends with them. Moreover, thanks to these findings, we know today that Plotinus' Gnostic friends were Valentinian Gnostics. In the light of these new discoveries, one therefore has to ask whether — historically speaking — Plotinus was not more of a Gnostic than the classical philologists were willing to admit.

However, Plotinus is a subject which I dare mention only with great trepidation. Jonas never published his third volume on Plotinus, nor did Henri-Charles Puech ever publish his book about Plotinus' relationship with the Gnostics. Where such great scholars hesitated, I feel I must tread softly. There is only one thing I should like to suggest: in tracing back Plotinus' ideas to classicism, it seems to me that the classical philologists failed to provide a classical parallel to one of the fundamental concepts in Plotinian philosophy, namely the emanation. On the other hand, we know for sure that in Egyptian tradition, the concept of emanation plays an important role. Moreover, emanation was traditional among the Valentinian Gnostics. This is all we know. Valentinus was a mythopoeic person. He said the world originated in the tears and the smile of Wisdom. This is very beautiful, very impressive but it is mythology, a mythology that also expressed the idea of emanation. It is not barely possible that Plotinus was told something about this Gnostic emanation by his Gnostic friends in Rome?

As to Origen, two facts are reported about his life [8]. The first is that, when he was only a little boy, his father, who died as a martyr, made him learn the

---

[7] Cf. G. Quispel and H.-Ch. Puech, Le quatrième écrit gnostique du Codex Jung in 'Vigiliae Christianae', 9, 1955, pp. 65-102. The publication of the *Tractatus Tripartitus* is scheduled for 1973, Francke Verlag, Bern.

[8] Eusebius, *Hist. Eccl.*, VI, 2, 7 ff. and 13 ff.

Bible by heart. I believe that as a child this must have made a deep impression on Origen. The second fact concerns Origen as a young man of about sixteen or seventeen years. At that time, a wealthy lady in Alexandria took Origen, who was very poor, into her house. Another of the lady's protégés living in her home was a Gnostic, who lectured to visiting philosophers and Gnostics. The anecdote rings perfectly true. A wealthy anthroposophist lady of our day might well know a young man, whom she might introduce to anthroposophy in this manner. I do not know whether the story is actually true, but one cannot help assuming that Origen was strongly influenced by Gnosis in his youth.

From the historical point of view the thesis of Jonas can therefore be defended. Even though Plotinus and Origen were not Gnostics themselves, it is well possible that they were subjected to strong Gnostic influences. Whether Gnosis developed from mythology to philosophy is another question, but both of Jonas' theses are closely interrelated. It still remains to be seen, however, whether Gnosis is a vulgarized form of philosophy or the reverse, whether philosophy does indeed owe much to the mythology of Gnosis.

At this point I should like to use another example to illustrate the development from mythos to logos. It is an important one and belongs here. We all know how Greek culture developed from mythos to logos. Wilhelm Nestle published a very famous book on this subject and it carried the very title *Vom Mythos zum Logos* [9]. In this work Nestle gives a beautiful description of how the oriental peoples still lived in the mythos state, and how the great event in Greek culture had been the discovery of logical thinking. Later, Onians showed that although Homer's mode of thinking may still have been primitive, it did give rise to the foundations of European, that is, logical thinking. This is common knowledge. What we are concerned with here is the break-through of mythos that occurred at the beginning of our era in the Greek-Hellenistic world, a culture with a rational approach to the universe. How could it happen? To answer this question, we have to go back to the authors of the Gnostic heresy, Simon Magus and his Helen, who also were the prototypes for Goethe's Faust and Helen.

Around 225 A.D., Hippolytus transmitted to us a systematization of Simonean Gnosis that was probably written 150 years after the death of Simon Magus [10]. In this unique document no reference is made to sin. Furthermore, the name of Christ never appears, which is noteworthy because Gnosis is always looked upon as a Christian heresy, whereas in this document of Simonean Gnosis there is no suggestion of Christian religion, nor is the name of Christ

---

[9] W. Nestle, *Vom Mythos zum Logos*, 2nd ed., Stuttgart, 1942 (reprint: Aalen, 1966).
[10] Hippolytus, *Refutatio*, VI, 9, 3-18, 7.

mentioned. What is more, there is no reference to God. One is tempted to speak of an *absentia realis*. To the pseudo-Simon, the author of the document, the foundation of the universe consists of infinite energy that both generates and permeates everything. On the analogy that a point in itself is nothing but can form a line by being added to other points, the author claims that this infinite energy is also present in man. According to him, the purpose of human life is to develop this zero point into an image, to the state of "being-in-the-image" (*Ebenbildlichkeit*). This is a very impressive concept and we have to see it in the light of the Stoic concept of *zotikè dynamis*, the life energy that permeates everything. It is a form of Gnosis, perhaps a vitalistic philosophy, but in any event it is also philosophy.

To find out something about this Gnostic philosophy, we must try to discover its mythological roots. We therefore have to look at Simon and Helen. We are told that Simon lived in Samaria and was married to a prostitute by the name of Helen. The Helen in question was said to have been the cosmogonic potency that created the world and was subsequently overwhelmed by the *archontes*, the rulers of the world. In the perspective of "being-in-the-image" we can understand this, although it is difficult to discover the right approach. After all we know that in Antiquity Helen was revered as a goddess, since her images and shrines were found everywhere, including Samaria. Moreover, we are familiar with a Pythagorean exegesis of the myth about Helen of Troy. The Pythagoreans thought that the name, Helen, was somehow connected with Selene, the moon. They said that Helen had actually been a moon virgin and had once lived in the moon. Subsequently, she had been abducted, just as Helen of Troy had been abducted by Paris, and like her, she had to live on this earth until she was allowed to return to the moon. The Pythagoreans therefore saw in Homer's story a reenactment of the myth about the soul which had lived in the moon and after an exile in our world had returned to its place of origin. It becomes quite clear that for the Greeks Helen originally symbolized the anima. But nothing in the Greek sources indicates that Helen was considered to be a cosmogonic potency. This aspect has to be viewed in another perspective.

It should be recalled that Helen was also called Sophia, i.e., Wisdom. Even in *The Proverbs* and in *Sophia Salomonis*, Wisdom, ḥokhmah, seems to tend towards hypostasis. Furthermore, in a recently discovered "targum of fragments" we find an interesting variant of this story [11]. Because in Judaism it was assumed that as God's mediator Wisdom had been present during

---

[11] H. R. Weiss, *Untersuchungen zur Kosmologie des hellenistischen und palästinensischen Judentums*, Berlin, 1966, p. 199.

creation, the beginning of the Bible was read differently from the way we do:
In the "targum of fragments", the Hebrew *be-reschit* (in the beginning) —
"In the beginning God created the heavens and the earth", — was replaced
by *be-ḥokhmah*, and we thus read: "In His Wisdom God created the heavens
and the earth".

The remarkable thing is that in Samaritan liturgy, which has survived down to
our day, the same tradition can be found [12]. Here we read that in the beginning,
God in His Wisdom created the heavens. This seems to me to be the light
in which we have to view the myth of Helen, who was sent to earth by God
in order to create the rulers of the world, the angels; subsequently, she was
overpowered by them and was to be delivered from her exile on earth.

The increased emphasis placed by scholars on the Jewish background of Gnosis
is still highly contested. Some opponents of this thesis say that the origins of
Gnosis are not to be found in Judaism properly speaking, but in the vicinity
of Judaism, in other words, the Samaritan sect. That is all right, but the
Samaritans have to be looked upon as Jewish heretics. Especially the above
quotation that "In His Wisdom God created the heavens" shows the inter-
relationship between Simonean Gnosis and beliefs held by the Samaritans, as
well as certain Jewish circles. In trying to get to the bottom of this vitalistic
philosophy we came across the extraordinary Samaritan myth of *ḥokhmah*, the
cosmogonic potency.

According to a later Simonean tradition, Sophia is said to have shown herself
to the archons, the rulers of the world, sometimes in the form of a man and at
other times in the form of a woman [13]. The answer to the question whether
this is a true tradition can only be found in another document discovered at
Nag Hammadi, the *Apocryphon of John* written around 100 A.D.[14]. It contains
a grandiose description of the unknown God, the Gnostics' *agnostos theos*,
who is beyond the concept of God, a "non ground-of-being". Quite singularly
he was accompanied by a female figure, who was brought forth because God
reflected Himself in the water of His light and who was named Barbelo, an
unintelligible word. In the *Apocryphon of John*, this female figure or goddess
is called a *metropatōr*, which Martin Krause translated as "grandfather" in his
edition of the *Apocryphon of John*. To any normal person the idea that God
was married to his grandfather seems rather peculiar. It therefore becomes
eminently clear that a mere grammatical grounding in Coptic is not enough.

---

12 *Samaritan Liturgy* XVI, 1 (ed. Heidenheim 25).
13 Epiphanius, *Pan.*, XXI, 3, 2.
14 M. Krause and P. Labib, *Die drei Versionen des Apokryphon des Johannes im Koptischen
Museum zu Alt-Kairo*, Wiesbaden, 1962.

On the contrary, to know Coptic too well can even be harmful at times, because all these texts were translated from the Greek. In this instance the confusion wrought by translators who have a fair knowledge of Coptic but who do not know enough Greek, becomes obvious. If only Martin Krause had read Christian Morgenstern's "Song to Mary", where he speaks of Mary, the goddess of ultimate tragedy, ultimate happiness and suffering, both mother and mistress. Christian Morgenstern would have understood the expression "mother-father", he could have conceived of a female figure who was both mother and father. This notion coincides with the comments made by the Jewish philosopher, Philo of Alexandria, about Wisdom or Sophia. In his work, *Cherubim*, 49, Sophia is seen as virgin earth, which is impregnated by the seed of God. This becomes still clearer in *De Profugis*, 9, where she becomes even more like our *metropator*, the feminine "mother-father" or "father-mother". Here Sophia is God's virgin daughter, whose nature is male. In terms of Judaism, the remarks of this Jewish philosopher are just as heretical as Simon Magus' concept of Sophia, according to which she is both male and female. The question that arises is where the idea came from. I do not know whether it is possible to trace it to the pre-Jewish, Canaanitic concepts about Anat in Ugarit or those found in Bethel, where a *Synhedra* of God (Goddess) is mentioned, and those discovered in Elephantine in Egypt. The only thing I can state with certainty is that any mention of an androgynous deity belongs to the realm of mythology. As to the *Apocryphon of John*, the introduction has Christian content, but the actual system shows no trace of Christian religion. It has therefore been rightly concluded that the *Apocryphon of John* is an early Gnostic text with elements of Greek philosophy and Jewish religion. At the same time, it also suggests a critical attitude to orthodox Jewish concepts, such as the distinction between the Creator and the Highest God, but in any event it does not reflect the influence of Christian religion.

Even Irenaeus stated as early as 200 A.D. that Valentinus had developed an existing form of Gnosis into a Christian Gnosis. It has always been my view that this line of thinking was correct and I feel that it has been confirmed by the publication of the *Apocryphon of John*. It becomes much more apparent that Valentinus — this extraordinary mythologist who conceived of the universe in terms of tears and smiles, — undoubtedly knew the myth we find in the *Apocryphon of John*. Viewed in this perspective, we realize that the whole system of thought — many of its elements, such as the fall of Sophia —, used by Valentinus, was already present in the *Apocryphon of John*. However, he cristianized the system and not just superficially; for the Christian element became basic for him. In Valentinus' interpretation of these existing Gnostic myths, Christ carried and revealed the awareness of the unconscious Self to mankind. According to Valentinus, spirit is present in man, but it is dormand. Only the word of Christ, which awakens and reveals it, can lead to self-knowledge. This concept is demonstrated most beautifully and described most poetically in the *Gospel of Truth*. In Dutch we have a very nice expression: we do not speak of revelation but of *openbaring*. Carrying a play on words to its extreme, we might say that *open-baring* (revelation) is also an "opening up", which might be equated with giving birth. Through the word of revelation we are reborn, that is, opened up in order to receive the self. By means of a Gnostic interpretation of the Christian religion Valentinus provided us with a very original approach, which is not the Word and the Spirit, or the Word and the Sacrament, but the Word and the Self.

As to Origen, I think it is somewhat daring to talk about him in the presence of Ernst Benz, the editor of his writings. However, what I now propose to discuss is a new interpretation of Origen in the light of the *Nouvelle Théologie*. Jean Daniélou and above all Henri de Lubac, whom I consider to be one of the greatest theologians of our day, reiterated time and again that Origen was a biblical theologian. De Lubac emphasized that Origen's symbolical and spiritual interpretation of the Bible had not only been of great historical importance but was also timely for present day ecclesiastical tradition, especially since the Church always stressed the symbolical and spiritual interpretation of the Bible. De Lubac's recent books such as *L'Exégèse médiévale, Histoire et Esprit,* etc., are very interesting in this respect and place great emphasis on the fact that Origen's interpretation has been preserved in the course of time [15].

On the other hand Origen did not only write Bible commentaries, he was also the author of *De Principiis,* and this is why some Gnostic influence on Origen cannot be denied. Now that the fourth text from the *Jung Codex* is to be published in the near future, it will no longer be possible to believe that his ideas arose out of nothing. The fourth document from the *Jung Codex,* the *Tractatus Tripartitus,* is a very unique piece of writing. It consists of approximately one hundred pages, in which the history of the universe is told from its inception in God until its final return to Him. It is an extremely obscure text. I had always thought that the *Phenomenology of the Spirit* by Hegel was the most difficult piece of writing, but this last document from the *Jung Codex* is even more puzzling. One of the reasons for this is that it was translated from Greek into Coptic by someone who did not even understand what he was translating. The document is, however, extremely important, first of all

[15]   H. de Lubac, *Exégèse médiévale. Les quatres sens de l'Écriture,* 4 vols., Paris, 1959-1964; idem, *Histoire et Esprit. L'Intelligence de l'Écriture d'après Origène,* Paris, 1950.

because it provides a parallel to Valentinian Gnosis as described by Irenaeus and because it shows that Irenaeus, althought he was by no means dishonest, did not understand Gnosis. What is even more important is that it shows the great influence Gnosis had on Origen. The text also includes a very impressive, profound and beautiful description of the unknown God as the primal cause of the All. This God is called Father, and the name leads to the logical conclusion that whenever God has been a father, he must have had a son. If God is a father in eternity, he eternally begets a son. These speculations about the eternal birth of the son can also be found — with the same argumentation — in Origen's writings and in those of his school.

The author of the *Tractatus Tripartitus* was probably a man by the name of Heracleon and, as we pointed out earlier, he was living in Rome around 160 A.D. He was a disciple of Valentinus, who had come to Rome about 140 A.D. After his death there was a schism in the school of Valentinus; the Oriental group remained faithful to the principles of Valentinus, whereas the Western group sought a rapprochement with the Catholic Church. The leaders of the Western or Italic school included a certain Ptolemy, as well as Heracleon, who wrote a commentary on the Gospel of John, many fragments of which have come down to us [16]. To recapitulate, Valentinus lived around 150 A.D. and Heracleon around 160. The latter catholicized, or rather christianized the doctrine. We, furthermore, know that Origen lived around 225 A.D. The interesting thing is that the fourth document from the *Jung Codex*, the *Tractatus Tripartitus*, must be dated somewhere between Valentinus and Origen. Obviously, there was a gradual transition from Valentinus to Heracleon, and from Heracleon to Origen. For Valentinus, the primal cause was a quaternio, which consisted of the depth and silence from which emanated *nous*, that is, consciousness, and truth. This quaternio was a sort of *tetractys*, from which the entire world of the spirit and thus also the entire universe had emanated. Valentinus' quaternity was, however, replaced by a trinity with Heracleon. For, Heracleon knew a trinity consisting of God, the Son and in addition, strangely enough, the Church, a female hypostasis, which one cannot help but identify with the Holy Spirit. A quaternity was replaced by a trinity, but it was accompanied by a doctrine of eternal birth just as we find it later in Origin. We therefore note a twofold correspondence between Heracleon and Origen.

You probably remember the basic principles of the Valentinian system: the pleroma, the world of the spirit, emanated from the deity; the aeons, half angels, half ideas, do not know the deity but are filled with desire for it; this desire

---

[16] W. Völker, *Quellen zur Geschichte der christlichen Gnosis*, Tübingen, 1932, pp. 63-86.

becomes excessive and turns to passion. It is a sort of disease that first develops in one part of the body and then breaks out in another place. In the same manner, this perverted desire, or passion for God, broke out in the last aeon, i.e., in the aeon of Wisdom. Wisdom wanted to penetrate God's mystery and her *superbia* was her downfall. The emergence of Evil was therefore a process that took place in the divine. According to Valentinus, Evil was a kind of neurosis in the pleroma that developed in the aeon of Wisdom.

Heracleon's approach was very different. In this writing he emphasized that although Wisdom fell from grace, this had been due to her own free will, her own decision, her *autexousion*. Until recently, we had always thought that the emphasis on free will had been the decisive characteristic that made Origen's theology non-Gnostic. For Origen the fall was pre-existent to the creation of the world. But the theologians believed the essential thing to have been Origen's emphasis on freedom of will in contrast to Valentinus, for whom the fall was a divine process. Now we have to admit that Origen's concept was in fact prefigured in Heracleon's Gnosis. It shows how gradual the transition from mythos to logos, from Gnosis to orthodoxy was. Where we used to see sharp contradictions, we now see gradual transitions. Slowly and by stages, Gnosis was transformed into the orthodoxy of Origen.

Another aspect of this was that Origen, in contrast to the Gnostics, attributed great importance to the doctrine of the creator. The Gnostics differentiated between the creator of the world and the highest deity. As a matter of fact, the Demiurge can still be found in the *Tractatus Tripartitus*, but here, too, we see a change, which can only be explained as a rapprochement with Catholicism. Whereas Valentinus — just as the *Apocryphon of John* — still displays a hostile attitude toward the Demiurge, the approach to the Demiurge in the *Tractatus Tripartitus* is quite friendly and positive. He is merely the hand and the eye of Wisdom and no longer has any specific function of his own. Here the universe is guided by Wisdom, which in this context is called Logos. Again we see the gradual transition from Valentinian Gnosis to the theology of Origen.

However, the most important idea expressed in the *Tractatus Tripartitus* is that of *pronoia* and *paideusis*, i.e., providence and the eductation of mankind. We might have known this because in the Latin translation of Irenaeus, there was a sentence, which said that man was imbued with spirit because spirit required psychic or sensuous exercise, and that this was the reason for which the world had been created. In other words, the universe exists in order to educate the spirit. For its *paideia*, education, spirit needs psyche, that is, ethics, religion and sensuousness, that is, materia. Unfortunately, Epiphanius' version read differently, namely that the soul required sensuous exercise. This is what the scholars picked up, completely misunderstanding the meaning of Valentinian Gnosis. The interpretation that should have been given to Irenaeus' text is spelled out quite clearly in this tractate, which states that the world had been created for the purpose of rendering spirit conscious, but that to this end spirit also required an ethical and religious foundation. The Gnostics were not nearly so wild as the Church Fathers described them. They consciously emphasized that although spiritual life differed from ethical or religious life, spiritual life cannot exist unless it has an ethical and religious basis. The idea that spirit needs psychic as well as sensuous, material exercise is expressed much more clearly in the *Tractatus Tripartitus,* which stresses that Evil is also necessary to the historical process, in the course of which spirit is educated. This comes as a great surprise to a Gnostic scholar. Never would he have expected any-thing like this from a Gnostic, but in two places the text states that Evil is also useful for the education of spirit and that for this reason Evil, too, is predestined. The author of this tractate is not afraid to assert that Evil is divine Providence in the life of man. The unique philosophy of history which makes up a major portion of the tractate is founded on the simple premise that spirit has to go through this ethical, religious and material, sensuous exercise in order to become conscious of itself. We are reminded of Dante's *Divine Comedy,* where the poet has to go through the inferno and purgatory in order to enter paradise. What is described here is similar, but instead of being a Divine Comedy it is a Divine Tragedy: after passing through the inferno of sensuousness and materiality, as well as the purgatory of morality and religion, spirit achieves freedom.

Heracleon also differentiates between these three stages of development in history. The first is the hylic, i.e., the material stage, which corresponds to the period when Greek philosophy flourished. According to Heracleon, everything that came in the beginning, the primordial, was materialist. Man was unable to transcend matter. Greek philosophy, Heracleon claimed, was therefore full of contradictions; it was simply hylic. For this reason, the Greek philosophers debated the existence of Providence, the question whether the world is a mechanism or nature, whether there is freedom of will or determinism. According to him, everything that was debated in the schools of the philosophers was materialism.

Heracleon had much greater regard for the Jewish religion. He considered the era of Judaism to have been the higher, the psychic phase, because there were prophets who proclaimed *one* God as well as the Messiah; and in contrast to the Greek philosophers, the prophets were all in agreement. However, the Jews also had various Bible interpretations. These gave rise to a number of heresies, which the author was well acquainted with. According to some of these heresies,

God is *one*, whereas according to others, there are many gods. Some said that God was the source of Good only. Others said that God was the source of Good and Evil. Some said the world had been created by God, and others that it had been created by the angels. In any event, Heracleon had a very high opinion of the Jewish religion, especially the Old Testament. This again shows how close he was to Catholicism. Of course, in the history of spirit, this was not the last, the pneumatic phase, beginning with the advent of Christ. When Christ came and revealed his Gnosis, the pneumatics, who are all light, came to him, heard his word and followed him.

The world will continue to exist until all spiritual human beings have become conscious of themselves and of God. Then the end will come: the hylics, the materialists, will perish; the psychics will be blessed in their fashion; and the pneumatics will enter the pleroma, the bridal chamber, where they unite as brides with the male angels, their higher selves, attaining perfection and contemplating God eternally — the *mysterium conjunctionis*.

This overwhelming, difficult and important document makes a tremendous impression on anyone who is familiar with the field of Gnosis. In his *History of Western Philosophy in Antiquity*, written many years ago, Windelband described the Gnostics as the first philosophers of history because they considered the advent of Christ not only to have been the central event in history but in the universe at large [17]. I am convinced that the new findings, especially the tractate by Heracleon, will show that the venerable historian of philosophy was right. In his own way Heracleon was one of the first philosophers who looked on history as the evolution of mankind from the inferno of sensuousness to the freedom of the spirit via religion and morality. Christ came to free mankind. The evolutionary approach is presented here in the form of a cosmic-historical process and its similarity to that of Origen is obvious. Hal Koch entitled his book on Origen *Pronoia and Paideusis*, precisely because Origen conceived of providence as education designed to make pneumatics of human beings. The correspondence between Heracleon and Origen in this respect is as manifest as it is in the case of eternal birth and the freedom of Sophia.

---

[17] W. Windelband, Germ. ed., München, 1923, p. 279.

II

THE JEWISH ORIGIN OF GNOSTICISM

DER GNOSTISCHE ANTHROPOS
UND DIE JÜDISCHE TRADITION

Einleitung

Mit dieser Untersuchung löse ich ein Versprechen ein, welches ich in meinem Buch „Gnosis als Weltreligion" gegeben habe. Dort deutete ich ganz kurz an, warum ich die iranische Urmenschhypothese für „far-fetched" hielt und warum meiner Ansicht nach die jüdische Adam-Mythologie einbezogen werden müsste, um die Gestalt des gnostischen Anthropos zu verstehen, und kündete an, dass ich sonstwo darauf zurückkommen werde. Inzwischen hat mein Kollege Prof. Th. C. Vriezen in bezug auf diese meine Ansicht die Frage gestellt, ob wirklich mit dem Anthropos des hermetischen Poimandres Adam gemeint war. Das war für mich eine Veranlassung, mich tiefer mit dem Problem zu befassen und mit noch mehr Argumenten meine These zu erhärten. Doch konnte es bei der Behandlung dieser Detailfrage nicht bleiben. Es musste der ganze Komplex der iranischen Urmenschhypothese herangezogen werden.

Man hat in den letzten Jahren sehr viel über eine vorchristliche Gnosis und einen vorchristlichen gnostischen Erlöser gesprochen. Es gibt nicht wenige Autoren, die eifrig nachbeten, was andere darüber gesagt haben: man tut einfach, als ob das Bestehen eines iranischen Erlösungsmysteriums bewiesen sei. Man redet von einem erlösten Erlöser, der dem persischen Gayomart entspricht, als ob so etwas wirklich in den iranischen Quellen zu finden wäre. Ich aber muss bekennen, dass die Lektüre der Bücher Reitzensteins, Schaeders und Kraelings mich enttäuscht hat. Nur die schwarze Kunst einer bedenklichen Quellenforschung, so scheint es mir, erlaubt es diesen Forschern, ein iranisches Erlösungsmysterium zu rekonstruieren, das es wohl nie gegeben hat.

Anstatt dessen aber fand ich, dass das heterodoxe Judentum einen wichtigen Beitrag zur Entstehung der gnostischen Anthroposlehre geliefert hat. Es wurde mir immer deutlicher, dass samaritanische und jüdische Gnostiker an der Quelle der grossen Strömung gestanden haben, welche in den Manichäismus ausmündet. Und nicht selten lässt sich die Abhängigkeit dieser jüdischen Gnostiker von rabbinischen und haggadischen Exegesen einfach beweisen. Obwohl es nun für mich ein Wagnis ist, dieses Gebiet zu betreten, habe ich doch nicht gezögert, die Vorarbeit zu unternehmen, in der Hoffnung, dass jemand sie verbessern wird. An dieser Stelle möchte ich meine Verpflichtung an Erik Peterson dankbar hervorheben, der in seiner Untersuchung über die Befreiung Adams aus der Macht des Schicksals das Entscheidende schon gesagt hat [1]. Obwohl mir natürlich die Werke der Reitzensteinschen Schule

---

[1] Frühkirche, Judentum und Gnosis, Rom, 1959, pp. 107-128.

einigermassen bekannt sind, habe ich es nicht für nötig gehalten, ausführlich gegen sie zu polemisieren. Nur dann und wann, wenn ihre Interpretationen allzu kühn wurden, habe ich sie mit einigen Worten abgelehnt. Es sei aber nachdrücklich hervorgehoben, dass es sich hier um einen Versuch handelt, und nur um einen Versuch, das brennendste Problem der heutigen Gnosisforschung einer Lösung näher zu bringen. Mir stand als Ziel vor Augen, die Entwicklung der gnostischen Anthroposlehre aus dem heterodoxen Judentum genetisch darzustellen. Wenn diese historische Beweisführung mir gelingen würde, wäre ja sowieso die iranische Hypothese ausgeschlossen. So sei es mir denn gestattet, in zwei Kapiteln über die gnostische Interpretation von Chokma und Adam als Urbilder des Menschseins zu sprechen.

I. DIE KOSMOGONISCHE PHASE

Es wird im neugefundenen Apokryphon Johannis über die Schöpfung des Menschen erzählt, dass Gott sein Bild reflektiert im Wasser des Urchaos den sieben Planetenkönigen des bösen Weltschöpfers Jaldabaoth zeigte. Diese Archonten waren so beeindruckt von der Schönheit dieses Bildes, dass sie die Entscheidung fassten: „Lasset uns einen Menschen machen nach dem Bilde Gottes". Sie fingen unmittelbar mit der Arbeit an. Jeder gab sein Bestes, um das neue Wesen so schön wie möglich zu machen. Das Resultat entsprach ihren Versuchen: das neue Wesen, Adam, war ausserordentlich schön; aber obwohl er ganz vollkommen schien, konnte er sich nicht bewegen [2]. Als er dann durch eine List auch das göttliche Pneuma empfängt, wird er zum „vollkommenen Menschen", zum Vater aller Pneumatiker, welche „das unbewegliche Geschlecht des *vollkommenen Menschen*" genannt werden [3].

Das Apokryphon Johannis, das in Ägypten gefunden wurde, scheint eine alexandrinische Gnosis zu enthalten und kann schon um 120 verfasst worden sein [4]. Schon hier begegnet uns das eigentliche Thema der gnostischen Anthropologie, das Verhältnis vom göttlichen Urbild und menschlichen Abbild, welches als eine Einheit und Wesensgleichheit der Gegensätze auf gefasst wird. Dieses Thema kehrt nun, wie wir sehen werden, in tausendfachen Variationen in der Geschichte der Gnosis wieder. Und doch kann sogar eine so altertümliche und archaische Fassung, wie sie im Apokryphon Johannis vorliegt, nicht ursprünglich sein. Sogar dieser Mythos zeigt schon die Spuren einer sekundären Fortbildung und späteren Übermalung. Wir müssen annehmen, dass die komplizierten gnostischen Systeme des zweiten Jahrhunderts sich aus einer viel einfacheren Form entwickelt haben. Im Apokryphon

---

[2] W. Till, The Gnostic Apocryphon of John, Journal of Ecclesiastical History III, 1, p. 19.
[3] So ist zu lesen. Vgl. Carl Schmidt, Philotesia Kleinert, Berlin, 1907, p. 317 sqq.
[4] G. Quispel, De oudste vorm van de gnostische mythe, Ned. Theol. Tijdschrift 1953.

Johannis wird zwischen der *Ennoia* der höchsten Gottheit, der Idee, der Barbelo und der gefallenen Sophia, *Prounikos*, unterschieden. Dass kann nicht ursprünglich sein. Nach den Archontikern wohnt die höchste Sophia oderhalb der sieben Archonten in der Ogdoas (Epiph. Pan. 40) [5]. Es wird erzählt, dass diese Sophia, also die Idee, das höchste Gegenbild der Gottheit, die Archonten erzeugt hat, dann aber von ihnen festgehalten worden ist, damit sie nicht zurückkehre (Iren. 1, 23, 2). Zweifelsohne hat die Spaltung der Sophia in eine höhere und eine niedrigere Hypostase zum Zweck, die abgründige Einsicht zu verhüllen, dass es einen Bruch und eine Spaltung innerhalb der Gottheit gibt. Aber weil diese gnostische Auffassung nicht zu verdecken ist und bis in die spätesten Mythenbildungen überall durchschimmert, muss die einfachere Gestalt des Mythos als die ursprünglichere gelten.

Diese Überlegung führt uns von Alexandrien in den Bereich der syrischen Gnosis. Saturninus von Antiochen lehrte, *ähnlich wie der Samariter* Menander, dass der eine unbekannte Gott die Engel, Erzengel, Kräfte und Mächte gemacht hat (Iren. 1, 2, 4, 1). Ein Vergleich mit der Lehre des früheren Menander zeigt, was das bedeutet. Er, Saturninus, muss gelehrt haben, dass die Gottheit, vermittels ihrer weiblichen Hypostase, der Ennoia (der Sophia), die Archonten gezeugt hat. Sophia ist die Mutter der Sieben. Die Welt ist geschaffen von den bekannten sieben Planetengeistern, und ebenso der erste Mensch, Adam. Es erschien nämlich (das heisst im Urwasser des Chaos) ein leuchtendes Bild von der höchsten Kraft oben (von der Sophia?); die Archonten versuchten dies zu greifen, aber konnten es nicht fassen, weil es sofort wieder emporstieg. Darauf sagten sie sich: „Lasset uns einen Menschen schaffen nach dem Bilde und der Ähnlichkeit". Das geschah. Aber wegen der Schwäche der Engel konnte sich dies Gebilde nach seiner Erschaffung nicht aufrichten, sondern es kroch wie ein Wurm daher. Da erbarmte sich seiner die Kraft von oben (die Sophia?) und entsandte einen Funken des Lebens: dieser richtete den Menschen auf und gab ihm das Leben. Die Thematik der Ebenbildlichkeit ist dieselbe. Die Fassung der Sophia aber ist viel einfacher. Es gibt hier nur eine Sophia, die Ennoia Gottes. Und doch sind wir gezwungen, noch einen bedeutenden Abstrich zu machen, um die ursprüngliche Gestalt des Mythos wiederzugewinnen. Saturninus lehrt, dass der Judengott einer der Engel war. Er kennt also die Trennung zwischen Schöpfergott und höchstem Gott, welche so charakteristisch für die Gnosis des zweiten Jahrhunderts ist.

Aber am Anfang des zweiten Jahrhunderts war diese Scheidung in der syrischen Gnosis noch nicht vollzogen: Ignatius von Antiochien († 117), welcher die judaisierende Gnosis seiner Zeit heftig bekämpft hat und gewiss eine solche

---

[5] H.-Ch. Puech, s.v. Archontiker, in Reallexikon für Antike und Christentum, p. 633.

Verirrung mit der grössten Entrüstung gemeldet haben würde, falls er sie gekannt hätte, erwähnt diese Trennung auffallenderweise nicht. Weiter scheint der Name dieses Demiurgen, Jaldabaoth, vielleicht יַלְדָּא בָהוּת , „Sohn des Chaos", darauf hinzuweisen, dass er als Archon von Sophia aus dem Chaos erzeugt ist; und in der Tat bezeichnet er den Planeten Saturn, den höchsten der „Sieben", und hat wohl ursprünglich mit dem Judengott nichts zu tun [6]. In der syrischen Gnosis vom Anfang des zweiten Jahrhunderts war also Sophia noch die weibliche Hypostase des jüdischen Gottes: sie erzeugte die sieben Planeten, unter denen Saturn natürlich eine hervorragende Stellung einnahm. Die judaisierende Gnosis, welche Ignatius erwähnt, muss ungefähr diese Gestalt gekannt haben. Daneben findet sich nun, und gerade in einer sehr altertümlichen Quelle, die Ansicht, dass auch die Welt ihre Ebenbildlichkeit dem Bilde der Lichtjungfrau in dem Wasser des Chaos verdankt. Basilides berichtet aus einer „barbarischen" Quelle, welche also jedenfalls vor 140 nach Christus geschrieben sein muss, wie im Anfang Licht und Finsternis sich vermischt haben (Acta Archelai 67, 4-12).

Als die Finsternisse das Licht gesehen hatten, begehrten sie es und verfolgten sie es, weil sie sich mit ihm vermischen (in geschlechtlichem Sinne) und Anteil an ihm haben wollten. Das Licht aber verspürte nur die Lust, nach unten zu blicken, und schaute wie *in* einen Spiegel (velut per speculum, ὡς δι' ἐσόπτρου). Es ist dieses Licht nichts anderes als die kosmogonische Psyche, denn, wie Marius Victorinus sagt, wird diese eine lebenerzeugende Macht, wenn sie nach unten schaut, weil sie libidinös ist (Marius Victorinus, c. Arianos 1086c, si vero in inferiora respexit, cum sit petulans, potentia vivificandi fit). So entsteht ein Bild (ἔμφασις), und nur ein Bild des Lichtes bei den Finsternissen: das Licht selbst zieht sich zurück, ohne mit den Finsternissen in Berührung zu kommen. Es ist dieser Abglanz des Lichtes ein *intuitus* und *ein Bild in der Materie* (ὕλης ἔμφασις), das auch eine *species lucis*, ein εἶδος τοῦ φωτός genannt wird: es ist damit wohl das Formprinzip der Materie gemeint, welche ein aristotelisch beeinflusster Platonismus neben dem ewigen Urbild, der ἰδέα, annahm. Der nicht ganz sicher überlieferte Text berichtet dann, dass die Finsternisse sich dieses Schattenbildes bemächtigt und es zerrissen haben (traxerunt, ἔσπασαν). So erklärt es sich, dass die Kreaturen die sichtbare Welt erzeugt haben als eine *similitudo*, ein Gleichnis, weil das Licht sich mit allen vermischt hat.

---

[6] Origenes, c. Celsum VI, 32, weist darauf hin, dass Jaldabaoth der Magie entstammt, cf. Bousset, Hauptprobleme, p. 351; es fragt sich, ob es sich hier nicht um eine Beziehung zur phönizischen Religion handelt: W. H. C. Frend, The Gnostic-Manichaean Tradition in Roman North Africa, Journal Ecclesiastical History IV, 1, p. 19.

Wir dürfen nach Vergleich mit anderen Versionen den Mythos wohl so transponieren, dass die Lichtjungfrau, die Sophia, ihr Eidolon in den Spiegel der Urwasser projiziert; daraufhin bemächtigen sich die Weltmächte, die Archonten, dieses Schattenbildes und bilden den sichtbaren Kosmos als ein Gleichnis der Lichtwelt. Was bedeutet es nun aber, dass dieses Schattenbild der Lichtjungfrau von den Archonten zerrissen wird?

Der Dionysoskult kannte den Ritus des σπαραγμός, welcher so erklärt wird: „Ein Schaf wurde in die Mitte der Teilnehmer am Kult geworfen, welche dieses Tier dann Glied für Glied zerrissen und roh auffrassen" [7]. Dieser Ritus, welcher noch bis tief in das dritte vorchristliche Jahrhundert bestand, wurde natürlich von den Platonikern allegorisiert und auf die Zerrissenheit der Psyche in dieser Welt gedeutet. Auf diesem Weg scheint sie auch zu den Gnostikern gekommen zu sein.

Ganz deutlich ist aber in diesem Fragment, dass die Welt ebenbildlich ist, weil die Lichtjungfrau einmal ihr Eidolon in die Materie projiziert hat.

Nicht nur der Mensch, sondern auch die Welt ist nach gewissen Gnostikern ein Abbild der Sophia, oder wie man dieses göttliche Urbild nennen will. Und weil, wie wir sehen werden, diese Vorstellung vom Eidolon der Sophia sich schon in den Kreisen um Simon Magus findet, muss eine verwandte Form des Mythos schon in einer judaisierenden Gnosis bestanden haben.

So werden wir dann auf den Bereich der jüdischen Magie verwiesen, wo die Samariter Simon und Menander wirklich ähnliches gelehrt haben: vor allem ist auffallend, dass bei ihnen die Trennung von höchstem Gott und Schöpfergott fehlt. Aber andererseits müssen wir bedenken, dass die jüdischen Anschauungen, welche in späteren gnostischen Systemen zu finden sind, doch wohl nur durch Vermittlung dieser Kreise in die antijüdische Gnosis eingedrungen sind. Es will dabei beachtet sein, dass die neugefundenen gnostischen Texte über Häresien unter den Juden berichten; Codex Jung 112, 17: „Sie haben zahlreiche Häresien gebildet, welche bis heute bei den Juden bestehen. Einige sagen, dass Gott ein einziger ist, der gesprochen hat in den alten Schriften, andere sagen, dass es viele Götter gibt; einige sagen, dass Gott einig ist und einfaltig in seinem Wesen, andere sagen, dass sein Handeln zweifaltig ist und die Ursache von Gutem und Bösem; einige sagen, dass er der Demiurg des Bestehenden ist, andere sagen, dass er durch seine Engel geschaffen hat". Hier wird also als Lehre einer jüdischen Häresie angegeben, was bei Simon, Menander und Saturnin wiederkehrt, dass es die Engel waren, welche die Welt und den Menschen geschaffen haben.

---

[7] E. R. Dodds, The Greek and the Irrational, 1951, p. 276.

So haben wir dann die Möglichkeit, das Modell einer jüdischen Gnosis zu entwerfen, und zwar ein Modell in dem modernen wissenschaftlichen Sinne des Wortes. Ob es eine solche Urgnosis wirklich gegeben hat, bleibt dabei unentschieden. Es handelt sich um eine Hypothese, welche die historischen Gebilde in ihrer Entwicklung verständlich macht. Ich halte es dann auch für erlaubt, auf Grund der ältesten gnostischen Quellen, welche eben über judaisierende Strömungen innerhalb der Gnosis berichten, ein System der jüdischen Gnosis zu entwerfen.

Dann ergibt sich etwa folgendes Bild:

Gott schafft aus dem Chaos die sieben Archonten durch Vermittlung seiner *Chokma,* der humectatio luminis oder Lichttau (Iren. I, 30)[8]. Die Chokma wirft ihr Eidolon, ihr Schattenbild, auf die Urwasser des Tohuwabohu. Daraufhin bilden die Archonten die Welt und den Körper des Menschen, der auf der Erde wie ein Wurm kriecht. Die Chokma schenkt ihm den Geist. Weiter lässt sich nun folgendes aus späteren gnostischen Quellen vermuten.

Die Verführung der Eva bestand darin, dass der Teufel, in der Gestalt der Schlange, mit ihr geschlechtliche Gemeinschaft hatte und so Kain und Abel zeugte [9]. Die Ursünde ist also die Geschlechtlichkeit.

Nach dem Fall besteht auf der Erde ein Kampf zwischen den Söhnen Seths und den Kindern Kains. Als aber die Töchter Kains die Sethiten verführen, bringt die Chokma die Sintflut über die Welt [10].

Aber die Bemühungen der Sophia hörten wahrscheinlich damit nicht auf: sie schickte sieben Propheten, entsprechend den sieben Planeten, von Moses bis Esra [11].

So etwa bildet sich das Modell des Mythos in seiner ursprünglichen Gestalt, das den verschiedenen gnostischen Systemen zugrunde liegt und sich auch, wie es mir scheint, in den Ausführungen des *Apokryphon Johannis* und im System, das Irenaeus 1, 30 wiedergegeben wird, leicht wiedererkennen lässt.

---

[8] E. Preuschen, Die apokryphen gnostischen Adamschriften, Festgruss B. Stade, Giessen, 1900, p. 225, gibt die talmudischen Stellen an: Talm. bab., tr. Chagiga, f. 12b; „Nach den Pirkê Rabbi Eliezer 34 kommt dieser Tau vom Haupte Gottes. Als von Gott ausgehend, heisst dieser Tau hier mit Recht ἰκμὰς τοῦ φωτός.

[9] Die Nachricht, dass Kain und Abel vom Teufel bei Eva erzeugt sind, bei Epiphanius, Pan. 40, 5, 3. Verwandte Auffassungen bei den Gnostikern hat H.-Ch. Puech verzeichnet in seinem Aufsatz: Fragments retrouvés de l'Apocalypse d'Allogène, Mélanges Franz Cumont, Bruxelles, 1936, p. 993, 948, 954. Vgl. auch unter Archontiker und Audianer im R. A. C.

[10] Epiphanius, Panarion 39, 1, 4 (ps. Tert. adv. omnes haereses 3, Philastrius).

[11] Rekonstruktion von E. Preuschen, o.c., p. 232.

Dieser Mythos ist durchaus Sophia-Mythos. Von einem Erlöser oder von einem Urmenschen ist vorläufig noch nicht die Rede. Woher stammt nun dieser Mythos? Solche Spekulationen konnten in einem Kreis entstehen, wo man über die Schöpfungsgeschichte der Genesis unterrichtet war. Die Interpretation der Genesis hat ja im Altertum solche merkwürdigen Anschauungen veranlasst: Gott sollte die Welt geschaffen haben, indem er wie eine schöne Gestalt oder auch ein Magnet der überströmenden Materie sich näherte [12]; auch wird gesagt, der Geist habe sich am Anfang wie eine Seele mit dem Urwasser vermischt, um zu verhindern, dass die Finsternis mit dem Himmel in Berührung käme [13].

Das scheinen nur einfache Metaphern, welche an der Hand des heiligen Textes zu verdeutlichen suchten, wie am Anfang aus Chaos Ordnung entstanden ist. Aber diese Metaphern, die schöne Gestalt, der Magnet, dieser Stein der Weisen, sind in gewissen Umständen so geladen, dass sie sehr leicht die Bilderwelt der Seele heraufbeschwören können. Wo das geschehen ist, ist die Gnosis geboren. So weiss dann auch eine sehr altertümliche Darstellung zu berichten, dass der Geist, ein weibliches Wesen, die Finsternisse, die Tiefe und das Wasser schied; dann aber haben die Finsternisse sich auf ihn gestürtzt und ihn vergewaltigt [14].

Hier ist nun der Geist aus Gen. 1 weiblich aufgefasst, weil Ruaḥ im Hebräischen *feminini generis* ist. Das dürfte wohl zeigen, dass dieser Mythos im jüdischen Bereich entstanden ist. Aber auch von Sophia wird immer wieder gesagt, dass sie $\epsilon\pi\epsilon\phi\epsilon\rho\epsilon\tau o$ [15]: es wird dargestellt, dass die Archonten sich an sie heften wie an einen Magneten oder sie begehren wie eine schöne Frau. Geist und Sophia, Ekklesia und Jerusalem, Ruaḥ, Chokma, Kenesseth Israel und Shekhina, all diese Gestalten, welche das Judentum sogar in seinen kühnsten Augenblicken noch so peinlich und reinlich geschieden hat, werden auf einmal verbunden und verwischt, als ob ein erwachendes mythisches Bewusstsein jetzt auf einmal seine Chance bekäme und überall Anknüpfungspunkte fände, sogar bei einer so unmythischen Religion, wie es das Judentum ist.

Das Material, aus dem dieser Mythos gebildet wurde, ist ungnostische und entstammt zum grössten Teil dem kontemporären Judentum.

---

[12] Tert., adv. Herm. 44: facit mundum apparens sicut *decor* et *magnes* attrahens ferrum.
[13] Theophilus ad Autolyc. II, 13; vgl. Ps. Clem. Hom. 11, 22, 3; 13, 12, 1.
[14] Philastrius 33, Marx, p. 18, 4: ante erant solum tenebrae et profundum et aqua, atque ex his divisio facta est in medio, et spiritus separavit haec elementa. Tunc ergo tenebrae irruentes in spiritum …
[15] Till, *o.c.*, p. 18.

Es wird als jüdische Häresie überliefert, dass die Engel den Körper von Adam gebildet haben: ἀγγέλων ποίημα ἦν τὸ σῶμα τὸ ἀνθρώπειον, (Justinus, Dialogus 62)[16] Das ist nun an sich nicht verwunderlich. Gnostisch wird diese Vorstellung erst, wenn die Archonten dies in Gegensatz oder in Rebellion gegen die Gottheit oder ihre Sophia tun. Es wird uns überliefert, dass auch der samaritische Gnostiker Menander aus dem ersten Jahrhundert gelehrt hat, dass der Körper eine Schöpfung der Engel sei (etsi angelorum fuisset operatio, ut *Menandro* et Marco placet; Tert., Res. 5). Es kann also über die heterodox-jüdische Herkunft dieser Anschauung kein Zweifel bestehen. Und um den jüdischen Ursprung noch zu betonen, wird im Mythos angedeutet, dass der Körper an sich schon ebenbildlich ist. Das ist eine Auffassung, die in jüdischen und juden-christlichen Quellen ausgesprochen wird und sich von den spiritualisierenden Tendenzen der Kirchenväter merkwürdig abhebt.

Diese jüdische Grundlage wird nun astrologisch gedeutet: die Engel sind als die sieben Planeten aufgefasst, die jeder für sich einen bestimmten Teil des Körpers, der mit ihren Aspekten korrespondiert, beigetragen haben. So ist der Körper ein Erzeugnis der sieben Archonten im Sinne der astrologischen Melothesie [17]. Selbst wenn nun in einer gnostischen Schrift diese astrologische Interpretation der Schöpfung Adams als chaldäische Weisheit bezeichnet würde, dann sollte man daraus nicht schliessen, dass dann eine heidnische, mesopotamische Quelle zitiert wird, welche das älteste aller datierbaren Elemente der Tradition über den persischen Urmenschen enthält [18]. Zu solchen

---

[16]	Vgl. z.B. Philo, de Opif. Mundi 24; de Conf. Ling. 35. Es muss beachtet werden, dass nach dem slawischen Henoch Adam aus sieben Elementen geschaffen worden ist (Bonwetsch, 28, 9), cf. Hippolytus, *Ref.* V, 26, 7: οἱ τοῦ Ἐλωεὶμ ἄγγελοι ... ποιοῦσιν τὸν ἄνθρωπον.

[17]	Wie das bei dem Samariter Menander zu denken ist, zeigt wieder das Apokryphon Johannis, Till, *o.c.*, p. 18. Für die planetarische Melothesie im Hermetismus cf. A. J. Festugière, La révélation d'Hermès Trismégiste, Paris, 1944, I, p. 130.

[18]	Es handelt sich hier um die bekannte Naassenerpredigt, Hippolytus, Ref. V, 7, 6, wo es heisst, dass die Chaldäer den ersten Menschen Adam nennen und dass dieser Mensch, ein Bild des höheren Menschen Adam, unbeweglich lag, geschaffen von den vielen Mächten. Nun ist zu beachten, dass im Text nicht steht, dass dies die Lehre der Chaldäer war, aber es ist zuzu-geben, dass die Schöpfung Adams durch die Archonten eine astrologische Übermalung der jüdischen Ansichten ist. Wenn Theodor bar Konai im Apokryphon Johannis liest, dass die Planeten den Leib Adams gebildet haben, bemerkt er: Et cela, il l'a emprunté aux Chaldéens (Puech, o.c., p. 939). Um nun diese Stelle doch zu einer Stütze der iranischen Urmensch-hypothesen machen zu können, bemerkt Carl H. Kraeling, Anthropos and Son of Man, p. 51: „The 'Chaldean Tale', as we shall call it, is of importance for the analysis of the Anthropos tradition in a number of ways. It is, in all probability, the oldest of the datable elements of this tradition. It takes us out of the litoral Orient and back to Mesopotamia. It shows us that in Mesopotamia there existed long before Manicheism and the systems of the Syrian Gnostics a mythological celebrity, known as the Great or Upper Man, and said to have been embroiled

vorschnellen und weitreichenden Schlüssen geben unsere Texte keinerlei Veranlassung. Vielmehr sollte man bedenken, dass chaldäisch eben „astrologisch" bedeutet: es ist durchaus möglich, dass eine jüdische Heterodoxie die Schöpfungsgeschichte Adams astrologisch interpretiert hat.

Ebenso ist es jüdische, rabbinische *Mythopoiese*, dass Adam anfänglich ein riesenförmiges Monstrum war, das sich nur kriechend wie ein Wurm bewegen konnte [19]. Dass er dann nachher den Hauch bekommt, der ihn aufrichtet und zum Anthropos macht, ist natürlich auch Fortbildung der Erzählung in der Genesis.

Wir haben angenommen, dass in der ursprünglichen jüdischen Gnosis es der Teufel war, der Kain und Abel erzeugte. Das taten wir, weil dies die Ansicht der Archontiker ist, eine Strömung, die ein sehr altertümliches Gepräge hat [20]; sie findet sich aber auch in Pirke R. Elieser im Talmud von Babylon und wird auf altjüdische Adamssagen zurückgehen [21].

Nicht aus dem Bibeltext ist zu erklären, dass nach den Sethianern die Vermischung dieser zwei Klassen, der Sethiten mit den Kainiten, der Anlass zur Sintflut war (Epiphanius, haer. 39, 5): als besonders seltsam berührt es, dass es die Mutter ist, Sophia, die zur Vergeltung (ad vindictam) die Sintflut über die Menschen bringt [22]. Da ist doch ein geschichtlich-ethisches Handeln vorausgesetzt, das mir von meinen gnostischen Studien her nicht bekannt ist. Und in der Tat wird in den armenischen Adamsbüchern erzählt, „wie die Töchter der Kainiten sich schmückten und als Tänzerinnen gekleidet die Nachkommen Seths zu verführen wussten. Über diese Vermischung der beiden Geschlechter ergrimmte Gott und sandte die Sintflut" [23]. Das ist doch wohl

---

in a primordial conflict of desastrous results". Das alles scheint mir haltlos. Die Stelle sagt nur, dass die Astrologen, in Anlehnung an die Genesiserzählung, über die Melothesie von Adam sprachen. Damit verbinden die Naassener dann Spekulationen, welche uns schon aus Saturninus und dem Apokryphon Johannis bekannt sind. Dass der Adamas hier an Stelle der Sophia getreten ist, beweist meiner Ansicht nach, dass wir hier mit einer späteren Ausbildung des Mythologems zu tun haben. Sophia ist primär. Der Versuch Reitzensteins, in der Naassenerpredigt (eine heidnische und) eine jüdische Quelle von späteren christlichen Zutaten zu scheiden, scheint mir nicht gelungen. Die Naassenerpredigt scheint mir ein gnostisches Dokument des zweiten Jahrhunderts zu sein. Auch der samaritische Gnostiker Menander kennt die Schöpfung des Menschen durch die Engel, aber er redet nicht vom Anthropos, sondern von der Ennoia. Das ist die älteste Fassung des Mythos, welche uns bekannt ist.

[19] Stellen bei E. Preuschen, *o.c.*, p. 227.

[20] Epiphanius, Panar. 40, 5.

[21] V. Aptowitzer, Kain und Abel in der Agada (1922), pp. 128-131.

[22] Ps. Tert. adv. omnes haer. 2, Kr. p. 218: permixtiones enim dicunt angelorum et hominum iniquas fuisse, ob quam causam ... matrem ad vindictam etiam cataclysmum inducere.

[23] E. Preuschen, *o.c.*, p. 244.

der jüdische Kontext, dem die Sethianen ihre Ansichten entnommen haben. Die Tatsache, dass hier nun wirklich überall jüdische Hintergründe durchschimmern, ermutigt mich zu der Hypothese, dass die Sophia schon in der jüdischen Gnosis eine bestimmte Zahl von Propheten inspirierte. Diese Ansicht ist bekanntlich zum Grunddogma der manichäischen Anthroposophie geworden, welche jeden Religionsgründer als Apostel des Lichtnous fasste. Dergleichen wird auch in den Schriften von Nag Hammadi ausgeführt und muss als gnostisches Erbgut betrachtet werden. Nun findet sich aber im Judenchristentum die Ansicht, dass sieben Propheten als die sieben Säulen gedacht werden müssen, worauf nach den Proverbien die Sophia ihr Haus gebaut hat (ps. Clem. Hom. 18, 14). In der simonianischen, also in der samaritischen Gnosis wird über die drei Stufen gesprochen, am Sinai, in Jerusalem und in Samaria, durch die sich das Göttliche geoffenbart hat [24]. Daraus würde man schliessen, dass die judenchristliche Lehre vom wahren Propheten, welcher sich in wechselnder Gestalt zu verschieden zeigt, eine jüdische Vorstufe hatte.

Und in der Tat heisst es nun in einem gnostischen System, das noch überall die jüdischen Anschauungen unter christlicher Übermalung durchschimmern lässt, dass die sieben Archonten, „die heilige Hebdomas", sich aus dem jüdischen Volke Propheten erwählt haben. „Und ein jeder von ihnen nimmt sich seinen Herold um Gott zu verherrlichen, und zu verkünden" (Iren. I, 30, 5). Und weiter heisst es, dass „auch Sophia selbst durch sie viel gesprochen hat". Ursprünglich war doch wohl, dass Sophia sich durch diese sieben Propheten bekundete: das waren nun die sieben Säulen der Weisheit in chronologischer Folge. Es scheint mir also, dass auch die Lehre der Inspiration der Propheten durch Sophia in einer jüdischen, vorchristlichen Gnosis ihren Ort gehabt hat [25]. In der Sophia Salomonis VII, 27, wird gesagt: καὶ κατὰ γενεὰς εἰς ψυχὰς ὁσίας μεταβαίνουσα φίλους θεοῦ καὶ προφήτας κατασκευάζει. Und in Hagiga 12b wird angeführt, die sieben Säulen seien im Grunde nur einer, hazadiq, der Prophet.

Es ist aber noch nicht klargeworden, woher die merkwürdige Lehre stammt,

---

[24] Gnosis als Weltreligion, p. 58.
[25] Wertvolles Material für diese These bietet W. Staerk, Die Sieben Säulen der Welt und des Hauses der Weisheit, Zeitschrift für neutestamentliche Wissenschaft 35, 1936, pp. 232-261. Dagegen hat Geo Widengren, The Great Vohu Manah and the Apostle of God, Uppsala Universitets Årsskrift 1945, 5, mit einer sehr gekünstelten Beweisführung darzustellen versucht, dass die Lehre von den verschiedenen Propheten im Manichäismus unmittelbar der iranischen Religion entnommen sei. Was nun auch die Vorlagen der jüdischen Vorstellung sein mögen, welche in Sap. Sal. VII, 27, durchschimmert, sicher ist dass der Manichäismus in dieser Hinsicht Erbe einer gnostischen Tradition ist, dessen älteste Belege jüdisch sind oder doch auf das Judentum zurückgehen.

a) das die Sophia sieben Archonten erzeugt, welche ihre Mutter vergewaltigen, oder dass sie b) ihr Schattenbild in die Urwasser des Chaos projiziert und so auch wieder die Mächte der Finsternis nach ihrer Tochter begierig macht.

Aber es scheint möglich, die Vorlagen dieser Vorstellungen anzugeben. Die Entwicklung zeigt hier besonders lehrreich, dass die historische Ableitung die gnostischen Phänomene zwar verdeutlichen, aber nicht erklären kann, weil ganz harmlose Vorstellungen hier ganz gewaltige psychische Regungen auslösen und wie die Stichworte beim Assoziationsexperiment wirken.

a)   Man muss sich nämlich immer vor Augen halten, dass die Sophia der Gnostiker so etwas darstellt wie die *anima mundi* und sich mit griechischen Vorstellungen über die Weltseele berührt; diese Weltseele hat nun in der Tat wie ein Magnet alle möglichen Metaphern und Vergleiche der hebräischen Literatur an sich gezogen. In dem bekannten Naassenerpsalm wird im Anschluss an die Genesis dargestellt, wie „der erstgeborene Geist", die Gottheit, dass allgemeine Prinzip des Alls war; das zweite war das Chaos, das Tohuwabohu. „Als dritte aber empfing die Seele in Mühsal das Gesetz". Es ist die *ruah*, welche über dem Urwasser schwebte und zugleich als Gotteshauch im Menschen (ἀπὸ σῆς πνοίης) über der Erde irrt, wie bei Sirach 24 die Sophia in der Tiefe der Abgründe wandelt und Ruhe sucht; diese Weltseele müht sich in der Gestalt der Hindin, wie die Seele in Psalm 41 schreit wie ein Hirsch. Diese Weltseele kann ganz stoisch aufgefasst werden als ein Pneuma, dass das All durchwaltet. Die stoische Ansicht leiht sich nämlich vorzüglich für das eigentliche Anliegen gewisser Gnostiker, welche darstellen wollen, wie der gestaltlose Logos, der Weltgrund, im Menschen göttliche Gestalt bekommen kann, wie er mit sich selbst identisch ist und sich doch von sich selbst unterscheidet. Wenn Posidonius sagt, dass „Gott ein geistiges und feuriges Pneuma ist, das keine *Gestalt hat,* sich aber verwandelt in das, was es will, und sich allem angleicht[26], so kehrt das beinahe wörtlich wieder bei gewissen Gnostikern: „Sie sagen nun über das Wesen des Pneuma, das die Ursache von allem ist, das wird, dass es ... all das Werdende erzeugt und schafft, indem sie sagen: 'Ich werde, was ich will, und ich bin, was ich bin' ". Es ist also nicht zu leugnen, dass die Weltseele der Gnostiker sich in manchen mit verwandten stoischen Anschauungen berührt. Auch wenn die weibliche Hypostase der Gottheit, die Barbelo, oder wie sie heissen mag, als erste Ennoia bezeichnet wird, liegt eine Entleihung aus der Stoa vor: denn auch die Stoiker haben die Athena πρώτη ἔννοια τοῦ Διός

---

26 Aëtius in Diels, Doxogr. p. 320: Ποσειδώνιος θεὸν εἶναι πνεῦμα νοερὸν καὶ πυρῶδες, οὐκ ἔχον μὲν μορφὴν μεταβάλλον δὲ εἰς ἃ βούλεται καὶ συνεξομοιούμενον πᾶσι. — Naassenerpredigt, Hipp. V, 7, 25: λέγουσιν οὖν περὶ τῆς τοῦ πνεύματος οὐσίας, ἥτις ἐστὶ πάντων τῶν γινομένων αἰτία, ὅτι ... γεννᾷ δὲ καὶ ποιεῖ πάντα τὰ γινόμενα, λέγοντες οὕτως· γίνομαι ὃ θέλω καὶ εἰμὶ ὃ εἰμί.

genannt [27]. Trotz all diesen Übernahmen aber lag der stoische Immanentismus und Optimismus dem tragischen Weltgefühl der Gnostiker ferne: der gnostische Mensch empfand sich als Abspaltung einer transzendenten Ganzheit, welche nicht in diese Welt gehörte; so tief er auch in sich hinabstieg und über die personalen Begrenzungen seines Individuums hinausging, so fand er in den tiefsten Schichten seines Wesens doch nichts als die unendliche Melancholie der Gottesferne und Weltverfallenheit. Das bedeutete ihm das Mythologem der gefallenen Sophia, welche auch als Weltseele weltfremd war.

Es ist doch wohl bezeichnend für die Tatsache, dass die griechischen Elemente nur formal von der Gnosis übernommen wurden, dass das Mythologem der Mutter mit den Sieben letztes Endes einem sehr weltbejahenden und diesseitigen Platonismus entnommen ist. Wer die helle Freude und den kosmischen Enthusiasmus der pseudoplatonischen Epinomis kennt, wird wohl keinen Augenblick auf den Gedanken verfallen, dass diese kosmische Religion phänomenologisch etwas mit dem gnostischen Akosmismus zu tun hat. Und doch finde ich in dieser Schrift die formale Vorstufe des gnostischen Mythologems einer Weltseele, welche sieben Planeten erzeugt.

Der Autor der Epinomis will eine Astralreligion verkünden; sein Anliegen ist die Einführung des Kultes der sichtbaren Götter, der Gestirne. Deswegen trägt er auch seine Weltentstehungslehre als eine Theogonie vor: es gibt fünf Elemente, Feuer, Wasser, Luft, Erde und Äther. Daraus bildet die Weltseele als *Demiurg* die Elementargeister oder Lebewesen. Während man im Timaeus noch darüber zweifeln kann, wer mit dem Demiurgen gemeint ist, wird im Epinomis deutlich ausgesprochen, *dass die Weltseele als Demiurg auftritt (981b)*. Aus dem Element des Feuers schafft die Weltseele die Elementargeister, welche am Himmel sichtbar sind, ,,das göttliche Geschlecht der Sterne, welches den schönsten Körper bekommen hat und die glücklichste und beste Seele''. Diese seligen Gestirngötter sind vernunftbegabt und bewegen sich in vollkommener Ordnung. ,,Nachdem die Weltseele als Demiurg dies alles geschaffen hat (δημιουργήσασαν), erfüllte sie den ganzen Himmel mit Gestirngeistern'' (984c). Diese sichtbaren Götter müssen kultisch verehrt werden: es werden der Fixsternhimmel, die Sonne, der Mond und die fünf übrigen Planeten erwähnt. Es hat also die *Psyche* als *Demiurg* die Sieben hervorgebracht. Es scheint mir, dass dies die älteste uns bekannte Vorstufe der gnostischen Vorstellung ist, dass die Sophia als Weltschöpferin aus der Materie die sieben Archonten erzeugt hat. Und obwohl nun ein anderes Weltgefühl im Laufe der Zeit diese Vorstellung mit anderm Geist gefüllt hat, schimmert der platonische Hintergrund doch nicht selten durch.

---

[27] Justinus, Apologie I, 64, 5.

Es gab auch gewisse Äusserungen späterer Platonisten über die Weltseele, welche dem gnostischen Empfinden entgegenkamen: die Weltseele kann „*einschlafen*, erfüllt vom Vergessen ihrer Eigentlichkeit" [28]; oder es heisst, dass sie aus *tiefem Schlaf* geweckt wird, damit sie, sehend auf die geistigen Wesenheiten, die Formen der Welt empfangen kann [29]. Man hört sogar, dass die Seele sich einmal aufrichtet zum Licht der Erkenntnis, dann wieder durch Ermüdung hinunterfällt [30]. Solche Äusserungen könnten bei den Gnostikern Verständnis finden, weil eine gewisse Form des Platonismus ihrer religiösen Erfahrung gemäss war. Und obwohl nun die Gnosis noch ganz andere als philosophische Motive hatte, wenn sie über die gefallene Weltseele sprach, so muss man für die Ursprungsfrage doch wohl auch seine Aufmerksamkeit auf gewisse Anknüpfungspunkte im Platonismus richten.

Es heisst im Naassenerpsalm über die Weltseele [31]:

> Bald hat sie Herrschaft und schaut das Licht,
> bald weint sie, in Elend geworfen,
> bald lacht sie, bald weint sie,
> bald stirbt sie, bald wird sie,
> und, im Labyrinth irrend,
> sucht vergebens sie den Ausweg.

Das lässt sich von den oben erwähnten Ansichten der Platoniker nicht scheiden.

So kommen wir zum Ergebnis, dass die Gnostiker für ihre Anschauungen über die Sophia als Weltseele der griechischen Philosophie verpflichtet sind und dass besonders das Mythologem über die Mutter der sieben Archonten in der Epinomis seine letzte Vorstufe hat. Ein babylonisches Mythologem zu rekonstruieren, wie W. Bousset das gemacht hat, is unnötig. Die Anlehnung an griechische Vorbilder ist zu deutlich [32].

---

[28] Plutarchus, de an. procr. 1026.
[29] Albinus, Eisagoge 14, .3
[30] Augustinus, de Lib. Arbitr. I, 22.
[31] Zögernd schlage ich vor, den verdorbenen Text so zu lesen (Hipp., Ref. V, 10, 2):

ποτὲ μὲν βασίλειον ἔχουσα βλέπει τὸ Φῶς
ποτὲ δ' εἰς ἐλεεὶν ἐκριπτομένη κλάει,
ποτὲ δὲ χαίρει, ποτὲ δὲ κλάίει
ποτὲ δὲ κρίνεται, ποτὲ δὲ γίνεται
κἀνέξοδος ἡ μελέα κακῶν
λαβύρινθον ἐσῆλθε πλανωμένη
(cf. Hesychius: κρινομένους: ἀποθνῄσκοντας).

[32] Gegen die orientalische Herkunft eines solchen Mythologems spricht die wörtliche Übereinstimmung der gnostischen Äusserungen über die Weltseele mit platonischen und stoischen Philosophemen. Diese Überzeugung scheidet uns von W. Staerk (siehe Anm. 25), W. Bousset, Hauptprobleme der Gnosis, p. 9, und Geo Widengren, The Great Vohu Manah and the Apostle of God, Uppsala, 1945.

b)   Wir müssen jetzt die merkwürdige Lehre besprechen, dass die weibliche Göttin ihr Abbild in das Urwasser des Chaos projiziert. Eine solche Vorstellung steht in der Gnosis nicht vereinzelt da. Die erwähnte Quelle des Basilides, also ein uraltes Dokument, berichtet, dass die Finsternisse, als sie das Licht (also die Lichtjungfrau) sahen, sie begierig verfolgten. Die Lichtjungfrau ihrerseits hat diese Mächte nur angeschaut „wie in einem Spiegel" [33]. So ist nur ein Abbild (emphasis) des Lichtes zu den Finsternissen gekommen, das diese bösen Wesen dann zerrissen haben. So kommt es, dass die Welt nur ein Gleichnis der Lichtwelt ist.

Auch hier scheint also die Lichtmagd ihr Abbild in die Urwasser des Chaos reflektiert zu haben.

Die Gnostiker bei Plotin behaupten, dass die Weltseele, die Sophia, nicht heruntergekommen ist, sondern nur die Finsternisse erleuchtet hat: daraus ist ein Bild ($\varepsilon\H\iota\delta\omega\lambda o\nu$) in der Materie entstanden (II, 9, 10).

Es muss diese Vorstellung auch in der samaritischen Gnosis des Simon Magus bestanden haben: die Simonianer erzählen, dass die kämpfenden Griechen und Barbaren nur ein Bild der Helena gesehen, aber sie selbst, wie sie war, bestimmt nicht gekannt haben, weil sie beim ersten und einzigen Gott war [34]. Die Simonianer haben also die Geschichte der griechischen Helena allegorisch erklärt: wie nach der Sage die Griechen und Troier ein *Eidolon* der Helena umkämpften, so haben die Archonten nur ein Abbild der Sophia umkämpft, während diese selbst beim höchsten Gott war. Nun ist es an sich nicht merkwürdig, dass in einem jüdischen Dokument der Kampf des Lichtes und der Finsternis dargestellt wird. Dazu lud die Genesis geradezu ein, indem sie erzählte, dass es eine Urfinsternis und ein Urlicht gab, noch ehe Sonne und Mond geschaffen wurden. Dass diese miteinander kämpfen, ehe Licht und Finsternis geschieden wurden, galt in dieser Zeit für selbstverständlich [35]. Damit aber ist die merkwürdige Anschauung, welche hier vorliegt, noch nicht erklärt.

Überall handelt es sich also darum, dass die Sophia ihren Schatten in die Materie projiziert hat. Und es verdient Beachtung, dass diese Vorstellung sich in Dokumenten findet, die teilweise sehr altertümlich sind und keine oder sehr geringfügige christliche Einflüsse aufzeigen. Dass auch die Simonianer so

---

[33]   Hegemonius, Acta Archelai 67, 9: et quidem et respexit eas velut per speculum ($\H\omega\varsigma$ $\delta\iota'$ $\varepsilon\sigma\acute o\pi\tau\rho o\upsilon$). Enfasis igitur ... ad tenebras factus est solus.

[34]   Pseudo-Clemens, Recognitiones 10, 12: Graeci et Barbari confligentes *imaginem* quidem eius aliqua ex parte videre potuerunt, ipsam vero ut est penitus ignorarunt, quippe quae apud illum primum omnium et solum habitaret deum.

[35]   Philo, de Opificio Mundi 9.

lehrten, lässt vermuten, dass dieses Mythologem in der jüdischen Gnosis aufgenommen war. Woher nun diese Lehrmeinung?

Plotin stellt dar, wie die Seele bei der Geburt hinuntersteigt; wenn sie sich hinunterneigt, erzeugt sie ein *Eidolon*, die niedrige Seele, welche hinuntersteigt und vom Körper Besitz nimmt: so wird die untere Welt erleuchtet (Enn. I, 1, 12: ἡ νεῦσις ἔλλαμψις πρὸς τὸ κάτω). Es wird hier also zwischen einer erleuchtenden Seele und ihrem Schattenbild im Körper unterschieden. Die Seele versenkt sich also nicht in die Materie, sondern erleuchtet sie: was mit der Körperlichkeit in Berührung kommt, ist ihr Eidolon, ihr Schattenbild, das sie nach unten projiziert. Es ist wahr, dass dies eine der platonischen Tradition unbekannte Auffassung ist. So ist es nicht verwunderlich, dass man an Beeinflussung von seiten der indischen Sankyaphilosophie gedacht hat. Franz Cumont hat aber nachgewiesen, dass es sich hier um eine uralte pythagoräische Auffassung handelt [36].

Dann aber muss auch das gnostische Mythologem von hier verstanden werden. Wenn es heisst, dass die Sophia ihr Eidolon ins Urwasser des Chaos projiziert, dann ist das eine Amplifikation der pythagoräischen Ansicht, welche Plotin der philosophischen Tradition entnommen hat. Diese Vorstellung hat sich nun durch Vermittlung der gnostischen Tradition auch im Manichäismus bewahrt. Es heisst, dass Adam von den Archonten geschaffen ist nach dem Bilde des dritten Gesandten: „Als aber die Archonten ihn sahen, da begehrten sie ein Bild und bildeten nach seinem Bilde Adam" (136, 21). Es wird nun aber doch zwischen diesem Gesandten und seinem Eikon unterschieden: „Er hat sich offenbart in der Vollendung der Menschen in seinem Lichtschiff. Er hat ... die Lebendige Seele, die geglänzt hat in Vollkommenheit und Vollendung über den Welten der Feindschaft" (Keph. 87). Ebenso wird zwischen dem Urmenschen und seinem Eikon unterschieden: „Der selige, herrliche Mensch war in verborgener Weise in seinem *Eikon* ... in seiner heiligen Jungfrau, welche die *Jungfrau des Lichts* ist" (84, 17). Diese Jungfrau ist die Seele des Urmenschen, seine Lichtglieder, sein Eikon: "When the Watcher (?) stood in the boundaries of Light, he shewed to them his Maiden, who is his soul; they bestirred theirselves in their abyss, desiring to exalt themselves over her, they opened their mouth desiring to swallow her" (Psalms 10, 10).

Es ist klar, dass sich die Vorstellung nicht wesentlich geändert hat. Zugrunde liegt überall die Vorstellung, dass die Seele ihr Schattenbild in die Finsternis projiziert und so den Weltprozess oder die Menschenschöpfung in Bewegung bringt. Ursprünglich war das die Sophia, später sind es andere Gestalten

---

[36] Lux Perpetua, p. 354 und 413.

geworden. Das wichtige aber ist, dass zwischen der *Psyche* und ihrem Eidolon unterschieden wird.

Wir scheinen also in der griechischen Welt die Vorstufe eines wichtigen gnostischen Mythologems gefunden zu haben. Und wir müssen betonen, dass das Motiv der Projektion des Schattenbildes im Kontext des Seelenmythos zu Hause ist. Wenn wir es später in Verbindung mit anderen Vorstellungen antreffen, kann es dort nicht unsprünglich sein. Wir stellen hier schon fest, dass in iranischen Quellen weder die Mutter der Sieben noch das Eidolon der Psyche in der Hyle zu finden ist. Der gnostische Mythos war offenbar zuerst und in seinen frühesten Anfängen Sophia-Mythos, in Anlehnung an gewisse hellenistische Vorbilder. Zuerst tritt in diesem Prozess die weibliche Gestalt der *anima mundi* auf; später wird das Bild des männlichen *Anthropos* heraufbeschworen, wie es vom Standpunkt der Psychologie auch sehr verständlich ist.

Vorläufig stellen wir fest, dass die Gnosis, wie wir sie bisher kennengelernt haben, aus einem Konflikt geboren ist, und zwar aus der Auseinandersetzung des jüdischen oder samaritanischen Menschen mit gewissen hellenistischen Vorstellungen. Aus diesem Kampf, so scheint es, ist eine neue Religion geboren, welche sich vom Judentum und Hellenismus grundsätzlich unterscheidet, weil ihre Vorstellungen mythischer Natur sind: böse Archonten vergewaltigen ihre Mutter oder verfolgen den Schatten dieser Mutter. Vor allem fällt es auf, dass der *Eros* als das Grundübel empfunden wird, wie das auch im Apokryphon Johannis gesagt wird. Entsprechend wird nun auch die Sophia als Prounikos bezeichnet, weil die Lüsternheit Ursache ihres Falles war. Der Ursprung dieses Mythos, so scheint mir, kann nur in der Seele der damaligen Menschen gefunden werden.

II. DIE ANTHROPOLOGISCHE PHASE

a. Es dient der Sophia-Mythos nicht zuletzt dazu, die Situation des Menschen als eines gefallenen und doch ebenbildlichen Gottes zu begründen und ihm den Weg der Rückkehr zu seinem Ursprung zu weisen. Und so sehr richtet sich das Interesse auf die anthropologischen Gesichtspunkte, dass die ursprüngliche Verbindung mit der Weltschöpfung verlorengehen kann und die Gestalt des Anthropos an die Stelle der Sophia tritt. Da knüpft dann die Gnosis meistens an haggadische und sonstige Traditionen über Adam an.

Nun gab es eine Menge von Sagen und Erzählungen über Adam, welche unschwer mit gnostischem Gefühl geladen werden konnten. In den armenischen Adamsbüchern wird erzählt, dass die Eva den Adam nach seinem Tode im Traume sah ,,gleich einem Licht, wie vordem, als sie in dem Garten waren" [37].

---

[37] E. Preuschen, o.c., p. 187.

Adam war also, wenn ich mich so ausdrücken darf, vor dem Falle mit einem Lichtleib bekleidet. Der erste Mensch hatte nach rabbinischen Quellen Anteil am kabod Gottes [38]. Er war ein leuchtendes Wesen, dessen Ferse den Sonnenball verdunkelt, ja er war sogar nach jüdischen Quellen das Licht der Welt [39]. So kommt es, nebenbei gesagt, dass Adam in gnostischen und manichäischen Quellen als Φωστηρ, Leuchter, bezeichnet wird [40].

Neben der bekannten jüdischen Anschauung, dass Adam teilhatte am Lichtglanz Gottes (kabod), gibt es nun noch eine andere Überlieferung, welche weniger bekannt und doch für unser Thema von gewisser Bedeutung ist. Adam ist ein baal teschubah [41], der nach seinem Fall seine Sünde bekannt hat, Busse getan hat und zum Paradies zurückgekehrt ist. Tertullian sagt es so prägnant: Adam exomologesi restitutus in paradisum suum (De Paen. 12, 9). Und zwar ist es, nach der Apocalypsis Mosis 37, 4, das Paradies im dritten der sieben Himmel, wohin Adam versetzt worden ist: „Lift him up into Paradise unto the third heaven, and leave him there until that fearful day of my reckoning, which I will make in the world. Then Michael took Adam and left him where God told him".

Diese Wiederkehr ins Paradies hat nun zu Spekulationen über Adam geführt, welche eine gnostische Interpretation vorbereiteten. Es heisst in der Sophia Salomonis X, 1, dass es *die Sophia* war, welche „den Protoplasten, den Vater der Welt", *aus seinem Fall* aufhob, womit auf eine Errettung von Adam angespielt wird, von der in der Genesis nichts zu lesen ist. Besonders bedeutsam sind die jüdisch-magischen Anschauungen, welche ein genialer Forscher in gewissen magischen Papyri wiedergefunden hat, über die Errettung Adams aus der Macht des Schicksals [42]. Darin wird Adam dargestellt als ein Sklave der astralen Mächte: seine ursprügliche Gestalt ist ihm verlorengegangen, aber dadurch, dass er den heiligen Gottesnamen rezitiert, steigt er zum Himmel empor und kehrt wieder in das Paradies zurück. Peterson nimmt an, dass diese Spekulation über Adam bis in die früheste Zeit des Hellenismus zurückgeht.

Und zuletzt muss noch erwähnt werden, dass nach der jüdischen Apokalyptik und der Haggada der Leib Adams eine Quaternio bildete, weil es aus einem

---

[38] Gen. r. XI, 2. B. Murmelstein, Adam, ein Beitrag zur Messiaslehre, Wiener Zeitschrift zur Kunde des Morgenlandes 35, 1928, p. 255, 3.

[39] Adam, Licht der Welt: Philo, de Opificio Mundi 143, 144, 148; Jeruschalmi Sabbath II, 35b; Genesis r. 17, 8; Tan. Noa § 1; Murmelstein, o.c., p. 255, 3.

[40] Hippol. Ref. V, 8, 40 (Naassenerpredigt): Φωστήρ τέλειος Kephalaia LXV, p. 158: Er (Adam) wurde Erleuchter (Φωστήρ) in ihrer Schöpfung an Stelle des Lichtes des Bildes des Gesandten, der sich ihnen droben offenbart hatte.

[41] H. J. Schoeps, Aus frühchristlicher Zeit, p. 10, 3.

[42] E. Peterson, La libération d'Adam de l'ἀνάγκη, Revue Biblique LV, 1948, p. 199.

nördlichen, südlichen, östlichen und westlichen Element gebildet war. Adam war selbst tetragrammaton [43].

Mir scheint, dass diese Sagen über Adam eine Stelle verdeutlichen, welche beim Alchemisten Zosimos aufbewahrt worden ist; dieser gibt selbst als Quelle den gnostischen Propheten Nikotheos an [44]. Nach der Meinung vieler Forscher enthält die Stelle eine gnostische Darstellung, welche nicht wesentlich vom Christentum beeinflusst ist. Dort wird ausgeführt, dass Adam ein symbolischer Name ist, weil er den vier Windrichtungen entspricht. Dies aber ist nur der äussere Adam. Der innere Adam, der geistige Mensch, welcher in diesem Körper enthalten ist, hat einen offenbaren und einen verborgenen Namen. Dieser offenbare Name ist *Phos*, Lichtmensch [45].

Als dieser Lichtmensch, dieser Phōs, sich im Paradiese erholte, haben die Archonten auf Instigation des Schicksals ihn, der ja unschuldig und ausserhalb ihrer Wirkung ($\dot{\alpha}\nu\varepsilon\nu\dot{\varepsilon}\rho\gamma\eta\tau\sigma\varsigma$) war, überredet, den von ihnen gebildeten Adam anzuziehen, der dem Schicksal entstammte und gebildet war aus den vier Elementen. Und er, harmlos, wie er war, wies diesen Vorschlag nicht ab. Die Archonten aber brüsteten sich, weil sie ihn in die Sklaverei geführt hatten.

Es muss nun aber beachtet werden, dass Adam in dieser Erzählung des Zosimos nach seinem Fall *bereut hat* und das Paradies wieder aufgesucht hat. ($\ddot{\sigma}\mu\omega\varsigma$ $\varkappa\alpha\grave{\iota}$ $\sigma\Phi\alpha\lambda\epsilon\grave{\iota}\varsigma$ $\varkappa\alpha\grave{\iota}$ $\mu\epsilon\tau\alpha\nu\sigma\acute{\eta}\sigma\alpha\varsigma$ $\varkappa\alpha\grave{\iota}$ $\tau\grave{\sigma}\nu$ $\epsilon\dot{\upsilon}\delta\alpha\acute{\iota}\mu\sigma\nu\alpha$ $\chi\tilde{\omega}\rho\sigma\nu$ $\zeta\eta\tau\acute{\eta}\sigma\alpha\varsigma$)

Das Gnostische an der Erzählung liegt in der ausgesprochenen Feindschaft der Archonten gegen den Lichtmenschen, dessen Paradies sich oberhalb ihres Wirkungskreises befindet, und im betonten Gegensatz von Seele und Körper. Sonst aber finden wir uns schon bekannte Motive wieder: die Archonten bilden den Leib des Adam, eine Seele kommt von oben her. Er ist Sklave des Schicksals und kehrt wieder zum Lande seines Ursprungs zurück, nachdem er Busse getan hat. Und so ist natürlich auch der Phōs, der Lichtmensch im Paradies, kein anderer als der Phōster, der Leuchter Adam, der jüdischen Tradition. Dann wird es auch deutlich, dass der Rekurs auf den persischen Gayomart abwegig und unnötig ist. Ein neues Daseinsverständnis hat hier das bestehende jüdische Material in seinem Sinne interpretiert und mit neuem Gehalt erfüllt: der Mensch ein Sklave des Schicksals, dem er entrinnen muss, ein Gefangener seines

---

[43] Tanchuma, Pehude § 3, Pirke R. Elieser XI: „Gott begann den Körper des ersten Adam von allen vier Seiten der Welt zu sammeln". Andere Belegstellen bei: A. J. Festugière, La Révélation d'Hermès Trismegiste I, p. 269, 2.

[44] Über Nikotheos, dessen Schrift in Nag Hammadi gefunden wurde: H.-Ch. Puech, Coptic Studies in Honor of W. E. Crum, p. 134.

[45] Text bei R. Reitzenstein, Poimandres, p. 102. Übersetzung bei: A. J. Festugière, o.c., p. 263.

Körpers, den er töten muss, das sind die Stimmungen, welche in die bestehenden Mythologeme hineinempfunden werden.

b. Das neue Lebensgefühl, womit die Gnosis die bestehenden Vorstellungen ladet, so dass der weltanschauliche Rahmen gesprengt wird und immer neuere und verwirrendere Systemgebilde zustande kommen, kennzeichnet sich nicht zuletzt durch die Verneinung des Eros: die Sophia fällt wegen ihrer Lüsternheit, die transpersonalen Mächte vergewaltigen das Schattenbild der Seele, der Teufel erzeugt mit Eva ihre Söhne, und die Schöpfung ist Nachgeburt der Hurerei des Weltgeistes. Ja, überall schimmert die Vorstellung durch, dass das Böse aus einem Bruch in der Gottheit stammt und mit dem Eros identisch ist. Ein Verständnis dieser Vorstellung kann nicht zustande kommen, wenn der Blick an dem sexualen und libidinosen Aspekt dieser Bilder haften bleibt. Wir verstehen, so scheint es, die Gnostiker besser, wenn wir den Eros ganz allgemein als Lebensdurst und Lebensdrang fassen. Der Fall des Menschen ist seine Verfallenheit an das Leben in der Welt, sein Absturz in die Sklaverei von Leben und Tod. Seine Schuld besteht darin, dass er sich von einer transzendentalen Ganzheit abgespalten hat und selbständiges Dasein führt, kurz, seine eigentliche Schuld ist die Individuation. Die Gnosis wird dann auch nicht zuletzt darin bestehen, dass er durch den Mythos seine eigene Verklammerung in dem blinden und unbewussten Willen durchschaut und dadurch auch die Welt als Vorstellung aufhebt. Die Erlösung ist Loslösung vom Lebensdurst und Preisgabe der Individuation. Diese ebenso unhellenische wie unjüdische Stimmung hat das gnostische Weltgefühl nun wieder in eine gewisse platonische Ausführung hineingelesen, so dass es dann und wann scheinen kann, als ob die Gnosis eine Auslese aus Plato darstellte. Es kann aber eine so abgründige Weltanschauung, welche die tiefverwurzelte Abscheu des Menschen vor seiner individuierten Gestalt ausdrückt und seine radikale Verfallenheit an die Lebensmächte veranschaulicht, welche die ganze Last des Menschen aus seinem Lebensdurst erklärt und gegen die Geschöpflichkeit rebelliert, doch wohl nicht aus blosser Plato-Lektüre abgeleitet werden. On ne lit jamais un livre, on se lit à travers des livres. Wenn es auch wahr ist, dass gewisse Platoniker den Eros als Ursache der Verkörperung der Seele aufgefasst haben, so hat doch anderseits Plato den Eros ganz positiv gewertet. Die Gnostiker haben sich selbst in Plato wiedergefunden.

Was war nun die gnostische Auslese aus Plato? Zwei Motive müssen hier besonders erwähnt werden: 1. der Fall der Seele in die Welt von Geburt und Tod und 2. die Kreuzigung der Seele am Körper.

1. Die orphische Ansicht, welche von Plato übernommen wurde, dass die Seele vom Himmel gefallen ist, war im Altertum allgemein verbreitet. Dieses „Niederkommen" hatte nun auch für den antiken Menschen eine Assoziation

mit der Geburt des Kindes. Weil das Gebären auf der Erde stattfand, sagte man, dass das Kind auf die Erde fiel. Das Kind wird mit dem Kopf nach unten geboren: man sagt, dass es „mit dem Kopf nach unten auf die Erde stürzt". Ganz allgemein heisst es, dass der Neugeborene „zwischen die Füsse der Mutter fällt" [46].

Die platonische Tradition hat versucht, diese Seelenlehre auch durch Mythendeutung zu bestätigen. Man allegorisierte die Erzählung von Attis und der Grossen Mutter und fand darin kosmogonische, aber zugleich auch psychologische Wahrheiten, wie die Seele abgestürzt war in die Materie und zur Ideenwelt zurückkehrte. Dabei werden nun doch gewisse romantische Ansichten laut, die bei Plato noch nicht zu finden sind. Attis verlässt die Grosse Mutter und verliebt sich in eine Nymphe; dann bringt die Mutter ihn zur Raserei, er haut seine Genitalien ab und kehrt zur Mutter wieder. Das wird so erklärt: die Mutter ist die archetypische Welt, „die Quelle der geistigen und schöpferischen Götter, die Herrin alles Lebens, die Ursache alles Werdens, eine mutterlose Magd, die Beisitzerin des höchsten Gottes und wahrlich Mutter aller Götter" [47]; kurz gesagt: sie ist der Ort der Urbilder.

Attis ist der Demiurg alles Werdenden und Vergehenden oder auch das Formprinzip der materiellen Welt, der bis an die Enden des Kosmos abgestiegen ist und sich mit dem Feuchten der Materie vermischt, die Potenz der Mutter, durch welche sie die Hefe der Materie ordnet, man würde sagen, das Eidolon der Psyche, welche selbst oben bleibt. Es enthält die Entmannung des Attis die Weisung an die Menschen, „die wir ja auch vom Himmel gefallen sind und mit der Nymphe geschlechtlichen Umgang haben, um den weiteren Fortgang der Prokreation abzuhauen" [48]. Es werden Attis und wir alle, die wir einmal vom Himmel zur Erde geflattert und gefallen sind, aufgerufen, „zur Einheit hinaufzuschnellen" [49]. Was abgehauen, abgeschnitten, kastriert werden muss, ist der *Eros zum Werden* (Julianus 171 D: ὀργᾷ εἰς τὴν γένεσιν; 173 C: τὸ τῆς γενέσεως αἴτιον ἀποτέμνεται; Sallustius 4: ἡμῶν ἀποκοπτομένων τὴν περαιτέρω τῆς γενέσεως πρόοδον).

Gewisse Gnostiker haben eine Version dieser platonischen Mytheninter-

---

[46] Waszink, de Anima, p. 278; (Callisthen.) 1, 12, 9: πεσόντος ἐπὶ γῆς τοῦ βρέφους; Mart. Petri 13: sicenim nascimur, ut proni videamur in terram effundi; Hom., Ilias 19, 110: πέσῃ μετὰ ποσσὶ γυναικός.

[47] Julianus Apostata, Oratio V, 166B.

[48] Sallustius, Concerning the Gods IV, Nock, 8.

[49] Julianus 169C: ὅσοι ποτὲ οὐρανόθεν ἔπτημεν εἰς τὴν γῆν καὶ ἐπέσομεν ... ἐπὶ ... αὐτὸ τὸ ἓν ἀνατρέχειν.

pretation gekannt [50]. Ihre eigenen Darstellungen schliessen daran unmittelbar an. Es wird von einem Wesen gesagt, dass es seine Mutter verlässt, seinen Schatten abhaut und hinaufschnellt zum Pleroma [51]. Es ist auch hier wie bei Attis die Kastrierung so gemeint, dass der Lebensdurst ausgelöscht werden sollte. Was abgeschnitten wird, ist der Eros zur Gnesis. Wenn die heidnischen Gnostiker bei Arnobius sagen, dass die Seelen kopfüber in die Wollüste gestürzt sind, ist wohl dasselbe gemeint (II, 44).

2. Die Kreuzigung der Seele an den Körper hat mit christlichen Anschauungen nichts zu tun und lässt sich bis auf Platos Phaidon verfolgen. Jede Lust und jener Schmerz, so heisst es dort, nagelt die Seele wie mit Nägeln an den Leib (83 d). Der Tor schlägt sich selbst ans Kreuz und wird durch ebenso viele Kreuze als Begierden auseinandergerissen; der Weise versucht sich von seinem Kreuz zu lösen [52]. Auch die Gnostiker des Arnobius meinen, dass sie mit Nägeln am Leibe angeheftet sind (II, 13).

Es konnte unter diesen Umständen natürlich nicht ausbleiben, dass auch der Fall Adams buchstäblich als Absturz aus dem himmlischen Paradies aufgefasst wurde. Es ist dies nicht nur in gnostischen Schriften der Fall: Cyrillus von Jerusalem sagt, dass Adam (aus dem Paradies) gefallen und heruntergestürzt, aber auf Grund seiner Busse erlöst ist [53]. Methodius von Olympus formuliert es so, dass der Protoplast auf die Erde gefallen ist (De Resurrectione 1, 37, 6: πεσεῖν πρωτόπλαστον εἰς χθόνα. Wenn Petrus mit dem Kopf nach unten gekreuzigt wird, deutet er das als ein Bild des ersten Menschen, der erstmalig in die Genesis gekommen ist (τοῦ πρώτως εἰς γένεσιν χωρήσαντος ἀνθρώπου) (Mart. Petri 9). „Denn *der erste Mensch,* dessen Bild ich trage, mit dem Kopf nach unten abgestürzt, stellte eine Genesis her, welche früher nicht

---

[50] Der Autor der Naassenerpredigt kennt eine ähnliche platonische Deutung des Attis-Mythos. *Nur die platonische Deutung erlaubte ihm,* sich auf diesen Mythos zu beziehen. Er hat dasselbe getan, wie die Simonianer, die ihre sophianische Erfahrung auf Helena übertrugen, weil Helena schon in der griechischen Welt zum Symbol der abstürzenden und wiederkehrenden Seele geworden war. Eusthatius, p. 154, ad IV, 121: σεληναίαν ἄνθρωπον τὴν Ἑλένην ἐπλάσαντο ὡς ἐκ τοῦ κατὰ σέληνην κόσμου πεσοῦσαν, καὶ αὖθις δὲ ἄνω ἁρπαγῆναι αὐτὴν ἐμυθεύσαντο; Tatianus, Or. 10, 3: τὴν ἐκπορνεύσασαν εἰς Ἡλύσια πεδία μετατεθεικώς.

[51] Excerpta ex Theodoto 32, 3: οὗτος δέ, καταλείψας τὴν Μητέρα, ἀνελθὼν εἰς τὸ πλήρωμα; Irenaeus I, 11,1: καὶ τοῦτον μέν, ἅτε ἄρρενα ὑπάρχοντα, ἀποκόψαντα ἀφ' ἑαυτοῦ τὴν σκιάν, ἀναδραμεῖν εἰς τὸ πλήρωμα.

[52] Seneca, De Beata Vita 19, 2: Cum refigere se crucibus conentur, in quas unusquisque vestrum clavos suos ipse adigit, ad supplicium tamen acti stipitibus singulis pendent; hi qui in se ipsi animum advertunt, quot cupiditatibus tot crucibus distrahuntur.

[53] Cyrillus, Cat. II. 7, über Adam: ἵνα βλέπων ὅθεν ἐξέπεσε καὶ ἐξ οἵων εἰς οἷα κατηνέχθη, λοιπὸν ἐκ μετανοίας σωθῇ.

bestand [54]. Der sterbende Petrus ist ein Gegenbild von Adam, der in die
Welt von Geburt und Tod stürzte. Die Askese, welche in dieser Schrift gelehrt
wird, beabsichtigt die Tötung des Lebensdranges und der Verhaftung an den
Körper. Diese Betrachtung des Eros ist der gnostischen sehr nahe.

So finden wir denn auch in der Gnosis die Ansicht, dass Adam und Eva aus
dem Paradies hinausgeworfen sind und vom Himmel in diese Welt geworfen
(dejectos de caelo in hunc mundum; Iren. I, 30, 3). Und daraus sehen wir,
dass das Paradies ursprünglich im Himmel, oberhalb des Machtbereichs der
Archonten gedacht wird. So wird es immer deutlicher, was das Mythologem
von Adam für den Gnostiker bedeutet. Er empfindet die Regierung der
Weltmächte der Archonten als eine Last und Sklaverei, aber er kennt auch die
Möglichkeit eines freien Daseins, das hinter und vor seiner Situation liegt; die
Frage, wie dann der Mensch dieser Sklaverei verfallen ist, beantwortet er
dann und wann mit der Deutung, dass der Eros Ursache seiner Verfallenheit
an das Leben ist: dies besagt das Mythologem des Falles Adams in das
Werden.

Gegen diese Hintergründe gesehen, wird es nun doch auch wahrscheinlich,
dass mit dem Anthropos, von dem im Poimandres des Corpus Hermeticum die
Rede ist, Adam gemeint ist. Es ist dies um so mehr einleuchtend, als auch im
übrigen der Poimandres der grossen Linie der biblischen Schöpfungsgeschichte
folgt und eine allerdings wunderliche Exegese der Genesis gibt [55]; und es ist
doch nicht wohl denkbar, dass der Autor dabei auf einmal einen iranischen
Fremdkörper eingeschaltet hätte über ein Wesen, das merkwürdigerweise den
gleichen Namen wie Adam hat. Es ist hier doch wohl, wie bei Cyrillus, im
Martyrium Petri, bei Zosimos und bei den Gnostikern von Irenaeus I, 30, mit
dem fallenden Gotteskind Adam visiert. Dann aber könnte gewissermassen der
Poimandres als das Dokument einer judaisierenden Gnosis betrachtet werden.

Es wird erzählt, dass die Gottheit einen Anthropos erzeugt, der ihm gleich ist.
Dieser schaute durch das Gefüge der Sphären hinunter, nachdem er ihre
Umhüllung durchbrochen hat, und zeigte der niedrigen Natur die schöne
Gestalt Gottes, gespiegelt in den Wassern des Chaos.

Die Natur schaut das Bild des Anthropos ($\varepsilon\tilde{\iota}\delta o\varsigma$) im Wasser und seinen
Schatten auf der Erde und verliebt sich in ihn. Seinerseits verliebt sich der
Anthropos, als er die ihm ähnliche Gestalt im Wasser der Natur gespiegelt
sieht und nimmt Wohnung in der *vernunftlosen Gestalt* (14).

---

[54] Martyrium Petri 9, Lipsius-Bonnet, p. 94: $\dot{o}$ $\gamma\grave{\alpha}\rho$ $\pi\rho\tilde{\omega}\tau o\varsigma$ $\check{\alpha}\nu\vartheta\rho\omega\pi o\varsigma$, $o\tilde{\upsilon}$ $\gamma\acute{\epsilon}\nu o\varsigma$ $\dot{\epsilon}\nu$ $\epsilon\check{\iota}\delta\epsilon\iota$
$\check{\epsilon}\chi\omega$ $\dot{\epsilon}\gamma\acute{\omega}$, $\kappa\alpha\tau\grave{\alpha}$ $\kappa\epsilon\phi\alpha\lambda\grave{\eta}\nu$ $\dot{\epsilon}\nu\epsilon\chi\vartheta\epsilon\grave{\iota}\varsigma$ $\check{\epsilon}\delta\epsilon\iota\xi\epsilon\nu$ $\gamma\acute{\epsilon}\nu\epsilon\sigma\iota\nu$ $\tau\grave{\eta}\nu$ $o\dot{\upsilon}\kappa$ $o\tilde{\upsilon}\sigma\alpha\nu$ $\pi\acute{\alpha}\lambda\alpha\iota$.
[55] C. H. Dodd, The Bible and the Greeks.

Wenn es richtig ist, dass mit dieser vernunftlosen Gestalt der Körper des Anthropos gemeint ist, fällt der Zusammenhang zwischen dem Bild im Wasser und dem menschlichen Körper auf, von denen wir oben sprachen. In verschiedener Hinsicht sind diese Spekulationen über Adam ein Abklatsch des Sophia-Mythos. Übereinstimmend ist die *spectandi libido*, der Reflex des Gottesbildes im Urwasser des Chaos, der Eros als Grundübel, der Körper als Abbild des Urbildes. Der Mythos vom Anthropos will, ebenso wie der Sophia-Mythos, begründen, dass der Mensch ein Sklave des Schicksals und dass der Eros schuld am Tode ist. Aber wir sehen ganz klar, dass verschiedene Motive, welche dort ursprünglich waren und am richtigen Ort, hier in abgeleiter Form wiederkehren. Der kosmogonische Mythos der Sophia hat dem anthropologischen Mythos des aus dem himmlischen Paradies abstürzenden Adam seine Farben verliehen. Wenn aber die Schuld des Eros und die Macht der versklavenden Gestirne so betont werden, zeigt es sich von neuem, dass jüdisches und griechisches Material als Symbol des revoltierenden, lebenverneinenden gnostischen Weltgefühls hat dienen müssen.

Wir halten hier einen Augenblick inne und versuchen die bisherigen Ergebnisse unserer Untersuchung zu überblicken. Es wurde wahrscheinlich, dass es eine vielleicht vorchristliche, judaisierende Gnosis gegeben hat, welche griechische Anschauungen über die Weltseele mit biblischen Gestalten, wie Chokma und Ruaḥ, verband und mythologisch deutete. Daneben und danach fanden wir die Ansicht, dass der Fall Adams als ein Absturz aus dem Lichtreich des Paradieses in die Welt von Geburt und Tod aufgefasst werden muss: da spielt platonische Seelenlehre hinein. Das Astrologische hat dem Ganzen eine eigentümliche Färbung gegeben. Das Bedeutsame ist nun, dass das neue gnostische Weltgefühl diesen bestehenden Vorstellungen einen neuen Sinn gegeben hat. Dass es einen Bruch in der Gottheit gibt oder auch dass der Lebenswille zu verneinen ist, darf nicht als hellenistisch oder jüdisch gelten. Und doch ist die jüdische Vorstellungswelt und die hellenistische Vulgärphilosophie und Astrologie zureichend zur Erklärung der Ursprungsfrage. Iranische Vorstellungen sind uns nicht begegnet. Und vollends hat die Gnosis, soweit wir sie bisher kennengelernt haben, keine Erlösergestalt gekannt: es ist unrichtig, den Anthropos, den Adam, im Poimandres als Erlöser vorzustellen. Wenn es auch vielleicht eine vorchristliche Gnosis gab, so doch nimmermehr einen vorchristlichen gnostischen Erlöser.

[The writing „Bronté or Perfect Nous", found at Nag Hammadi, contains a pre-gnostic Sophia myth which reminds us of Isis and of Helen: M. Krause, Gnostische und hermetische Schriften aus Codex II und Codex VI, Glückstadt, 1972, pp. 122-132].

GNOSTICISM AND THE NEW TESTAMENT

When we consider the problem of Gnosticism and Christianity, we must take into account certain facts about the history of the Church.

Paul's opponents in Palestine did not disappear without leaving any trace. Their views were inherited and developed by a group of Jewish Christians existing somewhere in Western Syria; it was this group that was largely responsible for the views expressed in the Pseudo-Clementine writings. It is, of course, exceedingly difficult to assess just to what extent the older views are present in these later writings. But there is no doubt that some continuity does exist. Attempts to deny this continuity or to explain it away by citing parallels from Gnosticism should be dismissed as apologetics. The Pseudo-Clementine writings may be somewhat fantastic, but certainly are not gnostic. They are moreover valuable to the historian of the Church, both for the concept which we find there of Jesus as the promised prophet and because they show us that animosity towards Paul continued to persist in certain Jewish Christian quarters.

Nor should we assume that the Christian community of Jerusalem — that recognized Paul, but did not accept his views on the Law — vanished into the air after A.D. 70, or even after 135. If the Acts of the Apostles say nothing about the Christian mission to Egypt or Eastern Syria and Mesopotamia, we must not conclude that nothing of the kind existed. Egypt is very near to Palestine; consequently there were many Jews living in Alexandria. So it is possible that Jewish Christians came to Alexandria at a very early date to preach the Messiah, especially to their compatriots. In any case Jewish Christians must have lived there before A.D. 200, because both Clement of Alexandria and Origen quote with some respect from their Gospel, the *Gospel According to the Hebrews*.

Relations between Palestine and Edessa are better substantiated. Tradition tells us that a certain Addai, a name abbreviated from the Hebrew Adonya, was sent from Jerusalem to Edessa to preach the gospel and was very well received there by the local Jews. Burkitt and Vööbus agree that there must be some truth in this story. As a matter of fact, we must consider the Aramaic-speaking Christendom of Palestine and Syria as a special unit with its own traditions, strongly influenced by its Jewish surroundings and not very interested in the ontological interpretation of Christianity which developed on Greek soil. This isolation explains, for example, why the concept of the Holy Ghost as a Mother, a concept well attested in the Jewish Christian Gospel tradition and quite understandable in a religion of Semitic language, continued to persist everywhere in Syria and can even be found in the fourth-century Syrian mystic Makarios.

All this, of course, has nothing to do with Gnosticism. It is against this background, however, that we must see the Gospel tradition in the *Gospel of Thomas*, which for several reasons should be located in the Christian community of Edessa and dated about A.D. 140. This collection of Sayings contains evidence of a Gospel tradition transmitted in a Jewish Christian milieu. In fact, one saying is even based upon a quotation from the *Gospel according to the Hebrews* (1.2). In logion 12, James is seen as the primate of the whole church, a view also attested by the Pseudo-Clementine writings (*Rec.* 1 : 43); this reflects the precedence of James in the primitive community, of which Paul also gives witness when, in Galatians 2 : 9, he puts James before Peter. If the Western Text gives the names in the opposite order and thus shows that at a very early date somebody in Rome may have had a different opinion, this only proves that the original wording was no mere coincidence. But the *Gospel of Thomas* also shows that it was Jewish rather than Gentile Christians who brought Christianity to Eastern Syria. Its author often uses, and even inserts into his sources, the word *monachos* in the sense of "bachelor", thereby showing that this was a technical term in his milieu. As a matter of fact, this word, of central importance in the *Gospel of Thomas*, has until now not been found in any known gnostic writing unless one wants to claim that the *Gospel of Thomas* is such, and so its presence is certainly no evidence for this text being gnostic. In fact its use here tends to show that the *Gospel of Thomas* is not gnostic at all. For the word *monachos* here, as in the Bible translation of the Jewish Christian Symmachus, seems to be the translation of the Hebrew *yāḥid*, which is invested with the same meaning of "bachelor" in some rabbinic passages. The concept continued to exist in Syrian asceticism, expressed by the technical term *iḥidaya*, which conveys exactly the same idea.

We find the same relation between Jewish Christianity and Syrian asceticism in logion 42, "become passers-by". Some gnosticizing interpreters of the *Gospel of Thomas* have translated it, "come into being as you pass away". Consideration of the Greek, Coptic, and Hebrew languages show that this translation is very impressive, incomprehensible, and faulty. Joachim Jeremias has pointed out that "passer-by" is a literal translation of the Hebrew word *'ôbēr*, which means "wanderer", "wandering teacher". The logion says, "become wanderers". Obedient to this commandment the Syrian ascetics kept wandering until the fourth century and even later.

It would seem that this ascetic mood of the Jewish Christians is responsible for the distortion of the parable of the invitations, as found in the *Gospel of Thomas*, logion 64. Following the example of certain OT prophets, Zephaniah

(1 : 11) and Zechariah (14 : 21), this writing shows a certain animosity towards commerce and business. "Tradesmen and merchants shall not enter the seats (lit. places) of my Father". But exactly the same application and interpretation of the parable is to be found in Aphraates (Parisot, pp. 249-50: *qui adsumit iugum sanctorum, negotiationem a se removeat*). Vööbus was certainly right when he pointed out that Syrian asceticism and Christian asceticism in general had a Jewish Christian background. A gnosticizing, arbitrary, and unhistorical interpretation of the *Gospel of Thomas* obscures this insight into the history of the early Church.

Historians of the early Church have recently stressed the importance of Encratism and the fact that its roots lay in primitive Christianity. These two realizations have a direct bearing upon the much debated problem of Gnosticism and Christianity. Much would be gained for our study of the NT if it were established once and for all that Encratism is not the same as Gnosticism. Henry Chadwick, in an article for *Reallexikon für Antike und Christentum,* has shown that Christianity has been accompanied by Encratism since its very beginning. Perhaps it was present in Corinth, where Paul exhorts the Encratites not to give up marriage in spiritually overrating their all too human frames. Certainly it is there too in the pastoral letters, where Jewish Encratites proclaim that the resurrection has already taken place and that marriage should be abolished. Later, Encratism remained a current within the Catholic Church until finally, in some quarters of the Western Church, the Encratites were declared heretics and expelled. I must add that in Syria the Encratites in fact remained within the Church much longer. Tatian was not considered a heretic there; on the contrary his Gospel harmony, which contained Encratitic corrections, was accepted for use in the Church. The *Acts of Thomas,* written about A.D. 225 in Edessa, reflects the main stream of Syrian Christianity when it proclaims divorce as the essential Christian teaching. The Syrian *Liber Graduum,* rightly considered by its editor Kmosko to be Encratitic, shows no evidence that it was written outside the Church. The fourth-century Syrian mystic Makarios (38 : 1) identified the Church with its unmarried ascetics — a characteristic view of Encratitic doctrine. But although his views are certainly in tune with the specific teachings of the Syrian Messalians, we cannot prove that in his lifetime Messalianism led a heterodox existence outside the Church. Our sources show rather that their expulsion took place only towards the end of the fourth century. Messalianism then was probably a revival of a very old indigenous spirituality, which had existed in Syria for many centuries.

Encratism seems to have differed from Catholicism mainly in that it prescribed celibacy, whereas the Western Church in general only preferred it. Celibacy was for the Encratites a requirement for baptism. According to our sources they considered marriage to be fornication and corruption; from this it followed that everyone who had not left his father and his mother was to be considered the son of a prostitute. Moreover, birth was considered to be deplorable, because it inevitably led to death.

Our main source for the history of Encratism, the third book of Clement of Alexandria's *Stromateis*, reveals a more sophisticated and profound interpretation of the Christian faith and gives us reason to suppose that a certain continuity between the NT and the early Church can also be found to exist in the case of Encratism.

In the *Stromateis*, marriage is considered in its eschatological perspective. Jesus had taught that in the eschatological era marriage would not exist any more (Mark 12 : 25 par.). But now eschatology has been realized. Christ has risen from the dead, the faithful participate in his resurrection, and therefore marriage should be abolished. It is possible that this reasoning also lies behind the words of the Encratites in II Tim. 2 : 18, saying that the resurrection has already taken place.

Clement also transmits the pessimistic view of these Encratites on love and marriage; reproduction and generation only serve to nourish death. But the basis of their theology is biblical — they follow the Lord who was poor and unmarried. Redemption, moreover, is a deliverance from desire, because the Fall, according to their interpretation, was a Fall out of innocence into sexuality. The tree of knowledge, from which man ate, symbolized sexual intercourse. Jesus by his life and message delivered the Christian from this urge and drive for life.

When we have read and understood the views of the Encratites in the third book of the *Stromateis*, we clearly see that this is the real theology of the *Gospel of Thomas*. It teaches that

1. only those who are unmarried can be saved (1. 75);

2. the resurrection has already taken place (1. 51);

3. marriage is fornication (1. 105);

4. the earthly mother produces children for death, but the heavenly Mother regenerates them for eternal life (1. 101);

5. before the Fall, man lived in a state of innocence, where the differentiation between the sexes had not yet taken place (1. 37, 1. 11). When man returns to the sexual innocence of the child, and only then, he regains Paradise (1. 22); he realizes the original unity and identity with himself which he had lost.

All this is Encratitic and in accord with the information given by Clement of Alexandria concerning the Encratites. This proves that the *Gospel of Thomas* is Encratitic. The activity of Tatian in Eastern Syria and the Acts of Thomas attest to the existence of Encratites in the Syrian Church of Edessa. The *Gospel of Thomas* proves that they were already there about A.D. 140. Unlike Gnosticism the *Gospel of Thomas* does not teach an inferior demiurge, docetism, the divine consubstantiality of the human Self, nor the mythical expression of self-experience. Where is Achamoth, where Barbelo, where are the Aeons? Those who claim that the author of the *Gospel of Thomas* was a Gnostic, must first prove that there were Gnostics in second-century Edessa and that the author of this writing was one of them. I know of no sources which contain such information. The adherents of the gnostic interpretation, moreover, must explain how the author could possibly say that the buried *corpse* could rise again (logion 5, Greek version) and that Jesus manifested himself, quite undocetically, in the *flesh* (l. 28, cf. Baruch 3 : 38).

I think, on the contrary, that we can adduce a decisive argument to prove that the *Gospel of Thomas* is Syrian and Encratitic. Working quite independently of each other, Dom Baker and G. Quispel have recently established that the Syrian mystic Makarios knew and used the *Gospel of Thomas*. Makarios quotes one saying almost word for word: "The Kingdom of God is spread upon the earth and men do not see it" (1 : 113). There are, moreover, many clear allusions to the *Gospel of Thomas* and there are also very many similarities in theology. For both Makarios and the author of the *Gospel of Thomas* Christ is our Father, and the Holy Spirit our Mother; man should be one, because God is one. Man originates in the heavenly Paradise, and has fallen because he has tasted the bitterness of desire and has drunk the venom with which the serpent infected the fruit of knowledge. But now eschatology has been realized, the resurrection is already there, owing to Christ. Therefore, man should dissolve his marriage, leave his wife and children, follow Christ and identify himself with Him, in order to regain Paradise here and now.

Nobody has ever said that Makarios was a Gnostic. Then neither is the *Gospel of Thomas*. We should envision this writing in its historical milieu and thus in its proper perspective, in order to discern its message. Encratism is not Gnosticism — not even the Encratism of the NT, which should be interpreted in the light of the Encratitic sources that are available, in both Greek and Syriac, although they are of a somewhat later date.

With this in mind, we turn to the so-called *Hymn of the Pearl*, which occurs in the *Acts of Thomas* (chs. 108-113). This hymn is sometimes considered the key to the pre-Christian Iranian myth of the Saved Savior, which is supposed to lie behind the teaching of the NT, especially the Fourth Gospel. The poem tells us about a prince, who as a child was living in the kingdom of his father. He is sent away from home with a "load" (*phortion*) of precious stones to fetch a pearl in Egypt. When he arrives there he clothes himself in the dress of the Egyptians and forgets about his mission. Then a letter is sent to him from home which reminds him of his task. He charms the serpent that guards the pearl, "the one pearl" (line 12), and he takes this pearl away and returns to his father. The robe which he had formerly worn is given back to him. In this he recognizes his real nature. He invests himself with this robe and gives the pearl to his father.

There is no doubt that this hymn is Christian in origin. It is based upon the parable of the pearl, of which it is a poetical amplification and illustration. More especially it is based upon the version of this parable contained in the *Gospel of Thomas,* l. 76. "The Kingdom of the Father is like a man, a merchant, who possessed merchandise (*phortion*) and discovered a pearl. That merchant was prudent. He sold the merchandise, and bought 'the one pearl' for himself".

This parable must have existed outside the *Gospel of Thomas* in the Jewish Christian and Syrian Gospel traditions. In the Pseudo-Clementine *Recognitions* (3 : 62) we also read that the merchant was *sapiens* and that he bought *unam margaritam* ("the one pearl"). Likewise, *sapiens* is the reading of Ephrem Syrus and the *Life of Rabbula*. But the *Hymn of the Pearl,* too, has the variants *phortion* and "the one pearl" in common with the *Gospel of Thomas.* If the *Acts of Thomas* was written at Edessa about A.D. 225, this Christian hymn must have been composed sometime before 225 and after the introduction of Christianity into Edessa by Jewish Christians. Nor is there any doubt that its basic ideas are also to be found in the Syrian Makarios. For in Makarios as well, we find that man receives again the garment of glory that he had lost when the soul fell from its height and became the slave of the true Pharaoh (47 : 6). Or again he likens Christians to the sons whom a father sent to a foreign country with drugs to soothe and kill the dragons that attack them (26 : 24). Moreover in Makarios, Scripture is the letter, written by a king (39).

In this historical context the underlying idea of the *Hymn of the Pearl* is revealed. The soul, born in the heavenly Paradise, must be reminded of its task in the body, so it can return to Paradise and receive the original garment of the Spirit. The concept of the preexistence of the soul in Paradise, of Jewish origin and understandable in a Christian milieu so profoundly influenced by Judaism, persisted in Syria at least until the time of Makarios (25 : 7). The *Hymn of the Pearl* is not gnostic at all, but rather an orthodox Christian hymn tinged with Judaistic colors.

Perhaps these conclusions will give us some second thoughts about the apodictic and uncritical statements of Geo Widengren and others concerning the

Iranian myth of the Saved Savior. We are reminded of the sober criticism by
Gershom Scholem in his great book, *Jewish Gnosticism,* where he writes

Theories that the origin of Gnosticism is to be found outside the scope of
Judaism have been widely discussed. It is one of many marvels confronting
the explorer in the field that scholars who have been looking far and wide to
establish the source from which it all has come have been remarkably reluctant,
or, rather, unwilling to allow the theory that Gnostic tendencies may have
developed in the very midst of Judaism itself, whether in its classical forms or
on its heterodox and sectarian fringes. The more far-fetched the explanation,
the better. The theories of Reitzenstein in particular, on the Iranian origin of
Gnosticism, have had considerable influence for some time. Even when, on
closer inspection, they have been found disappointing and highly speculative,
they still linger on — if only in a somewhat emasculated form. One is often
left wondering about the methods used in this approach; and one is no less
amazed by the stupendous ignorance of Jewish sources that warps the
conclusions and even the basic approach of some of the finest scholars. Since
the appearance of the excellent collection of rabbinic source material in Strack-
Billerbeck's *Commentary on the New Testament,* we have, furthermore, been
vouchsafed a new kind of fake scholarship, one that feeds on this work and
takes it for granted that what is not in Billerbeck is not in existence [1].

I think we must agree with Scholem. Gnosticism is not a late chapter of the
history of Greek philosophy and therefore a Christian heresy, an acute
Hellenization of the Christian religion. Nor is it a fossilized survival of old
Iranian or even Indian religious concepts, and certainly it is not derived from
a presupposed, consistent Iranian myth of the Saved Savior. It is rather a
religion of its own, with its own phenomenological structure, characterized by
the mythical expression of self-experience through the revelation of the
"Word", or, in other words, by an awareness of a tragic split within the
Deity itself. And as such it owes not a little to Judaism. When we try to
discern the relations between Judaism and Gnosticism, the problem of
Gnosticism and the NT may be seen in a new and illuminating perspective.
For clarity's sake we shall distinguish between three milieus: first, circles at
the outskirts of Judaism, namely in Samaria; second, the milieu of esoteric lore
transmitted within the very heart of Palestinian Pharisaism; and third, certain
baptist sects in Palestine which seem to have had some relation to the Jewish
religion. The Hellenistic Judaism of Alexandria as represented by Philo,
however, does not seem to have the same relevance to our subject.

The female counterpart of God is called "Helen" in the Gnosis of Simon the
Magician, "Barbelo" in the *Apocryphon of John,* and "Silence" in the

---

[1] *Jewish Gnosticism, Merkabah Mysticism, and Talmudic Tradition* (New York: Jewish
Theological Seminary of New York, 1960), pp. 1-2.

Valentinian school. Perhaps all these names are important illustrations of the syncretistic character of Gnosticism. Helen was a goddess, venerated everywhere in the Hellenistic world and in Samaria. Depth and Silence always have had, as they did then, a mystical flavor. "Barbelo" is more problematical, for its etymology is uncertain. In a magical papyrus which I acquired in Berlin in 1956, the name is found spelled Abrbelôth, together with Io, Ialtaboth(?), El, Adonai, Gabriel(?), Istrael, Mikael, Ouriel, (B)ainchoooch, and Abrasax. This sounds very Jewish, but does not necessarily prove that Abrbelôth was venerated in Jewish circles. In Greek magical papyri we find such forms as these: barbarioth (Preisendanz, 1 : 70), Barbar Adonai (1 : 84), Brabēl (1 : 102), Abraiaoth (1 : 106), Abraal (1 : 180), Abriēl (2 : 43). The only thing we can say is that Abrbelôth is related to Jewish-Hellenistic magic.

But the fact is that these references and affiliations do not help us very much to discern the real issue of Gnostic theology, which is to my mind the concept of the suffering God, the fallen God. Yet the Gnostic sources are quite explicit in this respect. God suffers detriment to his soul (*Ev. Ver.* 41 : 36); Iao redeems his soul (Iren. 1 : 21-3); Christ redeems his soul (*Gospel of Philip,* 9). In a way this is also the basic idea of Manicheism, that primordial Man, the Self of God, is overwhelmed by the powers of darkness and vanquished, until the call from above redeems him. God, in redeeming man, redeems himself.

We must remove the Hellenistic accretions and rigorously examine the Gnostic conception against its Jewish background, to understand what this means and what was happening in the transition from Judaism to Gnosticism. The female counterpart of the Godhead in Gnosticism is the Wisdom of Judaism, the more or less personified *ḥokmâ* of Prov. 9 : 1, and of the Wisdom of Solomon, who according to Jewish teaching was instrumental in creating the world; and who, according to some versions of the story, descended from heaven to dwell among man but was not accepted and so returned to her abode in heaven.

It would seem that in the Gnosis of Simon the Magician, Wisdom herself fell — that is to say, the Fall is a split within the Deity. It is true that, according to one report, Wisdom herself remained completely unknown to the Rulers of this world, and only her image was overpowered by the lower powers (Pseudo-Clementine *Recognitions* 2 : 12). This then would mean that already at a very early date there existed among Samaritans (heterodox Jews) the concept of a double Wisdom. In any case, that is what we find in the *Apocryphon of John.* There Barbelo, the female counterpart of God, is called the "first idea", a Stoic expression equally attributed to Simon's Helen, and understandable as a title of Wisdom; but the last of the aeons, who falls because of her lascivity, is called Sophia. And it would seem that this is a complication of the more simple concept, that Wisdom herself falls. The Valentinian system, as conceived by Ptolemaeus, is still further differentiated. There Sige, the mother of the Pleroma, is distinguished from the thirtieth aeon, Sophia, who falls because of her desire to understand God, and then brings forth a lower Wisdom who is expelled from the Pleroma. But that we have here a far echo of Jewish Wisdom speculations, is proved by the fact that this female is called Achamoth, the Jewish *ḥokmâ* (Iren. 1.4.1).

Once again we must turn to syncretism and astrology to find some explanation for the gnostic demiurge. In the *Apocryphon of John,* now available in its three Coptic versions edited by M. Krause, and in a good English translation by Sōren Giversen, we read that this demiurge, Ialdabaoth, has the aspect of a lion and a serpent. Evidently he is a monstrous figure with the head of a lion and the body of a serpent, like Chnoubis or Abrasax on magical amulets. More helpful is the information that Ialdabaoth has been borrowed from magic and represents the planet *Saturnus* (Origen, *Contra Celsum* 6 : 33). Ialdabaoth, says the *Apocryphon of John,* had eyes like burning lightning that flashed. He is the God, who brings about Heimarmene. All this fits in very well with astrological lore. Saturn, the highest planet with the most malignant influence, is represented in Africa as Baal Hammon with the head of a lion, and Arnobius speaks about him as the lion-headed Frugifer (*Adv. Gentes* 6 : 10). Saturnus as Kronos, and therefore Chronos ("time"), is described by Plutarch (*de Iside* 44.) as the creator of the world, because Time in its course brings forth everything. Saturnus is also the god of lightning. He is related to the monstrous figure in the Mithraic mysteries, with the head of a lion and covered by snakes, who symbolizes Time and Fate. And certainly it is characteristic of Gnosticism to abhor and reject time and history. "This archon who was weak had three names: the first name is Ialdabaoth; the second is Saklas; the third is Sammael. But he was ungodly in his ignorance which is in him for he said: I am God and there is no other God but me" (*ibid.,* 59 : 15-20). Ialdabaoth is Aramaic for "Son of Chaos", an etymology which has long been suspected, and one which does not shed much light on our problem. Sammael means "the blind one" and is a name of the devil in Jewish sources. This shows that the demiurge in the *Apocryphon of John* was identified with the devil, who in certain passages of the NT is conceived of as the Ruler of this world, or even the God of this world.

Still more illuminating is the etymology of Saklas. "Sakla" is Aramaic for "fool". This lends an Aramaic color to the story and reveals the basic idea of the writing. The *Apocryphon of John* dramatically describes the persistent struggle between Ialdabaoth and Barbelo, or some related female figure, whom he does not know. But if *sakla* means "fool", this means (in less mythological and more abstract terms) that the conflict between hidden wisdom and worldly folly is a persistent theme in history.

The original and spirited dualism of the *Apocryphon of John* is not, in the last analysis, a dualism of good and evil in the world, as in Manicheism, but of the Divine and the world. But at this point, the learned Gnostics Basilides and Valentinus follow a different course. They consider the demiurge to be an ignorant tool of a higher purpose. I think theirs is a conscious modification. It would seem to me that the original form of the myth contained in the *Apocryphon of John* is more primitive and archaic than the profound and learned elaborations of Basilides and Valentinus. If we accept this as a working hypothesis, we may discern how much Basilides and Valentinus contributed of their own account, and how each in his own way Hellenized and Christianized an earlier Gnosis of a much more mythological character, and one which showed a relative absence of Christian elements and the strong influence of a Jewish milieu. Basilides had a speculative mind, Valentinus was enthusiastic and poetical, but they did not create out of nothing. They developed an already existing gnostic myth, which at least must have been similar to the teaching of the *Apocryphon of John*. Then we can discern that they radically changed a primitive dualism into a much more monistic setting.

Basilides was perhaps not as original or as bold as he seemed to be, when he started his system with an impressive statement about the "non-existent God". In the *Apocryphon of John* we find a similar negative theology. It might be, then, that this was the traditional way of starting a gnostic system. What is really new is that Basilides replaced emanation and fall with creation and evolution, and conceived of Christ as the exclusive, central source of revelation, whereas the *Apocryphon* seems to teach several interventions by Barbelo. The Ruler of the world is not described as a hostile monster: he serves the hidden purpose of God and is instrumental in its fulfilment. But he originates from chaos and thus reminds us of Ialdabaoth, which seems to mean "Son of Chaos". He is called Abrasax and so recalls the well-known figure of the magic gems with the head of a cock, the tail of a serpent, and a whip in his hand. Most characteristically, this highest Ruler of the world does not know that there is a God above him. So this theme seems to have been taken from an already existing gnostic system.

Valentinus appears to have followed the version in the *Apocryphon of John* more closely. It is said in a Valentinian source that Sophia suffered her passion apart from the embrace of her consort (Iren. 1.2.12); this feature also plays an important and detailed role in the newly published *Apocryphon* (Krause 135 : 30). Moreover, in certain Valentinian sources, she prays, and the aeons intercede for her (Hipp. 6 : 31). When in 1947 a reconstruction of the original doctrine of Valentinus was published, this was supposed to have been the teaching of the Gnostic teacher himself, though no document from his school had exactly preserved this sequel of events. It was moreover suggested that the scheme of the myth was borrowed from some already existing oriental gnosticizing sects [2]. It is gratifying to find, so many years later, something rather similar in the *Apocryphon of John* (61 : 35): "She repented with much weeping, and the whole Pleroma heard the prayer of her repentance and praised the invisible, virginal spirit for her sake". This seems to prove that Valentinus must have known this or a similar writing.

What is more, when we find in a Valentinian document that the demiurge is called "foolish", *mōros* (Hipp. *Ref.* 6.33.1; 6.34.8), like "Sakla" in the *Apocryphon of John,* we must assume that it is a traditional motif taken from an earlier Gnosis. For in the *Apocryphon* "fool" has a very special, Jewish meaning. A fool is a man who says in his heart that there is no God. But that is exactly what the Ruler of this world is thought to say. Therefore he is "foolish"; God and his Wisdom are hidden from him.

This concept that the Wisdom of God is a hidden Wisdom, seems to be of Jewish origin. It is found already in Job 28 : 12 ff. An adherent of Simon Magus seems to have taught that Divine Wisdom was completely unknown to the Rulers of this world (Pseudo-Clementine *Recognitiones* 2 : 12: *ipsam vero ut est penitus ignorarunt*). The theme of the foolish Ruler of the world seems to be traditional in Gnosticism and seems to be derived from a Jewish milieu.

This would explain its curious similarity to some views held by St. Paul. The view that Wisdom has fallen is absent from the N.T. Therefore, when we find in the Synoptic Gospels (as in Matt. 11 : 28) that Jesus speaks as the embodiment of Wisdom, we should not explain it in terms of a gnostic influence, but rather explain it in terms of a common Jewish background. Likewise, when St. Paul in the first two chapters of I Corinthians proclaims a Divine Wisdom unknown to the Rulers of this world, he is not necessarily under the influence of Jewish gnostic sects. But he does say that the Wisdom of God is hidden and unknown to the Rulers of this world; for if the Rulers had known the hidden purpose of salvation, they would not have crucified the Lord of Glory (2 : 7-8). They were foolish enough to serve God without knowing it. But God in his act of salvation unmasked worldly wisdom as folly (1 : 20). And we might also add that the works of Paul imply that the wisdom of the Rulers of this world is equally foolish and godless. In the light of the Cross, that wisdom which the angels of the nations supposedly transmitted to

---

[2] "The Original Doctrine of Valentine", *Vig. Chr.* I (1947), pp. 43-73. See above pp. 27-36.

the several peoples, is shown to be worldly, autonomous, and godless wisdom
— it is essentially "folly" in the Hebrew sense of the word. All this suggests
that Paul did not think about earthly kings and authorities, but rather about
spiritual entities located somewhere in space, the ambivalent spiritual powers
behind the earthly authorities. This way of looking at things would seem to be
very near to the gnostic dualism of *hokmâ* and *sakla*. It is not just a
mythological concept of the universe that Paul and the gnostics have in
common. It is rather the awareness that the profoundest motives of this world
are absurd and that our rational philosophies, inspired as they are by these
innerworldly motivations, are equally absurd — because our world as such is
absurd.

But even if Gnosticism and Christianity shared a common Jewish background,
there is yet another aspect of their relationship which bears investigation —
namely, that the Gnostics may have preserved archaic Christian material not
attested elsewhere. For a certain period they belonged to the Christian Church
(in some congregations longer than in others) and participated in the social,
liturgical, and sacramental life of the local churches. But by nature the Gnostics
were not inclined to have any special appreciation for the massive objectivity
of ritual acts. They tended rather to spiritualize exterior rites and thought that
it was not only baptism which saved men, but also the Gnosis, "what we are,
where we come from, whither we go". Therefore we have recently learned to
appreciate gnostic writings, not only for the specific gnostic doctrine they
contain, but also for the traces of primitive archaic theology expressing
Christian views in Semitic categories which we find imbedded in the gnostic
doctrine itself. Whatever interpretation one finds for these remarkable
theological data, he sometimes cannot help but assume that these primitive and
undoubtedly Jewish concepts and expressions sometimes lead us back a long
way from Gnosticism to Palestinian Christianity, especially where sacramental
views are concerned.

On the other hand, the Mandaean problem has become an open question again,
since Torgny Säve Söderbergh has shown that the Manichaean *Psalms of
Thomas* were based upon some extant Mandaean hymns, thus proving that
the Mandaean sect in Iraq must have had a very long prehistory. Kurt Rudolph
argued in his useful monograph on the Mandaeans that this sect was of
Western Palestinian origin, and there is much to say in favor of his thesis.
The curious expression "Lord of Greatness" in Mandean writings has been
found in the Qumran *Genesis apocryphon*. Moreover, I cannot explain the
parallels between the names of Mandaean divinities and those found in the
Hellenistic magical papyri unless the Mandaeans have very old Western roots.
We should also note that in the Mandaean sect ritual ablutions in "living"

streams of water have a central place. The Swedish scholar Segelberg has argued that there exist some curious parallels between the Mandaean and the Roman rite of baptism, and concludes that they had a common pre-Christian background in Palestine. His studies deserve very attentive consideration.

Furthermore, Niels Dahl has pointed out that justification in Paul has baptismal implications. Basing himself upon Qumran material, he has shown that in the Essene sect the same combination of ablution and justification was found as in Paul. "But you were washed, you were sanctified, you were justified in the Name of the Lord Jesus Christ and in the Spirit of our God" (I Cor. 6 : 11). It goes without saying that rebirth in the *Gospel of John* also has its sacramental implications. Now the *Gospel of John,* more than any other writing of the NT, has stylistic and conceptual parallels with Mandaean literature. Even if Mandaeism turns out to be neither so old nor of Palestinian origin, obligatory reading of Mandaean writings could serve students of the NT as good preparation for the right understanding of the Fourth Gospel.

All this tends to show that baptism was very important in primitive Christianity, and may have had its prefiguration in the Jewish sects of Palestine.

A primitive survival of sacramental language seems to have been preserved in the *Gospel of Philip,* Saying 12.

One single Name they do not utter in the world, the Name which the Father gave to the Son, which is above all things, which is the Name of the Father. For the Son would not become Father except *he clothe himself with the Name of the Father.*

It has been proven long ago that the speculations about Jesus as the Name of the Father, so frequent in documents of Valentinian Gnosis, presuppose esoteric Jewish lore about the Name of the Lord and have parallels in NT passages, especially John 17 : 11 ("keep them in Thy name which Thou hast given me") and Phil. 2 : 9 ("bestowed on him the Name which is above every name"). Here the gnostics have a common background with John and Paul, a background which is Jewish or even Jewish Christian. But the curious expression "to clothe oneself with the Name" needs further clarification. There is a parallel for it in another source of Valentinian Gnosis, a sacramental formula quoted by Irenaeus 1.21.3, "The hidden Name with which Jesus the Nazarene invested himself...." It is possible that these words contain an allusion to the baptism of Jesus in the Jordan, for the Valentinians thought that at that moment the Name of God had descended upon Jesus (*Excerpta ex Theodoto* 22 : 6). The same expression occurs in the *Odes of Solomon* which I consider to be evidence for Syrian Christianity in Edessa.

Put on, therefore, *the Name of the Most High* and
know Him:
and you shall cross without danger,
while the rivers shall be subject to you (39 : 8).

If we assume that Christianity in Edessa was of Palestinian origin, there is some possibility that the concept of the believer "putting on the Name" is of Jewish Christian origin. In any case we also find the theology of the Name elsewhere in Syria.

In the *Acts of Thomas* (ch. 27) "the holy Name of Christ which is above every name" is invoked in a sacramental context. The "true Name", that is, the *tetragrammaton* is distinguished from the convential name "Jesus Christ". "Thou art not able to hear his true Name now at this time, but the name that is given to him is Jesus the Messiah" (ch. 163). If we find the same curious expression in the Syrian Christianity of Edessa and in circles of Valentinian Gnostics somewhere in the West, this seems to point to a common background in Jewish Christianity.

As far as I know, the expression "to put on the Name" is not found in the O.T. But we find there a similar conception, that namely the Spirit of God "invests" man, so that he is "clad" with the Spirit (cf. LXX Judges 6 : 34 ms A; I Chron. 12 : 19; II Chron. 24 : 20). In a magical Jewish writing of later date, "describing a highly ceremonious rite in which the magician impregnates himself, as it were, with the great Name of God, i.e. performs a symbolic act by clothing himself in a garment into whose texture the Name has been woven", it is said, "Then go into the water up to your loins and *put on* the glorious and terrible Name in the midst of the water" (*Sēfer Hammalbush*, Br. Mus. 752). From this passage we may conclude that the idiomatic Hebrew phrase for "putting on the Name" was *labuš eth ha-šēm*.

The same expression was current among the Samaritans. In a Samaritan hymn it is said about Moses: "Mighty is the great prophet, who *clad* himself *in the Name* of the Godhead" [3]. I think this material is relevant for the interpretation of Paul's remark, "As many of you as were baptized into Christ, you have *put on* Christ" (Gal. 3 : 27). The wording seems to be thoroughly Jewish. It reveals to us the Jewish perspective of Paul's sacramental convictions. It also leaves open the possibility that this drastic imagery was not personally invented by Paul, but was inherited by him from a common faith and even perhaps prefigured in some pre-Christian sect of Jewish baptists.

Gnostic materials, then, can be instrumental in our discerning the sacramental

---

[3] A. E. Cowley, *The Samaritan Liturgy*, I, 54.

implications and Jewish presuppositions of some NT authors, if only we admit that the Mandaean problem and, more generally, the history of Jewish sects have to be taken into account.

The most important Jewish contribution, however, both to Gnosticism and to early Christianity, seems to have come from esoteric circles in the heart of Palestinian Judaism. Gershom Scholem has shown that there existed within Judaism esoteric traditions which had very old roots and went back to Pharisaic circles of the first century A.D. And he has pointed out that St. Paul as well as some Gnostics must have known these traditions. I accept his view. The Valentinian Gnostic Marcus the Magician, who gives us a phantastic description of the "body of Truth", is indebted to Jewish esoteric traditions about the measuring of the body of the Schechina. When the *Pistis Sophia* mentions a *Yahweh qātōn* and a *Yahweh gādōl*, this writing reveals a familiarity with the shocking terminology of earlier Jewish mystics. We must add that the speculations in the Valentinian *Gospel of Truth* about Christ as the "proper Name" of the hidden God must have the same origin. For in the *Apocalypse of Abraham* (ch. 10), the oldest document of Jewish mysticism, we find that Jaoel the vicegerent of God second only to God himself has received the ineffable Name that is dwelling in him. Speculations on the Name, moreover, were characteristic of esoteric Jewish lore. I think I can mention a new argument in favor of the thesis that Jewish esoteric teaching concerning the *kābôd* as the "form like the appearance of a Man" or the "body of God" influenced Gnostic thought. It is taken from the *Treatise on the Three Natures*, the fourth book of the Jung Codex, where it is said about Christ: "He alone is truly worthy, the *Man* of the Father, who is ..., the *form* of the formless, (the body) of the bodiless, the *face* of the invisible, the *word* of the inutterable, the *thought* of the unthinkable" (p. 66, 1 : 10-16).

We see then that the Gnostics have been influenced by a very specific current within Judaism, namely the esoteric traditions of Palestinian Pharisees. This should stop once and for all the idle talk of dogmatic minds about Gnosticism having nothing in common with Judaism proper. On the other hand, the comparison shows how far the Gnostics have removed themselves from these Jewish origins. The Gnostics teach the consubstantiality of God and man; the Jewish mystics underline the gulf that separates man from God, even in the ecstasy of vision. The Jewish mystics know of no split within the Deity, nor do they admit that the creator of the world is a lower demiurge.

Early Christianity, too, seems to have been influenced by these esoteric traditions. In his book, *Jewish Gnosticism,* Scholem proves that Paul is expressing himself in the terminology of the rabbinic ecstatics, when he says that he has been lifted up towards the Paradise in the third heaven (II Cor.

12 : 2). It is certainly reasonable to suppose that a former Pharisee knew the traditions of esoteric Pharisaism.

This perspective might also throw a new light on other passages of the NT. On this occasion I will only remark that the Western text of Luke 11 : 52 (paralleled by logion 39 of the *Gospel of Thomas*) shows an awareness of this secret tradition when it states that the teachers of the Law, especially the Pharisees, have *hidden* the key of knowledge, that is, the oral interpretation of the Law.

But also the Gospel of John can become more understandable in the light of these traditions. The attention of the Jewish mystics was focused upon such chapters as Isa. 6 and Ezek. 1, where the prophets described the manifestation of God upon his throne. The mystics were concerned to behold this *kābôd*, this "body" or "form like the appearance of a Man". Is it not remarkable, then, that in the Fourth Gospel Jesus reproaches the Jews that they have not seen the *eidos* of God (John 5 : 37), implying that God has a form?

Elsewhere (12 : 41) John states that Isaiah beheld the glory of Christ. This could be interpreted to mean that the prophet beheld Christ eternal upon the Throne; in that case Christ is identified with the *kābôd* which, according to the mystics, manifests itself upon the throne. This is not only a matter of parallels and historical influences. It reveals a deep affinity with the basic motives of Jewish mysticism, a common conception of God and a similar answer to the challenge of a particular historical situation. Again it is Gershom Scholem who proves to be a trustworthy guide and a eye-opener on our way. His book *Von der mystischen Gestalt der Gottheit* contains a learned discussion of the problem of the image in monotheism. The latter opposes the use of images in the cultus. But this does not imply that God has no form. The Bible explicitly states that God has a "form" (Num. 12 : 8), and is full of anthropomorphic imagery. Under the influence of Greek philosophy, Hellenistic Judaism tried to spiritualize these conceptions and to assimilate them into the abstract generalizations of a rational world civilization.

Completely the opposite reaction to philosophy is to be found in the Palestinian circles which brought forth Jewish mysticism. In these conservative, even reactionary quarters, it is stressed that God has a "form". Anthropomorphism is reasserted in a challenging and provocative way. Such bold symbolic speech naturally leads to the break-through of authentic mythological patterns — and this did not happen at the outskirts of Judaism, but in the center of Palestinian Judaism. Such a Gnosis is completely Jewish-orthodox. Its aim is to maintain that the God of Israel is not an unmoved first mover, but a hidden God who reveals himself to man. This basic issue of the biblical religion is formulated in a radical way. The astonishing imagery serves a thoroughly conservative purpose, the preservation of the Jewish identity.

Against this background we see more clearly how Jewish early Christianity was. It was part of that movement of the "revolt of the images" on Palestinian soil, already reflected in Jewish apocalypticism and continued in esoteric Pharisaism, the eventual result of which was the birth of Gnosticism proper, at the fringe of Judaism. We may consider this movement as an endeavor in the face of the Hellenistic world civilization to maintain the faith in a living God who is moved and reveals himself. At the same time it represents a swing within the Jewish soul away from reason and moralism towards freedom and the image.

In Christianity, in contradistinction to Gnosticism, man remains man. God is moved, but not split, and the redeemer is also the creator. In spite of this, we must conclude that Gnosticism and Christianity have much in common, because they have in part a common background and a certain historic affinity for one another. Therefore careful consideration of the Gnostic materials can help us to discern how Jewish the NT is, and how lively was the Jewish mind at all times, and especially at the beginning of our era. So much so that both Judaism and Christianity would not only contrast the folly of this world with a transcendent Wisdom which lies beyond our grasp, but would stress the sacramental implications of salvation, and the possibility of beholding the glory of the hidden Lord.

THE ORIGINS OF THE GNOSTIC DEMIURGE

The theory that Gnosticism has its roots, or some of its roots, in Judaism, has been opposed by Hans Jonas. In an address to the centennial meeting of the Society of Biblical Literature, held in New York, December 28-30, 1964, he revealed to an excited and restive audience the unheard-of background of this new view. On the one hand there was the vanity of Jewish scholars who are ready to accept the Jewish origin even of what is disreputable. On the other hand there were certain decadent psychological circles which are ready to concoct an exciting, nay soul-shaking spectacle: the greatest iconoclasm before modernity erupting in Judaism. Against all this, Jonas firmly held that the relation of Gnosticism to Judaism is defined by the anti-Jewish animus with which it is saturated. Gnosticism is "the greatest case of metaphysical anti-Semitism" [1].

Even if there are some traces of animosity against the Jewish people in Gnostic texts, this does not necessarily mean that the writers of these texts were not Jews. Such expressions of *Selbsthass* are possible, because there are historical parallels for them. Anti-semitism has very deep roots in utopian and Marxist socialism. It seems to me that the real issue is this: most Gnostics were against the Jewish God who created the world and gave the Law. Is it possible that this doctrine is of Jewish origin? This problem has not been discussed until now. Even those who do accept that many Gnostic views are to be derived from Judaism, seem to have avoided this theme.

In our times Erik Peterson was the first to point out that Gnosticism is of Jewish origin. He considered Gnostic dualism as a cosmic amplification of the conflict of the good and the evil inclination in the heart of man according to Jewish sources [2]. When the Valentinian "Gospel of Truth", found at Nag Hammadi, was acquired by the present author on 10 May 1952, this writing was found to contain very elaborate speculations on Christ as the Name, even the Proper Name, of God. This was supposed to go back to Jewish apocalyptic views on the Name [3]. This hypothesis was partly accepted, partly criticised by Jean Daniélou. The latter pointed out that the concept of Christ as the Name could also be traced to the oldest strata of Christian tradition, viz. the community of Jerusalem. So the speculations on Christ as the Name of God could also have been borrowed by the Gnostics from Jewish Christians [4].

---

[1] *The Bible in Modern Scholarship*, Nashville-New York, 1965, p. 288.

[2] Article "Gnosi", in *the Encyclopedia Cattolica Italiana*.

[3] *The Jung Codex*, London, 1955, p. 73. See above p. 23.

[4] J. Daniélou, *Théologie du Judéo-Christianisme*, Tournay, 1958, p. 199.

Now there can be no doubt that the Gospel of Truth is Gnostic and Valentinian. But it must be admitted that the concept of Christ as the Name can also have been borrowed by the Gnostics from Christians of Jewish origin or influenced by Jewish Christian tradition. This could happen for instance in Egypt, the homeland of Valentinus. Direct contact of the Gnostics with Jewish esoteric or apocalyptic lore has not been proved in this case.

On the other hand Gershom Scholem showed convincingly that at least one Valentinian Gnostic, Marc the Magician, was familiar with esoteric traditions among the Palestinian Jews about the "body" of God [5]. In any case the relationship between Gnosticism and Judaism is firmly established. And this relationship does not show any animosity or caricature whatsoever.

The same is the case with the Gnostic Sophia or Achamoth. There is no doubt that this very characteristic figure of Gnostic mythology is derived from biblical and Jewish Wisdom. Of course there are differences: no Jew until Simon the Magician of Samaria seems to have conceived Sophia (Helen) as a symbol of the split within the deity. This view, however, is not a parody of the Jewish faith, but another interpretation, and a profound one, of a traditional symbol in Jewish religion. It is possible to reconstruct the hypothetical model of a Jewish Gnosis, in which Adam and Sophia played a prominent part [6].

After many years it is possible to criticise the article of 1954, in which these views were expounded. The fact is that the author was perhaps not right, but that others at that time were so fantastically wrong. It was considered absurd at that moment to suppose any relation between Gnosticism and Judaism. It should be observed that the learned studies of Grant [7], Macl. Wilson [8] and Böhlig [9], who all accept the enormous influence of Judaism upon Gnosticism, are of a later date.

Against this background we must place the problem which we want to discuss in this paper, namely the origin of the concept of a lower Demiurge. We must not exclude the possibility that it arose among the Jews. A trustworthy tradition tells us that there were Marcionites among the Aramaic speaking Jews of Palestine: Tertullian, adv. Marc. 3, 12: *invenies apud Hebraeos, Christianos, immo et Marcionitas, Emmanuhelem nominare, cum volunt dicere ... nobiscum deus.* (You will find that, among the Hebrews, Christians, nay even adherents of Marcion, say "Immanuel", when they want to say "God is with us"). Jews

---

[5] *Jewish Gnosticism, Merkabah Mysticism, and Talmudic Tradition,* New York, 1960.
[6] *Eranos Jahrbuch* XXII, 1954, pp. 195-234. See above pp. 173-195.
[7] R. M. Grant, *Gnosticism and Early Christianity,* New York, 1959.
[8] *Gnosis and the New Testament,* Oxford, 1969, p. 144.
[9] *Le origini dello Gnosticismo,* Leiden, 1967, pp. 109-140.

were not allergic to this concept. There is however, as far as I know, only one Jewish text, which attests that there were Jews who taught a highest God and an inferior creator of the world. This is Al-Qirqisānī's Account of the Jewish Sects [10]. It tells us that the pre-Christian Jewish sect of the Magharians in Palestine distinguished between God, who is beyond anthropomorphism, and one of his angels, who is responsible for all the anthropomorphic features contained in the Old Testament, and who is the creator of the world: "They do not strip such anthropomorphic descriptions of God (in scripture) of their literal sense, but they rather think that these descriptions apply to one of the angels, namely the one who created the world".

This report is of a late date (Qirqisānī lived in the 10th century). Moreover it seems impossible that the author refers to members of the Qumran community (though the Magharians were called so, because their writings were found in a cave). In the Dead Sea Scrolls this curious concept cannot be found. On the other hand the views expounded are so remarkable and unique, that it is difficult to consider them as a medieval hoax. Therefore, I think we must suppose that such a group did exist before the Christian era in Palestine. It is possible that the angel referred to is the so-called "Angel of the Lord". In that case the views of the Magharians could be the outcome of an inner Jewish process. Already in the Old Testament we find several passages, in which the bold anthropomorphism of the source has been toned down and the name of the Lord has been replaced by the more cautious expression, "The Angel of the Lord". It is a well known fact that towards the beginning of our era the Jewish concept of God became more and more transcendent and that Jewish scholars explained away anthropomorphisms in Holy Scripture. These sectarians seem to have gone so far as to attribute even the creation of the world to the Angel of the Lord, because this is described in the Bible as a creation by the word or by handicraft, both anthropomorphisms.

Of course we may not exclude the possibility that these Jewish sectarians were also influenced by the Timaeus of Plato, according to which the visible world was brought into order by a divine being of inferior status, the demiurge. There is, however, no evidence in our sources that the Magharians were familiar with Platonic philosophy.

Harry Wolfson has suggested that the Gnostics, who almost unanimously considered the Demiurge to be an angel, derived their views from this Jewish sect [11]. It would seem that this is correct. It would explain to a certain

---

[10] L. Nemoy, Al-Qirqisānī's Account of the Jewish Sects, *Hebrew Union College Annual*, 7 (1930), pp. 317-397.

[11] The pre-existent angel of the Magharians and Al-Nahāwandi, *Jewish Quarterly Review*, XI, 1960, p. 97.

extent the curious fact that the Gnostics in general did not deny the truth of the Old Testament, but accepted it in a literal sense, like the Magharians. The gnostic solution of the problem of the Old Testament has too much in common with the solution of the Magharians to be sheer coincidence. The way from the Jewish sectarians to the great Gnostics of the second century is beset with pitfalls and difficulties. This is mainly the case because our evidence for the earliest Gnostics like Simon the Magician and Cerinthus is not above suspicion.

In *de praescriptione haereticorum*, c. 34, Tertullian says explicitly that the distinction between the highest God and the lower demiurge was unknown to the heresies of the apostolic times:

Et tamen nullam invenimus institutionem inter tot diversitates perversitatum, quae de deo creatore universorum controversiam moverit. Nemo alterum deum ausus est suspicari — facilius de filio quam de patre haesitabatur — donec Marcion praeter creatorem alium deum solius bonitatis induceret, Apelles creatorem angelum nescio quem gloriosum superioris dei faceret ...

It is true that the Acts of the Apostles (c. 8) do not accuse Simon the Magician of such heresy. Justin Martyr does not say with so many words that Simon was opposed to the Creator (I Apol. 26). According to Cyrill of Jerusalem Simon pretended to have manifested himself on Mount Sinai as the Father (Cat. VI, 14). This would imply that Simon acknowledged the Jewish God and identified himself with Him. And in the Simonian system transmitted by Hippolytus (VI, 9, 3 sqq.) not a trace can be found of this gnostic doctrine. Against this it may be observed that according to Irenaeus (1, 23, 2) Ennoia (= Wisdom) brought forth the angels and powers, by whom this world has been made. So at a certain moment the Simonian school may have admitted the teaching of a lower, angelic demiurge.

Still more important for our purpose are the Pseudo-Clementine writings, where Simon is sometime considered as a Samaritan and other times as a Jew. In the Recognitiones (2, 39) he accepts the authority of the Law: *Ita enim ab eo, qui mundum condidit, scripta est, ut in ipsa rerum fides habeatur.* Simon here strongly stresses the fact that there is one God. He proves however from the Law that there are many Gods beside Him, namely those who created man (*hi qui hominem fecere*). One of them has been allotted to the Jewish people. In the same work (2, 57) it is said that this God has been sent by the highest God, whom he does not know: *ipse misit creatorem deum, ut conderet mundum.* It has often been observed that Simon in the Clementine writings is a mask for Paul, or Marcion, or Apelles. But in the quoted passages this cannot be the case. There a Jewish teacher proves from the Law, which he accepts, that there is one God and besides a lower creator. This resembles very much the conceptions of the Magharians. So it would seem possible that there existed such a doctrine on Jewish soil, either in the school of Simon or somewhere else. It is clear that the author of the Clementines, or its source, has not invented this doctrine. The author of the Fourth Treatise of the Jung Codex, possibly the Valentinian Heracleon, may refer to such doctrines, when he observes that there are numerous heresies among the Jews: "Some say that He is the creator of what exists: others say that He created through His angels". (p. 112, 33-113, 1). It is not quite certain, that Simon the Magician taught a subordinate angel who was the creator of the world. Another theme however of gnostic mythology is well attested to him. Both Irenaeus and the Clementines speak us about the ignorance of the angels. According to Irenaeus, Simon assumed that the angels who created the world were completely ignorant of the existence of the highest God (Iren. I, 23, 2: *ipsum enim se in totum ignoratum ab ipsis*). On the other hand it is suggested that these powers did not know the real Helena, who is Wisdom above (Rec. 2, 12: *ipsam vero ut est penitus ignorarunt*).

We find a similar concept in the first Letter to the Corinthians of St. Paul (2, 8). There it is said that the Rulers of this world would not have crucified the Lord of Glory, if they would have known the hidden wisdom. Paul and Simon were roughly contemporaries. Both seem dependent here upon a common Jewish background. It is by no means excluded that the theme of the ignorance of the angels has been developed under the influence of a non-Jewish religion. I know, however, of no earlier or contemporary sources who could have influenced Simon and Paul in this respect.

Next to Simon there is another Gnostic whose views may possibly be considered as Jewish, namely Cerinthus. According to a legend transmitted by Irenaeus (III, 3, 4) the disciple John left the bath when he saw Cerinthus there. We may wonder what were the teachings of the latter that were so abhorrent to the disciple. It is said that Cerinthus taught an adoptionist Christology, a realistic eschatology of an earthly millennium and that he practised circumcision and observed the Sabbath [12]. All this tends to show that he was a Jewish Christian. These doctrines are no reason to leave the bath. If there is any truth in the legend about John and Cerinthus, the latter must have adhered to a quite repellent doctrine. This lends some support to our sources who explicitly declare that Cerinthus assumed a lower demiurge. Iren. I, 26, 1: *non a primo deo factum esse mundum docuit, sed a virtute quadam valde separata et distante ab ea principalitate quae est super universa et*

---

[12] A. Hilgenfeld, *Die Ketzergeschichte des Urchristentums*, Darmstadt, 1963, p. 41 sqq.

ignorante eum qui est super omnia deum. Ps. Tert., Adv. Omnes Haereses 3:
*nam et ipse mundum institutum esse ab angelis dicit ... ipsam quoque legem
ab angelis datam perhibens, Judaeorum deum non dominum, sed angelum
promens.*

If this is a trustworthy tradition, Cerinthus has been a Jewish Christian who
differed from other Jewish Christians by his belief that the world was created
by an angel. We would hardly believe that a realistic eschatology, which is an
acceptance of the created world, could be combined with the assumpt-
ion that the world was created by an inferior and ignorant angel,
were it not that we have now the evidence of the Jewish Magharians who also
accepted a creation by an angel. If our evidence about Cerinthus is trustworthy,
it would seem that a Jew was among the first to develop the Gnostic conception
of a demiurge. This is understandable. A non-Jew, when suffering under the
misery of the world, would simply have declared that the Genesis story was a
myth without truth. He could not have cared less about the origin of the Jewish
law which he despised. Only people who had been brought up to believe every
word of the Bible and to cling to the faith, that God is one, and yet found
reason to rebel against Law and Order, may have inclined towards the Gnostic
solution: God is one and the Bible is right, but anthropomorphisms like creation
and lawgiving are to be attributed to a subordinate angel.

I think there is a strong argument in favour of the Jewish origin. That is the
fact that this angel is often called Saklas. Saklas means "fool" in Aramaic.
The angel who created the world is called foolish, because he does not know
that there is a God above him. That is a very peculiar concept of folly, but
understandable in a Jewish milieu, where the man who says in his heart that
there is no God, is named a fool [13].

This is the simple model upon which several later Gnostic systems are based:
there is one God, who dwells on high with Wisdom; underneath there is His
Angel, who created the world and gave the Law. We find this model in the
teaching of the *Archontics*; in the seven heavens there are Rulers, Archonts,
dominated by the tyrant of the seventh heaven, Sabaoth. Above them is God
and the Mother in the Ogdoas (Epiphanius, Panarion 40). No Christian
influence can be detected here. Nor do we find any anti-Jewish animus. Why
should one opposed to the Jews accept their concept of one God and His

---

[13] If, as the editor Alexander Böhlig supposes (*Koptisch-Gnostische Apokalypsen*, Halle, 1963,
p. 95), *the Apocalypse of Adam* is pre-Christian and Jewish, the name Saklas for the demiurge
would have been used even before the Christian era: o.c., 74, 3, p. 106 Böhlig: *sie werden zu
Saklas, ihrem Gott gehen.*

personified Wisdom. It must be from such a model that the system of the Apokryphon of John was developed, which I would date about 100 A.D. [14]. There Sophia engenders an archon (= angel) who creates the world: his name is Jaltabaoth (= Aram. "Son of Chaos") and Sammael (= "the blind one") and Saklas (= "the fool"). The latter name is explained as follows: "But he was ungodly in his ignorance, which is in him, for he said: I am God and there is no other God but me". It is my considered opinion that the learned Gnostics, Basilides, Valentinus, Marcion, and Apelles must have been familiar with some form of the vulgar Gnosis as contained in the Apokryphon of John. The Valentinians still adhered to the archaic conception that the demiurge is an angel (Iren. I, 5, 2: *demiurgum et ipsum angelum, deo autem similem*). The same is true of Apelles (Tertullianus, *de Carne Christi* 8: *angelum quendam inclytum nominant, qui mundum hunc instituerit*). In the Western School of Valentinian Gnosis a certain rehabilitation of the Demiurge has taken place. This is particularly clear in the Fourth Treatise of the Jung Codex, possibly written by Heracleon [15]. According to this writing the demiurge is called God and Father and King:

Therefore he is embellished with all the names, which are an image of Him (= the highest God), who possesses all the attributes and all the honours. For he (the demiurge) too is called father and god and demiurge and king and judge and place and dwelling and law (p. 100, 25-30).

The basic model, however, has remained the same. Notwithstanding his lofty titles, the demiurge is an angel, a subordinate ruler, and nothing more. "For he (Sophia) placed an *archon* over all the images, whom nobody commanded, because he is the lord of all of them" (p. 100, 18-21).

We conclude then that the characteristic feature, which distinguishes Gnosticism from Gnosis in a general sense, originated in Palestine among rebellious and heterodox Jews. If we keep this in mind, we see that absolute dualism, as attested by Marcion and Mani, is a secondary and later development. Much has been said lately about the relationship of the "Iranian" (= absolutely dualistic) and the "Syro-Egyptian" (= relatively dualistic) type of Gnosticism. If we are willing to admit the Jewish roots of Gnosticism, we see

---

[14] *Apocryphon Johannis,* Codex II, 10, 2-23, Krause pp. 136-137. S. Giversen, *Apocryphon Johannis,* Copenhagen, 1963, pp. 65-66.

[15] H.-Ch. Puech and G. Quispel, *Le quatrième écrit du Codex Jung, Vig. Chr.* IX, 2, 1955, pp. 65-102. The fact that in the quoted passage the demiurge is called "king", because he is an image and symbol of God (who is also king) seems to indicate that the author of the Fourth Treatise is Heracleon. The latter considered the demiurge as "a little king subordinated to the universal king" (God) (Or., *in Joh.* XIII, 60).

that this terminology is misleading and that absolute dualism is a later development, based upon and originating from the relative dualism of Jewish Gnosticism.

[An unpublished writing from Nag Hammadi opposing the Demiurge contains so many Hebrew and Aramaic expressions that the Jewish origins of the Gnostic Demiurge cannot be doubled anymore. Birger Pearson, *Jewish Haggadic Traditions in The Testimony of Truth from Nag Hammadi, (CG IX, 3)* Ex Orbe Religionum I, Leyde, 1972, pp. 457-470.]

THE BIRTH OF THE CHILD
Some Gnostic and Jewish Aspects

In his book *Eclipse of God* the Jewish philosopher Martin Buber described the psychologist C. G. Jung as a Gnostic. The statement was not intended as a compliment, because, according to Buber, Gnosticism and not atheism is the true enemy and opponent of faith in the Jewish or Christian sense of the word. His attitude was based on the view that Judaism and Gnosticism never had anything in common and therefore were irreconcilable antagonists even during the first centuries of the Christian era. The same view is held by Hans Jonas, who did not even mention Judaism as the root and background of Gnosticism in his epoch-making book entitled *Gnosis und spätantiker Geist.* Any views to the contrary were considered by him to represent the futile vanity of certain Jewish scholars on the one hand and that of decadent psychological circles on the other [1]. According to him, Gnosticism cannot possibly be derived from Judaism, and wherever it uses Jewish concepts, as that of a creator of the universe or demiurge, it distorts them. Furthermore, he claimed that the Jewish material that had been incorporated by Gnosticism had been given a purely negative interpretation.

As long as research into Gnosis confines itself to the phenomenological method, it can hardly come up with another evaluation. For, in looking at the essence of the Gnostic religion, it becomes obvious that there is a fundamental difference between the Jewish and the Gnostic approach. Gnosis is based on the idea that there is something in man, his unconscious spirit, which is related to the ground of being. In order to restore the wholeness it has lost, the deity has an interest in redeeming this spiritual principle in man. Phenomenologically speaking, this concept has nothing in common with the Jews' reality affirming approach to creation.

What may seem phenomenologically impossible, may, however, prove to be quite possible in historical terms. The Gnostic records found near Nag Hammadi in Egypt seem the show that the influence of Judaism on Gnosticism was considerable.

This became evident as soon as the first document of the discovery at Nag Hammadi, the Valentinian *Gospel of Truth,* was published in 1956. The

---

[1] G. Quispel, Gnosticism and the New Testament, in *The Bible in modern scholarship,* ed. by J. Ph. Hyatt, Nashville, 1965, 252-271; *idem, The Origins of the Gnostic Demiurge,* in *Kyriakon. Festschrift Johannes Quasten,* ed. by P. Granfield and J. A. Jungmann, Münster, 1970, 271-276. See above pp. 196-212 and pp. 213-220.

meditations on Christ and the Self include extensive commentaries on Christ as the proper name of God, i.e., as revealing His essence. *Kurion onoma* as such is, of course, a *terminus technicus* used in Stoic philosophy. However, it was apparently taken over by the Jews to hint at the hidden, secret, unmentionable name of God. *Shem hammephorash* is identical with *shem hammejuhhad* (proper name) in Jewish source material, and in esoteric Judaism this name author of the *Gospel of Truth* took over and incorporated a Jewish concept.

In its present form, the *Gospel according to Thomas*, a collection of *Logia* also found at Hag Hammadi, seems to indicate that its author was a Gnostic, at least on the basis of present interpretations. Some of the words attributed to Jesus in this Gospel reveal an independent tradition and were transmitted by Jewish Christian circles. Evidence to this effect is provided by the fact that the Lord's brother James, the Pope of Jewish Christianity, appears in this document as Jesus' legitimate heir and the ruler of the entire Church. Jewish Christianity was, however, a Jewish sect, which, it would seem, influenced Gnosticism in this respect.

Furthermore, it became increasingly obvious that the figure of Sophia, which played a central role in many Gnostic systems as a world spirit in exile and as a cosmogonic power, must be traced back to the Jewish *Hokhma* of the Old Testament and to Jewish schools of Wisdom.

It is perfectly possible that, as tradition has it, the transition from the Jewish to the Gnostic concept of wisdom took place in the school of Simon Magus of Samaria. In the Palestinian Targum as well as in Samaritan liturgy, "beginning" was the equivalent of "wisdom". "In the beginning God created the heaven and the earth" eventually became "in his wisdom God created the heaven and the earth". This is the premise for Simon's view, according to which Helena, or Sophia, emerged from God in order to create the rulers of the world, who then, however, overwhelmed and imprisoned her.

It should be recalled that the Samaritans were a heterodox Jewish group, and the question concerning the relationship between Gnosis and Judaism cannot be answered as long as we identify present-day Rabbinical Judaism with the Judaism of those days. At that time, Palestine harboured not only Pharisees, but also Essenes, Baptists, Samaritans, Wisdom teachers, Jewish Christians, as well as a host of heretics of all kinds. As Gershom Sholem demonstrated, there were even a number of strict Pharisees in Palestine, who handed down esoteric traditions known to the Gnostics and which later gave rise to a truly Jewish form of Gnosis, the *Kabbalah*.

Until recently it seemed impossible to find convincing evidence to show that the classic Gnosis of antiquity developed or was able to develop out of Judaism.

The Cologne *Mani Codex* seems to be of particular importance in this connection, because it shows how Gnosis evolved out of Judaism, or Jewish Christianity, as a result of a dialectical process [2].

On the other hand there is no doubt that the Manichaean myth described a Gnostic experience, namely the encounter with the Self. The Codex tells how "the Twin" revealed himself to Mani at the age of 25:

> I recognized him
> and understood that he was my Self,
> from whom I had been separated [3].

On the other hand we now have proof that from the age of four to twenty-five, i.e., before he had this experience, Mani had been — like his father Patek before him — a member of the Jewish Christian Elkesaite sect in Babylonia.

The new discovery not only confirms the most recent theories about the origins of Gnosticism; it also seems to coincide with the latest findings in the field of Syrian Church history.

Not long ago we discovered that, in contrast to Mediterranean Christianity of the Greek and Latin variety, neither the origins nor the essence of Aramaic Christianity had ever been catholic. The historical picture is therefore very clearcut: a Latin form of Christianity, which was practical and legalistic, wrestling with sin and atonement, strove to establish a theocratic world order through the medium of the papacy. This form subsequently gave rise to Protestantism and later to Roman Catholicism. Furthermore, there was Greek, ontological Christianity, which was concerned with the synthesis of being and time, thus creating an impressive type of Christology. Its heirs are the Slavic Churches and the Monophysitic Churches of Egypt, Ethopia and Armenia. In addition, however, there was Aramaic Christianity, whose center was in Edessa and which lives on in the Thomas Christians of India and in other remnants of Nestorianism. This was a pluriform and colourful kind of Christianity, whose adepts could be found among the wandering and the poor (and as I pointed out earlier, it never was catholic). The reason was that it did not have its origins in Gentile Christianity, but in Palestinian Judaism [4].

From Jean Cardinal Daniélou's contribution to *The Crucible of Christianity*, it becomes quite apparent that for a long time Christianity continued to exist as a Jewish sect, whose activities paralleled and even went counter to those of

---

[2] A. Henrichs und L. Koenen, Ein griechischer Mani-Codex, *Zeitschrift für Papyrologie und Epigraphik*, 5, 1970, 97-216.

[3] Kölner Codex 29, 9-11: cf. *Henrichs und Koenen*, 168 f.

[4] G. Quispel, *Makarius, das Thomasevangelium und das Lied von der Perle*, Leiden, 1967.

St. Paul. This sect was responsible for the beginnings of Christianity in Egypt, Carthage and Rome [5]. There, it was soon replaced by Gentile Christianity, but outside the Roman Empire, i.e., in Babylonia and Mesopotamia this was not the case. I fail to understand how scholars can possibly deny the Jewish Christian elements in Aramaic Christianity, especially since Jerome reported that in Aleppo he had visited Jewish Christians in the fourth century. According to him, they had their own gospel, the *Nazorean Gospel,* and adhered to Jewish law. On the other hand, the *Gospel of Thomas,* written in neighbouring Edessa around 140 A.D., proves that the Nazoreans had existed in Mesopotamia much earlier, as it contains elements of Jewish Christian Gospel tradition [6].

Moreover, Hippolytus reported that the Jewish Christian prophet Elkesai had a vision in Parthia around 100 A.D. [7]. At that time, Babylonia, where millions of Jews lived, belonged to the Parthian Empire. It can therefore be assumed that Elkesai was active in Babylonia, and as a result, it thus becomes understandable how Mani happened to grow up among the Elkesaites in southern Babylonia.

In addition, there were also Encratites in Mesopotamia. They rejected marriage, the drinking of wine, the eating of meat and held other unusual ideas. We know them from the Encratitic *Logia* in the *Gospel of St. Thomas,* as well as from Tatian's *Diatessaron,* which was written in Mesopotamia around 170 A.D. The brilliant scholar Erik Peterson [8] rightly saw in these Encratites the founders of Manichaeism, although in developing this thesis he made a mistake. According to tradition, Mani's father heard in the heathen temple: "Patek, do not eat meat, drink no wine and abstain from women", and this led Peterson to conclude that the Baptists, to whom Mani and his father belonged, were Encratites. However, there is no reason to believe that the Elkesaites were ascetics. Other scholars, who erroneously identified these Baptists with the non-ascetic Mandaeans, made tremendous scholarly efforts to prove that the Mandaeans had indeed been ascetics at one time, although it is eminently clear that these words did not refer to any historical facts, but were simply an expression of tendentious Manichaean propaganda. On the onther hand, Peterson was quite correct in pointing out that it would be difficult to explain Mani's experience with the Twin without the *Acts of*

[5] J. Daniélou, 'That the Scripture might be fulfilled'. Christianity as a Jewish Sect, in *The Crucible of Christianity,* ed. by A. Toynbee, London, 1969, 261-282.
[6] G. Quispel, *Het Evangelie van Thomas en de Nederlanden,* Amsterdam, 1971.
[7] Hippolytus, *Refutatio,* IX, 13.
[8] E. Peterson, Bemerkungen zum hamburger Papyrusfragment der Acta Pauli, in *Frühkirche, Judentum und Gnosis,* Rom-Freiburg-Wien, 1951, 204 ff.

Thomas (in which Thomas is looked upon as Jesus' twin), or even the Manichaean condemnation of sexual intercourse without the influence of the Encratites [9].

Inasmuch as the religious life of Edessa was by no means monolithic, mention must also be made of Bardesanes. There are many conflicting notions regarding the original doctrine of this highly gifted man. In any event, he taught the pre-existence of matter, a theory that must have been known to Mani.

It is impossible to prove that the Mesopotamian Christians also included Marcionites and Gnostics. Yet, we must assume that this was so, because Marcion must have been the premise for Mani's and his disciple Addai's criticism of the *Old Testament* and because the name Mani gave to the Creator of Man, Saclas, i.e., the Fool, presupposes the myth of the *Apocryphon of John.*

In visualizing Aramaic Christianity as it existed in those days, one could easily imagine that the founding of the Manichaean religion meant little more for its author than Erik Peterson's or Heinrich Schlier's "conversion", i.e., simply a transition from one variety of Christianity to another. To the extent that they can be ascertained clearly, any Buddhist or Iranian elements in the Manichaean system are completely secondary. This applies in particular to Manichaean dualism.

The ideas of the Elkesaites are fairly well-known to us from the *Pseudo-Clementine Homilies,* and they are strikingly Jewish. In these writings, everything is concretized. The eschatology is concrete: the kingdom of Heaven is to be realized on earth. The concept of God is concrete: God is considered a figure and not an idea or a principle. Thus, even evil was viewed realistically as one of God's creatures and not as a *privatio boni* or as matter. Satan is described as having been created out of a mixture of the elements and as a servant of God, his "left" hand [10]. It was a very courageous and consistent form of monotheism, which can also be found in the *Old Testament* as well as the *Dead Sea Scrolls,* and which has remained characteristic of Jewish mysticism. As the Clementine Gospel quotations show, the Elkesaites placed strong emphasis on this concept.

All Matthew (10 : 29) said was that no sparrow falls to the ground without God — an expression which provides the possibility of side-stepping the issue. The pseudo-Clementines were much more radical in saying that no sparrow is

---

[9] G. Quispel, Das ewige Ebenbild der Menschen. Zur Begegnung mit dem Selbst in der Gnosis, *Eranos Jahrbuch* 36, 1967, 23 ff. See above pp. 140-157.
[10] *Ps. Clem. Homiliae,* XX, 4, 6.

caught in a snare without the will of God (XII, 31). Even the tragic fate of a
helpless bird caught through human meanness is attributed to the will of God.
In the *Pseudo-Clementinae Homiliae* (XII, 29) Jesus says:

> That which is good must be brought about
> And blessed is he, who brings it about.
> That which is evil has to come about
> But woe onto him, who brings it about.

In history both good and evil occur, because God so wills it. These same
quotations, as so many others of Jewish Christian origin, can also be found in
Mani's own or other Manichaean writings for the simple reason that Mani
grew up in a Jewish Christian community and took over a number of sayings
that did not coincide with his own convictions. His only real concern was to
prove that God was not responsible for the bird being caught in the snare, i.e.,
for the occurrence of evil in the history of man.

Tertullian once said that Marcion and many others, especially heretics, who
struggled with the question of *unde malum*, were induced to postulate a better
God upon reading the following words of God in Isaiah: "Ego sum, qui condo
mala" (*Adv. Marc.* I, 2). This is undoubtedly the existential core of the
problem in man that gave rise to Gnosticism. Moreover, as shown by the
Pseudo-Clementines, it should be recalled that the Elkesaites' view hardened
in the course of their struggle against Marcion. In other words, Mani did not
militate against Christianity in general or against Catholicism, but against this
specific Jewish Christian doctrine. Time and again he condemns the idea that
God is the source of evil. According to him, evil is the "non-thing" which God
did not want, but which will forever exist side by side with Him. Manichaean
dualism is Mani's reaction against the Jewish Christian faith of his youth. Even
he postulated, however, that the original antithesis was not light and darkness,
but God and Satan and he, too, held that Satan was created out of the
primordial elements, which shows that he was unable to escape the influence
of his opponent. To understand Mani's attitude toward Christianity, it must be
remembered that his canon differed from ours. It is a fact that he did not
recognize the *Acts of Luke*, but on the other hand considered the so-called
apocryphal acts of the apostles to be canonical. Let us not forget that the *Acts
of Thomas* originated in Edessa around 225 in Encratitic circles. However,
the *Acts of John* also had a strong influence on him and contributed to the
development of the doctrine of *Jesus patibilis*. For, in the *Acts of John*, Christ
says that he suffers with all those who are suffering innocently [11]. The
beginning of his *Epistula Fundamenti* shows that Mani had knowledge of the

---

[11]   *Acta Johannis*, 96.

Gospel of Thomas. On the other hand it is not known who transmitted the letters of Paul to him.

The most important thing that should be remembered is that most probably he did not know the canonical gospels, for the simple reason that in those days and for a long time to come Tatian's *Diatessaron* was the recognized gospel of Aramaic Christianity. We have no evidence that translations of the gospels existed in Edessa at that time or anywhere in the Persian Empire, where Mani used to live. In contrast, the Manichaean fragments prove that Mani both knew and used the Tatian's *Diatessaron* [12]. This must be taken into consideration in attempting to answer the question about Mani's attitude toward Christianity.

A number of Manichaean witnesses claimed that Jesus said he would send the Holy Spirit to mankind. Thus, St. Augustine quotes the Manichaean Felix as follows: *mittam vobis Spiritum Sanctum Paracletum* (I, 2). According to the Cologne Papyrus, Mani himself said: Κύριος ἀπέστειλέν μοι σύζυγον (The Lord sent me a partner) (p. 120). In An-Nadim's *Fihrist* the "Twin" says to Mani: Greetings to you, Mani, from myself and the Lord, who has sent me to you and has chosen you for His mission (Flügel, *Mani,* p. 84). It had always been assumed that this was an allusion to the *Gospel according to John* (14 : 16). It should, however, be noticed that the wording in the Fourth Gospel is different: And I will pray the Father, and *he* shall *give* you another Paraclete (14 : 16). On the basis of Ephrem Syrus' Commentary on the *Diatessaron,* we have evidence that Tatian actually changed this wording, because he did not read: "He shall give", but "I shall send". According to Tatian's view, Christ himself would send the Paraclete. This was what Mani read in his copy of the *Diatessaron* and it acquired fundamental importance for him.

Mani's religious experience was not in fact unique. Encounters with the Self as a guardian angel can also be found in Valentinian Gnosticism as well as in Jewish and Islamic mysticism [13]. The Greeks, especially the Pythagoreans, conceived of the *daimon* as the counterpart image of man's Self. This idea was taken over by Judaism and thus crept into Jewish and Syrian Christianity. In the *Gospel of Thomas* it is of central importance. Moreover, it is a notion that is found not only in religion but also in literature, such as German Romanticism and in the poems of the Dutch poet A. Roland Holst. It is a recurrent *topos* in history. The encounter with one's own Self does not seem to be a rare

---

12   C. Peters, *Das Diatessaron Tatians,* Orientalia Christiana Analecta 123, Rome, 1939, 125 ff.
13   G. Quispel, Das ewige Ebenbild der Menschen, 9-20. See above pp. 140-149.

occurrence. The unique and important aspect of Mani's religious experience was that he thought his Self to be the Paraclete and that on the basis of Tatian's *Diatessaron* he was able to give his experience a Christian interpretation.

The title "Apostle of Jesus Christ", which Mani applied to himself, should also be viewed against this background. The fact that he used it was neither an attempt at imitation, nor a pretext but resulted from true conviction. Mani assumed the name of Apostle because he interpreted his Twin as the Paraclete and because he had read in Tatian that Christ would send the Paraclete. Augustine pointed out quite correctly that:

"Unde se in suis litteris Jesu Christi apostolum dicit eo quod *Jesus Christus* se *missurum* esse promiserit atque in illo miserit spiritum sanctum". (*De haeresibus,* 46). (In his letters he therefore styles himself as Apostle of Jesus Christ because Jesus Christ promised he would send him and in him he sent the Holy Spirit.)

Mani's understanding of the Self can be properly evaluated only on the basis of the variant in Tatian. He did not indulge in self-deification; not his empirical ego, but his transcendental Self was the Paraclete.

On the other hand there can be no doubt that Mani himself interpreted the Twin as the Paraclete mentioned in John, despite the attempts that were made time and again to question this interpretation. As early as 1734, Isaac de Beausobre wrote that Mani had never claimed to be the Paraclete (*Histoire du Manichéisme* I, 103). The extent to which phenomenology and the history of religion have failed to make any progress in the last 250 years is shown in the work of L. J. R. Ort, who, despite the lack of any evidence or knowledge of the *Diatessaron,* claimed that the title of Paraclete for Mani was an invention of Western Manichaeism, an assimilation to Christianity for missionary purposes [14]. Tatian's variant, which was known to Mani, however, disproves these theories.

There is no reason to assume, as Geo Widengren did in his book on Mani, that a Buddhist shrine existed in Seleukia-Ktesifon, that there was an ascetic trend in Mandaeism, that the incarnation of the divine Self was of Iranian origin, or that there had been a Mandaean period in Mani's life, not to mention the theory of a substratum of the old Mesopotamian religion as it manifested itself in Gnostic Baptism — suppositions which are all without foundations [15]. A careful reading of the Fourth Gospel will prove much more enlightening.

---

[14] L. J. R. Ort, *Mani. A religio-historical description of his personality,* Leiden, 1967, 259.
[15] G. Widengren, *Mani und der Manichäismus,* Stuttgart, 1961.

Mani, however, owes still another of the doctrines he followed to Jewish Christianity. According to the *Pseudo-Clementines*, Jesus was the true Prophet. On the other hand, the true Prophet had already appeared once before. The Holy Spirit had incarnated itself earlier in Adam and later revealed itself to the patriarchs of the *Old Testament*, such as Abraham and Moses, until, having appeared in varying shapes over a period of centuries, it came to rest in Jesus. Mani took up this idea and amplified it. According to him, Buddha, Zarathustra as well as Jesus were sent out to different nations at different times as emanations of the same principle that manifested itself with finality and perfection in Mani, the Paraclete.

Mani's dualism as well as his doctrine of the successive incarnations can therefore be explained on the basis of his Jewish Christian background.

This throws some new and unexpected light on the origins of Islam. Mohammed's concept of his mission had always appeared to bear a striking resemblance to the Jewish Christian concept of the true Prophet. Not only was Jesus, according to him, a prophet like other prophets before him, but Mohammed himself was the true and final Prophet, the Seal of the Prophets. Until recently, it had not been possible to find any evidence of Mohammed's connection with Jewish Christianity. It had been assumed that the Jewish Christians had lived exclusively in Transjordania and had gradually become extinct. Owing to the discovery of the *Cologne Codex*, we now know, however, that southern Babylonia had also been inhabited by Elkesaites, who had called themselves Baptists, because after the actual baptism, they practised certain additional ablutions for the purification and atonement of their sins.

Baptists (Sabians) were mentioned in the Koran in three places (II, 59; V, 73; XXII, 17) as members of a recognized religion of the Book, which, according to Mohammed's precepts, was to be tolerated along with Judaism and Christianity. It is too early to make any definitive statement in this matter, because the whole problem will have to be investigated by a scholar specialized in Islamic studies. But as a working hypothesis we are quite justified in assuming even now that these Sabians, the Baptists of the Koran, should be identified with the Jewish Christian Elkesaites. This would mean that Mohammed was acquainted both with the existence and the views of the Jewish Christians. The parallelism in concept regarding the true Prophet would thus have to be attributed to Jewish Christianity's historically verifiable influence on Mohammed. In this context it should also be recalled that, just like Islam, Jewish Christianity is basically a legalistic religion, which remained faithful to Jewish law, although it recognized Jesus as the Messiah of the Jewish people. If one follows this line of thought, it becomes much more apparent that it was actually St. Paul, who cast Christianity as a faith with freedom from law and as a religion of the spirit. Paul's true greatness comes to light only when viewed in this perspective. Therefore, the actual dialogue between Christianity of the one hand, and Islam, as well as Judaism on the other, should be concerned with Paul's concept of the Law.

It also comes as somewhat of a surprise to see how fertile and productive Jewish Christianity was in Asia. In a sense, it gave rise to two religions, i.e., Manichaeism and Islam, which, looked at in this perspective, become Christian heresies.

Moreover, it also becomes completely clear to what extent the theses developed by the so-called School of the History of Religion were wrong. Reitzenstein, in his time, used Manichaeism as a point of departure in order to explain that Gnosticism and Christianity had Iranian origins. In a Manichaean fragment he found a dialogue between the Ego and the Self and decided that it must be Iranian. Hereafter, he was certain that both Mandaeism and Manichaeism were purely Iranian and that these religions should be used to explain Christianity, which after all was more than 200 years older. The premise for this assertion was, of course, that Mani had spent his early years among the Mandaeans.

Geo Widengren set out to prove these extravagant hypotheses with great thoroughness. According to him, Manichaeism was a mixture of Mesopotamian and Iranian religions. He claimed that the doctrine of the Prophet originated in Mesopotamia and that the idea of a succession of prophets stemmed from Iran. Widengren was convinced that before Mani's time both views had been merged in Gnostic Mandaeism, to which Mani was supposed to have belonged.

In the meantime, the story transmitted by the Arabian writer An-Nadim was systematically neglected. According to An-Nadim, Mani never belonged to the Mandaean sect in his youth but to the Jewish Christian sect of the Elkesaites [16]. This was also confirmed by the Cologne papyrus. One must ask oneself, whether a science that dares to drop written tradition by the wayside to follow up valueless fantasies is really worth the name. We now know that as a child Mani was a Jewish boy, that he was circumcised and celebrated the Sabbath. Indeed, it must even be doubted that this parents were of Parthian and royal origin, a fact that was mentioned by An-Nadim, but not in the Cologne papyrus. Most probably this was a legend which arose out of the desire to rediscover in the person of Mani the Parthian prince mentioned in the *Song of the Pearl*.

---

[16] G. Flügel, *Mani, seine Lehre und seine Schriften*, Osnabrück, 1969 (= Nachdruck der Ausgabe 1862), 133.

Mani was a Jewish Christian. For this reason, his basic experience, the encounter with the Self, should be explained against this background. In this case, it should, however, also be possible to understand the fundamental concepts of Manichaeism, the identity of the ego and the self, the empirical ego and the guardian angel, in terms of his Jewish Christian origins. We would thus have to interpret Manichaeism, a religion without sacraments, as a spiritualization of Jewish Christian baptism.

II

I wonder whether at Eranos I even dare mention Christian baptism. I suppose that it is somewhat risky, but in order to understand the early Christian baptismal tradition, you will have to forget everything Karl Barth wrote in his Dogmatics about baptism. Karl Barth not only claimed that child christening was nonsense but that baptism was not a sacrament at all. An assertion of this kind is incomprehensible to anyone who knows the documents of the Early Church or even just the New Testament. Perhaps we should also forget all that has been said in the West about baptism, for we must remember that all such statements were subject to the influence of St. Augustine, who thought that baptism absolves us from original sin and the primordial guilt of concupiscence. This concept is very interesting but was little known in the Christian Church in the centuries preceding St. Augustine. One might conjecture that Augustine was indebted to Manichaeism for this notion, as he had been a Manichaean himself for over nine years. There actually are some indications to this effect, but I shall not dwell on them in this context. We therefore have to delve a little further into the past and ask what the Early Christians taught about baptism and how they practised it. We soon realize that the concept of rebirth coincided with that of baptism. In other words, in the view of the Early Church the inner event of a new birth coincided with the outer ritual of baptism. It is important to remember this in order to understand the purpose and the deeper meaning which the Christians attributed to baptism and rebirth.

The Early Gentile Church engaged in a whole of rituals, beautiful and highly symbolic acts which were not entirely archaic. People were immersed three times in the name of the Father, the Son and the Holy Ghost, whereupon the venue of the Holy Ghost was called down upon them by imposition of the hands. This cannot have been the original concept and to discover it, we might do well to disregard even the views of St. Paul on this matter.

You all know that in *Romans* 6, Paul expressed very profound views about the nature of baptism. You will recall that for Paul Christ's death and resurrection were almost more important than His life. His views of Christian

baptism have to be regarded against this background. We might summarize
them in Goethe's words:

"Until you have grasped this — Die and be transformed! — You will be
nothing but a sorry guest on the sombre earth". (*Selige Sehnsucht*)

While Paul would have agreed with this entirely, "die and be transformed"
would also have meant to him the outer ritual act of baptism. For, according
to Paul, baptism is a form of death, a submersion in water and a re-emergence,
i.e., a resurrection in union with Christ and in Christ. In *Romans* 6, Paul said
that when we are baptized into union with Christ Jezus we are baptized into
His death, immersed in it; and he clearly stated that the sacrament of the holy
baptism is an image of Christ's death. Thus, whenever an initiate is immersed
in water and re-emerges, the image of Christ's death is re-enacted in him.

Paul's concept inevitably brings to mind the Greek mysteries, because in many
of them — irrespective of whether they were devoted to Osiris, Attis or Adonis
— a young god who embodies living nature dies and is reborn. A great deal
has been written about the relationship between the Greek mysteries and the
Christian sacraments. I do not intend to go into the matter, but simply want to
point out that in describing the holy baptism as an image of death Paul is using
the language of the Greek mysteries. The mysteries of Adonis, for instance,
were looked upon as an image of Adonis' death. The mythical event of the
young god's death was ritually re-enacted during every celebration of the
mystery. The very expression "image of death" used to refer to the mysteries
of Adonis. Ovid used it in describing the death of Adonis and the mourning
women: "repetitaque mortis imago annua plangoris peraget simulamina nostri
(the image of the death is re-enacted annually by the celebration of our
sorrow)[17].

The expression used in relation to the Adonis mysteries is therefore the same
as that used by Paul in his Epistle to the Romans: the mystery of baptism as
an image of Christ's death; Christ in his death and resurrection must therefore
be assumed to have been present at the baptism in the same manner as Adonis
was presumed to have been present at the mysteries. Along with Hugo Rahner,
who discussed this topic so eloquently at *Eranos,* I therefore do not preclude
the possibility that, in writing about baptism Paul may have been using the
language of the Greek mysteries [18]. This does not help us, however, in our
investigations of Jewish Christian baptism. You undoubtedly know that the
Jewish Christians differed from Paul precisely in that for them it was not

---

[17] Ovid, *Metam.,* X. 726-727.
[18] H. Rahner, *Griechische Mythen in christlicher Deutung,* 3. Aufl., Darmstadt, 1966, 19-54.

Christ's death which brought salvation, although they recognized His resurrection. The Jewish Christian source material says nothing about baptism being associated with Christ's death. Furthermore, it is extremely difficult for us to imagine that these Palestinian Christians — very humble people living in Transjordania — had been influenced by the Greek mysteries. We shall see, however, that their ideas regarding the mystery to a large extent paralleled those of the Greeks.

I would tend to agree with Odo Casel, who repeatedly emphasized this point in his study of the sacraments as the Christian mysteries. According to him, Christianity was not influenced by the Greek mysteries to any great extent. Yet, according to Casel, the cult *eidos* of the Christian sacrament — the idea that the rite was a re-enactment of the original myth — was quite comparable to the cult *eidos* of the Greek mysteries. A rather ingenious mind once formulated the idea as follows: Christianity was not influenced by the Greek mysteries precisely because in its origin and essence it was already a mystery religion. I would be inclined to accept this definition, provided, however, that Jewish Christian baptism is viewed as a product of Judaism and that form of Christianity which was based on Judaism. Jean Cardinal Daniélou and Georg Kretschmar provided us with detailed studies describing the original Jewish Christian baptismal rites [19]. From the works of these learned scholars we infer that this form of baptism was not characterized by simplicity. On the contrary, it was apparently much more complex, meaningful and symbolic than our present-day baptism. There is no doubt that Jewish Christian baptism had a deeply spiritual, symbolic content. These people lived in a symbolic world and, as Gershom Scholem pointed out, in a period when a breakthrough of images occurred in Jewish culture. In fact all aspects of Jewish Christian baptism are related to Judaism; not to the Rabbinical or Pharisaic variety, of course, but to heterodox forms of Judaism. I am thinking here of the Essenes or the Baptists (followers of John the Baptist), a hitherto wholly unknown aspect of Judaism which was discovered only quite recently.

The origins of baptism are entirely Jewish. The Essenes practised ablutions which probably influenced the Jewish Christians. Christian baptism is therefore not only highly symbolic and mythological, it is also very Jewish. As erudite scholars have discussed this topic at length, I shall confine myself to a very brief description of the baptismal rites performed in those days. Among other things, baptism was required to take place in "living" water, i.e., a spring,

---

[19] J. Daniélou, *Théologie du judéo-christianisme*, Tournai, 1958, 369-386; G. Kretschmar, *Die Geschichte des Taufgottesdienstes in der alten Kirche*, in *Leiturgia*, V, Kassel, 1970 (= 1964), 14-58.

a river, especially the Jordan, or the sea. Even much later, the baptismal water was frequently referred to merely as "the Jordan". The *datio salis,* the giving of salt, which continues to be a Roman Catholic rite today, is undoubtedly of Jewish origin, too, because we now have evidence that the salt was considered to be essential to the covenant aspect of baptism. However, I shall refrain from giving you any further examples and simply provide you with a schematic outline of the probable course of events.

Baptism for the absolution of sins existed even prior to Jesus as evidenced by the story of John the Baptist. This concept of baptism is thus pre-Christian. On the other hand, the words of John the Baptist "He will baptize you with the Holy Spirit" show that the Spirit was added as a new element. This was the content of Jewish Christian baptism, whereas the profound interpretation symbolizing death and resurrection must be attributed to Paul and his co-Hellenists.

After this brief outline I shall now discuss three aspects of Jewish Christian baptism, i.e. anointment, rebirth and the bridal chamber.

In contrast to the practices of the western Gentile Church, anointment preceded the actual baptismal bath in the rites of the Jewish Christians as well as the Syrian Christians, whose practices evolved out of those of their Jewish brethern. Some passages in the *New Testament* (*Acts* 10, 44; 1 *Cor.* 10, 2) imply that this rite existed in the pre-Pauline era. What does this mean? The Jewish Christians believed that Jesus became Christ at His baptism. A number of present-day occult sects continue to hold this view, but it is very ancient and originated with the Jewish Christians. Jesus was believed to have become the Messiah, because during His baptism the Holy Spirit descended upon Him. Messiah, of course, means the Anointed One. On the one hand, what took place here was a spiritualization of the Jewish Messiah ideal, the Anointed One being he who was anointed with the Holy Spirit. On the other, it explains to us why anointment became part of the baptismal ritual. For, to lead a Christian existence according to the Jewish Christan concept, one had to follow in Christ's footsteps and even imitate his life. In describing the baptism of Jesus the Jewish Christian Gospel says: "My Son Thou art, ... this day I have begotten Thee". This notion was taken over by the Syrian Christians, whose priests say to the initiate while anointing him: "My Son Thou art, this day I have begotten Thee". Through baptism man became God's child; this was expressed by the practice of anointing the entire body of the Christian adept prior to his baptism.

We know a great deal about this custom as it was practised in Syria. However, we also know that it existed among the Jewish Christians of Palestine, who even went so far as to call themselves *Christoi*, i.e. the Anointed Ones. They did not mean to imply that they resembled the Messiah in every respect, but they believed that, in *imitatio* of him, they were anointed with the Holy Spirit. The Holy Spirit descended to earth when Jesus became Christ at His baptism and this has been repeated in the lives of all initiates ever since [20].

The ceremony of anointment is well known from the Old Testament, where we read of kings, priests and prophets being anointed. As a result of anointment one becomes a king, priest, or prophet. All these notions are embodied in the ritual of anointment and it is difficult to differentiate between them. One might say that, since Christ was the true prophet for the Jewish Christians, every Christian must possess a prophetic quality. This idea cannot be dissociated from the Christians' belief that they were a people of kings and priests. This belief is the fulfilment of God's word to Moses, which according to the Bible foretold that the Jews "shall be unto Me a Kingdom of priests and a holy nation". (Exodus 19 : 6). The meaning of anointment can only be understood in the Jewish perspective. The Christian innovation was that anyone, even the humble and the poor, could be anointed. Using a rather controversial but unavoidable expression, we would have to call it the democratization caused by the advent of Christianity. I am quite aware of the fact that democracy is a loaded word. Usually I try to avoid it in my lectures, but at times it seems to be impossible. In this case, we have to admit that Early Christianity had a democratic quality owing to the fact that even the humblest person was able to receive the Holy Spirit and to belong to the kingdom of priests. There were other non-Christian religious movements in antiquity that reserved the mysteries for the spiritual elite. Now anointment came to mean that anyone could have access to the Spirit.

In Iraq and Iran the Mandeans have survived as a sect to this day, and it is highly probable that they continue to practice the form of baptism advocated by John the Baptist. Very scholarly investigations have shown that anointment was not originally a Mandean practice [21]. As far as we can tell, it is of no importance to them. In this connection, I am always reminded of the Baptist's word regarding Jesus: "I have baptized you with water" — which is the customary practice among the Mandeans — "He will baptize you with the Holy Spirit", which is expressed in the symbolism of anointment.

In addition, baptism is also the mystery of rebirth. It involves absolution from sin and liberation from concupiscence. According to the Pseudo-Clementines,

---

[20] Hippolytus, *Refutatio*, VII, 34, 2.
[21] E. Segelberg, *Masbuta. Studies in the ritual of the Mandaean Baptism*, Uppsala, 1958, 130 ff.

the essential meaning of baptism is, however, that man comes to understand his origins. This was misinterpreted to mean that the sacrament of rebirth enlightened man about his origins, existence and future. In actual fact, through baptism man comes to know his divine origin; both his Father, i.e., God, as well as his Mother. This point is made very clear in one passage of the *Pseudo-Clementines* where it is stated that through the bath of rebirth man shall know his parents — *gennesantes* — i.e., God and the Mother [22]. Again, we cannot help but be astounded, because we had always thought of Christianity as a thoroughly patriarchal religion. Now, it turns out that originally this was not so.

The Jewish Christians were entirely convinced that the Holy Spirit was a feminine hypostasis. A fragment from the Jewish Christian Gospels reads as follows: "Even so did my Mother, the Holy Spirit, take me by one of my hairs and carry me away onto the great mountain Tabor". In another fragment, the Holy Spirit says to Jesus at his baptism: "My Son, in all the prophets I was waiting for Thee" [23]. The idea expressed in these passages was that Jesus was reborn at His baptism which for Him, too, was the bath of rebirth. Every Jewish Christian should therefore be thought of as having been reborn by his mother the Holy Spirit after emerging from complete immersion in the baptismal bath. Here, we come to a very simple realization: just as birth requires a mother, so rebirth requires a spiritual mother. Originally, the Christian term "rebirth" must therefore have been associated with the concept of the spirit as a feminine hypostasis.

Let us reflect on what this implies. In the *Gospel according to John,* Jesus says to Nicodemus: "In truth, in very truth I tell you, unless a man has been born over again he cannot see the kingdom of God" (John 3 : 3). The same wording can also be found in the *Pseudo-Clementines.* Since they were not aquainted with the Fourth Gospel, these words are clearly taken from a free Palestinian tradition. Actually the Pseudo-Clementine wording is much simpler: "Unless you are reborn, you shall not enter the kingdom of Heaven" [24]. The Jewish Christians, therefore, also handed down these words of Jesus as part of their tradition. They seem to have believed that a rebirth was a true act of pro-creation, a birth by the Holy Spirit. I cannot excape the notion that this may have been the original meaning of Christ's word.

The re-enactment of birth in a mystery inevitably brings to mind the Greek

---

[22] *Homiliae,* XI, 3, 6.

[23] E. Hennecke, *New Testament Apocryphs,* Eng. translation by R. Mc. L. Wilson, London, 1963, p. 164.

[24] *Homiliae,* XI, 26, 2.

mysteries, although the idea is not always rendered in the same manner. It has been pointed out that in the blood baptism of the Attis mysteries the expression *renatus in aeternum*, reborn in eternity, was used, but blood baptism does not signify a birth by a mother. It may well be that in this respect the Attis mysteries were influenced by Christianity.

Apuleius mentioned the fact that he was, as it were, reborn, *quodam modo renatus*, when he was initiated into the Isis mysteries [25]. According to his reports, this initiation in no way involved birth by a mother, but referred to a cosmic experience, which is a rebirth only in a metaphorical sense.

The only parallel I know of can be found in the Eleusinian mysteries, although no historical connection can be established with the Christian tradition. Recent research into the Eleusinian mysteries uncovered some important material. I should like to draw your attention to a specific action and a vision which formed a part of these mysteries.

It seems that, after the fast and after having drunk the *kykeon*, the mystes took something out of a large basket, then performed "the act" and replaced "the something" in the basket. The reference is very mysterious. What was in the basket. Even in antiquity some people seemed to have thought that it was a phallus. However, Theodoret reported that the basket in the Eleusinian mysteries contained a womb [26]. A. Körte assumed that the mystes passed the womb under his garments, then dropped it on the ground and replaced it in the basket: a very peculiar rite, which can probably be interpreted as an adoption rite [27]. According to a Greek author, Diodorus Siculus (V, 39), Hera at one time adopted Heracles as her son pressing him against her body and then dropping him on the ground to simulate a birth. We must assume that this strange gesture should be understood as an adoption rite.

In my view such an interpretation would explain the mysterious words belonging to the Orphic doctrine which were inscribed on a gold tablet found in southern Italy. On it we read: "I have sunk beneath the bossom of Despoina, the Queen of the Underworld". Probably this meant that, in death, the author of these words, an Orphic, was adopted by the Goddess of the Underworld, i.e., Persephone. He thus became a child of the chthonic Mother. As the vision in Eleusis seems to indicate, the mystes is adopted as a child of the divine mother through the performance of this rite, which constitutes a valid parallel to Jewish Christian baptism. Evoking the ineffable holy thing, the Hierophant

---

[25] Apuleius, *Metam.*, XI, 16, 4.

[26] Theodoret of Cyrus, *Graec. aff. cur.*, VII, 11.

[27] A. Körte, *Archiv für Religionswissenschaft*, 18, 1915, 119.

proclaimed in a loud voice: "The Mistress has given birth to a holy boy. Brimo has given birth to Brimos, that is the Strong One to the Strong One". In his vision the mystes evidently saw the birth of the child from the Earth Goddess and by re-enacting the mystery, he must have felt that somehow he had become the child of the Mother.

We should by no means draw the conclusion that the Jewish Christians were influenced by the Eleusinian mysteries. The symbolism developed spontaneously. The Pseudo-Clementines said that in the beginning the Spirit hovered over the waters, and inasmuch as everything was created out of water and Spirit, the Spirit or Mother, also created man anew by hovering over the baptismal waters. The premise for this statement is, of course, that the Holy Spirit is feminine [28].

Finally, brief reference should be made to the bridal clamber. This custom seems to have been practiced by the Valentinians, as well as the Manichaeans, and we find mention of it in the recently discovered *Gospel of Philip*, written by a Valentinian in Antioch around 200 B.C. It is unlikely that the ceremony of the bridal chamber is of Gnostic origin, because it is also part of Syrian Church practices. It should probably be attributed to Jewish Christianity, for in the *Pseudo-Clementines* we read: "When illuminated by the Spirit and sown with the True Prophet's White Word of Truth, every human being is a bride" [29].

Once a person has been baptized a new symbol has been enacted and the man or woman becomes a bride. We find here another strange parallel, this time to the Mithras mysteries. In these mysteries it was traditional for the initiate to have the following lines sung to him: "Sing on *nymphè*, rejoice oh *nymphè*, rejoice oh new light". Scholars used to argue a great deal about the meaning of the Greek word *nymphè*. Some people wanted to change it to *nymphos*, bridegroom, until it was found that the initiates in the Mithras mysteries, who were all men, were conceived of as male brides. Once again, we should not conclude that the Mithras mysteries influenced Jewish Christianity. Both traditions simply developed the same imagery. We do not actually know how the scene was enacted by the Jewish Christians. The *Gospel* of Philip intimates that a bridal chamber was built, to which the new adept was led after his or her baptism. Here, the holy nuptial, the *mysterium coniunctionis*, took place. One can hardly help thinking that the rite symbolized the union of the soul with Christ. There is undoubtedly some connection here,

---

[28] *Homiliae*, XI, 26, 3.
[29] *Homiliae*, III, 27, 3.

but the *Gospel of Philip* tells us that, in the mystery of the bridal chamber, man is joined in marriage to his Guardian Angel, who is the Self. No doubt the true content of this mystery is man's union, the *mysterium coniunctionis*, with his Guardian Angel, his *Daimon*, or the Self. I do not think we can exclude the possibility that this concept goes back to Jewish Christian tradition. The fact that in Jewish Christian baptism the initiate wears a white garment, which is after all a symbol of the Self, points to a union of the existential Ego with the spiritual Self, not eschatologically, but in the here and now. For, both the guardian angel and the heavenly robe can symbolize the transcendental Self.

I am therefore inclined to think that Mani's religious experience, his encounter with the Self, presupposes and spiritualizes the symbolism of anointment, rebirth and the *mysterium coniunctonis* of Jewish Christian baptism [30].

---

[30] Translated from German by Ruth Horine.

94